Social Problems in America

Edited by KENNETH L. CULVER

Rinehart Press / Holt, Rinehart and Winston

SAN FRANCISCO

To Lillian

who has enriched my life

Library of Congress Cataloging in Publication Data

Culver, Kenneth L   comp.
    Social problems in America.

    1. United States—Social conditions—1960—
—Addresses, essays, lectures. I. Title.
HN65.C84   309.1'73'092   74-1218
ISBN 0-03-006561-5

Cover design by Jane Bacher.

All photos by Geoffrey Gove except:
Pages 17, bottom; 193, bottom;
195, top left: Ford Foundation;
Pages 4, bottom; 76, bottom left: John C. Goodwin;
Page 17, middle: National Association for Mental Health;
Pages 5, bottom; 14, top; 193, top right;
195, top right and bottom: Salvation Army;
Page 2, top left: Charles Steiner;
Pages 4, middle; 5, top right: Wide World.

© 1974 by Rinehart Press
5643 Paradise Drive
Corte Madera, Calif. 94925

A division of Holt, Rinehart and Winston, Inc.

PRINTED IN THE UNITED STATES OF AMERICA

4 5 6 7   006   9 8 7 6 5 4 3 2 1

Contents

Preface

Over the years America's social problems have become difficult, intricate, and hydra-headed, pervading the entire social, economic, and political structure. They touch every individual and press upon every segment of the community. Inadequate housing, poverty, unemployment, public welfare, social conflicts, deviant behavior, minorities, and the aged are among the perennial problems. Nominal success has been achieved in such problems as slum clearance, crime prevention, race relations, welfare programs, and public health, but much more needs to be done.

In addition, as a result of spectacular progress in science and technology during the last fifty years, we face not only the old problems but also new and vastly more urgent ones. Technical advances in transportation, communication, automation, and medicine have deeply affected our way of living, stirring up unrest, sowing seeds of dissension, and undermining mores. Traditional ways of dealing with sex, minorities, women, and youth are being questioned. We have reached a fork in the road. What happens in the future will depend on how we go about solving, resolving, and dissolving this mass of problems.

Holding top priority is our expanding population. Between 1945 and 1974, a high birth rate and a life span extended by advances in medicine caused the population to skyrocket from 150,000,000 to well over 200,000,000. These fifty million people have changed the whole environment; they have meant more mouths to feed, more bodies to house and clothe, and more minds to educate. The pressures on resources and the environment compel us to ask: What will happen if the birth rate is not controlled?

Amazing growth of the cities and suburbs, triggered by World War II and accelerated by an expanding economy and technological developments, has accompanied the increase in population. Urbanization has produced congestion, pollution, slums, and violence and has intensified conflict, tension, frustration, and anxiety in individuals and within communities.

In the expanding economy stimulated by World War II and the conflicts in Korea and Vietnam, the commercial, industrial, military, and government establishments have flourished. The entire social, economic, and political world has been computerized and enmeshed by this system.

If the situation had earlier failed to engender a sense of urgency, the energy crisis will force everyone to realize that the dangers of population growth, pollution of air and water, the spoilation of natural resources, the growth of crime, and urbanization require immediate constructive action. If business, labor, government, and military leaders do not recognize their responsibilities and respond to the challenges, then new leaders must arise. All groups within the community must cooperate and work for the welfare of America. There must be an "overriding sense of collective responsibility."

This anthology describes the problems. I have tried to choose articles that illustrate the most pressing, threatening problems. They present an array of viewpoints and arguments from political scientists, lawyers, sociologists, economists, criminals, and students. They focus on population, pollution, permissiveness, poverty, race, crime, and the military. They deal with injustice, youth, anomie, and alienation. Perhaps by seeing the reality, we can gain the courage and wisdom to find solutions. A better world need not be an idle dream.

Special thanks go to Professor S. Christodoulou (Manhattan College), David King, Sherry DeMatteo, Mary Klein, Clifford Snyder, and Robert deVilleneuve for their criticisms and suggestions; each knows the special contribution that was made.

Kenneth L. Culver

Part 1
The Question

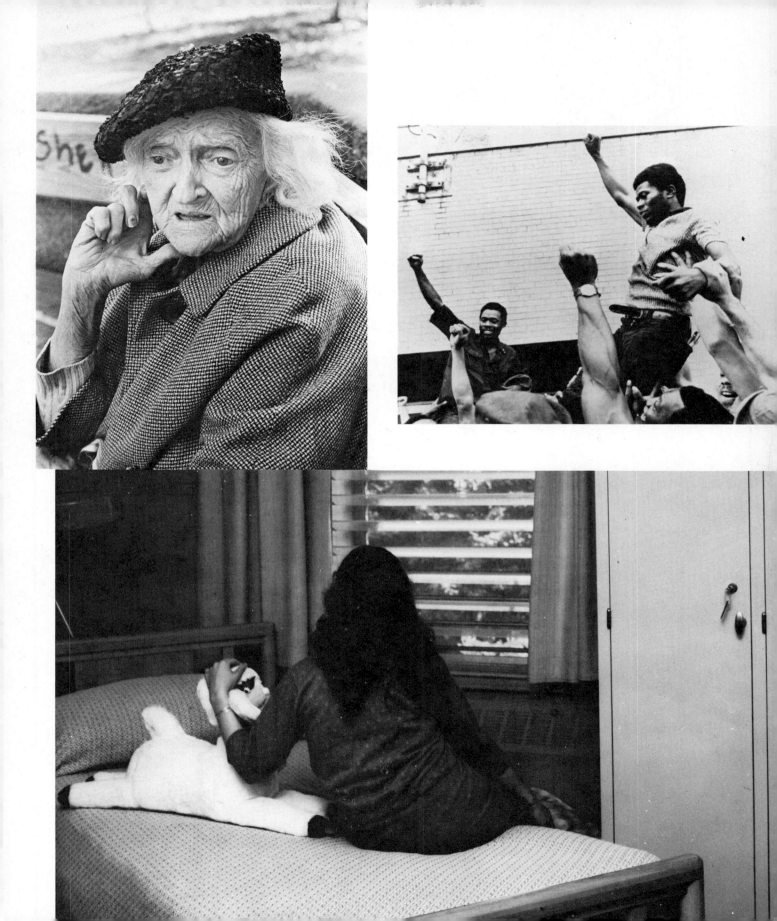

1 DEFINING A SOCIAL PROBLEM

What Is a Social Problem?

Neil H. Jacoby

From *The Center Magazine* (July-August, 1971), 35–40. Reprinted, with permission, from the July/August 1971 issue of *The Center Magazine*, a publication of the Center for the Study of Democratic Institutions, Santa Barbara, California.

Former Dean of Business Administration at UCLA, Dr. Jacoby is presently Professor of Business Economics with extensive governmental and public service. Among his publications is European Economics: East and West *(1967).*

It is widely believed that the American nation confronts serious social problems. Many hold that our society is being shaken by a succession of overlapping and interrelated crises, including population growth and concentration, environmental pollution, poverty, crime, drugs, racial enmity, malnutrition, urban blight, and the [late] war in Southeast Asia. Most of those in the New Left aver that unresolved problems are mounting in intensity. Changes in social institutions are occurring too slowly, they say, to accommodate changes in the goals, beliefs, and expectations of the public. Hence, the potentiality of a political revolution—of a sudden drastic restructuring of our social institutions—is rising. Indeed, extremist groups like the Weathermen and the Black Panthers, along with such mentors as Professor Herbert Marcuse, are actively fomenting revolution. They deliberately reject the course of working peacefully within the social system to shape its development along desired lines. The mounting level of violence in American society throughout the sixties suggests that not a few persons have given credence to this line of thought.

It is therefore timely to examine the meaning of social problems. How do they arise? By what process do they escalate into crises? How can they be ameliorated or resolved?

A basic premise of our inquiry is that peaceful evolution is nearly always to be preferred to violent revolution as a path of social reform. Although revolution may in some circumstances be necessary, man's history shows that it is an extremely wasteful mode of social change. Revolution destroys physical and social capital and leaves in its wake a large reservoir of wrongs and inequities that require generations to liquidate. Evolutionary social change can avoid these setbacks. It can steadily augment social justice and material well-being. It can yield progress without hiatus.

Let us consider the nature of a "social problem." In January, 1969, the distinguished Panel on Social Indicators appointed by the Secretary of Health, Education, and Welfare reported that, by nearly all measures, the well-being of the American people had improved materially since

World War II. Yet it found that public disaffection had also risen markedly. The reason was, it wisely observed, that people's expectations had risen faster than reality could improve.

The phenomenon noted by the Panel on Social Indicators was the same as that observed by Toqueville in eighteenth-century France:

> The evil which was suffered patiently as inevitable, seems unendurable as soon as the idea of escaping from it crosses men's minds. All the abuses then removed call attention to those that remain, and they now appear more galling. The evil, it is true, has become less, but sensibility to it has become more acute.

A social problem, then, may be defined as a gap between society's expectations of social conditions and the present social realities. Social expectations are the set of demands and priorities held by the people of a society at a given time. Social realities mean the set of laws, regulations, customs, and organizations, along with the pertinent economic, political, and social processes that prevail at a given time.

Social problems are created by public awareness of, or belief in, the existence of an expectation-reality gap. They are basically psychological phenomena—ideas held in the minds of people—about the disparity between what should be, and what is, in our society. Social problems are not definable solely in physical or biological terms, such as so many calories of food intake per day, or so many square feet of housing per capita. They must be defined in terms of the extent of the expectation-reality gap.

One may illustrate the independence of a social problem from any particular social condition by considering the example of poverty. Poverty is now perceived by Americans to be an important social problem in the United States, because in 1970 eleven percent of the population had incomes under the official poverty level (about $3,500 per year for a family of four), whereas Americans generally believe that no one should live under the poverty line. Poverty was

not perceived to be an important social problem in 1947, although twenty-seven percent of the population then lived under the poverty line by 1970 standards. Despite an astonishing gain in the real incomes of those in the lowest brackets, public expectations outraced realities. Hence the expectation-reality gap with respect to poverty is wider today than it was in 1947. The problem of poverty has become more serious at the same time that the incidence of poverty has been cut sixty percent and continues to decline.

Once the concept is grasped that a social problem is a gap between public expectations of social conditions and social realities, it becomes clear that our society, and especially its political leaders, must pay as much attention to the forces that determine public expectations as to those that shape social realities. They should seek to keep the gap at a tolerable size and thereby avoid violent or disruptive social behavior.

The expectation-reality gap is, of course, a dynamic system that changes through time. Public expectations change as a consequence of the expanding size and concentration of the human population, of rising affluence, or of technological advances. Thus, the high priority now assigned to the problem of environmental pollution reflects an elevation in the social expectations of clean air and water and other environmental amenities by a richer and more crowded population. Public expectations are also shaped by the flow of information, words, and pictures that they receive from the mass media of communication—newspapers, magazines, radio, and television. Expectations are likewise heavily influenced by publicly expressed views of political leaders. For example, President Eisenhower raised the nation's expectations for better highways with his support of the interstate highway system in the fifties; President Johnson boosted public expectations of an end to poverty with his "war on poverty" in the sixties.

Changes in social expectations require responsive changes in social realities, if a rise in social tensions—that is, in revolutionary potential—is to be avoided. For example, racial tensions have risen in the United States partly because the rising social expectation of racial integration of the public-school system, called for by the 1954 *Brown* decision of the Supreme Court, has not yet produced a commensurate shift in the racial structure of the educational system. As with the social problem of poverty, the realities of educational integration have improved, but have been outrun by the rise in public expectations.

Revolutionary potential—the degree of public frustration caused by a gap between expectations and realities—is also a function of time. It will rise as the time lapse lengthens between a given expectation and responsive change in social institutions and processes. The American Revolution of 1776 exploded when a sufficiently large number of colonials found that the gap between their long-reiterated demands for a larger voice in their own government and the intransigency of the British Crown was no longer endurable. Timely action by the British to delegate powers of self-government would have reduced the revolutionary potential and even possibly avoided a political revolution.

There have been periods in American history when popular expectations of social improvement have been extremely low. During the Great Depression, for example, the revolutionary potential was surprisingly weak. Public expectations of social improvement had become so deflated by 1933 that only a small gap separated them from the grim social realities of those times. President Roosevelt and his New Deal performed a magnificent act of political leadership in regenerating public expectations.

The mass media play an important role in the creation and magnification of social problems. They do this by increasing public awareness of gaps between social goals and current realities, and also by magnifying public perceptions of such gaps. Millions of Americans read about and see on their television screens crime on the streets, slums in the cities, deprivation in the ghettos, smog in the air, and sewage in the water. The American public was only remotely informed about these conditions fifty years ago. The mass media are frighteningly effective in widening public awareness of the chasms that separate man's expectations of peace, plenty,

justice, and stability from the realities of the human condition. Thus they create social problems where none had existed before, and they escalate minor problems into major crises.

If the mass media operated simply as faithful transmitters of printed and pictorial images of society as it is, one could not complain about their effect on the public's perception of reality or the size of the expectation-reality gap. However, they are more than mere transmitters. They are selectors of the information and images presented to people. Because they thrive on the shocking, the extreme, the bizarre, they have little interest in conveying to their audiences the normal life or the quiet incremental progress of society. The mass media tend to screen out words and images that reveal normality, and to transmit those that show deprivation, injustice, suffering, and maladjustment, on the one hand, and those that depict wealth, extravagance, or conspicuous consumption, on the other. Thus they function as magnifiers or amplifiers of the expectation-reality gap that previously existed in the public's mind. Expectations of social improvement are elevated even higher; social realities are seen to be even worse than before.

Art Buchwald recently recounted how George III suppressed television in Britain during the latter eighteenth century, because TV pictures of British mercenaries suppressing colonial Americans were inciting the British public to a state of rebellion against its colonial policies. Despite its humorous approach, the proposal has a serious point. Buchwald used this imaginary analogy to suggest that the U.S. government should suppress all television coverage of the late war in Southeast Asia.

A recent example of journalistic distortion was the pronouncement by *The New York Times* and the Washington *Post* that the police have killed twenty-eight Black Panthers since January 1, 1968. This "news" statement was widely copied, and followed by editorial speculation that the police were conspiring to wipe out Black Panther leadership. The Negro community reacted in anger. In a carefully researched article in the *New Yorker* of February 13, 1971, Edward J. Epstein showed that the source of this inflammatory statement was Charles R. Garry, counsel for the Panther organization, and that it was false. Ten of the twenty-eight Panthers had been killed by their own political opponents. With two possible exceptions about which the facts are unclear, a study of the other sixteen deaths showed that in every case the Panthers were armed, threatened the police, and shot first. There was not a shred of evidence to support the conspiracy thesis.

If the mass media are a powerful instrument in the formation of public attitudes and expectations, it becomes vitally important that they present accurate and balanced word-and-picture images of events within their proper historical contexts. No one would suggest governmental censorship of information flows to the public. What is proposed is self-disciplined objectivity so that the mass media will perform their function of accurate and objective transmission of information that can be the basis of rational and realistic public attitudes and expectations.

Our political system of representative democracy also tends to create or to expand social problems by raising public expectations of social gains and by exaggerating gaps between expectations and realities. Politicians generally do not challenge the validity of existing public expectations, or seek to reduce them to realizable levels. The basic reason for their one-sided influence is clear enough. It is in the professional interest of the politician to inflate rather than deflate unrealistic expectations. Politicians are elected by "viewing with alarm" the empty records of their opponents in office and by leading the voters to believe that the incumbent scoundrels have prevented them from getting their share of the good things of life. If only the electorate turns the rascals out, change will bring great improvements. Of course, by the time of the next election the roles of politicians in the two parties are often reversed; the "great society" still has not been achieved and the people are more frustrated than ever. The expectation-reality gap has widened.

Intellectuals are also traditional "viewers with alarm" because any other attitude would compromise their professional reputations as social critics. They consider it a duty to decry gaps between the performance of the society and its potential. Otherwise their colleagues would believe that they had sold out to the Establishment or had lost their critical faculties. Given the strong propensity to hypercriticize in scholarly teaching and writing, and considering the now vast number of youths under academic influence in the higher educational system, it is no wonder that a rising fraction of the U.S. population has become alienated from society and its institutions.

Presidential Task Forces and Commissions and other public groups often generate or enlarge social problems by attention-getting public statements. Although such bodies are supposed to provide calm and objective assessments of social problems, their effort to compete with the tidal wave of information that daily inundates us all often leads them to make shocking statements that create distorted impressions or beliefs in the public mind. Because the whole truth is rarely dramatic, they tend to twist the truth or to convey partial truths in order to create shock value.

An instance of headline-grabbing by distortion is the 1968 Report of the National Advisory Commission on Racial Disorders, commonly known as the Kerner Report. Although this weighty document contained much wisdom, what stood out when it was issued was the inflammatory headlined statement that "this nation is moving toward two societies, black and white, separate and unequal." The vast majority of people who read this headline, but who did not read the whole report, concluded that the Kerner Commission found that racial inequality and separation in America was rising in all dimensions. The implications of the statement were extremely disruptive. By implying that the Establishment was failing to improve racial relations, and that the racial gap was widening, the Kerner Report added fuel to the fiery demands of militant groups for revolutionary changes. Seeds of bitterness were sown in the minds of the uninformed. Racial tensions were exacerbated at home. The nation was denigrated abroad.

Yet the truth is that our democratic political institutions and our market economy, despite imperfections, have been making steady progress in narrowing the economic, educational, political, and social inequalities between the races ever since World War II. The median income of nonwhite families rose from fifty-five percent of that of white families in 1950 to sixty-three percent in 1968; and, according to figures cited by Daniel Moynihan, the incomes of black young married couples had become equal to those of white young married couples in 1970. The proportionate reduction in poverty since 1959 has been almost as great among blacks as among whites. Whereas in 1947 black adult Americans completed thirty-four percent fewer years of schooling than the entire population, by 1969 this difference had narrowed to nineteen percent; and, for persons in the age bracket from twenty-five to twenty-nine years, it had nearly vanished. The differences between the life expectancies at birth of the two races diminished significantly during the postwar era. The steadily rising proportion of black citizens that are registered and vote in elections and of blacks in public office shows a narrowing of the political gap. Blacks themselves overwhelmingly believe that conditions are improving for their race in this country, as sociologist Gary T. Marx reported in his book *Protest and Prejudice*. All these facts demonstrate impressive postwar progress of the American Negro toward economic and political equality, although many will understandably say "too little and too late." The correct conclusion to be drawn, however, is to keep public policy on the present course and to try to accelerate its pace.

The gravity of the nation's social problems is also enlarged by the teachings and writings of the liberal left. Much liberal left social thought is based upon illusory concepts of the nature of man and society, well described by Professor Harold Demsetz as the "Nirvana," "other grass is greener," "free lunch," and "people could be different" fallacies (*Journal of Law and Economics*, April, 1960).

The "Nirvana" approach to social policy presents a choice between a theoretical ideal never approached in man's history and existing conditions. The vast distance between the two naturally creates a social "crisis." The true choice, however, lies between existing conditions and others that are feasible in the sense of being capable of attainment. Because the expectation-reality gap in the latter case is usually small, the "crisis" is reduced to a manageable problem.

The "other grass is greener" illusion credits an alternative social condition, usually in some foreign country, with great virtues said to be lacking in American society. Thus atmospheric pollution is said to be the product of capitalistic enterprise, and its cure is to adopt state socialism. This idea is repeated by social critics who have not taken the trouble to ascertain that pollution levels in socialist countries have risen, along with their G.N.P.'s, even faster than in capitalist countries.

The "free lunch" fallacy is that there are costless remedies for social ills. Since unemployment is an evil, say the critics, abolish it and reduce the unemployment ratio to zero. They choose to ignore the heavy social costs of such a policy in the form of restrictions on individual freedom, lowered productivity, and price inflation. Every decision that produces public benefits imposes costs, and the problem is to weigh both and determine the balance.

The "people could be different" fallacy is that the Good Society can be attained by radical changes in the moral and ethical behavior of people. Thus the "new communist man," imbued with a totally altruistic concern for the public welfare, was seen by the older Marxists as the condition for the ultimate transformation of socialism into true communism. Unfortunately, he has not yet appeared in sufficient numbers to make this possible; and he shows no sign of doing so. While moderate changes in men's values and behavior can occur over time (indeed, changes are essential if our society is to improve), sharp mutations in human nature are a fantasy. In reforming our society, we are wise to take human nature as a datum, and to design structures and processes for imperfect men and women rather than for saints or philosophers.

In his report to the nation on U.S. foreign

policy for the nineteen-seventies, President Nixon observed: "No nation has the wisdom and the understanding and the energy required to act wisely on all problems, at all times, in every part of the world." The statement is equally true and important if we substitute "nation" for "world." The number of different domestic problems that the people of a nation can cope with effectively at any given time is limited, not only by the stock of popular wisdom, energy, and understanding, but also by the available economic resources of the society. In view of the fact that available economic resources form a severe constraint upon national capability to improve real social conditions, whereas public expectations of social improvement can soar at a virtually unlimited rate, it is far more likely that a social problem will escalate into a "crisis" through an inordinate rise in expectations than by a failure of real conditions to improve.

If national political and intellectual leaders ignore the resource constraints upon real social improvements, they may, by dramatizing one social deficiency after another, stimulate public expectations so powerfully that multiple social "crises" are created in the public mind. During the Administration of President Johnson, for example, a "war on poverty" was followed by a "war on hunger" and a "war on slums" and so on. Faced by a "war" on a new social front every few months without having won any of those already in progress the American people became progressively confused, frustrated, angered, and alienated from their government. Failure of the national political leadership to hold social expectations within the boundaries of national capabilities led to the violence and disruptive behavior that marked the last half of the sixties.

By the end of 1968 public frustration and social tensions in the United States had reached a dangerous level. Americans demanded a quantity and variety of social improvements far beyond the capacity of this or any other society to produce. People's energies were being dissipated in dropoutism, absenteeism, and irrelevant protest rather than utilized in constructive action—as shown by a catastrophic drop in pro-

ductivity. Fortunately the succeeding Nixon Administration applied the remedies of "low profile" and "benign neglect," which succeeded in reducing many social "crises" into manageable problems by deflating exaggerated public expectations.

It is a mistaken view that real social progress only occurs after a "crisis" has been generated, or that a deflation of exaggerated public expectations is tantamount to foot-dragging in making necessary social reforms. On the contrary, there is a good deal of evidence that "crises"— especially if accompanied by violence—are inimical to long-run progress; and that the maintenance of a proper relation between expectations and realities avoids disruptive social behavior that retards real social progress. Thus, poverty in the United States was being rapidly reduced after World War II and there is no convincing evidence that the "war on poverty" launched in 1965 speeded up the process.

Our theory of social tensions helps to explain the almost pathological mood of self-criticism and self-deprecation that has descended upon Americans in recent years. William James said that an individual's self-esteem could be measured by the ratio of his success or achievement to his potential. By analogy, national self-esteem is the ratio of national achievement to national potential, as they are generally perceived by people. As national achievements (i.e., social realities) are depreciated, and national potentialities (i.e., social expectations) are exaggerated, the quotient of national self-esteem will fall to the vanishing point.

Our society is a dynamic system in which public values and expectations and social institutions and processes change through time. The central aims of public policy should be to maintain an optimal expectation-reality gap and to achieve an optimal rate of change in both social expectations and social realities.

An optimal expectation-reality gap is wide enough to preserve incentive and motive for beneficial changes in social institutions and processes. ("Man's reach should exceed his grasp, else what is Heaven for?") Yet it is not so wide as to cause public frustration and diversion of energy from constructive action to inaction or to disruptive behavior. Public goals and expectations should advance through time, fast enough to maintain social flexibility and adaptability, but not so rapidly as to lose contact with realities.

The real conditions of life should also be improved through time, fast enough to sustain a popular belief in progress but not so fast as to lead to malallocations of resources and social imbalances.

Because the rate of improvement in social conditions is determined within a fairly narrow range by well-known constraints upon the growth of production, whereas the rate of increase in public expectations is virtually unlimited, it is likely that political leaders will more frequently find it necessary to moderate public expectations than to raise them in order to avoid dangerous gaps. This appears especially probable in our society which, as has been seen, is institutionally organized to magnify expectation-reality gaps and in which high achievement is the normal goal.

The general strategy for approaching the optimum gap between expectations and realities will include the following elements: (1) accelerate desired institutional changes in the economic, political, and social systems to an optimum rate; (2) publicize the changes that are occurring in the society to reduce poverty, racial discrimination, crime, or to improve health, housing, and other conditions; (3) instruct the public in the political and economic processes of change and their time dimensions so that there will emerge a general appreciation of what is realistically possible; (4) develop through research more frequent and reliable indicators of social conditions and of the state of public expectations, and of their rates of change through time, as guides to social policy-makers. Social scientists should also try to measure the sustainable rates of change in social institutions. Leonard Lecht's pioneering effort to measure the dollar costs of attaining U.S. national goals, and to compare it with national production capacity is a type of research that should be expanded (*Goals, Priorities, and Dollars.* New York: Free Press, 1966).

Managing public expectations has become a vital new dimension of political leadership in the United States, of coordinate importance with the engineering of orderly reform of our social institutions. Political leaders need to observe expectation-reality gaps constantly in order to maintain the proper state of tension in society. The statesmen of the future will be those who know how to bring about orderly social change and also to keep public expectations in a productive relationship to realities. Thus they will enable our society to resolve successfully a constantly emerging set of new social problems.

Part 2
Problem Areas

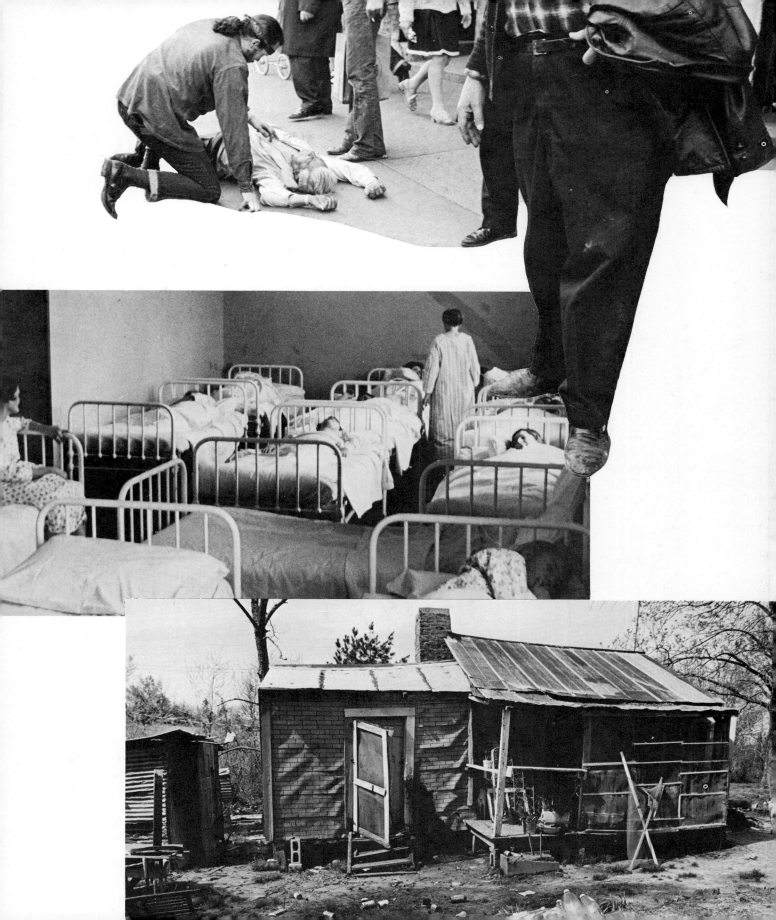

2 ENVIRONMENT—AT WHAT PRICE?

The High Cost of Protecting Our Future: Saving the Crusade

Peter F. Drucker

From *Harper's Magazine* (January, 1972), 66–71. Reprinted by permission of the author.

Peter F. Drucker is Professor of Social Science at the Claremont Graduate School and has taught at Bennington College and New York University. Among an extensive list of publications are The End of Economic Man *(1939),* The New Society *(1950),* The Effective Executive *(1967), and* Men, Ideas, and Politics *(1971).*

Everybody today is "for the environment." Laws and agencies designed to protect it multiply at all levels of government. Big corporations take full-color ads to explain how they're cleaning up, or at least trying to. Even you as a private citizen probably make some conscientious effort to curb pollution. At the same time, we have learned enough about the problem to make some progress toward restoring a balance between man and nature. The environmental crusade may well become the great cause of the Seventies—and not one moment too soon.

Yet the crusade is in real danger of running off the tracks, much like its immediate predecessor, the so-called war on poverty. Paradoxically, the most fervent environmentalists may be among the chief wreckers. Many are confused about the cause of our crisis and the ways in which we might resolve it. They ignore the diffi- cult decisions that must be made; they splinter the resources available for attacking environmental problems. Indeed, some of our leading crusaders seem almost perversely determined to sabotage their cause—and our future.

Consider, for example, the widespread illusion that a clean environment can be obtained by reducing or even abolishing our dependence on "technology." The growing pollution crisis does indeed raise fundamental questions about technology—its direction, uses, and future. But the relationship between technology and the environment is hardly as simple as much anti-technological rhetoric would have us believe. The invention that has probably had the greatest environmental impact in the past twenty-five years, for instance, is that seemingly insignificant gadget, the wire-screen window. The wire screen, rather than DDT or antibiotics, detonated the "population explosion" in underdeveloped countries, where only a few decades ago as many as four out of five children died of such insect borne diseases as "summer diarrhea" or malaria before their fifth birthday. Would even the most ardent environmentalist outlaw the screen window and expose those babies again to the flies?

The truth is that most environmental problems require technological solutions—and dozens of them. To control our biggest water pollutant, human wastes, we will have to draw on all sciences and technologies from biochemistry to thermodynamics. Similarly, we need the most advanced technology for adequate treatment of the effluents that mining and manufacturing spew into the world's waters. It will take even more new technology to repair the damage caused by the third major source of water pollution in this country—the activities of farmers and loggers.

Even the hope of genuine disarmament—and the arms race may be our worst and most dangerous pollutant—rests largely on complex technologies of remote inspection and surveillance. Environmental control, in other words, requires technology at a level at least as high as the technology whose misuse it is designed to correct. The sewage-treatment plants that are urgently needed all over the world will be designed, built, and kept running not by purity of heart, ballads, or Earth Days but by crew-cut engineers working in very large organizations, whether businesses, research labs, or government agencies.

The second and equally dangerous delusion abroad today is the common belief that the cost of cleaning the environment can be paid for out of "business profits." After taxes, the profits of all American businesses in a good year come to sixty or seventy billion dollars. And mining and manufacturing—the most polluting industries—account for less than half of this. But at the lowest estimate, the cleanup bill, even for just the most urgent jobs, will be three or four times as large as all business profits.

Consider the most efficient and most profitable electric-power company in the country (and probably in the world): the American Power Company, which operates a number of large power systems in the Midwest and upper South. It has always been far more ecology-minded than most other power companies, including the government's own TVA. Yet cleaning up American Power's plants to the point where they no longer befoul air and water will require, for many years to come, an annual outlay close to,

if not exceeding, the company's present annual profit of $100 million. The added expense caused by giving up strip mining of coal or by reclaiming strip-mined land might double the company's fuel bill, its single largest operating cost. No one can even guess what it would cost —if and when it can be done technologically—to put power transmission lines underground. It might well be a good deal more than power companies have ever earned.

We face an environmental crisis because for too long we have disregarded genuine costs. Now we must raise the costs, in a hurry, to where they should have been all along. The expense must be borne, eventually, by the great mass of the people as consumers and producers. The only choice we have is which of the costs will be borne by the consumer in the form of higher prices, and which by the taxpayer in the form of higher taxes.

It may be possible to convert part of this economic burden into economic opportunity, though not without hard work and, again, new technology. Many industrial or human wastes might be transformed into valuable products. The heat produced in generating electricity might be used in greenhouses and fish farming, or to punch "heat holes" into the layer of cold air over such places as Los Angeles, creating an updraft to draw off the smog. But these are long-range projects. The increased costs are here and now.

Closely related to the fallacy that "profit" can pay the environmental bill is the belief that we can solve the environmental crisis by reducing industrial output. In the highly developed affluent countries of the world, it is true that we may be about to de-emphasize the "production-orientation" of the past few hundred years. Indeed, the "growth sectors" of the developed economies are increasingly education, leisure activities, or health care rather than goods. But paradoxical as it may sound, the environmental crisis will force us to return to an emphasis on both growth and industrial output—at least for the next decade.

There are three reasons for this, each adequate in itself.

1) Practically every environmental task demands hugh amounts of electrical energy, way beyond anything now available. Sewage treatment is just one example; the difference between the traditional and wholly inadequate methods and a modern treatment plant that gets rid of human and industrial wastes and produces reasonably clear water is primarily electric power, and vast supplies of it. This poses a difficult dilemma. Power plants are themselves polluters. And one of their major pollution hazards, thermal pollution, is something we do not yet know how to handle.

Had we better postpone any serious attack on other environmental tasks until we have solved the pollution problems of electric-power generation? It would be a quixotic decision, but at least it would be a deliberate one. What is simply dishonest is the present hypocrisy that maintains we are serious about these other problems—industrial wastes, for instance, or sewage or pesticides—while we refuse to build the power plants we need to resolve them. I happen to be a member in good standing of the Sierra Club, and I share its concern for the environment. But the Sierra Club's opposition to any new power plant today—and the opposition of other groups to new power plants in other parts of the country (e.g., New York City)—has, in the first place, ensured that other ecological tasks cannot be done effectively for the next five or ten years. Secondly, it has made certain that the internal-combustion engine is going to remain our mainstay in transportation for a long time to come. An electrical automobile or electrified mass transportation—the only feasible alternatives—would require an even more rapid increase in electrical power than any now projected. And thirdly it may well, a few years hence, cause power shortages along the Atlantic Coast, which would mean unheated homes in winter, as well as widespread industrial shutdowns and unemployment. This would almost certainly start a "backlash" against the whole environmental crusade.

2) No matter how desirable a de-emphasis on production might be, the next decade is the wrong time for it in all the developed countries and especially in the U.S. The next decade will bring a surge in employment-seekers and in the formation of young families—both the inevitable result of the baby boom of the late Forties and early Fifties. Young adults need jobs; and unless there is a rapid expansion of jobs in production there will be massive unemployment, especially of low-skilled blacks and other minority group members. In addition to jobs, young families need goods—from housing and furniture to shoes for the baby. Even if the individual family's standard of consumption goes down quite a bit, total demand—barring only a severe depression—will go up sharply. If this is resisted in the name of ecology, environment will become a dirty word in the political vocabulary.

3) If there is no expansion of output equal to the additional cost of cleaning up the environment, the cost burden will—indeed, must—be met by cutting the funds available for education, health care, or the inner city, thus depriving the poor. It would be nice if the resources we need could come out of defense spending. But of the 6 or 7 percent of our national income that now goes for defense, a large part is cost of past wars, that is, veterans' pensions and disability benefits (which, incidentally, most other countries do not include in their defense budgets—a fact critics of "American militarism" often ignore). Even if we could—or should—cut defense spending, the "peace dividend" is going to be 1 or 2 percent of national income, at best.

But the total national outlay for education (7 to 8 percent), health care (another 7 to 8 percent), and the inner city and other poverty areas (almost 5 percent) comes to a fifth of total national income today. Unless we raise output and productivity fast enough to offset the added environmental cost, the voters will look to this sector for money. Indeed, in their rejection of school budgets across the nation and in their desperate attempts to cut welfare costs, voters have already begun to do so. That the shift of resources is likely to be accomplished in large part through inflation—essentially at the expense of the lower-income groups—will hardly make the environmental cause more popular with the poor.

The only way to avoid these evils is to expand the economy, probably at a rate of growth on the order of 4 percent a year for the next decade, a higher rate than we have been able to sustain in this country in the postwar years. This undoubtedly entails very great environmental risks. But the alternative is likely to mean no environmental action at all, and a rapid public turn—by no means confined to the "hard hats" —against all environmental concern whatever.

The final delusion is that the proper way to bring about a clean environment is through punitive legislation. We do need prohibitions and laws forbidding actions that endanger and degrade the environment. But more than that, we need incentives to preserve and improve it.

Punitive laws succeed only if the malefactors are few and the unlawful act is comparatively rare. Whenever the law attempts to prevent or control something everybody is doing, it degenerates into a huge but futile machine of informers, spies, bribe givers, and bribe takers. Today every one of us—in the underdeveloped countries almost as much as in the developed ones—is a polluter. Punitive laws and regulations can force automobile manufacturers to put emission controls into new cars, but they will never be able to force 100 million motorists to maintain this equipment. Yet this is going to be the central task if we are to stop automotive pollution.

What we should do is make it to everyone's advantage to reach environmental goals. And since the roots of the environmental crisis are so largely in economic activity, the incentives will have to be largely economic ones as well. Automobile owners who voluntarily maintain in working order the emission controls of their cars might, for instance, pay a much lower automobile registration fee, while those whose cars fall below accepted standards might pay a much higher fee. And if they were offered a sizable tax incentive, the automobile companies would put all their best energies to work to produce safer and emission-free cars, rather than fight delaying actions against punitive legislation.

Despite all the rhetoric on the campuses, we know by now that "capitalism" has nothing to do with the ecological crisis, which is fully as severe in the Communist countries. The bathing beaches for fifty miles around Stockholm have become completely unusable, not because of the wicked Swedish capitalists but because of the raw, untreated sewage from Communist Leningrad that drifts across the narrow Baltic. Moscow, even though it still has few automobiles, has as bad an air-pollution problem as Los Angeles—and has done less about it so far.

We should also know that "greed" has little to do with the environmental crisis. The two main causes are population pressures, especially the pressures of large metropolitan populations, and the desire—a highly commendable one—to bring a decent living at the lowest possible cost to the largest possible number of people.

The environmental crisis is the result of success—success in cutting down the mortality of infants (which has given us the population explosion), success in raising farm output sufficiently to prevent mass famine (which has given us contamination by insecticides, pesticides, and chemical fertilizers), success in getting people out of the noisome tenements of the nineteenth-century city and into the greenery and privacy of the single-family home in the suburbs (which has given us urban sprawl and traffic jams). The environmental crisis, in other words, is very largely the result of doing too much of the right sort of thing.

To overcome the problems success always creates, one has to build on it. The first step entails a willingness to take the risks involved in making decisions about complicated and perilous dilemmas:

What is the best "trade-off" between a cleaner environment and unemployment?

How can we prevent the environmental crusade from becoming a war of the rich against the poor, a new and particularly vicious "white racist imperialism"?

What can we do to harmonize the worldwide needs of the environment with the political and economic needs of other countries, and to keep American leadership from becoming American aggression?

How can we strike the least agonizing balance

of risks between environmental damage and mass starvation of poor children, or between environmental damage and large-scale epidemics?

More than twenty years ago, three young chemical engineers came to seek my advice. They were working for one of the big chemical companies, and its managers had told them to figure out what kind of new plants to put into West Virginia, where poverty was rampant. The three young men had drawn up a long-range plan for systematic job creation, but it included one project about which their top management was very dubious—a ferroalloy plant to be located in the very poorest area where almost everybody was unemployed. It would create 1,500 jobs in a dying small town of 12,000 people and another 800 jobs for unemployed coal miners—clean, healthy, safe jobs, since the new diggings would be strip mines.

But the plant would have to use an already obsolete high-cost process, the only one for which raw materials were locally available. It would therefore be marginal in both costs and product quality. Also the process was a singularly dirty one, and putting in the best available pollution controls would make it even less economical. Yet it was the only plant that could possibly be put in the neediest area. What did I think?

I said, "forget it"—which was, of course, not what the three young men wanted to hear and not the advice they followed.

This, as some readers have undoubtedly recognized, is the prehistory of what has become a notorious "environmental crime," the Union Carbide plant in Marietta, Ohio. When first opened in 1951 the plant was an "environmental pioneer." Its scrubbers captured three-quarters of the particles spewed out by the smelting furnaces; the standard at the time was half of that or less. Its smokestacks suppressed more fly ash than those of any other power plant then built, and so on.

But within ten years the plant had become an unbearable polluter to Vienna, West Virginia, the small town across the river whose unemploy-

ment it was built to relieve. And for the last five years the town and Union Carbide fought like wildcats. In the end Union Carbide lost. But while finally accepting federal and state orders to clean up an extremely dirty process, it also announced that it would have to lay off half the 1,500 men now working in the plant—and that's half the people employed in Vienna. The switch to cleaner coal (not to mention the abandonment of strip mining) would also put an end to the 800 or so coal-mining jobs in the poverty hollows of the back country.

There are scores of Viennas around the nation, where marginal plants are kept running precisely because they are the main or only employer in a depressed or decaying area. Should an uneconomical plant shut down, dumping its workers on the welfare rolls? Should the plant be subsidized (which would clearly open the way for everybody to put his hand in the public till)? Should environmental standards be disregarded or their application postponed in "hardship" cases?

If concern for the environment comes to be seen as an attack on the livelihood of workers, public sympathy and political support for it is likely to vanish. It is not too fanciful to anticipate, only a few years hence, the New (if aging) Left, the concerned kids on the campus, and the ministers in a protest march against "ecology" and in support of "the victims of bourgeois environmentalism."

In the poor, developing countries where men must struggle to make even a little progress in their fight against misery, any industry bears a heavy burden of high costs and low productivity. Burdening it further with the cost of environmental control might destroy it. Moreover, development in these countries—regardless of their political creed or social organization, in Mao's as well as in Chiang Kai-shek's China and in North as well as in South Vietnam—cannot occur without the four biggest ecological villains: a rapid increase in electric power, chemical fertilizers and pesticides, the automobile, and the large steel mill.

That poor countries regard those villains as

economic saviors confronts us with hard political choices. Should we help such countries get what they want (industrialization), or what we think the world needs (less pollution)? How do we avoid the charge, in either case, that our help is "imperialistic"? To complicate matters, there is a looming conflict between environmental concern and national sovereignty. The environment knows no national boundaries. Just as the smog of England befouls the air of Norway, so the chemical wastes of the French potash mines in Alsace destroy the fish of the lower Rhine in Belgium and Holland.

No matter what the statistics bandied about today, the U.S. is not the world's foremost polluter. Japan holds this dubious honor by a good margin. No American city can truly compete in air pollution with Tokyo, Milan, Budapest, Moscow, or Düsseldorf. No American river is as much of an open sewer as the lower Rhine, the Seine, or the rivers of the industrial Ukraine such as the lower Dnieper. And we are sheer amateurs in littering highways compared to the Italians, Danes, Germans, French, Swedes, Swiss, and Austrians—although the Japanese, especially in littering mountainsides and camp grounds, are clearly even more "advanced."

If not the worst polluter, however, the U.S. is clearly the largest one. More important, as the most affluent, most advanced, and biggest of the industrial countries, it is expected to set an example. If we do not launch the environmental crusade, no one else will.

We shall have to make sure, however, that other nations join with us. In the absence of international treaties and regulations, some countries—especially those with protectionist traditions, such as Japan, France, and even the United States—may be tempted to impose ecological standards on imports more severe than those they demand of their own producers. On the other hand, countries heavily dependent on exports, especially in Africa and Latin America, may try to gain a competitive advantage by lax enforcement of environmental standards.

One solution might be action by the United Nations to fix uniform rules obliging all its mem-

bers to protect the environment; and such action is, in fact, now under official study. The United States might help by changing its import regulations to keep out goods produced by flagrant polluters—allowing ample time for countries with severe poverty and unemployment problems to get the cleanup under way. We have good precedent for such an approach in our own history. Forty years ago we halted the evils of child labor by forbidding the transportation in interstate commerce of goods produced by children.

Such a course, however, will demand extraordinary judgment. Unless we persuade other nations to join with us—and set an example ourselves—we may well be accused of trying again to "police the world."

The hardest decisions ahead are even more unprecedented than those we have been discussing. What risks can we afford to take with the environment, and what risks can we *not* afford to take? What are the feasible trade-offs between man's various needs for survival?

Today, for example, no safe pesticides exist, nor are any in sight. We may ban DDT, but all the substitutes so far developed have highly undesirable properties. Yet if we try to do without pesticides altogether, we shall invite massive hazards of disease and starvation the world over. In Ceylon, where malaria was once endemic, it was almost wiped out by large-scale use of DDT; but in only a few years since spraying was halted, the country has suffered an almost explosive resurgence of the disease. In other tropical countries, warns the UN Food and Agricultural Organization, children are threatened with famine, because of insect and blight damage to crops resulting from restrictions on spraying. Similarly, anyone who has lately traveled the New England turnpike will have noticed whole forests defoliated by the gypsy moth, now that we have stopped aerial spraying.

What is the right trade-off between the health hazard to some women taking the pill and the risk of death to others from abortions? How do we balance the thermal and radiation dangers of nuclear power plants against the need for more electricity to fight other kinds of pollution? How should we choose between growing more food for the world's fast-multiplying millions and the banning of fertilizers that pollute streams, lakes, and oceans?

Such decisions should not be demanded of human beings. None of the great religions offers guidance. Neither do the modern "isms," from Maoism to the anarchism popular with the young. The ecological crisis forces man to play God. Despite the fact that we are unequal to the task, we can't avoid it: the risks inherent in refusing to tackle these problems are the greatest of all. We have to try, somehow, to choose some combination of lesser evils; doing nothing invites even greater catastrophe.

Cleaning up the environment requires determined, sustained effort with clear targets and deadlines. It requires, above all, concentration of effort. Up to now we have had almost complete diffusion. We have tried to do a little bit of everything—and tried to do it in the headlines—when what we ought to do first is draw up a list of priorities in their proper order.

First on such a list belong a few small but clearly definable and highly visible tasks that can be done fairly fast without tying up important resources. Removing the hazard of lead poisoning in old slum tenements might be such an action priority. What to do is well known: burn off the old paint. A substantial number of underemployed black adolescents could be easily recruited to do it.

Once visible successes have been achieved, the real task of priority-setting begins. Then one asks: 1) what are the biggest problems that we know how to solve, and (2) what are the really big ones that we don't know how to solve yet? Clean air should probably head the first list. It's a worldwide problem, and getting worse. We don't know all the answers, but we do have the technological competence to handle most of the problems of foul air today. Within ten years we should have real results to show for our efforts.

Within ten years, too, we should get major results in cleaning up the water around big industrial cities and we should have slowed (if not stopped) the massive pollution of the oceans, especially in the waters near our coastal cities.

As for research priorities, I suggest that the first is to develop birth-control methods that are cheaper, more effective, and more acceptable to people of all cultures than anything we now have. Secondly, we need to learn how to produce electric energy without thermal pollution. A third priority is to devise ways of raising crops for a rapidly growing world population without at the same time doing irreversible ecological damage through pesticides, herbicides, and chemical fertilizers.

Until we get the answers, I think we had better keep on building power plants and growing food with the help of fertilizers and such insect-controlling chemicals as we now have. The risks are now well known, thanks to the environmentalists. If they had not created a widespread public awareness of the ecological crisis, we wouldn't stand a chance. But such awareness by itself is not enough. Flaming manifestos and prophecies of doom are no longer much help, and a search for scapegoats can only make matters worse.

What we now need is a coherent, long-range program of action, and education of the public and our lawmakers about the steps necessary to carry it out. We must recognize—and we need the help of environmentalists in this task—that we can't do everything at once; that painful choices have to be made, as soon as possible, about what we should tackle first; and that every decision is going to involve high risks and costs, in money and in human lives. Often these will have to be decisions of conscience as well as economics. Is it better, for example, to risk famine or to risk global pollution of earth and water? Any course we adopt will involve a good deal of experimentation—and that means there will be some failures. Any course also will demand sacrifices, often from those least able to bear them: the poor, the unskilled, and the underdeveloped countries. To succeed, the environmental crusade needs support from all major groups in our society, and the mobilization of all our resources, material and intellectual, for years of hard, slow, and often discouraging effort.

Otherwise it will not only fail; it will, in the process, splinter domestic and international societies into warring factions.

Now that they have succeeded in awakening us to our ecological peril, I hope the environmentalists will turn their energies to the second and harder task: educating the public to accept the choices we must face, and to sustain a worldwide effort to carry through on the resulting decisions. The time for sensations and manifestos is about over; now we need rigorous analysis, united effort, and very hard work.

3 POPULATION—HOW MANY?

The Population Problem in the United States

Lincoln H. Day

Professor Day teaches sociology and public health at Yale University and is a specialist in demography. In addition to his journal articles and other studies, he has written Too Many Americans *(1964).*

"For most people the population problem exists for developing countries or some other place in the world, but they do not see it as a problem in the United States. No country can support even a low rate of population growth for an unlimited period of time. Regardless of the economy or level of living which people are willing to tolerate, there is an upper limit to the number of people that can live in a given area. The United States, like every other country on earth, must at some point reach the upper limit of its population growth. If at all possible, this upper limit should be achieved rationally in such a way as to make possible the maintenance of the style of living which the people of the country desire. If this upper limit is not achieved rationally by limitation of births, it will come, as Malthus said, by war, famine and plague.

Dr. Day points out that here in the United States our level of living is in greater danger from population pressure than in most other areas of the world. He also looks at the excess population growth to determine those segments of the population making the greatest contributions. The greatest contribution in total numbers comes from native whites of native parentage. In conclusion Dr. Day indicates some of the specific steps that should be taken in a program to reduce our rate of population growth here in the United States."*

Sixty-six years ago, we Americans entered the twentieth century with a population of 75 million, a population less than two-fifths (38 percent) as large as the 196 million we number today. Within the next thirty-four years, if the growth rate of the last five years continues, we will add another 122 million, bringing the total to enter the twenty-first century up to 318 million—four times as many of us as there were a century earlier. The sheer magnitude of this growth is remarkable—and something quite new in man's history. Already the fourth largest population in the world, we Americans increase each year by a number equal to the population of the whole San Francisco—Oakland urban area

*Comments by the editor, Daniel O. Price

and nearly a million larger than the entire Washington, D.C. urban area. These are not mere statistics. These are Americans, with American needs, with American hopes and American aspirations.

Few would hold that of all nations our population problems are the worst. All over the world man is multiplying at historically unprecedented rates and in many areas under conditions that threaten his very survival. But the fact that population growth has immediately disastrous consequences for peoples elsewhere in the world should not blind us to the very important consequences it has for life right here in the United States.

One thing is inescapable: no population can continue to increase indefinitely, nor can the population of the United States continue much longer to increase at the high rate we are experiencing today. Sooner or later there would come a point at which the burden of human numbers so reduced levels of living that the death rate would once more rise to preindustrial heights. Related to this is another demographic fact, one equally inescapable though often overlooked, when population increase *is* finally halted, it will be as a result either of lowering the birth rate or raising the death rate. There is no other way. This is worth remembering when we come to consider whether or not to take positive steps to curb population growth.

We must also bear in mind that the decisions we make about childbearing today will greatly determine the kind of society we and our children live in tomorrow, for population has a sleeper effect. The full impact of childbearing occurs not at conception, not even at birth. Rather, it steadily mounts as a child grows, becomes educated, seeks employment, sets up a separate household, and eventually becomes a parent himself. In our present enthusiasm for childbearing we in America are creating a situation in which our children may have available to them a quality of life in many ways markedly inferior to that of their parents.

In its simplest terms, then, the population dilemma in the United States can be reduced to this choice: continuation of the present, ultimately ruinous, pattern in which childbearing is regarded as the exclusive prerogative of the individual parent and no consideration is given to its social consequences; or recognition that the consequences of childbearing are as important to the society as they are to the individual parent and that individual and social interests coincide in the need to limit family size to two or—at the very most—three children.

This may sound extreme, but I propose to show why this difficult choice has become necessary. I shall describe the pertinent characteristics of American population growth, point out how much various groups in our population are contributing to this growth, and enumerate some questions we might consider if we are to do anything constructive about it.

I think it will help our understanding of the particular nature of American population growth if we first divide the world into two broad demographic categories, categories that reflect not only different demographic conditions but also different consequences arising out of these conditions and different problems to be overcome if population is to be humanely controlled by reducing the birth rate rather than by increasing the death rate.

In the one category human wastage from physical need is already widespread. Even a short-run continuation of present population growth rates will mean increased hunger and misery and quite possibly increased mortality as well. The countries in this category are the so-called "underdeveloped" countries. They contain approximately two-thirds of the world's people and include all Asian countries except Japan and Israel, together with most of the countries of Latin America and most of the populations of Africa. In these countries fairly extensive control is being exercised over deaths. The result is extremely rapid rates of population increase, rates that in many instances are high enough to double a population every twenty to twenty-five years.

In countries of the second category the situation—at least for the present—is quite different. Here there is extensive control on *both* sides of the demographic equation—over deaths *and* over births. By comparison with countries in the first category, growth in most of these "developed" countries—the United States being a notable exception—is now relatively slow, although still very rapid if viewed in historical terms. Even though there are different consequences for different classes of people in every country, the main threat of population growth in the poorer countries is to *life itself.* In the more affluent countries the threat is, instead, to the very *quality of life.*

In the nonindustrialized countries population increase denies the fulfillment of basic human needs—the need for enough to eat, for a place to live, for a job. In the industrialized countries it threatens to erode those personal freedoms and pleasures made possible once basic human needs are met. It is a matter of the *quality* of life, a matter of the kind of life one can lead in terms of diet, health, education, housing, work, play, and personal freedom.

Perhaps nowhere among the affluent countries is the threat of population growth to the quality of life so real as it is in our own United States. Of considerable importance in this is the very fact that we have the world's highest material (and I stress that word, "material") level of living. This high material level of living both obscures the dangers inherent in rapid growth (for example, how can things be getting worse when the Gross National Product keeps going up?) and, at the same time, exacerbates many of the difficulties such growth entails. Each year we spend an ever larger portion of our high Gross National Product merely to escape from the consequences of congestion and additions to our numbers. Population increase does not lead to crowded schools in a country of low educational levels, to traffic jams, if only a few own cars, to overcrowded vacation spots, if only a few have vacations, to losses of land for roads and municipal facilities, if only a few live in suburbs. But in combination with our high material levels of living population increase in this country has already necessitated greater restrictions on individual behavior, greater centralization in government, rising economic costs and taxes, crowded schools and recreation areas, van-

ishing countryside, air and water pollution, endless traffic jams, crowded court schedules, and a steady loss in time, solitude, quiet, beauty, and peace of mind. This deterioration we are experiencing right now. Yet half of us can expect to live long enough to see in this country, if present rates continue, a population of nearly 400 million and the difficulties attending population growth increased and magnified by the fact of *two* Americans for every *one* here now.

If we are to halt this deterioration and ultimately achieve population stability, the time to set the process in motion is *now,* not ten or twenty years from now. Even if tomorrow we managed somehow to cut our rate of growth in half, we would still be increasing by over a million people each year. There is no chance whatever of keeping our population at its present size. In fact, another surge of growth threatens just ahead as girls born during the "baby boom" of 1945–60 begin coming of age, increasing the population of potential mothers by some 75 percent in the thirty years between 1960 and 1990.

What, then, are the demographic characteristics of today's Americans that lead to this rapid growth in numbers? To some extent we Americans have always been a numerically expansive people. Rapid population increase has been a prominent feature of American life since before the founding of the Republic. The components of our population increase have undergone considerable change, however. In the past our high rate of growth was sustained by a combination of large-scale immigration and large-sized families. For example, in 1907, the peak year of immigration to this country, the number of migrants reached almost 1.3 million, while a leading demographer has estimated that with the high mortality of the time, American population increase in the early nineteenth century required an average of 8.3 births per mother. But today this is no longer the case. Migration figures but little in the total, while the large family of five or more children is a fairly unusual occurrence.

What accounts for our population growth today is a combination of four demographic conditions, each of which has become more pronounced in the years since World War II. These four conditions are: first, low death rates (ours are not the lowest in the world, but they are certainly among the lowest); second, nearly universal marriage (approximately 95 percent of us marry at least once in our lifetimes); third, marriage at what for a European population is a notably early age. (Half of the women who marry in this country do so before their twenty-first birthdays and about 90 percent before their twenty-fifth birthdays. By way of contrast, the proportions who marry this early in Europe are only about two-thirds as high). The fourth and final condition supporting our present growth is a clustering of family size within the range of two to four children: few couples with no children or one child only, and few with five or more.

With our population expanding rapidly it may come as a surprise to learn that very large families play only a minor role in this country's family patterns, and that family size is clustered within such a narrow range as two to four children. In historical terms this is quite a modest size. Even so recently as the turn of this century, nearly half of women survivors to age forty-five had borne at least five children. The proportion today is only about 10 percent. The present situation in this country thus illustrates a new and tremendously significant fact: no longer is the large family a requisite of population increase. The low mortality rates of today permit rapid, sustained population growth when family size is of only moderate dimensions.

We are thus in something of a predicament with respect to the possibility of reducing our growth rate by voluntary means. Unlike the peoples of the nonindustrialized countries, we Americans already limit the size of our families through extensive use of the most effective means of controlling birth. Only a minority of Americans fail to participate in this widespread cultural practice. Moreover, most Americans can comfortably afford to raise a moderate-sized family of three or four children; and, as public opinion polls show, most now seem to want that many and intend to have them. Yet three children is a substantially larger average than that needed to keep our population at a stable size.

With the marriage and death rates prevailing today the difference between a typical family of two children and a typical family of three is the difference between a population that is stabilized and a population that is doubling itself every forty to forty-five years.

Under such conditions as these what we must have to check our population growth is a setting in which couples who would ordinarily have three or more children will be induced to limit their childbearing to two, or—at the very most—three children, instead. This is not, I think, as impossible a task as it may, at first, appear. But before we can attempt to achieve it we must be thoroughly versed in the facts about differences in childbearing practices among different groups in the population. The clustering of family size in the two to four children range is, after all, an average for the country as a whole. The parents in some groups have fewer than the average; in others, more. In order to do anything about it, we must have a clear idea of the origins of excess childbearing, of the number of children born over and above the number necessary only to replace the population.

It is not easy to make such a determination, however. The main difficulty comes from the fact that childbearing is possible over a period of some twenty to thirty years in a woman's lifetime. As a consequence, substantial changes can occur in year-to-year birth rates without a corresponding change in total family size, and, conversely, a change that has actually occurred in family size cannot be finally determined until the women concerned reach the end of their childbearing period. We cannot know at this juncture, for example, whether recent declines in their birth rates mean that young women of today will ultimately bear fewer children than did their older sisters, or whether they are merely postponing a part of their childbearing to some later date.

Despite such limitations it is still instructive to attempt approximations of the proportions which various groups in the population contribute to our total growth. Those I have made are based primarily on materials from the census, supplemented by vital statistics data and various survey research findings. They are adjusted for age differences and, as much as possible, for differences in mortality. Some of my findings may surprise you, but it is on data such as these that any truly relevant program of population control must be predicated.

The most striking thing to note from these calculations is the very diffuseness of the responsibility for our excess reproduction. Almost every segment of our population contributes to this excess, some more than others, of course. The excess is derived to a proportionately greater extent from the reproduction of Negroes, Indians, Mexicans, and Puerto Ricans; white persons whose parents were born in the United States; rural and small town dwellers; farmers and manual workers, persons with less than five years of schooling; Catholics and Mormons. About the only groups in the population that seem *not* to be contributing to this excess are the foreign-born, the Jews, and the college-educated Negroes.

The pattern of Negro childbearing is particularly interesting, partly because of the size of this group and partly because of the alarums that have been sounded concerning its reproductive behavior. There can be no doubt whatever that Negroes are at the present time reproducing themselves at a faster rate than whites. Their birth rate is currently some 36 percent higher. But a comparison of the over-all birth rates of whites and Negroes can be misleading. There are differences in the age distributions of the two populations, and childbearing is more frequent at some ages than others. Standardizing for age differences—and also for the fact that the higher mortality among Negroes necessitates a somewhat higher birth rate for replacement purposes—I find that current Negro natality is still in excess of white, but by about 20 percent instead of the 36 percent figure calculated without standardization. This is a sizable reduction. Of even more interest is the fact that the higher natality of Negroes originates almost entirely in the far higher natality of those women who were born in the South and who continue to reside there. Average childbearing among Negro women living outside the South (approximately

half of the total) is virtually the same as that of the white population, and this despite the concentration of these women in those categories of the population having generally higher natality —that is, in the lower income, less schooled, manual occupation categories.

Knowing that one or another segment of the population contributes a disproportionate share to our excess childbearing is of considerable importance to the design of programs for population control. But it is only one side of the picture and, by itself, potentially misleading. Thus we find that nonwhites, while producing a proportionately larger share of the excess, still account for but *one-fifth* of the total, whereas whites account for *four-fifths*. Urban whites may produce a proportionately smaller share of the total excess, yet more than one-third of all excess births originate with them. On the other hand, were Puerto Ricans to stop reproduction tomorrow, the number of excess births would be reduced by less than one percent. Southern nonwhite laborers have as high a rate as any group in the population, yet they account for only 5 percent of the excess.

The figures themselves are unimportant. What I wish to show by introducing them here is this: first, the tremendous diversity in the origin of our excess natality; second, the great diffusion of responsibility for it; and third, the need for a population program the provisions of which, reflecting this diversity of needs and practices, will touch all segments of the childbearing population.

I have described the dimensions and particular characteristics of American population growth. What now can we do about it? There is no dearth of proposals. They range from compulsory sterilization after the second or third birth all the way to encouragement of homosexuality. It seems that where scientists abstain from making policy recommendations, the bizarre-ists are only too ready to rush in.

Actually, I see no need for such extreme measures. The foundation for population stability in this country has already been laid. We already have a well established small family system here. What is needed is further building on this system, not wholesale rejection of it for something less attuned either to our way of life or to our demographic needs.

Before enumerating some possible approaches, let me note a few of the more general considerations pertinent to any formulation of population policy.

First of all, we should recognize that population stability by control over childbearing—at least for the United States—is definitely attainable. There is no necessary reason for us to acquiesce in a limitless continuation either of our present high rate of growth, or of growth in general. As a people we have not yet lost control over our demographic destiny. Some of our behavior must be changed, of course. But these changes are minor compared with those that would be forced upon us if our population continued growing another twenty to thirty years at its present rate. Various European populations are now virtually stabilized as a result of extensive family limitation. We are capable of doing the same. Control by such means in this country can hardly be considered either alien or unattainable.

A second consideration is that motivation for family limitation—of whatever degree—is extremely complex and involves the interaction of *many* diverse elements. Attitudes toward childbearing do not evolve in a vacuum. They are responsive to what happens over the whole range of human experience—our living standards, our aspirations, our fears, our concepts of normal and abnormal, right and wrong.

Related to this is the fact that any given level of natality can result from a variety of causal conditions. We find both high and low natality in conditions of both poverty and affluence, of both crowded settlement and sparse settlement, high infant death rates and low infant death rates. There is, apparently, no one-to-one causal relationship between any particular level of natality and any particular condition of life. This makes the formulation of population programs a delicate undertaking, to say the least!

Fourth, we note that to the extent family size is subject to conscious control, the number of children couples elect to have will be a function of the needs that children are presumed to fulfil for their parents: a function, that is, of what parents expect to get out of having children.

Finally, we should remember that the sum total of rational decisions about family size on the part of *individuals* does not necessarily produce the demographic conditions best suited to an *entire society*. If it did, there would be no population problem.

We still know little about the consequences of specific programs undertaken to influence childbearing. None has been tried for very long, and where these programs have been tried, there were always unusual circumstances—war or depression, for example—which could account for the changes that occurred. Moreover, in view of the complexity of motivations and our, as yet, limited understanding of the relation between particular social conditions and particular levels of childbearing, any policy we undertake must be broadly based and subjected to a continuous scrutiny of its effects on demographic conditions. The effects of any demographically-inspired policy on other areas of social life must also be carefully weighed. Still, the situation calls for some kind of action. I should like to recommend, therefore, the following as first and minimal steps to be taken to bring our population into balance.

I have already said that the long-range purpose of any population policy for this country would be the preservation and extension of a high quality of life for all Americans. It follows that such a policy must work with democratic means and within a framework of democratic values, that it must work without coercion and without consigning anyone against his will to a state of celibacy or childlessness.

One type of measure would be of a sort to lower the proportion of the population exposed to the risk of childbearing by means of postponing the age of marriage or increasing inducements to remain single. Certainly we could afford to reduce substantially the strong pressures currently on young people to marry, to marry early, and, once married, to commence childbearing. But to make this approach effective as a means of lowering the birth rate would require either a prolonged period of sexual denial among single men and women, or social approval of contraception for the unmarried and liberalized access to abortion to compensate for contraceptive failure. As with all measures designed to influence the pattern of childbearing, difficult choices are unavoidable.

Another approach would be to assume that the proportions marrying and becoming parents, together with the timing of marriage and childbearing, would be little changed from what they are today. Under these conditions the greatest success would attach to a program of population control that sought to achieve four intermediate goals. These would be: 1) to increase public awareness about the facts of population growth, 2) to increase national concern for the value and healthy development of every child, 3) to decrease the dependence of adults on childbearing as a means of fulfilling various psychological and social needs, and 4) to expand the efficiency and availability of a variety of birth control techniques.

The first of these goals would be education of the public, and particularly of school children and young adults, to the relevance of population both to our way of life and to the attainment of our national goals. This education could occur in the schools, in churches, in public forums, through the media of mass communication. No one should leave high school without a basic understanding of population dynamics in a finite world and of the individual's part in shaping demographic conditions. Moreover, every high school student should be taught the facts of reproduction and the means by which to prevent conception. Each year nearly one-tenth of the girls fifteen to nineteen years of age bear a child. Many others become pregnant. Still others have sexual intercourse without becoming pregnant. The great majority of these experiences are out of wedlock. We cannot prudently wait till marriage or college to introduce our young people to the facts concerning both conception and contraception.

A second intermediate goal must be improvement of the lives of our children. If we are going to have fewer of them, we must guarantee to their parents that every effort is being made to ensure the health and well-being of those few we have. It does not seem too farfetched to suppose that cultural survival may figure as strongly in the decisions about family size as does physical survival. As long as there exist in this country such tremendous disparities in the quality of the environment for different groups of children, our stated national concern for child welfare will remain unconvincing. We must strive toward providing every child with adequate medical and dental care, decent housing, a good education, and security of employment when he becomes an adult. At the same time, we need a greater recognition of the importance and value of each individual child—regardless of his skin color, his parents' income, or his sex. In bluntly pragmatic terms there must be a much greater effort to conserve the human resources we already have in order to forestall any tendency to resort to excessive childbearing as a means of fulfilling parental and national needs.

The third intermediate goal should be to improve the lives of adults by making them more secure and by providing greater opportunities for rewarding activities and relationships outside the immediate family. This is indeed a broad goal and one that is difficult to translate into concrete proposals. The demographic rational for it is this: if couples are to limit voluntarily the number of their children to two or, at the most, three, they may need a strong sense of security about their place in society, and a sense of confidence that they can lead satisfying lives without undue dependence on family relationships.

The whole question of emotional support and response is an important one for childbearing in our society. As we have become a more specialized, less rural, larger, and more mobile society, our contacts have probably become less personal. Communities have more residents, doctors more patients, teachers more students, businessmen more customers. In the process, the relative importance of the individual is reduced and the competition for recognition heightened. In this mushrooming of size and anonymity the family stands out as a haven of intimacy, often providing the individual with his only retreat from the frustration, indifference, and sense of impotency encountered in his other social contacts. Children are seen as providing security, an antidote to the impersonality of one's other relationships, a sense of unique accomplishment. The question for population policy, then, becomes this: what kinds of alternatives to childbearing can be provided to meet these needs?

Moving toward a goal of increased cultural security for adults—as was the case with children—will require at the most basic level a greater acceptance of the importance of *every* adult and continuing efforts to eliminate the disabling effects of discrimination, whatever the grounds—sex, race, religion, income, or age.

Specific steps that could be taken to approach this goal are numerous, if piecemeal. To be really effective they would have to be tied in with a broad social policy aimed at improving the cultural atmosphere for American children and adults along many interrelated lines.

One of the possibilities would be the extension of opportunities for women to be interested and creative in activities outside the home. This should reduce the incentive to have additional children as an "adjustment" either to boredom or to the absence of satisfying alternatives. This will probably mean the opportunity for more women to combine a job with raising a family. Many married women are already employed, but there is room for improvement in the adjustment of working arrangements to suit their special needs. Opportunities for part-time work need to be expanded and the meager facilities for the daytime care of small children greatly enlarged.

Another avenue of adult activity for men as well as women could be the expansion of opportunities for adult education and vocational training—possibly as a prelude to undertaking a responsible volunteer job during leisure time. In any case, adults should be encouraged to continue their development beyond high school, college, or marriage. Much more attention should be paid to what happens to adults *after* their formal education, marriage, or retirement. The years after sixty-five are particularly marked

by cultural insecurity. We demographers often cite the need for security in old age as a factor maintaining high natality in the underdeveloped countries. Yet I wonder if this may not be a factor in developed countries as well. Certainly our aged suffer economically. They also suffer from vastly diminished social prestige, uselessness, and, in most cases, isolation. In a highly mobile society such as ours there may be an almost unconscious incentive to bear additional children in the hope that at least one will live nearby and provide emotional support and response.

There are others of this genre, relating to the planning of our cities, housing, the organization of work, the use of leisure time, that together could contribute substantially to greater cultural well-being for Americans. The relevancy of such measures to population control may seem obscure, but if a policy of rigorous family limitation is to rest on a democratic consensus, it may be just such imponderables as the quality of the cultural atmosphere for parents and children that in the long run are the most decisive determinants.

Let me turn now to the more direct, though not necessarily any more effective, means of influencing childbearing. Certainly the techniques of controlling births should be improved and made more accessible. A variety of means should be available to meet individual needs and preferences. All means, so long as they are effective and do not endanger the well-being of the persons involved, should be available. And I think they should be available to all who need them. By far the greatest effort should be concentrated on contraception, but I believe we will eventually have to come to terms also with the need to supplement this with a limited use of legal abortion as a last and, admittedly, less than satisfactory resort.

All this would undoubtedly work some reduction in our birth rate. But how much is uncertain, and I rather imagine the other three intermediate goals to natality control are at least as important in the United States today. Remember, with our low levels of mortality and our high proportions marrying, our population would still increase rapidly if the typical couple limited the number of its children to no more than three. Moreover, recent studies of family size expectations (as distinguished from actual practice) show little variation at all between different income and education groups in this country. The great majority of couples at all levels now want and expect to have at least three children. Thus, our rapid population increase derives only slightly from *unwanted* children.

It comes instead, from those third, fourth, fifth children whose parents want them—or who are, at the very least, not unwanted enough for their parents to exercise sufficient care to prevent their conception or birth. Contraception is important, but it cannot do the job alone. Couples must want—or at least be willing to have—fewer children.

A final observation, lest we decide we can leave to others the responsibility for curbing childbearing: if population stability is our goal, limitation to two, or—at the very most—three, children will have to extend to all levels of society. As we have already seen, nearly every section of the population contributes to our excess natality. Excessive childbearing among the poor is responsible for only a fraction of our large annual increase. By far the major portion comes from the middle and upper income majority, persons who have ready access to the means to plan the number of their children and who choose to have moderate-sized families.

No longer can we defend excessive reproduction by saying, "Well, *they* can afford it." The question is no longer simply whether *they* can or cannot afford it. The question now is whether the *country* can afford it. Reproduction may be a private act, but is has become one with far-reaching social consequences. This is particularly true of reproduction among the rich. The rich are more obvious. Their behavior is more likely to be imitated. Their style of life, with its second car, its summer house, larger property, greater amounts of travel, and generally more material possessions, requires a much higher consumption of those very things upon which population increase—in whatever class or country—places a premium: raw materials and space. Through our control over mortality we have reached a point where a parent's contribution can no longer be measured in terms of the *number* of his children—no matter who he is and no matter how much time, energy, and money he may expend on them.

Let us note that from a demographic point of view it is clear what we must have to stabilize population in this country. The way has already been pointed out by the experiences of several of the countries of western and central Europe. It represents no very great departure from the conditions of life that underlie the moderate-size family system we now have. On the assumption that we wish to achieve a demographic balance within the context of a democratically organized society, permitting parenthood to all couples except in cases clearly inadvisable on medical grounds, what we must work toward is a society in which no unwanted child is born; a society in which the decision to bear or not to bear a child is made solely by the potential parents; and, most important, a society in which this decision about childbearing is made in a social and cultural context that defines a three-child family as large.

4 ENVIRONMENT AND WASTE—WHERE WILL IT GO?

How Do You Get Rid of 3.5 Billion Tons of Waste a Year?

Peter Gwynne

Mr. Gwynne is an editor for Newsweek *and a specialist in several fields of science. He has written extensively for journals and magazines in his fields.*

America's most visible pollution problem is the towering mountain of solid wastes generated by more than 200 million consumers in our affluent, prepackaged society. At almost every turn we come upon piles of rubbish, overflowing trash baskets, or smelly garbage dumps that are filled to capacity. The countryside is dotted with ugly stacks of junked cars. Slag heaps stand black against the sky. Roadsides are littered with beer cans, pop bottles, and crumpled candy wrappers.

Americans discard garbage at a rate of 360 million tons a year, and the rate will certainly double by 1980. In 1970, we cast away 28 billion bottles, 48 billion cans, 30 million tons of paper, 4 million tons of plastic containers, 100 million tires, and 6.3 million automobiles. Farm animals added to the problem, producing 2 billion tons of their own waste. In all, Americans disposed of 3.5 billion tons of solid waste in 1970—an average of 5.3 pounds per person per day.

The capacity to cope with this avalanche of waste is shrinking fast. The traditional city dump is no longer just an eyesore; it may also be a health hazard. Many garbage dumps are already filled beyond capacity, and city incinerators produce extensive air pollution, even though they reduce the volume of garbage. Much of the refuse that is dumped into the oceans washes ashore, and other garbage forms stinking masses miles out at sea.

Nowhere is the problem more acute than in urban centers. According to Karl Wolf, special projects director of the American Public Works Administration, city dwellers "are standing in front of an avalanche, and it is threatening to bury them." This is not empty verbiage. At present, 10,000 people produce enough garbage in a single year to cover an acre of ground to a height of 7 feet.

Man's long neglect of his solid wastes has left a record that extends to prehistoric times. Indeed, the wastes of previous societies have given archaeologists many insights into ancient life. When German archaeologist Heinrich Schliemann discovered the ruins of the city of Troy in 1871 in what is now northwestern Turkey, he also found traces of eight other cities in the same mound. As early as 3000 B.C., the site had been level with the surrounding plain, but after the rise and fall of the cities of nine civilizations it had grown to a height of 16 feet. As each city died, its solid wastes formed the foundation for its successor. In effect, each city, once abandoned, became a garbage dump containing the wastes of the society of its time.

During the Middle Ages, garbage caused disease and death. Thrown slapdash into the streets, it fed a large rat population that carried plague fleas. The Black Death, caused by such fleas, killed an estimated 25 million people in Europe during the 1300s, and the great plague of London killed perhaps 1 of every 6 residents of that city during the years 1664 and 1665.

Today, of course, the worst health hazards of solid wastes have been overcome. Yet, increasingly, garbage is breeding sociological hazards. Uncollected trash in city slums not only gives ghetto inhabitants malodorous evidence of official neglect, it also may provide an excuse for riots and disruption. In June, 1970, for example, two New York City slum areas erupted when people began burning uncollected trash in the streets. The incidents ended in the looting of stores and fire-bombing of buildings.

The phenomenal increase in the amount of garbage is caused primarily by technological and marketing innovations. For example, the packaging industry has put vast new amounts of paper, cardboard, plastic, and aluminum into circulation since World War II. Some of these materials, particularly plastic and aluminum, do not naturally disintegrate over a period of time as do most other packaging materials. Paper and cloth, if they are left in a garbage dump long enough, will be absorbed into the soil, but not plastic containers. Aluminum cans do not rust and break down as do tin cans.

Surprisingly, there was a time when people took pride in the piles of waste that surrounded their communities. In Victorian England, for example, the plumes of smoke belching from grimy factories, and the towering slag heaps nearby, served as tangible reminders of the prosperity that the Industrial Revolution had

brought to countless towns. The word "muck," in the industrial north of England, became a slang expression for money, and the expression "rolling in it"—in muck, that is—came to mean blessed with great wealth. Today, however, muck is a source of disgust rather than local pride, not only in England, but throughout most of the world and particularly in the United States.

Now, the money in muck is almost entirely on the debit side of the ledger. Collecting and disposing of the wastes generated by our affluent society represents as great a financial as a technical problem. The Bureau of Solid Waste Management of the U.S. Department of Health, Education, and Welfare (HEW) reports that it costs the United States a staggering $4.5 billion each year to handle solid waste materials. Only education and highways take a larger share of municipal budgets. According to this same survey, our current methods of waste disposal are grossly inadequate. The bureau estimates that 18 percent more money—another $800 million a year—would be needed to handle our wastes adequately.

Awareness of this environmental problem has spurred research into new ways of handling solid wastes. Suggested solutions range from simple methods for separating and reclaiming minerals and other products from garbage by hand to using fusion—the nuclear reaction that provides both the sun and the hydrogen bomb with their immense energy—to destroy all traces of solid waste. At present, however, few of these solutions are ready for everyday use. Public apathy seems to be the major roadblock.

Most cities still dispose of their waste by throwing it on open dumps or burning it in incinerators. Yet dumps are smelly breeding grounds for flies, rats, and roaches, and rainwater that runs out of the dumps pollutes streams and underground water supplies. Some forms of garbage spontaneously catch fire if they are not compressed. The most compelling argument against this type of waste disposal, however, is the fact that the nation is running out of space. The country's 12,000 landfill sites are now close to capacity, and many cities are facing a major crisis because they have run out of possible landfill sites.

Incineration, at least as presently practiced, is a major source of air pollution, producing smoky wastes. When municipal officials do find an incinerator that operates within local air pollution standards, they still face the problems created when various types of garbage that cannot be burned are mixed with those that can. For example, a sheet of polyethylene that is processed with a bundle of books and pieces of wood may corrode and clog the furnace, or cause an explosion.

A 1969 HEW survey found that "94 percent of all land-disposal operations and 75 percent of municipal incinerators are unsatisfactory from the standpoint of public health, efficiency of operation, or protection of natural resources." The report called the situation "a national disgrace."

Ocean disposal hardly provides a shining contrast to these procedures. Scientists from the Sandy Hook Marine Laboratory in New Jersey pointed out, in February, 1970, that sewage sludge and dredging spoils, the industrial wastes scooped from rivers and ship channels, had produced a "dead sea" where they were dumped into the Atlantic Ocean 12 miles south of Long Island. A 20-square-mile area of muddy brown water was so befouled that it can no longer support marine life. On the West Coast, San Francisco has been forced to look elsewhere for a garbage dump. Its present practice of dumping garbage into San Francisco Bay is threatening to destroy fishing and to fill the bay itself. Norwegian explorer Thor Heyerdahl, who sailed a boat made of papyrus reed from Africa to Central America in 1970, reported seeing and smelling garbage and other wastes floating in the Atlantic Ocean hundreds of miles from any shore.

Merely collecting our wastes accounts for about 80 percent of the total disposal costs. Most of this is spent to haul the wastes to the dump, incinerator, or barge, if the material is to be thrown into the sea. The fact that the methods of collecting household garbage have hardly changed since before World War II is an indication of how little has been accomplished in the overall problem of disposal. As Charles C. Johnson, Jr., administrator of the U.S. Public Health Service, puts it: "The only real improvement we have made in waste disposal in the last 50 years was putting an engine instead of a horse in front of the garbage truck." Johnson was referring to the collection of household wastes, but the picture looks just as bad with industrial wastes. Experts bemoan the fact that, when architects design new plants and factories, refuse disposal is invariably the last factor to be considered.

Yet, bleak as this picture may appear, new technology for treating solid wastes, and perhaps even profiting from them, is under development at many government, university, and industrial centers. Many of these involve the general principle of producing or doing something useful with the garbage, treating it as a raw material rather than as waste. This approach—called recycling—is not new. Farmers have used manure and gardeners have used compost for many years. The reuse of today's peculiar forms of garbage, in the huge quantities in which they are generated, however, demands its own technology.

New solutions are easier to propose than to put into practice. Los Angeles, for example, tried the idea of grinding its garbage into fertilizer, but could find no market for its output. More promising are proposals for compaction—using tremendous pressure to squeeze garbage into small, odorless bales that can be dumped into landfills. One such plant has been built at Cambridge, Mass., by Reclamations Systems, Incorporated. It has 10 loading platforms and a 155-ton hydraulic press capable of compressing 5,000 pounds of trash into a cube 4 feet square.

Occasionally, compressed garbage of this sort is used to reclaim land from rivers and even from the ocean. Parts of the New York World's Fair of 1964 and Montreal's Expo 67 were built on such reclaimed land. Other schemes involving compressed garbage aim to utilize wasteland. Two of the most interesting and unusual projects of this type are under construction at Virginia Beach, Va., and in the flat countryside near Chicago, where vast quantities of landfill are being dumped to form large, man-made hills. The hills will be developed as recreational areas—the one in Virginia for soapbox derbies, the Chicago site for skiing and tobogganing.

Such landfill projects are only temporary solutions, however. Once the landfill is completed, the community must find another garbage-disposal site. Incineration, by contrast, can be continuous. Because of this fact, new methods of putting incinerated garbage to use are attracting much interest. In some incinerators, electricity is generated from steam or other hot gases produced by the heat from the burning garbage. Municipal garbage is a reasonably good fuel, in fact, with about one-third of the heating power of coal.

One incinerating unit now being developed by the Combustion Power Company of Palo Alto, Calif., and known as the CPU-400, should produce about 15,000 kilowatts of electricity daily in the course of burning 400 tons of municipal wastes. The unit achieves its efficiency by burning the material at extremely high temperatures and pressures—so high that most of the solids in the waste, including metals and glass, are melted during the process. Incineration produces hot gases that drive a turbine, and this turns a generator. The Bureau of Solid Waste Management estimates that such units, if they prove successful, could provide up to 10 percent of a community's electric power needs.

More spectacular than the CPU-400 are two giant incinerators already in action, one at Issy-les-Moulineaux, near Paris, France, and the other at Montreal, Canada. The first produces some of the electricity that is used throughout France. The second, a $14-million project with running costs amounting to $1 million a year, is the most modern incinerator on the North American continent. The Montreal incinerator produces steam that the city hopes to sell to companies that use steam in their manufacturing processes. Montreal officials intend to glean every possible piece of financial value from their wastes. They plan to sell the scrap metal found in the garbage,

about 20 tons a day from a total of 1,200 to 1,500 tons of wastes burned. Even the ashes that remain in the incinerator will be sold—very cheaply at first, according to Jean V. Arpin, Montreal's head of municipal services, while "we develop uses for them, and encourage others to do so." Such uses may include mixing the ashes with gravel for road construction.

A $275-million incinerator, to be built on the site of the former Brooklyn Navy Yard in New York City, is even more ambitious than the French and Canadian incinerators. In addition to burning 6,000 tons of trash each day, this unit will also have a treatment plant that will process 70 million gallons of sewage. The incinerator will be used to burn sewage sludge, while liquid wastes will be used to trap the fine ash and the other residue that is always given off in smoke when trash is incinerated.

Projects such as these are obviously more than just upgraded incinerators of the type used in most communities today. In order to produce heat energy efficiently and consistently, the wastes that feed these units must first be modified so that they are reasonably homogeneous when they enter the furnace. One way of doing this is to melt all the waste, as is done in the CPU-400 incinerator. Another way is to pulverize and shred the wastes before they are put into the furnace. If the fuel is evenly sized, it will burn more consistently. Buffalo, N.Y., has a new incinerator that can process 260 tons of waste per day. It has a huge crushing and shredding unit that can pulverize tree logs and items the size of refrigerators. But the Leonard S. Wegman Company, which built the incinerator, had to have a West German firm build the shredder. Units of this size could not be built in the United States, an indication of how far behind the times the United States is in garbage treatment.

A rotary-kiln incinerator built for the Dow Chemical Company's central waste-disposal facility in Midland, Mich., classifies garbage before it is fed into the incinerator. Wastes from the manufacture of 1,100 different products are divided into three categories before they go into the furnace—those that can be fed directly into the incinerator, such as trash and scrap plastic; pumpable wastes, such as tars and oils; and miscellaneous liquid wastes. The waste in each of these categories is further classified according to the time it takes to burn and the heat it produces on burning. The rates at which the different categories are fed into the furnace are then adjusted to produce an even rate of heat production.

Separation of this type is a key factor in the ultimate goal of reclaiming and reusing components of garbage. Indeed, the ability to separate garbage inexpensively and conveniently is one of the major economic considerations in deciding whether to recycle it or not. Recycling of metals, for example, may be less profitable than obtaining them from poor ores, so that recycling in such cases has no value beyond merely serving as one solution of the waste-disposal problem. Waste materials must compete effectively in the market place if they are to be used as raw materials for industry.

Separation methods now vary from sorting useful metals from garbage by hand to relatively sophisticated systems of separation by magnets and air currents. At one end of the line is the sorting of garbage at its source—in the kitchen—where the housewife separates it into metallic, paper, and organic wastes. Further up the line is the method used by Houston's Metropolitan Waste Conversion Corporation, a company that handles about 25 percent of Houston's garbage. The corporation tries to make a profit from the waste paper and iron it can separate from other garbage. Revolving magnets are used to remove the iron. Other forms of salable material are reclaimed by workers stationed along a moving belt that carries the garbage from one loading dock to another.

Given the high cost of labor, such a procedure is remarkably wasteful, and it is obvious that it should be mechanized, if at all possible. One promising approach to mechanization is an air-classification process developed by the Stanford Research Institute at Menlo Park, Calif. The pilot project successfully separated five different types of material by blowing jets of air through the garbage. The air jets separated material of specific size, density, and shape from the general mass. Another air scheme, now under research at the Massachusetts Institute of Technology, blows waste material around a vortex chamber where cutters shred it. Particles of waste can pass out of the vortex only when they have been shredded to a specific size.

The U.S. Department of Health, Education, and Welfare estimates that ordinary municipal wastes annually contain 10 million tons of iron, 1 million tons of nonferrous metals such as aluminum, copper, nickel, tin, lead, silver, gold, and zinc, and 15 million tons of glass. But only a few of these materials are reclaimed because of the high cost of collecting and processing them. About 50 percent of the copper, lead, and iron is recycled, and about 30 percent of the aluminum and 20 percent of the zinc are reused. But less than 10 percent of the textiles, rubber, and glass is reprocessed. Only about 20 percent of the paper, the largest component of municipal waste, is used again.

Reclamation technology is clearly most developed in the scrap-metal market, where the concept of the three R's of waste disposal—recovery, reuse, and recycling—is more than just wishful thinking. Aluminum cans hold out one of the brightest hopes in recycling because reclaimed aluminum is worth $200 a ton, compared with $20 for steel and $16 for waste paper. In Los Angeles, the Reynolds Metals Company is offering a bounty of one-half cent for each all-aluminum can turned in for reuse. The program yielded 195,000 pounds of used aluminum in one recent three-month period.

There was a time when people sold old newspapers and worn-out autos to junk dealers. Now the price for paper and scrap metal is so low, however, that most people believe it is no longer worth the trouble. Paper is thrown out with the household garbage, and old cars are abandoned in the streets. People also used to return empty bottles for a refund, but a two- or three-cent deposit isn't much anymore, and bottlers don't like the handling costs. The bottlers prefer nowadays to put their products in throwaways.

This has resulted in a massive glass disposal problem, and has prompted the introduction of four bills into Congress and proposed legislative action in 21 states to tax or ban nonreturnable containers, many of which are glass. Even though glass accounts for only 6 percent of the solid waste problem, it creates major difficulties because it is virtually indestructible if left on the garbage heap.

Bottle makers are trying to reduce the problem by developing "self-destruct" containers and by finding new uses for crushed glass. They are now testing soft drinks bottled in plastic, and research is underway on bottling materials that will disintegrate after long exposure in water. One team of British scientists at Birmingham University has developed a specially treated, self-destroying plastic that crumbles when exposed to the ultraviolet rays of sunlight. The material can be used for bottles, but each one would have to carry a warning of its tendency to disintegrate out of doors.

Meanwhile, the Glass Container Manufacturers Institute, which represents the major glassmakers, is following the lead of Reynolds Metals Company by setting up bottle-redemption centers in 21 states. It estimates that 11 billion bottles a year can be salvaged by these centers. The bottles will be ground up and used to make new bottles.

The idea of an incentive payment for junk automobiles is receiving serious study among government officials. One of the proposals under consideration would charge the initial purchaser of a car a fixed sum for a "bounty registration," perhaps $50. This would go with the car from owner to owner until the car was ready for the scrapheap. Regardless of the state of the scrap-metal market at the time, the ultimate owner would get $50 (plus whatever the car was worth as junk) by turning it in at an authorized auto graveyard. Governor Marvin Mandel (D., Md.) asked his state legislature, in 1969, to approve a plan to pay a bounty of $10 to anyone who brings an old car to a junk dealer, but no action was taken.

The primary difficulty with all these reclamation plans, however, is the lack of conclusive evidence that waste recovery can be profitable.

The Houston Metropolitan Waste Corporation charges the city $4.11 per ton for wastes that it recycles. Yet it loses some $2 per ton because the corporation cannot sell most of the paper and compost it reclaims, although the quality is good. Most companies, therefore, refuse for economic reasons to invest whole-heartedly in processes designed to recycle solid wastes.

Some experts believe that the trash crisis will not be solved until American industry develops what scientists call a "biodegradable" container, one that dissolves or rots quickly after use. The perfect example of such a container is the ice cream cone. It can be eaten, of course, but if it is not, it disintegrates easily in water or on a garbage heap. Another is a yet-to-be-marketed soup package that dissolves right along with its contents.

Meanwhile, researchers have come up with many new uses for products previously regarded as worthless. For example:

The construction industry is using some slag from blast furnaces as an aggregate for road-building.

Slag from coal ash has been used to make mineral wood, which scientists at West Virginia's coal research laboratory say is comparable to commercial insulating fibers.

Researchers in Japan have compressed solid wastes into rock-hard blocks, which are then coated with asphalt or cement and used as building materials. The procedure is still in an experimental stage.

Waste glass has been used in place of sand in certain forms of concrete.

Old rubber tires have been incinerated to produce a solid residue that can be used as a filter for sewage treatment.

If all these attempts at recycling and reusing wastes fail, we may have to turn ultimately to the hydrogen bomb as a garbage-disposal unit. This proposal by David R. Safrany of Bechtel Laboratory at Belmont, Calif., is under consideration by the U.S. Atomic Energy Commission as part of their Project Plowshare for finding peaceful uses for atomic energy. "All of the scientific problems have been worked out," Safrany told delegates to the American Chemical Society's 1970 meeting in Chicago. "All that remains are some technological problems." One of these is how to transport wastes to the bomb incinerator.

He believes that wastes could be piped to the huge underground salt dome caverns that dot the southwestern part of the United States. The wastes would be buried in these salt domes and then vaporized by hydrogen bombs. He estimated that 50 bombs, averaging 5 million tons of energy each, would be enough to handle the total waste problem. When the radioactive by-products cooled off, they might be siphoned from the ground for reuse. The process could be repeated years later when sufficient wastes had again accumulated.

But such a plan is now only a pipe dream of the future. The ironic fact remains that if nothing is done soon, the image of a nation standing knee-deep in garbage while firing rockets at the moon will become a stark reality. "The answer," U.S. Environmental Quality Control chairman Russell E. Train says, "isn't more efficient disposal, but lies in the production of things that become waste. If you produce them and they must be used, then develop recycling to keep them moving back into the system. In effect, keep them from becoming waste."

5 POVERTY— BENIGN AND NEGLECTED?

The Uses of Poverty: The Poor Pay All

Herbert J. Gans

From *Social Policy* (July–August, 1971), 20–24. Reprinted by permission of Social Policy Corporation, New York, New York 10010.

Dr. Gans, a specialist in urban studies and social problems, is Professor of Sociology at Columbia University. He has taught at the University of Pennsylvania and MIT. His major works are The Urban Villagers *(1962),* The Levittowners *(1967), and* Peoples and Plans *(1968).*

Some twenty years ago Robert K. Merton applied the notion of functional analysis to explain the continuing though maligned existence of the urban political machine: if it continued to exist, perhaps it fulfilled latent—unintended or unrecognized—positive functions. Clearly it did. Merton pointed out how the political machine provided central authority to get things done when a decentralized local government could not act, humanized the services of the impersonal bureaucracy for fearful citizens, offered concrete help (rather than abstract law or justice) to the poor, and otherwise performed services needed or demanded by many people but considered unconventional or even illegal by formal public agencies.

Today, poverty is more maligned than the political machine ever was; yet it, too, is a persistent social phenomenon. Consequently, there may be some merit in applying functional analysis to poverty, in asking whether it also has positive functions that explain its persistence.

Merton defined functions as "those observed consequences [of a phenomenon] which make for the adaptation or adjustment of a given [social] system." I shall use a slightly different definition; instead of identifying functions for an entire social system, I shall identify them for the interest groups, socio-economic classes, and other population aggregates with shared values that "inhabit" a social system. I suspect that in a modern heterogeneous society, few phenomena are functional or dysfunctional for the society as a whole, and that most result in benefits to some groups and costs to others. Nor are any phenomena indispensable; in most instances, one can suggest what Merton calls "functional alternatives" or equivalents for them, i.e., other social patterns or policies that achieve the same positive functions but avoid the dysfunctions.

Associating poverty with positive functions seems at first glance to be unimaginable. Of course, the slumlord and the loan shark are commonly known to profit from the existence of poverty, but they are viewed as evil men, so their activities are classified among the dysfunctions of poverty. However, what is less often recognized, at least by the conventional wisdom, is that poverty also makes possible the existence or expansion of respectable professions and occupations, for example, penology, criminology, social work, and public health. More recently, the poor have provided jobs for professional and paraprofessional "poverty warriors," and for journalists and social scientists, this author included, who have supplied the information demanded by the revival of public interest in poverty.

Clearly, then, poverty and the poor may well satisfy a number of positive functions for many nonpoor groups in American society. I shall describe thirteen such functions—economic, social, and political—that seem to me most significant.

THE FUNCTIONS OF POVERTY

First, the existence of poverty ensures that society's "dirty work" will be done. Every society has such work: physically dirty or dangerous, temporary, dead-end and underpaid, undignified and menial jobs. Society can fill these jobs by paying higher wages than for "clean" work, or it can force people who have no other choice to do the dirty work—and at low wages. In America, poverty functions to provide a low-wage labor pool that is willing—or, rather, unable to be *un*willing—to perform dirty work at low cost. Indeed, this function of the poor is so important that in some Southern states, welfare payments have been cut off during the summer months when the poor are needed to work in the fields. Moreover, much of the debate about the Negative Income Tax and the Family Assistance Plan has concerned their impact on the work incentive, by which is actually meant the incentive of the poor to do the needed dirty work if the wages therefrom are no larger than the income grant. Many economic activities that involve dirty work depend on the poor for their existence: restaurants, hospitals, parts of the garment industry, and "truck farming," among others, could not persist in their present form without the poor.

Second, because the poor are required to work at low wages, they subsidize a variety of economic activities that benefit the affluent. For example, domestics subsidize the upper middle and upper classes, making life easier for their employers and freeing affluent women for a variety of professional, cultural, civic, and partying activities. Similarly, because the poor pay a higher proportion of their income in property and sales taxes, among others, they subsidize many state and local governmental services that benefit more affluent groups. In addition, the poor support innovation in medical practice as patients in teaching and research hospitals and as guinea pigs in medical experiments.

Third, poverty creates jobs for a number of occupations and professions that serve or "service" the poor, or protect the rest of society from them. As already noted, penology would be minuscule without the poor, as would the police. Other activities and groups that flourish because of the existence of poverty are the numbers game, the sale of heroin and cheap wines and liquors, pentecostal ministers, faith healers, prostitutes, pawn shops, and the peacetime army, which recruits its enlisted men mainly from among the poor.

Fourth, the poor buy goods others do not want and thus prolong the economic usefulness of such goods—day-old bread, fruit and vegetables that would otherwise have to be thrown out, secondhand clothes, and deteriorating automobiles and buildings. They also provide incomes for doctors, lawyers, teachers, and others who are too old, poorly trained, or incompetent to attract more affluent clients.

In addition to economic functions, the poor perform a number of social functions.

Fifth, the poor can be identified and punished as alleged or real deviants in order to uphold the legitimacy of conventional norms. To justify the desirability of hard work, thrift, honesty, and monogamy, for example, the defenders of these norms must be able to find people who can be accused of being lazy, spendthrift, dishonest, and promiscuous. Although there is some evidence that the poor are about as moral and law-abiding as anyone else, they are more likely than middle-class transgressors to be caught and punished when they participate in deviant acts. Moreover, they lack the political and cultural power to correct the stereotypes that other people hold of them and thus continue to be thought of as lazy, spendthrift, etc., by those who need living proof that moral deviance does not pay.

Sixth, and conversely, the poor offer vicarious participation to the rest of the population in the uninhibited sexual, alcoholic, and narcotic behavior in which they are alleged to participate and which, being freed from the constraints of affluence, they are often thought to enjoy more than the middle classes. Thus many people, some social scientists included, believe that the poor not only are more given to uninhibited behavior (which may be true, although it is often motivated by despair more than by lack of inhibition) but derive more pleasure from it than affluent people (which research by Lee Rainwater, Walter Miller, and others shows to be patently untrue). However, whether the poor actually have more sex and enjoy it more is irrelevant; so long as middle-class people believe this to be true, they can participate in it vicariously when instances are reported in factual or fictional form.

Seventh, the poor also serve a direct cultural function when culture created by or for them is adopted by the more affluent. The rich often collect artifacts from extinct folk cultures of poor people; and almost all Americans listen to the blues, Negro spirituals, and country music, which originated among the Southern poor. Recently they have enjoyed the rock styles that were born, like the Beatles, in the slums; and in the last year, poetry written by ghetto children has become popular in literary circles. The poor also serve as culture heroes, particularly, of course, to the left; but the hobo, the cowboy, the hipster, and the mythical prostitute with a heart of gold have performed this function for a variety of groups.

Eighth, poverty helps to guarantee the status of those who are not poor. In every hierarchical society someone has to be at the bottom; but in American society, in which social mobility is an important goal for many and people need to know where they stand, the poor function as a reliable and relatively permanent measuring rod for status comparisons. This is particularly true for the working class, whose politics is influenced by the need to maintain status distinctions between themselves and the poor, much as the aristocracy must find ways of distinguishing itself from the *nouveaux riches*.

Ninth, the poor also aid the upward mobility of groups just above them in the class hierarchy. Thus a goodly number of Americans have entered the middle class through the profits earned from the provision of goods and services in the slums, including illegal or nonrespectable ones that upper-class and upper-middle-class businessmen shun because of their low prestige. As a result, members of almost every immigrant group have financed their upward mobility by providing slum housing, entertainment, gambling, narcotics, etc., to later arrivals—most recently to Blacks and Puerto Ricans.

Tenth, the poor help to keep the aristocracy busy, thus justifying its continued existence. "Society" uses the poor as clients of settlement houses and beneficiaries of charity affairs; indeed, the aristocracy must have the poor to demonstrate its superiority over other elites who devote themselves to earning money.

Eleventh, the poor, being powerless, can be made to absorb the costs of change and growth in American society. During the nineteenth century, they did the backbreaking work that built the cities; today, they are pushed out of their neighborhoods to make room for "progress." Urban renewal projects to hold middle-class taxpayers in the city and expressways to enable suburbanites to commute downtown have typically been located in poor neighborhoods, since no other group will allow itself to be displaced. For the same reason, universities, hospitals, and civic centers also expand into land occupied by the poor. The major costs of the industrialization of agriculture have been borne by the poor, who are pushed off the land without recompense; and they have paid a large share of the human cost of the growth of American power overseas, for they have provided many of the foot soldiers for Vietnam and other wars.

Twelfth, the poor facilitate and stabilize the American political process. Because they vote and participate in politics less than other groups, the political system is often free to ignore them. Moreover, since they can rarely support Republicans, they often provide the Democrats with a captive constituency that has no other place to go. As a result, the Democrats can count on their votes, and be more responsive to voters—for example, the white working class—who might otherwise switch to the Republicans.

Thirteen, the role of the poor in upholding conventional norms (see the *fifth* point, above) also has a significant political function. An economy based on the ideology of laissez faire requires a deprived population that is allegedly unwilling to work or that can be considered inferior because it must accept charity or welfare in order to survive. Not only does the alleged moral deviancy of the poor reduce the moral pressure on the present political economy to eliminate poverty but socialist alternatives can be made to look quite unattractive if those who will benefit most from them can be described as lazy, spendthrift, dishonest, and promiscuous.

THE ALTERNATIVES

I have described thirteen of the more important functions poverty and the poor satisfy in American society, enough to support the functionalist thesis that poverty, like any other social phenomenon, survives in part because it is useful to society or some of its parts. This analysis is not intended to suggest that because it is often functional, poverty *should* exist, or that it *must* exist. For one thing, poverty has many more dysfunctions than functions; for another, it is possible to suggest functional alternatives.

For example, society's dirty work could be done without poverty, either by automation or by paying "dirty workers" decent wages. Nor is it necessary for the poor to subsidize the many activities they support through their low-wage jobs. This would, however, drive up the costs of these activities, which would result in higher prices to their customers and clients. Similarly, many of the professionals who flourish because of the poor could be given other roles. Social workers could provide counseling to the affluent, as they prefer to do anyway; and the police could devote themselves to traffic and organized crime. Other roles would have to be found for badly trained or incompetent professionals now relegated to serving the poor, and someone else would have to pay their salaries. Fewer penologists would be employable, however. And pentecostal religion could probably not survive without the poor—nor would parts of the second- and third-hand-goods market. And in many cities, "used" housing that no one else wants would then have to be torn down at public expense.

Alternatives for the cultural functions of the poor could be found more easily and cheaply. Indeed, entertainers, hippies, and adolescents are already serving as the deviants needed to uphold traditional morality and as devotees of orgies to "staff" the fantasies of vicarious participation.

The status functions of the poor are another matter. In a hierarchical society, some people must be defined as inferior to everyone else with respect to a variety of attributes, but they need not be poor in the absolute sense. One could conceive of a society in which the "lower class," though last in the pecking order, received 75 percent of the median income, rather than 15-40 percent, as is now the case. Needless to say, this would require considerable income redistribution.

The contribution the poor make to the upward mobility of the groups that provide them with goods and services could also be maintained without the poor's having such low incomes. However, it is true that if the poor were more affluent, they would have access to enough capital to take over the provider role, thus competing with, and perhaps rejecting, the "outsiders." (Indeed, owing in part to antipoverty programs, this is already happening in a number of ghettos, where white storeowners are being replaced by Blacks.) Similarly, if the poor were more affluent, they would make less willing clients for upper-class philanthropy, although some would still use settlement houses to achieve upward mobility, as they do now. Thus "Society" could continue to run its philanthropic activities.

The political functions of the poor would be more difficult to replace. With increased affluence the poor would probably obtain more political power and be more active politically. With higher incomes and more political power, the poor would be likely to resist paying the costs of growth and change. Of course, it is possible to imagine urban renewal and highway projects that properly reimbursed the displaced people, but such projects would then become considerably more expensive, and many might never be built. This, in turn, would reduce the comfort and convenience of those who now benefit from urban renewal and expressways. Finally, hippies could serve also as more deviants to justify the existing political economy—as they already do. Presumably, however, if poverty were eliminated, there would be fewer attacks on that economy.

In sum, then, many of the functions served by the poor could be replaced if poverty were eliminated, but almost always at higher costs to others, particularly more affluent others. Consequently, a functional analysis must conclude that poverty persists not only because it fulfills a number of positive functions but also because many of the functional alternatives to poverty would be quite dysfunctional for the affluent members of society. A functional analysis thus ultimately arrives at much the same conclusion as radical sociology, except that radical thinkers treat as manifest what I describe as latent: that social phenomena that are functional for affluent or powerful groups and dysfunctional for poor or powerless ones persist; that when the elimination of such phenomena through functional alternatives would generate dysfunctions for the affluent or powerful, they will continue to persist; and that phenomena like poverty can be eliminated only when they become dysfunctional for the affluent or powerful, or when the powerless can obtain enough power to change society.

6 CRIME AND VIOLENCE— ALWAYS WITH US?

The Rat Packs of New York

Shane Stevens

From *The New York Times Magazine* (November 28, 1971), 91–95. © 1971/72 by The New York Times Company. Reprinted by permission.

Shane Stevens is active in the American Civil Liberties Union, contributes to the Saturday Review, New York Review, The Progressive, The Writer, *and* The New York Times, *and is the author of* Go Down Dead *(1967).*

By the start of the seventies, the country's racial rupture and economic inequalities had filtered through to consciousness in the minds of the youthful poor. Black Power—and the White Power backlash, especially among the frightened poor whites in the cities—set color as the determinant of one's enemies. The depressed economy meant even less money in the slums, and the young, as always, were the first to feel the crunch. Spending money had to be got from outside, and so the whole city became the arena. Rip offs were to be done anywhere, to anybody—preferably to a member of another race, religion, nationality or culture, but basically anyone with money. Violence became an accident of time and place.

The phenomenon is now seemingly endemic to large cities. In New York, as might be expected, it involves predominantly those youths who have the least opportunity and the most grievances—largely, but far from exclusively, black and Spanish-speaking residents. While the gangs and groups of the past fed on their own, today's rat packs, formed along racial lines—all white or Puerto Rican or black—feed on everybody else. For them, the city is one big cheese wheel.

Jumper is 16 and very cool. He has three friends he hangs around with. They're cool too. Johnny Apartment is 15, Wolfie and Chester are 14. They all go to the same junior high school in Central Harlem where they live. They like to play cards on a stoop, or maybe drink a little wine in a basement. Sometimes they go to the park with a girl or to throw a ball around. Most times they just hang out.

Sometimes they go downtown. "Just funnin' around, you know, man." A free ride on the subway and they're at a carnival. Times Square, Penn Station, Grand Central, East Side, West Side, all around the town—downtown, where the action is. They look and listen, watch and wait. Sometimes they pounce.

"Naw, we don't have no trouble with whites 'cause we don't have nothin' to do with them."

Wolfie laughs. "Yeah, that's right. 'Cept when we rip off something."

To get money to survive, Jumper and Johnny Apartment and Wolfie and Chester (their names and certain other data have been changed as part

47

of the terms of their cooperation) might rip off a stray white on a side street, or in Central Park, or even on a subway platform. A purse or handbag, a shoulder bag, a wallet or billfold, whatever they can get away with fast.

"You ask me why. You must be crazy to ask me that. We need money and white means money. That's it." No pretense at any racism here. Just an economic fact of life.

Sometimes assault is involved. If they hurt the victim that's his grief. Or hers. But they're not looking to hurt anybody: "We ain't into the kill thing. Anybody on that junk is workin' out of a fruit and nuts bag. We just want the money, like anybody else."

Just business as usual. But what about emotion? No hate there?

Johnny Apartment talks in a whisper, low and savage: "Hate? You wanna talk hate? Listen, Jim, I'll talk hate to you. I'm living with rats, man. Now you know and I know why I'm living like that; 'cause the white man put me there, and 'cause the white man keep me there."

"Say something slick for the Man."

"You wanna talk hate, I'll tell you somethin' about hate, Jim. The best way to hate whitey is to hate him before you born. That way you got a jump on the game."

"Dig it."

"Am I jiving on you?"

"Hey man, are we live or on tape?"

Jumper and the others don't think of themselves as a gang. They don't have any turf to protect, they have the whole city. And they don't need to fight other boys to prove their manhood. Quite the opposite: "Any man feeds off his own ain't got it together. He ain't behind it all." If they're not a gang they're not even a group. They have no special meeting place, no store, or club, or playground. No friends to defend, or enemies to defeat. No power and no feeling for power. They're floaters, here today, there tomorrow. Moving easy, sometimes on the spur of the moment, sometimes meeting with other strays for a day or a night. No pattern, moving haphazardly, perhaps meeting a white somewhere by chance and pulling a rip off if the circumstances are right.

What kind of life is this for a 14-year-old like Wolfie?

"Man, I been on the outlaw trail most all my life. Can't help it. What else you got for me?" How about school, maybe getting an education? "The best thing I like about school is after school." What about the real world out there? "The only real world is what I got in my hand. Everything else is make up."

Chester is 14 and he feels the same way. "The human race stinks, man. I'm glad I ain't in it."

But, of course, he is in it. And so are all of them, just as much involved with life as anybody else. Wolfie lives with his married sister, who is a nurse. Parents both dead, killed in a car crash when he was 6. Chester's mother, separated from his father, is on welfare and takes care of five younger children besides Chester. Only three years in New York, Chester's family came north from Louisiana. Both Wolfie and Chester have been left alone for much of their lives, and both are footloose.

Jumper's people fight a lot. His father, sick from some debilitating disease, drinks too much and his mother is always tired from her night job as a cleaning woman in a government building. He has an older brother who is doing time in a California state penitentiary. Jumper doesn't spend much time at home, using it mostly just for sleeping. He likes to keep moving and gets nervous when confined in any way.

Johnny Apartment has nobody. Mother dead, father unknown. A retarded sister is in a state institution. There might be other sisters he doesn't talk about. He was once in a city shelter and "a few times" in a detention facility. He sleeps in parked or abandoned cars, in basements or in friends' homes. For purposes of school, he is listed as living with a kindly building superintendent. He does have a small room there but doesn't often use it because the super is always drunk and there are too many rats.

This kind of existence is not untypical of the life style of many slum youth. For boys like these, life has little meaning and holds less promise. There is no sense of planning, no continuity. Talent and brains may well be there, but lack of opportunity and expression soon stifle ambition.

Disorder becomes the rule.

If they're not interested in any kind of organization, Jumper and the others are even less interested in politics or the black struggle. They laugh at the line, "Black Power is prune juice." They have no heroes except Malcolm X. "He was the baddest," they say in admiration. For them, there is no race struggle because the white man already has the game. Their job is to survive in a rip-off world they didn't make. If they cross the police or the courts they'll use their mother wit to get by.

"Man, it took me a long time to see that with the mother—whites the whole thing is honesty. Once you can fake that, you got it made with them."

In one respect, they are the least racist of all. They don't like any leaders and don't trust any leaders, in or out of Harlem. They instinctively suspect anybody—white or black—who would lead them, or "save" them, or even tell them what is right and wrong with them. All black leaders are put down the same way: "They all eat watermelon." About the only thing that is not scorned is the hustle for the dollar.

"What you got, man?"

"I'm tapped, man."

"Me too."

Jumper is 5 feet 11, medium frame. There's a hardness to him. Maybe he doesn't know all the angles, maybe he won't be around long enough to learn them, but he's playing with what he's got. Trying to survive.

"Let's take a walk 'round the park down there."

Through the gate before anyone spots them and down the stairs two at a time. Subway down to 59th Street. People look warily at the four of them, turn quickly away. They all wear the regulation uniform. White high-top Keds, blue jeans, denim jackets cut Western-style, sweat shirts or T-shirts underneath. Jumper and Wolfie have on their blue porkpie hats, soft, the brim pushed up all around. Johnny Apartment wears a racing cap, brown suede. Smooth.

Into the park by the pond, throwing pebbles at the ducks, badmouthing a few obvious homosexuals. Over to the zoo to look at the lions.

"Man, I wouldn't mess with that mother. Lookit them feet he got."

"Them's paws he got on."

"Mean mothers whatever they is."

Deeper into the park. It's early still, people walking, sitting. Past the statues and down the lake with the rowboats. Chester urinates on the grass.

"*Damn*, I just love this park. I love it 'cause the trees are close together and the people far 'part."

"Ain't far 'part enough for me."

"'Special when you got some action, ain't that right, man?"

"Only action he get is with his hand."

"What you talkin' about, man? I got chicks comin' outta my ear."

Jumper laughs. "Listen to this stud. And he ain't even half the man his mama is."

"Yeah, but his mama just nigger-struck is what she is."

Wolfie doesn't like that. "You sounding me, man?"

"He just runnin' his tongue, man."

"Yeah, stay loose, man."

A business suit walks by, paunchy, balding. Jumper goes up to him. "Hey, man, front me a quarter." The suit looks at him, sees the others. His right hand slips into his jacket.

In three hours of clowning around, knifing trees, verbally abusing some girls and stealing a radio from an elderly woman dozing on a bench, they make another half-dozen taps on people for change. As they leave the park a cop stands by the wall, watching them.

"Lookit that, man."

"I see him."

"Why he lookin' at us?"

"Maybe he jus' likes your Afro."

"And he a brother too."

"He got some white in him—lookin' like that."

"More'n that, man. He's just a whitey that come out the wrong color."

Sgt. William McCarthy, 15 years a policeman in Harlem, the last three as unit commander of the Youth Aid Division (Y.A.D.) in Central Harlem's sixth division, describes the rat pack's characteristic style:

"These kids lead a nomadic existence. They're like desert wanderers, roaming the city and committing crimes. They sometimes band together on the spur of the moment to go downtown for some action."

How far downtown?

"Penn Station, Times Square, the Upper East Side—anywhere they think there's money."

What about the Schleifer shooting on 110th Street?

"That's the borderline going south. We're getting increasing trouble in that whole area, mostly from juveniles. And much of it is violent crime. Schleifer was probably picked on the spur of the moment because he was white, and to a lot of these kids white means money." But how can they be called desert wanderers on 110th Street? "So this one was on the edge. But if Schleifer were 50 blocks downtown they might've jumped him or someone like him. The point is that they're mobile, they can appear anywhere."

Like wanderers in a desert. Or maybe a Disneyland. Where they can touch things they see on TV and know they will never have. Where they can rip off an executive because they'll never be one. Where they can cop a woman's handbag because they'll never be given credit cards and charge plates like she has. And where they can blow away a white man who put them where they are, and keeps them there.

"The Black Panthers and other black nationalist groups have told the kids that it's the white man who keeps them in the ghetto, and the only way to get him off their back is to go after him." McCarthy looks around his dismal office on the third floor of the 28th Precinct house, built in 1912. His eyes, stopping at a battered old school desk, seem to shrug. "If the white man has that kind of power then he's got the money to back it up, so he's a natural target," the sergeant says. He smiles. "Then, too, there's the practical matter of anonymity. Nobody knows them in any other areas."

Can anything be done? "It's got to start in the home, long before it gets to the streets and the police. There's no family supervision today.

When nobody cares about a kid, everything goes wrong. Youth crime is increasing. Sometimes I think maybe we're losing the war, all of us."[1]

Statistics bear this out. In the last 20 years reported juvenile incidents involving the police have increased more than 300 per cent in New York City. In McCarthy's division, taking in much of Central Harlem, the number of such incidents has doubled in the past decade; in 1970 alone, there were 297 arrests of juveniles (those under 16) for felonies and 3,401 "referrals" (which become part of a juvenile's record) for lesser offenses. City-wide the figures for last year were 17,944 arrests, of which more than 10,000 were for felonies, and 49,000 referrals. The 1970 figures for adolescents (those between 16 and 20) were just as dismal.

As a more recent example, in the first eight months of this year there were almost 800 reported robberies and a total of 1,135 felonies in Central Park. Both figures indicate a 20 percent rise over 1970 and a still larger increase over 1969. Police attribute much of this crime to city youths who roam the park, sometimes in packs of six or more, seeking victims. The growing use of drugs and increased migration of unskilled men and boys from the South and from Puerto Rico are the two major reasons cited for the escalation in criminal activity in the park.

But criminal activity is heavy in all areas of the city, and the rise in violent crime by youths is part of the picture. There has also been an increase in such crimes in other cities. Recently, an editorial in *The Times* noted that "reports from across the country confirm the dismal trend." But the real situation is even worse than statistics reveal, because many crimes of a semi-violent nature (such as purse snatching, which

[1] The Y.A.D. in Central Harlem has 20 people patrolling and investigating; each of the other 16 divisions in the city has about the same number. Acting as liaison between police and school, and police and family, the Y.A.D. concerns itself with juveniles. Legally, a juvenile delinquent is any youth over 7 and under 16 who does something which, if done by an adult, would be a crime. What crimes? A felony, any offense for which the sentence is more than one year, or a serious misdemeanor, such as unauthorized possession of a dangerous weapon, sex offenses or possession of dangerous drugs.

could lead to assault) are not reported unless the victim is injured.

There is no way to arrive at an estimate of how many city youths run in rat packs. The groups are amorphous, changing constantly, with no structure to them, no shape. There's no hard-core element, no criminal control, no Mafia management, no Fagin directing things. There's no common denominator among these youths beyond the desperate need for money. Some do it once and get scared. Some do it twice and get caught. Some move on to other things. Some just move. It's a childish kind of activity, grabbing a bag, hustling a wallet. Unfortunately, oftentimes children can hurt and even kill. But it's not man's work, it's not professional. It is, as one retired professional thief put it, "something for junkies and punks."

Punks. Most of them are living at home with parents or relatives; most attend school. On any school day hundreds of thousands of youngsters are traveling to different areas of an open city. Many rip offs are done on the way home from school. A rip off, almost by definition, is a spontaneous act done at a given moment because of favorable circumstances.

Under other circumstances, they might not do it. If they didn't need money, they might not. If they had some hope for the future, they might not. If they had a sense of responsibility, they might not. If family and community life were not deteriorating, they might not. Maybe, finally, if anyone cared, they might not.

In the matter of the ethnic background of rat packs, it is again impossible to arrive at any figure. Official juvenile statistics are hard to come by, since the law seems to guard them more zealously than adult figures. For instance, when asked for the percentages of white, black and Spanish-speaking juveniles arrested in 1970, the official police answer was, "This information is not available." In any case, economic need is color blind and there are slums in every corner of the city. And rat packs in all of them.

The public feels a widespread unease, a fear that something is radically wrong, a dread that "crime in the streets" may be getting out of control. The phrase means exactly that. Not crime committed by professionals but street rip offs committed largely by drug addicts and alienated elements of society, of which the roving packs of youngsters are a part.

Where will it end? "I don't know," said the young white man from the Lower East Side, a veteran rip-off artist at 18, "but long as you got your foot up my ass, I'm gonna have my knife at your throat."

"Yeah," said his 17-year-old friend, "and if that ain't enough, a gun at your head."

She was a model. Tall, sinewy; with long black hair reaching down over a tan jump jacket, framing a Pola Negri face. Her right hand held the model's black portfolio, proof of her identity. On her left shoulder hung a large beige bag, her fingers cupped around the wide strap. A big yellow "happy-face" button was pinned to the bag's flap. Black seamless stockings curved down to short Pucci boots with block heel and buckle buttons.

Walking south on Lexington Avenue and 85th Street, a slight wind teasing her hair, she seemed poised and confident. It was early, and she might well have been on her way to an important assignment on this bright autumn afternoon.

Chester saw her first. Coming around a corner, he spotted her across the street and motioned to Jumper and Wolfie. Jumper called over to Johnny Apartment, idling in front of a store. One look was enough for him. "Easy rider," he said softly. And started across the street, the others following.

She did not see them. Crossing behind her, keeping their distance, walking quietly, they caused no alarm or suspicion in the people on the street. If anyone noticed them in their sneakers and jeans, they were probably considered school kids going home or somewhere. What with all this school busing these days, you know. . . .

She was mid-block now. The sun's rays, warming the other side of Lexington Avenue, seemed to catch a sudden movement at the edge of shadow. A brief blurring of light as Wolfie ran up behind her and punched her with closed fist in the small of the back.

Involuntarily reacting to the blow, her arms opening in surprise much as a sea gull in startled flight, she dropped her portfolio just as her shoulder bag slipped to the sidewalk. With one quick scoop Jumper grabbed the bag, while Johnny Apartment reached for a ring on her outstretched hand. In a matter of seconds they were at the corner and around it, headed toward Third Avenue. After two blocks they split up, each to get home, with Jumper holding the money. The shoulder bag and its contents had already been tossed under a parked car. Like American merchants of an earlier time, only cash was acceptable. At least in a daylight rip off in enemy country where capture was always a possibility. And getting rid of evidence was a necessity.

The life of a nomad is never easy. With far horizons comes the burden of getting home safely. With the advantage of anonymity in a strange land comes the disadvantage of not knowing the terrain. Jumper and the others are aware of the dangers. They are also aware that, being minority youths, they could be stopped at any time by cops "vamping everybody in sight," who might put them "upside a wall and frisk our ass off." Normally they would be all right, but in a rip off their one goal is to get home fast or, if not that, to some other area. For this they need swift transportation.

The subway is their magic carpet. It takes them where they want to go, and away from where they don't want to be. It is a lifeline of sorts, providing both speed and anonymity. Small wonder that many rip offs occur near subway stations. Of course, in an area such as midtown Manhattan almost anywhere is near a subway station. One wonders what would happen to the rip-off rate of rat packs if the subways were closed at night.

Are youths like Jumper and Wolfie and Chester and Johnny Apartment worried about the possible consequences of getting caught? Not overly, apparently.

"First thing is, dig it. You gotta do some real wild-man stuff for them to come down on you. Most times they let you go home with your people right there."

"If you don't got too many raps on the sheet [juvenile record]."

"Yeah, that too. But if they keep you, then the judge'll let you go."

"That the God truth, man. I was there onct and that judge talkin' to me till I was catchin' a headache. Talk my ear clean off 'fore they let me go."

"Like I know some men they was sent somewhere and inside two weeks they back home."

"Sure, everybody know that."

For offenses that are not felonies or serious misdemeanors, a juvenile may either be held in custody for an appearance in Family Court or released to parents until the court appearance. This decision is made by the desk officer in the precinct. About 90 percent of such juveniles are so released, according to a high police official. The remaining 10 percent usually have a growing juvenile record. (A referral form—the YD 1—is made out by the Y.A.D. for juveniles and is, in effect, a record.)

If youths under 16 are considered juveniles and often let go with a referral and a verbal "spanking" or short-term detention, what of those over 16?

"That's a whole other thing, man. That's why a lotta men you see, they got papers on 'em saying they under 16. They could be 50, but they under 16. Am I jiving on you, man?"

"No man, that's just the way it is."

"That's 'cause if you over 16 they come down on you like you was King Kong. 'Special if you doing the heavy work [armed robbery, homicide with a gun]. Then they kick ass."

In New York adolescents between 16 and 20 are treated as adults under the Penal Code. That is, they are arraigned in Criminal Court, held in custody if bail is not set or posted, bound over to State Supreme Court if a grand jury hands down an indictment, tried in court and, if convicted, sentenced to prison. They are, however, separated from adult inmates.

Jumper, who just turned 16, isn't worried because "I got no record worth nothing. Long's I don't use a gun everything's cool." What about a knife? "Most times I don't even carry a blade. But if something goes wrong you can always throw it away fast."

What if a knife can't be thrown away fast enough?

"The thing is, we just grabbin' the stuff and run. That way nobody gets hurt. Nothin' can go real wrong."

But even if something does go "real wrong"— short of homicide, perhaps—a youth of 16 or 17 or even 18 with no prior felony conviction could still come out all right. If he were judged a "youthful offender," he would stand a chance of being put on probation or even receiving a conditional discharge (conditional on his behaving himself). And his record of conviction would be sealed; in effect, he would have no criminal record.

Popeye, an 18-year-old Puerto Rican punchman (one who punches a passing woman full in the face and then runs off with her bag) from the Lower East Side, was tried as a youthful offender and got probation on a Class B felony. "My woman, she rode me somethin' awful at night. She'd look me straight up the eye and she'd say, 'I need this' and 'I need that,' so I hadda get it for her."

His court-appointed lawyer ("If I listened to him I'd be talking to myself now") told him he'd be lucky to get five years, but instead he got a Y.O. and probation. "Not only that but now I got no record or nothin'. And all I hadda do was promise to go straight." Popeye laughs. "But you know, man, my woman is still there on my ear so I gotta go back to work. Only now I'm exter careful."

What if they found out he broke his word? It could mean prison.

That doesn't worry Popeye; he's a realist. "I didn't break my word, man, I just changed my mind. They understand."

Times Square is the watering hole of the jungle. Everybody who's anything in the nothing world of the hustle makes the scene sooner or later. The prossies walk their beat, early on Eighth Avenue, late on Broadway, their pimps sitting in little luncheonettes along Eighth in the 40's. Jockers and queens stand in front of sex bookstores on 42d Street or lounge in the back of cafeterias. Sharks and Murphy men patrol the bars near the bus terminal, while grifters of every shade work the side streets between Sixth and Eighth Avenues in the mid-40's. It's after 8 o'clock and the hustle is on, along with the bright lights of the neon jungle.[2]

Jumper and Johnny Apartment walk down Broadway, Wolfie and Chester trailing by a few steps. They like Times Square, the variety, the crazies, the quick ways to spend a buck. They come down at least once a week when they have the money. Movies, fast food, sometimes clothing and assorted junk.

"It's where to spend it. We don't mess 'round there 'cause it's too open, too many people. The whole place is leaking sounds."

For possible rip offs they go where it's not so noisy. Down to the Penn Station area or even farther, to 23d Street. Across town, west to east, all those blocks mostly quiet after business hours. The East 20's and 30's along Third and Second Avenues. Then around Grand Central and the U.N., working their way north through the moneyed 50's and 60's. The rich parks along the East River. The Upper East Side, going home. Baghdad on the subway. Or the bus.

Tonight they go to a 42d Street movie, eat at Nathan's ("Gimme ketchup on everything." "It's over there, pal") then walk around Broadway for a while. Wolfie's handwriting, analyzed, reveals that he "will make a lot of money in the near future." Chester, feeling sick from eating too much, turns salty. "I didn't eat too much, I was overserved."

As a goof, Jumper puts the make on a whore at 50th Street, but she turns away. Everybody laughs. "What she say, man?" Jumper shakes his head. "Says she only eats white bread."

"That's 'cause you didn't front no money."

"Make no difference. She don't burn no coal."

[2]A "jocker" is the aggressive partner in a homosexual relationship. A "Murphy man" accosts men in the street and tries to sell them a prostitute who he says is waiting in an apartment nearby; after receiving the money, he enters the building—telling the customer to wait while he makes preparations—then disappears, usually making his exit via the roof. A "grifter" is any kind of street hustler (the word is related to "graft").

"Hell, when a whore talking under her clothes she take any money."

"Not from me she don't."

"Ain't worth it, man."

"No woman worth the money."

" 'Special no whore."

"And a ugly old whore like that."

"Right on there, man."

It's well past midnight as the four of them move down Seventh Avenue. The street is dark. At 36th, a car's alarm system suddenly starts up by itself. They break into a run down the block, cursing the car, fearful that they'll be blamed. Into Penn Station, down the stairs, franks and Cokes at a stand, walk about a bit, then back outside.

On 33d Street a man headed toward the station is suddenly confronted by four youths who come upon him halfway up the deserted block. As they pass, Johnny Apartment turns quickly and shoves the tip of his blade into the man's back, up high on the shoulder, where it does little damage. The man, in pain, flails his arms, trying to reach the hurt. Jumper's hand is already inside the man's jacket, while Wolfie and Chester cut out his pants pockets with razors. Within 30 seconds they are away and racing for the corner. Once out of sight they will slow to a walk and immediately throw away everything but cash. Wallets and keys go down a sewer or basement. Checkbooks, credit cards, all go into the gutter unless there is no chance of being picked up by the cops. In which case they'll sell the cards, since there is no way they would ever be able to use them.

A walk to the next subway station, this time buying tokens so they cause no suspicion, and home. Just a night of fun and profit on the nomad circuit in the big city.

Is there any future in it?

Jumper doesn't think much about the future. Neither do the others. They find the present bad enough—or good enough, depending on their mood of the moment. Like many youngsters, they seek instant gratification and cannot readily handle long-term considerations. They don't like school and don't especially like to read. They know little about world affairs and couldn't care less. Yet they are infinitely more sophisticated than the gang members of years ago. They have been around the city, they have seen many things. They are aware of their rights and of society's wrongs. It would be hard to cheat them out of anything.

Only Johnny Apartment has a plan for the future. He's going to become a top pimp and "make plenty." He likes the way pimps dress, and the cars they drive, and how they handle their women. Most of all, he likes the idea of making it big. The point is not that he intends to be a pimp but that he's got all the ambition and drive and determination to rise to the top of his chosen profession, and that's just what every redblooded American boy is supposed to have.

Johnny Apartment is lucky, at least he knows what he wants. All Jumper and the others know is what they don't want. Which is more of the same they've had all their lives.

"What future?"

"I'm trying to forget my future."

Boys like Jumper and Johnny Apartment and Wolfie and Chester—thousands of them in rat packs all over the city, coming from every economic slum—ordinarily are not addicted to hard drugs. Those who do use drugs normally restrict themselves to snorting nonaddictive cocaine, when available. A longtime junkie does not have the coordination for the street rip off. Speed, steadiness, above all, control are needed. When a junkie does make the attempt, it is usually a more desperate—and for the victim, more dangerous—situation. A junkie often will use a gun, invariably one of the $10 "Saturday night specials." If not a gun, then a long knife held at the victim's throat or belly. Unfortunately, compliance is no guarantee of safety. Junkies are notoriously unpredictable.

The rat packs generally do not carry guns. They rely on surprise and speed, though knives are often shown for effect. If they use a weapon at times, it is a razor blade or the tip of a pocket knife, which distracts the victim momentarily. When guns are shown, it somehow changes the complexion, the "feel" of the crime from thievery to armed robbery, and places it in another, more premeditated category. Even then, the gun is seldom used. Those instances in which a victim is shot are usually the result of an act of bravado by the one holding the gun, who is perhaps challenged beyond the point of return by his companions.

In a time of social unrest and economic deprivation, lots of things go wrong. The emergence of rat packs is one of them. It is a problem for the city and for society, but even more of a problem for the youths themselves. Acts of hostility against anyone who crosses their path will in the long run destroy them. Cumulative degeneration is never pleasant to watch. Individual suicide is oftentimes tragic, but mass suicide, especially of the young, is always a national tragedy.

What can be done? Short of social evolution or biological revolution, perhaps nothing. Robbery—and violence—are increasing in every big city in the country, regardless of how much police officials like to pretend to the contrary. Based on the evidence, on statistics, on the rate of recidivism, nobody—not the police, not the courts, not the correction departments, and certainly not the prison systems—is taking care of its business. Rehabilitation is still in its infancy, community treatment has not yet even been born, and the concept of crime *prevention* rather than crime detection is still just a dream.

Albert Seedman, Chief of Detectives in New York, was recently quoted as saying: "Robbery grows out of social unrest, out of poverty and out of a society that is in flux. We can't do much about these root causes of robbery, but we can arrest more of the robbers."

That is an answer. It is not a solution.

What's going on? Maybe Jumper had it right after all. "Every turkey has its Thanksgiving, man."

Mugging as a Way of Life

David Freeman

From *U.S. Grant in the City*, 31–39, by David Freeman. Copyright © 1970 by David Freeman. Reprinted by permission of the Viking Press, Inc.

Mr. Freeman is a graduate of the Yale University School of Drama. He is a free-lance writer, having written several Off-Broadway plays and articles for The Voice, The New York Times, *and others. He is writing a novel, untitled at the moment.*

A few years ago, when the moon was made of paper and a pleasant old man was President, Hector D. moved with his mother, his grandmother, and a platoon of assorted relatives from the slums of north San Juan to El Barrio in the slums of north Manhattan. None of the family spoke English and there were ten people in three rooms, but the rooms were big, the plumbing was inside, and the older ones took strength in little Hector, who was nine and had eyes the color of ripe olives and who seemed to learn English faster than he grew. On Hector's eleventh birthday the family moved to Simpson Street in the south Bronx and Hector moved to the streets, where along with more English he learned the ways of the subway and of airplane glue.

Two years ago Hector moved from Simpson Street to Avenue C on the Lower East Side, where he changed his ectasy from glue to red wine in brown paper bags and then to heroin in glassine envelopes. Hector is still the only member of his family who can speak English and his eyes still look like olives, but green ones now, stuffed with red pimento. His relatives, or what's left of them, still live on Simpson Street, and Hector visits them occasionally. But Hector spends his days on the streets of the Lower East Side, where he and a friend named Louise share the nights in burnt-out buildings and support themselves by mugging their neighbors.

For a time, in the fifties, the streets that run east of Avenue A to the river and below Houston Street to the Brooklyn Bridge on New York's Lower East Side were almost a shrine, praised as the breeding ground of armies of doctors and lawyers, all of whom looked like Harry Golden. Praising the tenements of their youth ("Sure it was tough, but we had love and desire . . ."), Lower East Side alumni sounded like Nixon talking about his astronauts. Today the incipient Jewish judges are gone, and the hippies of a few years ago are mostly gone, departed for communes or the suburbs. The streets and the buildings, exhausted from generations of bright, aggressive youngsters followed by stoned hippies, look tired, as if they need a rest after sixty-five years of social ferment. Leo Gorcey and Huntz Hall are gone; the streets are lined with garbage now—human and automotive—and the people are mostly Puerto Rican. The billboards are in Spanish and in every store window a red sign screams, "How do you know you don't have V.D.? ¿Cómo sabe-Ud. que no tiene enfermedades venereas?" The old-law tenements are crumbling, collapsing, burnt-out hulks. Their windows are covered with tin and plywood and their roofs are ripped away so that the sunlight floods into the upper stories like shrapnel.

When Hector and Louise aren't mugging their neighbors, they live in these buildings, moving easily from a deserted tenement on Avenue D to another south of Houston Street, near the Bowery. Always a few steps ahead of the wreckers or the Board of Health, they squat their way across the Lower East Side like spiders, spinning a chaotic web, leaving bits and pieces of themselves in each apartment. Sometimes they stay a month, sometimes only a few days. As they leave, Hector and Louise set fire to the building, and as their house and with it their past burns, they head for the next block.

Louise is seventeen, and although she has not been there in some time, she is, for the record, an eighth grader at J.H.S. 71 on Avenue B. Louise was born in Bedford-Stuyvesant, but grew up on Avenue C, where her grandmother still lives. Hector met her about a year ago in Tompkins Square Park, where they were both listening to a rhythm concert in the band shell. Louise was moving to the Afro-Latin sounds drummed on resonant empty fifty-five-gallon oil drums and Day-Glo-blue bongos. The six stoned Lower East Side drummers and the triangle man were deep in a private communal riff when Hector got up from a bench and began moving with her. They've been together ever since. Louise is slightly taller than Hector, heavier, and more muscular. Her skin is deep black and her short natural hair gives her a masculine look. Louise usually wears blue jeans cut off like pedal pushers and wedge-heeled sandals that expose her silver-trimmed toes. She has a bullet pendant that dangles from a rawhide loop around her neck and settles gently between her breasts. The fingers of her right hand are decorated with Cracker Jack and midway claw-machine trophies: a red glass ruby, a skull and crossbones, and a narrow aluminum band that Louise says has the entire Lord's Prayer inscribed on it. C-H-I-C-O is tattooed on the knuckles of her left hand. These days Louise wears loose-fitting sleeveless blouses that expose her muscular biceps. The flowing blouse drapes easily over her swelling stomach and rests on the denim-covered haunches. Louise is five months pregnant.

Hector's jaw, pitted with clusters of bullet-hole acne marks, hangs open and occasionally dribbles a stream of spit across his delicate throat where the scars give way to bubbling, festering sores. At twenty-one, Hector is compact and wiry, and although his eyes are usually glazed and he often spends days on end in one of his apartments, picking at the scars on his arms and face, shooting up and nodding out, Hector is actually in better shape now, on heroin, than he was a year and a half ago when he was living on red wine. Hector, juiced out at nineteen, according to friends, was so filled with wine that his brain started going soft. Hector had been living on rotgut for about three months before he wandered over to the rhythm concert in Tompkins Square. Louise, who admits to having had her eye on him for some time before the concert, recalls his state easily, saying, "He was so drunk that if you would cut him, his veins spurted Dago Red. Guys would go after him with a knife just to get a drink." Louise, who finds wine disgusting, changed all that when she introduced Hector to her very old friend, Snow White. Louise says she first took heroin when she was twelve. Unlike Hector, she seems able to take it in small doses and stop when she cares to. Hector says proudly, "Since I got on the horse, I didn't take a drink at all. Juice is bad for you, make you mushy. I'm all over that now."

Hector and Louise usually work whatever neighborhood they're living in. They knock over every old man on the block, every young man who follows Louise's swinging hips and pocketbook, and every young girl attracted by Hector's olive eyes. They rough up all of them, take whatever money is there, and then move on.

Their procedure is classically simple. Louise swings her purse and her hips and walks casually down the street. When someone starts following her, and someone always does, Louise wanders aimlessly toward Hector, who steps out of inner space and puts a knife to the man's throat. Hector tells him—only once—to keep his mouth shut. Louise, who has been standing there looking confused, starts to grin and steers her new friend into the shadows or into an empty hallway to rifle his pockets and take his wallet. The whole thing takes two minutes and then Hector and Louise leave as suddenly as they appeared. Occasionally a victim screams and Hector covers the man's mouth to shut him up. If that doesn't help, Hector must make a choice: cut or run. If he cuts, he usually gets excited and cuts again. If he runs, Louise will laugh at him. Usually he

cuts. Not to kill, but to silence. Hector doesn't know if he's killed anyone. He remembers cutting one old man pretty badly, but he doesn't know if the man died. "He bleeded a lot. Like anything—thass all I know."

When Louise has picked up a likely candidate and wandered into Hector's shadow, she stops, lets the man catch up, and smiles and lets him move in. On Avenue D, that means a few sweet words and then some action. The victim starts pushing Louise into the shadows, pawing and babbling what he thinks is smooth talk. She giggles and protests mildly. Then Hector moves in. If the man has been rough with her, Louise sometimes takes the opportunity to spit in his face or kick him in the crotch. If it's a woman and she turns out not to have any money, Hector occasionally rapes her. Louise helps him by gagging the girl and holding her arms or spreading her legs. Like the cook who loved Mother Courage, Hector usually takes his women standing up. Often he threatens to rape the girl and then, instead of consummating it, urinates on her while Louise laughs. Then they both kick the girl a few times and run. If her clothes look good to Louise, she takes them along, leaving the girl to wander Avenue D bruised and naked.

Although Hector and Louise have no permanent home, they have established a bit of middle-class comfort in their lives. Hector and Louise are car owners, or more precisely, truck owners. Several months ago a dry cleaner on Avenue B left the ignition key in his delivery truck. Hector jumped in, and he'd been driving the truck every since. Hector has no driver's license and in fact can barely drive, but he and Louise practiced, careening around the streets until now they can both manage to maneuver the truck, a Ford, without too much trouble. They hid it in a garbage-covered lot on 6th Street until Louise produced three gallons of blue house paint appropriated from a renewal project on Avenue C, and the two of them painted their mobile home with rollers and a whisk broom. When they can afford gas, Hector and Louise joyride around the Lower East Side at night. When they can't find an abandoned building, they sleep in the back of the truck. With a can of red spray paint Hector has scrawled "*Quiere me*" on the right fender.

It's not hard to throw away a car on the Lower East Side—in fact it's hard not to. Park it, take off the license plates, and twenty-four hours later it will be stripped, an engineless metal shell, covered with children swarming like ants, jumping on the roof, trying to cave it in. Like an executioner offering his victim a last cigarette, a car vulture on the Lower East Side will always slide a metal milk crate under the axle, so that the machine doesn't fall to the pavement while it's being stripped of its wheels. The fleecing is done by children and adults in search of spark plugs, hub caps, and the like for fun and profit. Hector and Louise have escalated the war in order to equip their panel truck. In need of windshield wipers, they found them on a delivery van on Avenue D. Since that first set of wiper blades, Hector has taken to stripping loose parts from any car he sees, abandoned or not, and attaching the trophies to his truck. The truck now has four aerials and a myriad of reflectors, mudflaps, and tail lights. Much of the time Hector is not sure what he'll do with the parts. It's hard to sell spare auto parts in his neighborhood, where they are in endless supply, parked by the curb, free for the taking.

Hector and Louise, restless and broke—Hector with heroin but no reason, Louise indifferent—follow an old man in a long gray topcoat east on Houston Street past "Yonah Schimmel's Knishes," toward First Avenue. Hector walks casually, almost bopping to amuse Louise, keeping plenty of distance from the old man. Louise watches Hector's eyes follow the man's progress.

"What you looking at, boy?"

"Thass dinner up there."

"That's a nickel bag, that's what that is. That's a nickel bag of Snow White."

"Thass what I mean. Dinner. *Comprende?*"

Hector, staring at the man's back, walks a little faster, his hand in his hip pocket. Louise tugs at her bullet pendant and quickens her step to keep up. She touches Hector's elbow as they gain on him.

"He looks pretty old."

"Sure."

"Maybe he's a police."

"Some old man is all."

"A police, like an old man."

"Maybe."

As they pass an alley near First Avenue, Hector moves up on the man's left. Louise steps to his right, slides her arm into his, and begins to pull him gently toward her. As he turns to Louise, smiling and starting to tell her "No, no, I'm not interested," Hector pushes him sharply into the alley. Louise changes her gentle grip to a yank and pulls him into the dark. Hector follows with his knife open, swearing. Louise drops the man's arm and puts a tight yoke grip around his neck as Hector holds the knife to his stomach and fumbles for his wallet. The man begins to gag for breath and flutter his free arm. Louise tells him to shut up and draws the yoke tighter. Hector presses the knife against the man's stomach, cutting the fabric of his coat. He turns the blade upward and in one sweep slices the buttons off the coat. Louise knocks his wire-rimmed glasses to the ground and smashes them as Hector pushes the old man backward, across two open garbage cans. Two five-dollar bills. Hector pockets the money along with some loose change and he and Louise run for Avenue D.

Louise leans heavily into a broken door near the end of a dark and private hallway at her current address. She pushes it open with her shoulder and looks for Hector. He is sitting next to a shaft of light that melts through a broken window overlooking 7th Street. Nodding in the corner, his knees drawn up tightly against his bare chest, his electric-blue net polo shirt wrapped like a tourniquet around his left arm, Hector looks but doesn't notice her. Hector stares at the dust in the light, then moves his arm carefully into it, watching the specks settle on his forearm. He stares curiously at the red hole just below his elbow. The sores on his shoulder drip white fluid down his arm underneath the shirt tourniquet, to blend with the heroin on the lips of the red crater he is carefully cultivating on his inner arm, to avoid needle marks. Hector is always very careful to insert his needle in exactly the same spot each time. Hector touches the opening, caressing its edges. He purses his lips silently. As Louise stares, a pair of roaches crawl over Hector's works on the floor next to him. The bugs work their way across his needle on the way to the tin spoon, where they stop and stare at each other in the stoned safety of the spoon's bowl. Louise, carrying two cans of collard greens stolen from the shelves of the Pioneer Supermarket on Avenue A, stands in the doorway and smiles at him. "You want some food to eat? Greens?" She holds up her trophies and crosses to him so he can inspect the cans more closely. As she walks, her sandals sink into the carpet of roaches that covers the floor. Louise, amused at the sound, listens to her weight crush the brown shells. Halfway across the room she stops and turns her heels on the wooden floor, as if she were doing the Twist. She looks at Hector's eyes, lifting his lids to peer at the traces of burst veins. Hector mumbles in Spanish and smiles back at her. Louise tugs at his short black hair and says, giggling, "Man, are you stoned." She pokes through his pocket for matches. "I'll make some greens." In the kitchen, she fills a tin saucepan from a gallon jug of water and lights a small wood fire in the sink. She adds the greens to the water and rests the pan in the fire. As Louise's makeshift stove flares up, it heats the greens and broils a geyser of roaches and ants that burst up from the drain into the flames.

Hector, moving down Avenue C away from his current home on 2nd Street, turns suddenly and heads west, searching vaguely for Louise. Suffering from extreme morning sickness, Louise has awakened early and headed toward First Avenue, looking for a free clinic she has heard about. Hector can't remember for certain whether Louise has left this morning or the morning before. Up till now Hector has been casual about becoming a father, preferring to let Louise worry about it. Sometimes he claims not to know about the pregnancy, other times he seems pleased with it. When Hector gets to Avenue A he begins to get edgy—anything west of A

is alien territory and Hector knows it. Alien to Hector, and the home of the Alien Nomads. But this morning none of the Nomads seem to be out. It's a little past eight a.m. and the street is empty. Hector, following a private signal, like a bloodhound, Louise's scent in his nostrils, turns suddenly and heads toward Tompkins Square. "She gone to the cleen-ik, the cleen-ik," is all he can say. He keeps repeating it as he scans the streets. Near A and 7th, Hector finds what he's looking for. At the south end of the park Louise is curled on a stone bench, a few feet from a group of old men playing cards and rasping to each other in Ukrainian. Louise is moaning softly, a dark wet stain is traced on her lap and her throat is heavily bruised. The skin on her legs is shredded, hanging loosely, and a pool of vomit, flecked with collard greens, is on the ground in front of her. A trickle of blood drips steadily from her nose down onto the bullet pendant. Sensing his presence, Louise looks up at Hector, stares dully at him, and says, "Nomads."

"They beat you up?"

She nods and says, "I don't think there's no more baby, honey."

Hector sits on the bench, in the crook of her knees, touches the wet stain on her crotch and then dabs at her nose with his sleeve. "You get to the cleen-ik?"

"A whole bunch of Nomads. Gang banged me. Over there on Sixth Street."

"Sixth Street, huh?"

"There's some good houses in there. I was looking at the buildings. A whole bunch got me."

"You wanna move there? Sixth Street?"

"No, I wanna go to the clinic. Go home, get the truck so I could go to the clinic."

"Okay. I get it." Hector touches his sleeve to her nose again, and walks past the card game. At Avenue B he stops for a moment to talk to a man who wants to buy some heroin. Hector tells him he doesn't have any and then heads east toward Avenue C, trying to remember where he lives.

How to Make the City Safe Again—
Six Commentators in Search of a Crime Solution

From *The New York Times Magazine* (September 24, 1972), 14, 91–98. ©
1971/72 by The New York Times Company. Reprinted by permission.

1. GET THE COPS, COURTS, AND JAILS OUT OF THE PUBLIC-MORALS BUSINESS
Robert Daley

Formerly Deputy Commissioner, Public Affairs, New York City Police Department, Mr. Daley is author, photographer, and publicity agent. At one time he was publicity director for the New York Football Giants. He is the author of The World Beneath the City *(1959),* The Cruel Sport *(1963),* Only a Game *(1967), and* A Star in the Family *(1971) and has contributed articles to* Life, Vogue, *and* Playboy.

How to reduce crime—
How to reduce police corruption—
How to make the city safe again—

Of course I can offer suggestions. But one's first reaction is a feeling of impotence. It all seems so hopeless. The answers have been there so long they will sound like platitudes, and no one has the will and guts to act on them anyway.

Last winter I helped force through a decision by Commissioner Murphy that New York cops would no longer enforce the street-gambling laws. For decades the primary purpose of the police had been to suppress gambling—or so it seemed to every cop, each one, all of them. Some cops arrested gamblers and some pocketed gambling graft. Some did both. But gambling was on every cop's mind 24 hours a day, like sex on the mind of an adolescent boy.

The citizens, especially in the black enclaves, did not want these laws enforced, and in a city rife with muggers it seemed immoral for the cops to waste manpower enforcing them, and I

so convinced Commissioner Murphy and the police hierarchy over a period of days. Eventually, Chief of Patrol Donald Cawley was ordered to promulgate a decree, and he did so in a secret meeting with his borough commanders, and I leaked this secret on schedule to the press. Then we all waited for the storm, but it never came.

And so, at the cost of a few days' arguments by police brass, the single most important police-corruption hazard was eliminated, and a few million police hours and dollars per year were turned off gambling and onto street crime.

It seemed a small enough step then, but I get more impressed as I look back. Commissioner Murphy won that battle hands down, and also an earlier one in which he declined any longer, in the absence of a specific complaint, to enforce the Sabbath laws. More recently, to cut down on corruption, he ordered the noninvolvement of police in enforcement of certain anti-nuisance laws at construction sites. There was some criticism, not much.

There are three parts to the criminal justice system—the cops, the courts and correction. The implementation of a few dramatic ideas by the other two parties would be at least as effective as "selective" enforcement by police, and would reduce crime and corruption out of all proportion to their cost:

Enforce the gun laws. Everybody caught with an illegal gun goes to jail, instantly, instead of free, as now. Get those guns off the street and crime might drop. You'd be surprised.

I keep saying instantly. We live in a super-charged, high-velocity world. Everything takes place fast, except justice, which drags on for years. No wonder criminals laugh at it. It doesn't match the world. Trials should take place within a week. Before the witnesses have forgotten, or disappeared. Eliminate the delays which judges, prosecutors, defense attorneys (lawyers all) are so willing to accord each other. After conviction allow one appeal, also within a week, at which point the convicted criminal goes to jail for the duration of any other appeals.

I was personally involved in the arrests of two of New York's most successful professional car thieves. This was in October, 1971. It was the fifth arrest that year for one suspect, the third for the other. In May, 1972, I phoned the assistant district attorney who had the case. It was pending, he said; the two car thieves were out on bail and had another "operation" going in Queens: "We're trying to get another arrest on them."

Why do cases pend?

The jails must be changed. Also, felons must come out with a job waiting, and with some money. This isn't coddling criminals. The alternative is that each convict hits a fellow citizen on the head within an hour, in order to get money to eat, which is what is happening now.

Whole categories of crime must be eliminated. Get the cops, courts and jails out of the public-morals business. Let the Health Department cope with the prostitutes. Try summary justice: an instant fine. In France if you're stopped for a traffic violation, you must pay the gendarme the fine on the spot. Give the health inspectors this power and you can clear any street of prostitutes in a few seconds. At the sight of a health inspector they will sprint for the doorways. We admit we can't obliterate prostitution, right? We just want to control it, right?

Make heroin legal. Qualified buyers could purchase it at cost at the corner drugstore, with minimum practicable controls. Black leaders would call this genocide. We can't afford to listen to them, for they may be wrong. Doubtless when Prohibition ended certain men called this genocide too. How would the Irish race resist its fatal attraction for the bottle? Still, many of the Irish resist manfully, even today.

A victimless crime is not one where there is no victim, but one where there is no complainant. Laws cannot be enforced without complainants. The narcotic laws can't be enforced, for there are too many buyers and sellers. I have been out with police undercover teams that spent all day to find a certain dealer and buy $16 worth of heroin, seal it, trot it to the lab, await the result. Count one undercover buyer and two backup cops. All day for one buy. The D.A.'s demand two buys before prosecution. The arrest took place on a third day. Nine man-days for one arrest, plus court time, and an estimated 300,000 addicts buying and selling junk every day. It can't be done.

Make heroin legal. Wipe out the profit and you wipe out the pushers who hook our youth, and the organized crime overlords. Wipe out the expense of illegal heroin and you eliminate most of the 300,000 burglars, muggers and armed robbers. Burglars need to steal five times as much per day as their habits cost. Robbers may have to commit several crimes to get enough cash for one day's fix.

Change takes time. More than that, it takes will, and there is little of that around this year. In its absence, a few men can take a few giant steps on their own, at once, as Commissioner Murphy did with regard to gambling enforcement. The alternative is our current treadmill backward into the past.

2. IT'S THE DECENT PEOPLE VS. THE RIPOFFS, IN AND OUT OF UNIFORMS
Piri Thomas

Mr. Thomas is author of Down These Mean Streets *(1967), an account of his growing up in Spanish Harlem, and of* Savior, Savior, Hold My Hand *(1972). He has been associated with the Center for Urban Education since 1967.*

All my life in one way or the other I've lived in the Ghetto and ever since I can remember there was always some sort of violence going on—fights, muggings, purse-snatching, rapes, junkies and junk-pimps, faggots and prostitutes —and to enhance the ghetto world of violence around me, to help bring out its message of fear, hopelessness and despair was the embellishment of hot and cold running cockroaches and king-size rats, of exploitation beyond compare, of pride and prejudice. But lest the people in the pretty Pleasantville suburbs think that we of the ghetto dig violence and crime let it be known that the criminal element represents a comparatively small percentage of the total community. All the drugs that have been poured into our community by outside vested, organized interests have of course augmented the ripoffs by the junkies against the community via purse-snatching, burglaries, etc. But like, diggit, who brought hard-core drugs into our communities? It wasn't blacks or Puerto Ricans. It was another ethnic group that poured poison into our kids, and like I ought to know, having been a junkie myself a million years ago. I'd see the Lincoln Continentals cruise by and the big-time pusher's face was stone white and like he didn't have no Puerto Rican or black accent.

We are talking about violence. Well, this is part of what breeds it. But like what bugs me is that in the struggle of the greater part of the ghetto people for our right to justice, equality, dignity, for our right to first-class citizenship, we're being infiltrated by many who are out to fill their own bag, and under the guise of brotherhood, the cause, civil rights, these people have ripped off much bread from the commun-

ity. Others don't bother to name a cause. It's just out-and-out robbery, stomping, slashing, cutting, mugging, raping, like sucking the blood of the helpless innocents of their own ghetto communities and other communities. Except that in nicer communities, you call the police and *zap*, you got a friend indeed in your hour of need. In ghetto communities, you call the police and most of the time you better pray indeed in your hour of need.

I remember one time some years back looking out my window in Brooklyn, Bushwick section of Williamsburg. It was about 9:30 at night. There were about four or five white cats doing a number on (beating hell out of) a Puerto Rican near a candy store, and like they were doing their best to make him part of the sidewalk scene. I picked up the phone and dialed the police. A voice answered and I explained the situation: "Someone is getting killed." The voice on the other end (so help me, God) sounded bored as he asked, "Are they colored or Puerto Rican?" Diggit, my mind spun with the reality of his words. I asked him what did that matter. In the same bored tone, he said he'd like to know. I threw a look out the window at the Puerto Rican who was making those four or five white guys tired from beating on him and told the bored voice on the other end, "My God, those Puerto Ricans are practically killing that poor white guy!" And *zap*, some split minutes later the whole street was jumping with P.D. cars and light cavalry.

What I am saying is that our people in the ghetto complain to the police on crime, graft, drugs and like nothing happens. They get ripped off by those who prey on them and nothing happens. It is hard for a community to place trust in policemen who they see constantly on the make, taking bribes or monthly payoffs from known criminals, pushers of heroin and cocaine who have more than drug and crime connections. They get guaranteed police protection by renegade cops—the pity being that these ripoff cops make it hard on the good guys. But, like, ain't that like always?

In the ghettos are decent law-abiding citizens, regardless of race, creed or color, who despise the criminal element but are helpless, made more so by their unfortunate lack of confidence in the police (not unearned) and the growth of confidence on the part of the criminal elements who sense the helplessness of both police and community and rip away. We of the ghetto are definitely for law and order. We are against a criminal element which when arrested cries out, "Racism, bigotry." We want to raise our children as any other decent parents would like to.

We want to walk the streets without having to grow eyes in the back of our heads and the burden of having jumped paranoic. We want law and order, but it must be a law and order that is just and equal for all Americans no matter what their color or language may be. So help me, if the decent members of the communities and the decent law-enforcement people get together, the ripoffs in our society, both in and out of uniform, will have as much chance of scavenging on our society as a snowball in hell.

The ghettos and all the horrible conditions they breed are the problem, and the decent people who live there are desperately trying to be the solution to it. Together now—.

3. BUILD ANOTHER EAST VILLAGE IN THE DAKOTA BADLANDS
Roger Starr

Mr. Starr is Executive Director of the Citizens' Housing and Planning Council of New York.

No one can fairly promise full relief from the crime that confronts New Yorkers but they might draw comfort from a common resolution if they followed a tripartite policy which I will call, for the sake of mnemonics, Deterrence, Disease and Direction.

But first, some of the sackcloth in which good men have wrapped their heads should be unwound. Bernard Shaw expressed the liberal confusion on crime when he said wryly that stealing bread leads to prison while stealing railroads leads to Parliament. He meant to suggest that stealing a railroad is the more heinous offense, and that society's failure to condemn it as forcefully as a minor burglary illustrates the moral confusion that encourages petty crime. The thought is splendid paradox, but bad sense.

The theft of the Penn Central Railroad from its shareholders and creditors did not attack the morale and self-confidence of New Yorkers of every social class. But the street crime—the muggings, the smash-and-grab burglaries from cars, the breaking-and-entering from the fire escape

window, the rapes in the elevators and the alleyways and on the roofs—these chop up New York's cosmopolitan heart and mangle its cultural life. In this sense, petty crimes are far more serious than white-collar crimes, however large. But they are not a response, conscious or instinctive, to crime in high places. Instead, street crime is best understood as the inevitable concomitant of a wave of newcomers, displaced from peasantry, and trying, in many cases hopelessly, to adjust to the difficulties of city life.

Only 64 years ago, the Police Commissioner of New York City, Theodore Bingham, wrote in *The North American Review* that it was "not astonishing that with half a million Hebrews, mostly Russians, in the city (one-quarter of the population), perhaps half of the criminals should be of that race. . . . Though all crime is their province, pocket-picking is the one to which they take most naturally. . . . Among the most expert of all the street thieves are Hebrew boys under 16, who are brought up to lives of crime. . . ."

Similar comment was surely made about the Italians, the Irish, the Germans and now, of course, the blacks, the product of a combination of slavery and Jim Crow which could scarcely have been better designed to make difficult the adjustment from a rural to an industrial society, particularly at a time when the industrial society itself is passing through spasmic changes. Today's New Yorkers (like the residents of other Northern cities) are astonished by the present level of street crime because they believed that the relative peace of the nineteen-twenties and thirties was to become permanent. That peace— we see now—merely reflected the absence of significant demographic changes. European immigration had been stopped by the quotas while the mass of blacks were held on the farm by the manpower needs of Southern agriculture.

But what can be done today to cope with the wave of street crime following the wave of immigration? First—Deterrence. This relies on the police. Their efforts must be amplified by sharper individual security measures, until life becomes a series of precautions against invasion. Block associations, tradesmen's groups must mobilize and hire their own private guards when voluntary methods fail. Residents in housing projects must band together in formal auxiliary police forces.

These measures work—though sometimes merely in displacing street crime from one street or passageway to another—but their efforts carry with them an antilibertarian significance to those New Yorkers who still wish to believe that psychotherapy cures crime. In revulsion against this sudden flirtation with authoritarianism, conscience-troubled New Yorkers have suddenly discovered—in 1972!—Prison Reform.

Prisons should rehabilitate the offender, not merely punish him, they cry, too lately arrived on the scene to know that no prison system anywhere, no matter how humane its design and operation, reforms inmates systematically. Prisons should be humane because society should run humane institutions; to link such a policy to the frail hope of reforming inmates is dangerous to its permanence. The prison's purpose is twofold: it removes the offender to a place where he cannot hurt the public, and it satisfies the communal sense of justice. Prof. Martin Levin of Brandeis recently pointed out

that these ends are often inconsistent. If society wants protection against the likeliest recidivists, it would imprison youthful car thieves and muggers for the longest terms; contrariwise, it could safely parole most adult murderers without their serving a day. But these suggestions affront the communal sense of justice, which tells us that the young deserve another chance. The old can plead no mitigating primal innocence.

In his new awareness of the prison and its shortcomings, the urban citizen finds himself undermining the effectiveness of deterrence by re-examining the bail system. It is argued that the purpose of bail is to assure appearance on the date of trial, and that it is unconscionable to keep the unconvicted offender locked up in advance of the trial simply because a magistrate believes him likely, on the basis of his previous record, to commit further offenses before the trial date. I am sympathetic to all of these reservations, and to the implicit fear for everyone's liberties that, at least partly, motivate them. But I am convinced, equally, that more pervasive enforcement of the laws on street crime, expanded jails (and I hope more decent ones), and bail policies rooted in the public safety are necessary deterrents to street crime. I can sympathize with those who consider the price too high for the putative gain, but only if they will thereafter mute their complaints about the crimes themselves.

Second—Disease. I am convinced that the street crime characteristic of early waves of migration to the cities was ultimately brought under a measure of control by disease as well as deterrence. The street criminal's life was dangerous. He was exposed to all of the epidemic diseases of poverty that ravaged the slums 60 and 70 years ago, and on top of that he was menaced by the industrial accidents of casual labor and the dangers (from his colleagues as well as the police) of deadly assault. The familial chains of criminality were broken by deaths due to hazards no longer encountered.

Public-health and industrial improvements have removed the risks and lengthened the hereditary chain of the disorganized household. Yet man's ingenuity has developed a synthetic disease—heroin addiction—as deadly as its bacteriological predecessors. Hard-drug reactions ranked third among the most common causes of non-natural deaths in New York City last year—behind homicide and suicide. Can the craving for heroin be used to withdraw from the city those who derive an even more intoxicating flush from the drug itself than from carrying out a deadly assault? Suppose a consortium of foundations erected a replica of the East Village somewhere in the Badlands of the Dakotas, a place where all the heroin anyone could want would be placed neatly in his veins. Would that draw dangerous street criminals away from the cities, as the Western frontier drew off some of the city's less docile residents in the nineteenth century?

Perhaps cold-blooded realism should encourage a relaxation of the expensive and not very productive programs to "cure" drug addiction. If the disease were allowed to run its horrendous, illegal course, it would continue to terminate the careers of addicted street criminals not only by the effects of the drugs themselves, but by the deadly arguments that accompany their use and sale.

The segregation implicit in the first suggestion, the hopelessness of the second, will cause shudders of horror in the conscientious reader. Surely no one who has tried to help a heroin addict would wish to refuse him whatever relief may be discovered. But, in a more general sense, the discovery of a miraculous cure for heroin addiction would immediately lengthen the life span of addicts. Many of these, perhaps a majority, committed crimes of stealth and violence even before they became addicted. Unless a cure changes their basic personalities, the longer they live the more likely they are to commit more crimes, whether addicted or not.

The third part of the program—the Direction change—is the most important, the least hateful and the most difficult to achieve. It involves a change in the direction of the newly urbanized household so that younger members may take pride in some sort of social movement that will allow them a constructive discharge of the physical energies that otherwise inspire street crime. Prof. John Davis of C.C.N.Y. points out that the seduction of drugs rests not merely on physical addiction but on the membership they offer in a special, separate culture of which street crime is a part. Professor Davis points out that China is the prime example of a nation that conquered its narcotics problem, perhaps through the involvement of the susceptible age group in a movement—the Cultural Revolution—which conferred an identity. Through employment and clan membership, the American city offered this to the survivors of the previous waves of in-migration. If the city today cannot offer it to survivors of present street criminals, neither Deterrence nor Disease alone will succeed in the long run in reducing the incidence of street crime.

4. TREAT THIS PROBLEM LIKE A WAR EFFORT
Claude Brown

Claude Brown, a law student at Rutgers University, wrote his autobiography of his youth in Harlem, Manchild in the Promised Land, *"in the unvarnished language of a slum world whose ethos of violence dictates that a 'manchild' must fight to survive."*

On the cover of Morton Hunt's recently published book, *The Mugging*, there is an illustration of a dark-complexioned arm around the neck of a bald eagle holding a knife against the bird's throat. One possible interpretation of this picture is that white America is being mugged by black America—the symbolism is there. The cover of the same book tells us that mugging is America's most feared crime.

In truth, the vast majority of mugging victims are members of minority groups. Most muggings occur (contrary to popular misconception) in ghetto hallways and streets, not in Central Park or on Park Avenue. Common sense makes this obvious to all who might give the matter a moment's thought—for the same reasons which underlie the confinement of riots to the ghettos: The perpetrators possess lower visibility, greater anonymity and familiarity with the various escape routes in their own milieu.

Ever since the heroin plague struck big in this country (1950), the crime of mugging has been increasing in the major urban communities of America as though it's name were death and each new day was the Labor Day weekend. A continued increase in muggings is the only realistic prognosis presented so far.

Muggings are almost invariably committed by adult criminals with extremely low mentalities, impoverished ghetto youths or drug addicts. These three groups have one primary trait in common which makes them very dangerous: They are driven by a sense of ultimate desperation.

The most dangerous of the three principal types of muggers is the drug addict, for on his back he is carrying a starving monkey with which he cannot compromise. His drug habit must be fed frequently, like it or not. The monkey rules; the junkie simply obeys, he has no say in the matter. The nonaddict types might go out on a mugging venture one night and change their minds for a number of reasons. The drug addict must succeed. He has a psychological and physiological family of monsters who will devour him from the inside out, like pygmies eating their way out of a wounded, but living elephant, if he should even balk at feeding them.

An awareness of his own physical condition plays a major role in selecting the type of solid citizen who will be the addict's mugging victim. The addict knows that a well-thrown punch to the jaw will probably knock him into a comatose state and that a solid stomach blow will leave him convulsive. Therefore, he must limit his victims to persons who cannot defend themselves very well: women, the elderly, the physically handicapped, the timid, etc. As has often happened, the addict will hit some senior ghetto citizen on the head with a heavy metal object

and the weight of the object combined with the weight of the years will cause death; or if the victim is lucky, he will merely be left seriously and permanently injured. The addict, who has become the primary mugger on the American scene, is not particularly interested in hurting anyone. It's the monkey who has so little compassion for human suffering.

When certain criminal sources of income are eliminated for an addict, he must find others to replace them. If little old ladies in the ghetto are given protection when they go into the streets, the addict-mugger must stray beyond the boundaries of the ghetto to find unprotected prey—in "nice" sections of the city. When the addict-mugger is chased out of buses, taxicabs, subways and ghettos, he is simply being pushed out into other neighborhoods, other areas of crime and other streets. Crime is more noticeable when committed on the streets. People see the crime taking place, they become alarmed or outraged and report it to the police; this is the stuff from which statistics are made. An unfortunate and misleading feature of this real-life-statistics production company is that most communities soon learn to accept and live with this situation or cope with it as best they can. This attitude is highly infectious—it sometimes strikes the police before it afflicts the general citizenry.

To effectively combat the awesome spread of violent street crimes, solid citizens must seize the opportune moment to emit an earth-shaking hue and cry that politicians will be compelled to respond constructively to—this is election year. The greatly diversified civic groups must give the street-crime issue top priority and combine their efforts to solve this very urgent problem before they can each feel free to continue working on their pet projects. This problem must be treated as a war effort; we cannot afford to lose—at any cost—and victory is imperative.

We must give the street criminal an equal opportunity to commit the crimes which society deems acceptable: the crimes of lawyers, doctors, ministers, politicians, engineers, architects, etc. How many ghetto children will ever be charged with an antitrust violation when they grow up?

We might as well face the inescapable facts: Nothing will be done about this poor man's affliction until there is no longer any place for the privileged classes to run. Until the entire country becomes one gigantic ghetto street, late at night, and the politicians and bureaucrats are forced to live there too—with the rest of us prey.

5. STOP COUNTENANCING SELECTIVE OBEDIENCE TO THE LAW
Edgar Smith

Mr. Smith is author of Brief Against Death, *the story of his 1957 murder conviction and years on Death Row in New Jersey.*

When I was asked to contribute to this discussion of crime control in New York City, my reflex solution was pretty much the standard one: Hire more police, give them better training, get more of them out on foot patrol, pour in Federal funding for bigger guns, faster cars and louder radios, give the cops greater powers by repealing the Fourth, Fifth, Sixth and Fourteenth Amendments, and then build bigger jails to hold the increased number of criminals the more efficient police would arrest.

The trouble with such an approach is that while it would certainly bring smiles of satisfaction to the law-enforcement community—almost any cop on the street would say I was on the right track— it would fail to solve the problem. For in fact, such an approach is a response to the symptoms of the disease, not its root causes.

My own observations over the seven months since my release from prison convince me that what is needed is a whole new attitude toward crime, all crimes, from the biggest corporate price-fixing swindle to the theft of a car by a couple of kids out for a joy ride. Crime is not, as some people are beginning to think, part of normal daily life, something inevitable we have to learn to cope with, as we have learned to cope with foul air or a sanitation department that fails to pick up our garbage.

We have got to stop accepting crime. We have got to stop making excuses for those who commit crimes on behalf of causes with which we are sympathetic. We have got to stop countenancing selective obedience to the law. We can no longer afford selective outrage toward crime.

Muggers, armed robbers, and car thieves do not work in a vacuum; they work in the atmosphere we create when we excuse some crimes; when we excuse draft evasion or the theft of Government documents because we think the Vietnam war is wrong; when we laugh over the dinner table about how we cheated on our income taxes, excusing it on the basis that "everyone does it"; when we turn our backs on the breaking of drug laws because we don't think smoking a little grass ever hurt anyone; when we shrug our shoulders at price-fixing by a huge corporation because "that's the old business game," and we don't see how it directly affects us; even when we do something as seemingly insignificant as stealing a handful of paper clips from the office and excuse it because "they" can afford it. When we do any of these things, we are helping to create a climate of selective morality, of selective obedience to the law, that says to others, to the muggers and armed robbers and car thieves, "Look fellows, if you don't like the law, if you think the law or the society is unjust, if you think 'they' can afford it, go ahead and do your thing as the rest of us are doing."

There were those who warned us a decade ago that even as we overlooked lawbreaking by civil-rights advocates, however worthy that cause, and however unjust the laws, we were creating a climate in which others could say, "They get away with it, why can't we?"

A few years later, when we stood by and permitted senseless violence and destruction of property by antiwar protesters, excusing them because they were "our kids" and were protesting an unjust war, we were reinforcing the feeling among some that the law had become a sometime thing. Now, at the end of a decade of unrelenting increases in the incidence of crime, we look around and wonder why respect for the law is such an uncertain thing.

Surely it is not the whole answer to change our attitudes toward crime. The fact that the overwhelming majority of crimes today are being committed by men who have already been in prison for other crimes tells us that we desperately need changes in our correctional system, so that those we have in custody are changed for the better, not simply brutalized, dehumanized, embittered, and trained to be more efficient, more violent criminals when they are released back into society.

We *can* bring crime under control. We *can* turn back the tide. But if we are going to do it, we are going to have to stop tolerating it, stop believing there is nothing we can do about it, stop locking ourselves in at night and turning the streets over to those who believe we no longer care what they do.

6. MAKE SURE EVERY AMERICAN IS GIVEN THE OPPORTUNITIES
Jack Greenberg

Mr. Greenberg, author of Race Relations and American Law *(1959) and contributor to legal journals, is Director-Counsel, N.A.A.C.P. Legal Defense and Educational Fund.*

Count me with the "bleeding-heart" liberals who believe that "the most significant action that can be taken against crime is action designed to eliminate slums and ghettos, to improve education, to provide jobs, to make sure that every American is given the opportunities and the freedoms that will enable him to assume his responsibilities." In 1967 these were the words of the President's Commission on Law Enforcement and Administration of Justice, which included Lewis F. Powell, President Nixon's recent Supreme Court appointment, Leon Jaworski and Ross Malone, past presidents of the American Bar Association, William Rogers, Secretary of State, and others, none of whom are soft on crime.

Overwhelmingly, black and Puerto Rican New Yorkers are not only law-abiding but are the most frequent victims of violent crime. These crimes which they and whites suffer originate largely in such conditions as ghetto slum living, abject poverty and broken families. Socialization and character-building essential to law-abidingness have a hard time developing in the chaos of such communities. (Non-violent, non-fear-provoking white-collar crime is the domain of deviant, better-off whites.) The July 19 Census Bureau report depicts one-third of the black families in the New York area with incomes below $5,000, half below $7,000 and 63 percent of the Puerto Rican families below $7,000. The National Advisory Commission on Civil Disorders reported that in 1962 42.4 percent of New York's nonwhite-occupied housing units were deteriorated, dilapidated or without full plumbing. Since then, the situation has worsened. With a minuscule vacancy rate and high rentals compounded by racial discrimination in housing, it is nearly impossible for the ghetto dweller to escape to a less damaging environment. Yet when the State Urban Development Corporation recently proposed building a mere 100 subsidized apartments in each of nine Westchester towns, political uproar caused the plan to be shelved in five of the towns. The school busing backlash also reflects the reluctance of many white Americans to allow even part-time escape from the ghetto into their own better-off enclaves.

Not all remedies involve political and social controversies as sharp as those touched on above, nor financial cost so great. But resistance is heavy even to reforms that would have a direct impact on crime, the most important of which are: (1) Prison reform. Prisons generally instruct in crime rather than rehabilitate. (2) Sweeping changes in treatment of juveniles. Juvenile detention not only predictably sets young people off on lives of crime, but costs as much as the best psychiatric institutions or university educations. (3) Decriminalization of much socially disfavored conduct, *e.g.*, drunkenness, consensual sex offenses, gambling. (4) Gun control. The most modest proposals for control face enormous opposition. (5) Increasing the number of police on the streets. This costs money and dislocates established police work patterns.

The Crime Commission recommended many such changes, large and small, five years ago. But the recommendations have been so unheeded that Prof. James Vorenberg of Harvard, its executive director, recently wrote: "I find it hard to point to anything that is being done that is likely to reduce crime even to the level of five years ago."

Perhaps in the next few years, a growth in the political power of minority groups and idealistic young people, along with an end to the Vietnam war, releasing funds and, more important, moral energies, will lead to a consensus in favor of essential social changes, or at least experiments. Then, too, the median age of the population is getting somewhat older, a trend that should help lower the rate of crime, since the young commit a disproportionate number of violent crimes.

It is impossible to discuss crime in New York without dealing with heroin addiction. The experts disagree vigorously over the solution to this problem, and we cannot afford to wait years for answers. Yet, if we take the wrong approach without full information, we may make things worse.

There is a phenomenon known as the Hawthorne effect, perceived in early sociological research (at Hawthorne, N.Y.) in which it was found that subjects of social experiments often responded affirmatively merely *because* they were the subjects of the experiments. It may be that a massive group of experiments directed at drug addiction will produce a Hawthorne effect —at least a temporary defection from heroin in the addict population, sufficient to interfere with or break the cycle of addiction in which one addict recruits another.

Methadone maintenance and drug-free programs should be expanded to the limits of the numbers of addicts who will enroll. At the same time, despite the civil liberties problems, I would be willing to see a small experiment with involuntary civil commitment of addicts, necessarily coupled with treatment. While it has been said that treatment will not work when the addict is confined against his will, some who are knowledgeable about addiction argue to the contrary. And while I believe that heroin maintenance is an ultimately destructive program, I would be willing to see a small experiment with it on the slight chance that something beneficial for the addict and/or society may turn up. And with all this I would intensify police work against sellers.

Perhaps after a few years of such crash programs there will be a relapse to the old condition, but by then the cycle of addiction leading to more addiction may be broken and we may have learned more about how to deal with the problem. Maybe even now there is enough sentiment to undertake the effort and pay the cost of dealing with addiction on this intensive basis.

7 HEALTH CARE— A NATIONAL SICKNESS?

About Kennedy's Health Insurance Plan

Rick J. Carlson

From *Center Report* (February, 1973), 26–27. Reprinted, with permission, from the February, 1973, issue of the *Center Report*, a publication of the Center for the Study of Democratic Institutions, Santa Barbara, California.

Mr. Carlson is a Visiting Fellow at the Center for the Study of Democratic Institutions, Santa Barbara. He is an attorney and a member of the Institute for Interdisciplinary Studies, Minneapolis.

Almost everyone agrees that the health care system in the United States is in a deep condition of crisis. The litany is familiar; the cost of care is excessive; the structure of the system is anachronistic; resources are severely maldistributed; high quality is assumed but not proven; and everyone, even the rich, finds it difficult to gain access to care. A solution is now being sought through the enactment of a national health insurance program. Bills sponsored by the American Medical Association, Senator Jacob Javits, the National Health Insurance Association of America, the current Administration, Senator Edward Kennedy, AFL, CIO, the UAW and other labor groups, and the American Hospital Association all fall under the rubric of national health insurance.

Prominent among the proposals is that of Senator Kennedy. Not only is the proposal which the Senator introduced into the Senate more comprehensive than most other proposals; because of his looming candidacy in 1976, the bill assumes larger proportions. There is already evidence that he views the health issue to be a critical political issue for the next four years. President Nixon has also introduced a health proposal of his own, setting the stage for the clash. What are some of the salient features of Senator Kennedy's bill?

The Kennedy plan for a national health insurance would be established as "an integral part of the national social insurance system." It would provide compulsory health insurance for everyone, with the government acting as the insurer. Thus, the program would supplant most of the coverage now provided by private companies.

The plan would be paid for primarily by employers and employees but also by a substantial contribution from the government. The bill, as it now stands, provides that two-thirds of the cost would be derived from employer and employee contributions and the remaining one-third would come from general tax revenues.

The Kennedy plan, unlike some of the other plans, would require the installation of a new and larger bureaucracy resembling that which has already been put in place to administer Medicare. Comprehensive benefits would be provided, although they might be phased in. In distinction to some of the other plans, the Kennedy plan acknowledges the need for reorganization of the health care delivery system, but provides little in the way of direction for that reorganization, other than the inclusion of "incentives" to encourage group practice, regional planning, cost controls, etc. Beyond that the proposal provides that $1 billion would be skimmed off the top of the first year's revenues and allocated to delivery system reform.

The key arguments offered on behalf of Senator Kennedy's bill, as well as almost all the others, are that it would make health care services more available to everyone; reduce, if not eliminate, inequities in the current system in terms of purchasing power; and would give the Federal government a "handle" for regulating other aspects of the health care system in addition to cost, such as the quality of care.

In my view, despite these advantages, a national health insurance program will not effectively deal with all of the problems which currently plague the delivery of health care in this country. In fact, in some cases it may exacerbate them. For example, it is well known that the cost of care is approaching the prohibitive. With the passage of Medicare and Medicaid in the middle sixties, the costs of care skyrocketed because neither consumers nor providers were given incentives to hold down costs. As long as a third party pays the bill who cares what it costs? Passage of a comprehensive national health insurance plan without draconian cost control measures—*which are highly unlikely*—will steadily contribute to inflation in the health care sector.

Another of the "ills" of the current system is the severe maldistribution of health manpower. While it is possible to control the location of new capital facilities, such as hospitals, outpatient clinics, neighborhood clinics and so on, it runs against the American dream to dictate practice locations for physicians. Thus, given the expressed preferences of physicians for the affluent suburbs, it is unlikely that a national health insurance plan can do anything other than

exhort physicians to relocate where medical resources are scarce.

Whatever else a national health insurance plan may do, it will most certainly do no more than establish a floor of benefits for those who are eligible. Thus, although it will go a long way towards eliminating the dual nature of the current system, the failure of a national health insurance plan (largely because of cost considerations) to fix a "rich" package of benefits, will result in the affluent purchasing whatever care they believe they need, real or fanciful, with their own money. Thus, a kind of "rump" system providing benefits only to the rich will arise and thus inevitably resurrect the duality which passage of the plan seeks to eliminate.

A final and critical disadvantage is that national health insurance will not bring with it the means to determine the effectiveness of care. We don't know how to measure the benefits of health care with sufficient sophistication to allow us to make judgments about what kind of care we ought to buy, or whether why we should buy it at all. A recent study conducted by the Institute of Medicine reveals that the educational level of the parents is the single most important variable in the health status of children. If so, a dollar spent on education is more likely to have a beneficial impact on health than that same dollar spent on health care services. But the Institute of Medicine study is a rarity in health service research literature. Thus, in the absence of hard information about the cost-effectiveness of health care services, we as a society will not know what we are buying despite the fact that we keep on buying more and more of it.

"Scale" is yet another problem. While no definitive evidence exists correlating good or ill health with the scale of the treatment system, there are some disturbing implications. One of the "malaises" of our times is supposed to be alienation. This mood is alleged to depend in part on the inhospitability of large institutions. Under a national health insurance program, which is likely to include incentives for organizational development, the "unit" for delivery of care will increase in size. So will its concomitant: impersonality. This "scale" question may relate to well-being in ways which we can now only dimly perceive; or it may not. But factorial increases in the size of the units providing care inescapably further attenuates the patient's responsibility for his or her own health, and further removes the individual's access to the "tools" for self-care. Historically, with the rise of the professions in health, the individual has been relieved of responsibility for his own health. The advent of larger systems of care will force already dependent patients to relate to bricks, mortar and bureaucratic *triage*, whereas formerly their dependence was at least upon flesh and blood.

I've now reached my final and most important point. One of the major disadvantages of the current Congressional focus on a national health insurance plan is the concurrent neglect of a viable alternative: a national health service. One virtue we have been consistently willing to sacrifice to the prerogatives of physicians is egalitarianism. We have tolerated tiers of medical practice paralleling class structure and even have created classes of medical untouchables. Medicare and Medicaid have reduced many of these distinctions, but not all. The logical extension of these programs has always been some form of more comprehensive national health care services which would greatly expand public support of health care services while generally leaving the delivery system intact. But, a nationalized health insurance program is very different than a nationalized health care system, although the two are often confused. The first simply facilitates the purchase of care from providers who deploy themselves as they wish. The second would alter *both* the financing of care and the structure of the system.

The current debates are focused only on alternative health insurance plans, not on a national health service. Thus, the assault against inequitable access to care is proposed to be made with dollars rather than by structural reform. This indictment applies to all of the major national health insurance proposals including the polar approaches espoused by Senator Kennedy and the AMA. The current debate is proceeding along a narrow track which has been laid over Motherhood's capacious lap. Nowhere does one hear discussion of a third approach—a national health service. And this failure to engage in the issue could have two profound and irreversible consequences.

The first is that major expansion in the financing system will "lock in" the current structure for delivery of care for the indefinite future. This is the pitfall of this otherwise salutory means being taken to assault the inequities in health care through an expansion in purchasing power. The issue must be so stated to make it possible for reformers who wish to bring about a nationalized medical care system through a radical altering of its structure, to fix on the goal and not be deflected by the "good" which increased purchasing power through comprehensive health insurance represents.

The second is that underwriting the "costs" of the existing health care system through a comprehensive health insurance plan will inevitably result in even steeper escalations in the cost of care and more disproportionate consumption of the Gross National Product by health services expenditures. Enoch Powell, based upon his years of experience in administering England's health service (and leaving aside his animadversions on other subjects), has marveled at the capacity of patients to consume large doses of care. The passage of a national health insurance plan will kick out the last strut from under consumption constraint—the lack of uniform purchasing power—however much otherwise cruel. The result is that as a nation we will have decided to further "feed" an already bloated system and in so doing eschew not only a different way of organizing our health care system, but divert monies which could otherwise be spent to ameliorate social and environmental conditions such as poor housing and malnutrition which have a demonstrably greater impact on well-being.

In sum, then, the prospects for a nationalized system for health care, although never sanguine, may be less healthy than ever, and ironically, because the American poeple may be on the verge of finally deciding to put public monies to the task that private money and health care professionals haven't accomplished. For those who truly believe in a nationalized system for the provision of health care, even in the face of the limitations such a system has, this development poses a real and poignant conflict, because to continue to support nationalization requires rejection of a third party financing alternative through a national health insurance program. Yet if Anthony Lewis' eloquent words describing the English nationalized system are to serve to rally reformers, the alternative must be rejected:

"At its best, American medicine is superb, as British doctors often admiringly remark. But too few Americans get the best. That is why the United States is down further than might be expected in world health tables, not only in comparison with Britain. In infant mortality, for example, a 1969 United Nations report showed twenty-two countries with a lower rate than ours.

"'The characteristic, generous answer to such evident national failings is to spend more money. But we know by now that in the medical field, that alone is no solution. The United States spends about 6.9 percent of its gross national product on health and medical care, Britain only 4.9.

"What needs to be changed is the system of delivering medical care to the individual American. It is, as a British medical writer put it, 'a desperately inefficient as well as a heartless way of bringing the benefits of modern medicine to the population. Despite its wealth the health of America is poor.' "

Part 3
New Crusades

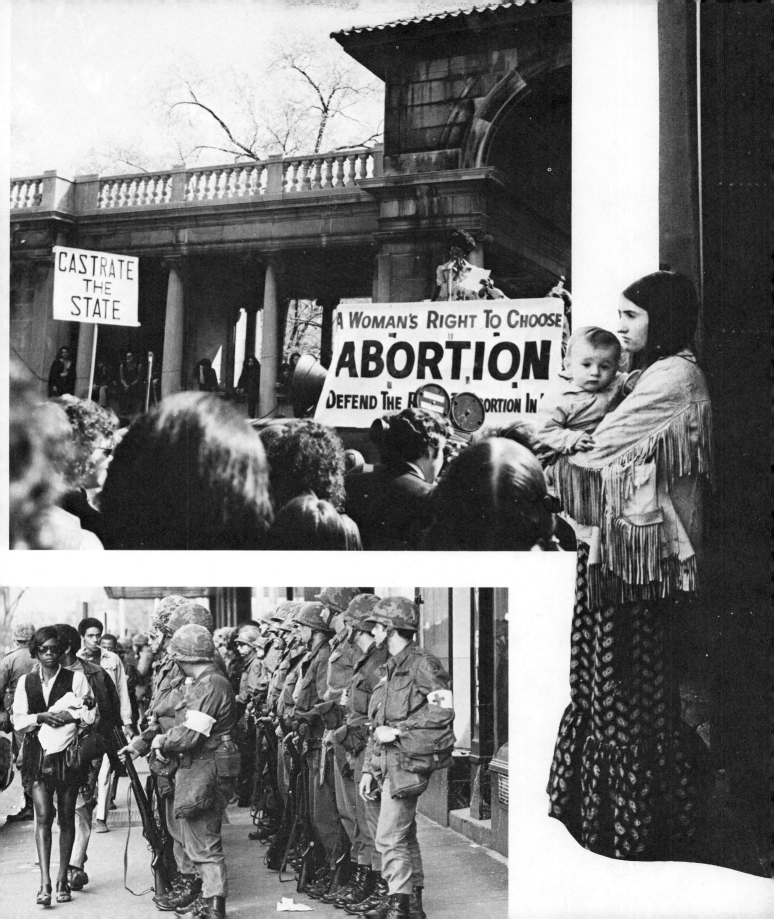

8 YOUTH CULTURE— NOTHING IS REVEALED?

Teen-Age Sex: Letting the Pendulum Swing

Time Magazine

From *Time Magazine* (August 21, 1972), 34–36. Reprinted by permission from *Time, The Weekly Newsmagazine*; copyright Time Inc.

Girls can score just as many times as boys if they want to. I've gone to bed with nine boys in the past two years. It's a natural thing, a nice thing and a nice high. It sure can clear up the blues.

> —*Mimi, 18, a June graduate of Tenafly (N.J.) High School*

I'm still a virgin. My friends last year blamed it on the fact that I was the youngest girl on campus. But I can't see having intercourse unless it's part of a tight emotional bond. My father has influenced me, but the fact that he is a minister has nothing to do with it. The church is not a stronghold against sex any more.

> —*Amanda, 16, a junior at Shimer College, Mount Carroll, Ill.*

They could hardly be more unlike, Mimi and Amanda.* Yet both are representative of American teen-agers in 1972. Though Amandas predominate among the nation's boys and girls between 13 and 19, there are enough Mimis so

*The names of the children and their parents in this story are fictitious.

that many parents are alarmed. Even some of the teen-agers themselves, especially those in college, are uneasy about their almost unlimited new sexual license. Along with a heady sense of freedom, it causes, they find, a sometimes unwelcome sense of pressure to take advantage of it. "I'm starting to feel the same way about getting laid as I did about getting into college," Dustin Hoffman confessed in *The Graduate*. A Columbia University psychiatrist reports that students come to him to find out what is wrong with them if they are not having intercourse. "My virginity was such a burden to me that I just went out to get rid of it," a junior at the University of Vermont revealed to a Boston sex counselor. "On a trip to Greece, I found any old Greek and did it so it wouldn't be an issue any more."

Was her trip necessary? Is there really a notable increase in teen-age sex? Foolproof statistics about sexual habits are hard to come by, but a recent survey prepared for the Nixon-appointed commission on population seems to offer reasonably reliable figures. Of 4,611 unmarried black and white girls living at home or in dormitories in 1971, more than 46 percent had lost their virginity by age 20, according to

80

Johns Hopkins Demographers Melvin Zelnik and John Kantner. Comparison with previous generations is difficult because earlier studies are incomplete; Alfred Kinsey, for example, author of the first large-scale studies of sexual behavior, did not include blacks in his statistics. However, Kinsey's 1953 survey of some 5,600 white women disclosed that 3 percent were nonvirgins at age 15, and 23 percent had had premarital intercourse by the time they were 21. By contrast, Zelnik and Kantner report that of the 3,132 whites in their sample, 11 percent of the 15-year-olds were nonvirgins, and 40 percent of all the girls had lost their virginity by the age of 20. In short, youth's sexual revolution is not just franker talk and greater openness; more teen-agers, and especially younger ones, are apparently having intercourse, at least occasionally.

Another indication of the reality of youthful sex is the rising incidence of VD, which has now reached epidemic proportions in high schools and colleges. After the ordinary cold, syphilis and gonorrhea are the most common infectious diseases among young people, outranking all cases of hepatitis, measles, mumps, scarlet fever, strep throat and tuberculosis put together. In 1970 there were at least 3,000 cases of syphilis among the 27 million U.S. teen-agers and 150,000 cases of gonorrhea, more than in any European country except Sweden and Denmark. From 1960 to 1970 the number of reported VD cases among girls 15 to 19 increased 144 percent, and that percentage does not begin to tell the story, because it is estimated that three out of four cases go unreported.

The spiraling rate of pregnancies among unmarried girls is yet another indicator of sexual activity by the young. Per thousand teen-agers, the number of illegitimate births has risen from 8.3 in 1940 to 19.8 in 1972. Of an estimated 1,500,000 abortions performed in the U.S. in 1971, it is believed that close to a third were performed on teen-agers. Last year women at one prominent Eastern university had 100 illegitimate pregnancies, while at another there were almost 400—a rate of one for every 15 students. Nationwide the college pregnancy rate runs from 6 percent to 15 percent.

In Perspective

"Anything that discourages heterosexuality encourages homosexuality," says Paul Gebhard, executive director of the Kinsey Institute for Sex Research. Is the opposite also true? Some psychiatrists speculate that the new sexual freedom enjoyed by teen-agers may lead to a decrease in homosexuality. "Because there are fewer sexual taboos in our society today, the adolescent is more likely to find a heterosexual pathway," says Dr. Judd Marmor of Los Angeles. Yet only a small number of adolescents are likely to be affected, Marmor contends, since generally "the origins of homosexuality derive from certain specific conditions in the home, and these conditions still exist." There are no recent statistical studies that show changes in the incidence of homosexuality among teen-agers. There are, however, some changes in attitudes. Just as there is a greater willingness to "come out of the closet" among their elders, younger men and women are more open about homosexuality, especially in cities and on campuses where there are organizations like the Gay Activist Alliance.

In heterosexual relationships, too, it is the teen-agers' attitudes that have probably changed more than the statistics. The different sexual experiences of two sisters, eight years apart in age, illustrate at least some of the changes that are taking place.

Sue Franklin, now 25, had a traditional middle-class Midwestern upbringing. In 1965, when she was 18 and a college freshman, her sorority sisters talked about their sexual feelings only with extremely close friends, and nearly all gossiped about girls they suspected of having affairs. "Virginity was all important," Sue remembers. Then her boy friend of five years' standing issued an ultimatum: "Either you go to bed with me or I'm leaving you." She gave in and was overcome with remorse. "My God," she thought, "what have I done? The more I learned about sex, the guiltier I felt, especially about enjoying it. I almost felt I had to deny myself any pleasure. My boy friend felt bad, too, because I was so hung up."

Sue's sister Pat, on the other hand, was just 15 and in high school when she first went to bed with a boy. Only one thing bothered her: fear of getting pregnant. She appealed to Sue, who helped her get contraceptive advice from a doctor. Since then, Pat has had one additional serious relationship that included sex. Observes Sue: "Pat had as healthy an attitude as could be imagined, as healthy as I wish mine could have been. She and her friends are more open. They're not blasé; they don't talk about sex as they would about what they're going to have for dinner. But when they do discuss it, there's no hemming and hawing around. And boys don't exploit them. With Pat and her boy friends, sex isn't a motivating factor. It's not like the pressure that builds when sex is denied or you feel guilty about it. It's kept in perspective, not something they're especially preoccupied with. They don't see sex as something you can do with everyone; they're not promiscuous."

Nor are most teen-agers. Though the number of very youthful marriages appears to be declining, a fourth of all 18- and 19-year-old girls are married. More often than not, they had already had intercourse: more than half of them got married because they were pregnant. But on the whole, teen-agers actually are not very active sexually, in spite of the large number of non-virgins. Of those questioned by the Johns Hopkins demographic team, 40 percent had not had intercourse at all in the month before the survey, and of the remainder 70 percent had done so only once or twice that month. About 60 percent had never had more than one partner, and in half the cases that one was the man they planned to marry. When promiscuity was reported, it was more often among whites: 16 percent admitted to four or more partners, while only 11 percent of blacks had had that many.

Teen-agers generally are woefully ignorant about sex. They may believe that "most teen-age boys can almost go crazy if they don't have intercourse," that "you can't get pregnant if he only comes one time," or that urination is impossible with a diaphragm in place. Other youths cherish the notion that withdrawal, douching, rhythm or luck will prevent conception. Overall, "the pervasiveness of risk taking" is appalling, Zelnik and Kantner discovered. More than 75 per cent of the girls they interviewed said they used contraceptives only occasionally or never.

To close the information gap, schools and colleges have begun to provide telephone hot lines, new courses, manuals of instruction and personal counseling. By dialing 933-5505, University of North Carolina students can get confidential information about pregnancy, abortion, contraception, sexual and marital relationships. More than 30 trained volunteer counselors answer 50 calls a week, with at least one man and one woman always on duty so that shy callers can consult someone of their own sex. Complex questions are referred to a dozen experts, mostly physicians, who have offered their help.

Away from the campus, counseling is hard to come by, but contraceptive advice is usually available, at least to urban teen-agers, from private social agencies and public health departments. This has not long been so. Birth Control Crusader Bill Baird was arrested in 1967 for giving out contraceptive devices to Boston University coeds. His conviction was overturned last March when the Supreme Court ruled that a state could not outlaw contraceptives for single people when they were legal for married couples. In most states the law is ambiguous about giving teen-agers birth control advice, particularly without parental consent. But nowadays many authorities interpret the law liberally, believing that since teen-age sex is a fact, it ought at least to be protected sex. In any court test, they believe, the trend toward recognizing the civil rights of minors would prevail.

The policy of Planned Parenthood in New York City is typical. Before 1968 it gave birth control information to unmarried teen-age girls only if they already had had a child. Observes Executive Vice President Alfred Moran: "We were saying, in effect: 'We'll be glad to provide protection if you buy the ticket of admission—one pregnancy.'" Realizing the illogic of that position and swept along with the "new ethos,"

YOUTH CULTURE — NOTHING IS REVEALED?

YOUTH CULTURE — NOTHING IS REVEALED?

the organization now serves almost everyone and estimates that nearly 40 percent of its new patients are 19 or under.

At Manhattan's Margaret Sanger Research Bureau, clinic workers include teen-agers like Kathy Hull, 17, who gets course credits at her Brooklyn high school for volunteering. Chocolate cookies are passed around at the rap sessions that patients attend before they are examined and given contraceptives; boy friends are invited to the meetings and may even be present at the pelvic examinations if their girl friends agree. Said one who did: "He held my hand, and I was glad he cared enough to be there."

Dolls with Breasts

What brought about the new sexual freedom among teen-agers? "Obviously," nine parents out of ten would probably say, "it's all this permissiveness." But permissiveness is just a word that stands for many things, and as with most societal changes, it is often difficult to tell what is cause and what is effect. One major factor is the "erotization of the social backdrop," as Sociologists John Gagnon and William Simon express it. American society is committed to sexuality, and even children's dolls have breasts and provocative outfits nowadays. Another frequently cited factor is the weakening of religious strictures on sex. Observes Social Critic Michael Harrington: "One of the great facts about our culture is the breakdown of organized religion and the disappearance of the inhibitions that religion once placed around sexual relationships." Sociologists have found an inverse relationship between churchgoing and sexual experimentation: the less of the former, the more of the latter. In fact, suggests Sociologist Ira Reiss, today's teen-agers may have more influence on religion than the other way round. Among liberal clergymen, at least, there is something of a scramble to keep up with youthful ideas on sex. Permissive Catholic priests let their views become known and so in effect encourage liberated youngsters to seek them out for confession. Unitarian churches give courses for 12- to

14-year olds "About Your Sexuality," complete with frank lectures and discussions, as well as films showing intercourse, masturbation and homosexuality.

Diminishing family influence has also shaken up the rules. The disillusionment of many youths with Viet Nam, pollution and corruption has sexual side effects, say Simon and Gagnon. It reinforces the idea of the older generation's moral inferiority. In fact, the two sociologists assert, many young people begin sexual activity in part as a "personal vendetta" against their parents. Nor does the older generation have a very good record of marital stability. Since there are now 357 divorces for every 1,000 marriages, it is little wonder that children do not necessarily heed their parents' advice or consider marriage their ultimate goal. "There's a healthy disrespect for the façade of respectability behind which Albee-like emotional torrents roll on," says Yale Chaplain William Sloane Coffin Jr.

Parents are not necessarily straightforward in their advice when they give it. Recalls Bob, a senior at the University of Pittsburgh: "When I was in high school, my father warned me about sex. It wasn't so much the moral part that bothered him; he was afraid I'd knock up a girl and have to get married and get a job. I think he knows I'm living with a girl now, but if it bothers him, he hasn't made any big deal about it. I guess he figures it will help keep me in college and away from someone who might have marriage in mind."

In the Sack

As with churches, some parents are following the lead of the children. One of these is a real estate executive in California, father of three sexually active teen-age girls. "I see sex being treated by young people more casually, yet with more respect and trust. This has had an effect on me and my wife," he asserts. In fact, he claims that it has transformed their 20-year marriage into "a damned exciting relationship." It has also led to a startling willingness to forgo privacy. One of the children recently asked her father at dinner: "Dad, how often do you masturbate?" And the children's mother confides: "Once in a while at breakfast Jim'll say, 'Gosh, we had a good time in the sack last night, didn't we?' " According to her, the girls "get a kick" out of this sort of confidence.

Many sensitive teen-agers find such "liberated" parents worse than old-fashioned ones. "In an attempt to be hip," says a recent Bard graduate, "parents and teachers can often rob an adolescent of his own private times, his first secret expressions of love. Over-liberal parents can make a child self-conscious and sexually conscious before he is ready. Sex cannot be isolated from the other mysteries of adolescence, which each person must explore for himself."

Disillusioned as they may be with their elders, teen-agers owe much of their sexual freedom to parental affluence. More of them than ever before can now afford the privacy of living away from home, either while holding jobs or going to college. The proliferation of coed dorms has eased the problem of where to make love; though such dorms are not the scenes of the orgies that adults conjure up, neither are they cloisters. A phenomenon that seemed shocking when it first appeared in the West and Midwest in the 1960s, two-sex housing is now found on 80 percent of the coed compuses across the country. At some colleges, boys and girls are segregated in separate wings of the same buildings; at others they live on separate floors; at still others, in adjacent rooms on the same floor.

Some behavioral experts claim that in these close quarters, brother-sister relationships develop, so that a kind of incest taboo curbs sex. Moreover, Sarah Warren, a June graduate of Yale, suggests that "if you've seen the girls with dirty hair, there's less pressure to take their clothes off." But Arizona Psychiatrist Donald Holmes insists that "where the sexual conjugation of man and woman is concerned, familiarity breeds consent." At a coed dorm at the University of Maryland recently, boys poured out of girls' rooms in droves when a fire alarm sounded in the middle of the night. At Bryn Mawr, one student explains: "When a boy and girl have been going together for a while, one of them drags his mattress into the other's room." A new kind of study problem has recently been brought to a college psychiatrist: what to do if your roommate's girl friend parades around your room nude. Ask her to get dressed? Or go elsewhere to study?

As for the Pill, nearly all laymen consider it a major cause of the new freedom, but a majority of professionals disagree. Because most girls dislike seeing themselves as on the lookout for sex, few go on the Pill until they are having intercourse regularly. Even then, because they are worried about its side effects, almost half choose other means, if indeed they use contraceptives at all. Just the same, Hartsdale, N.Y., Psychiatrist Laurence Loeb believes, the very existence of the Pill has important psychological effects because it means that pregnancy is avoidable.

Then why so many illegitimate births? A principal reason, say behavioral experts, is unconscious ambivalence about pregnancy—both wanting and not wanting it. According to Planned Parenthood, teen-agers may see pregnancy as a way of remaining childishly dependent on others or, conversely, as a step toward adulthood. Besides, adds Chicago Youth Counselor Merry Allen, "it's still a way to get married, if that's what you want."

According to popular opinion, the drug culture is yet another spur to sexual activity. "Once you've taken drugs and broken that rule, it is easier to break all the others," says a senior at the University of Pittsburgh. "Drugs and sexual exploration go hand in hand," insists Charlotte Richardson, a lay therapist in Atlanta. But many doctors doubt that drug use increases sexual experimentation (whether marijuana increases sexual pleasure is even a matter of some dispute). Stanford Psychiatrist Donald Lunde, among others, believes that drugs do not lead to sex but that depression causes many teen-agers to try both sex and drugs; each, he says, is a "temporary way of feeling good." Some kids actually use drugs to avoid sex. Says Daniel X. Freedman, University of Chicago professor of psychiatry and one of the most respected drug researchers: "You can't blame rising nonvirginity on drugs. A lot of adults do so, just as they blame pornography, when the real issue is how their children regulate themselves."

What about Women's Liberation? During the '20s, the feminist drive for equal rights for women was partly responsible for an increase in premarital sex even greater than the present acceleration. Today's extreme militants, who believe that the new wave of permissiveness is a conspiracy to exploit them, want to put a damper on sex. But for the vast majority of women, the movement stands in part for a new freedom in sexual matters.

Over the past four years, Philip and Lorna Sarrel, sex counselors at Yale, have asked 10,000 students to fill out anonymous questionnaires on sexual knowledge and attitudes. Once it was easy to tell which answers came from males and which from females. No more. "At last, both young men and women are beginning to express their sexuality without regard to stereotypes," Sarrel declares with satisfaction. "We're getting rid of the idea that sex is something men do to women." As Jonathan Goodman, 17, of Newton High remarks, "I'd probably want to talk it over with a girl, rather than just let it happen. Her reasons for doing it or not doing it would be as important as mine."

Most observers think the equality movement has weakened, though not demolished, the double standard, and reduced, though not ended, male preoccupation with virility. There is somewhat less boasting about sexual conquest. Jonathan, for one, asserts that "I respect my girl friend and our relationship enough not to tell everyone what we're doing." Anyway, reports recent Columbia Graduate Lou Dolinar, "Now that girls are living with their boy friends in the dorm, it's pretty hard to sit around with them and talk like a stud. Male bull sessions of sexual braggadocio have been replaced by coed bull sessions about sexual traumas."

Identity Crisis

Can teen sex be harmful, apart from causing such problems as illegitimate pregnancy and disease? Manhattan Psychoanalyst Peter Blos believes that the early adolescent, however phys-

ically developed, is psychologically a child and lacks the emotional maturity necessary to manage sexual relationships. If a child tries to grow up too fast, Blos says, he may never grow up at all. Says Catholic Author Sidney Cornelia Callahan: "Sexuality is very intimately related to your sense of self. It should not be taken too lightly. To become an individual, the adolescent has to master impulses, to be able to refuse as well as accept."

Even on campuses where sex is relaxed, says Sociologist Simon, "kids still experience losing their virginity as an identity crisis; a nonvirgin is something they did not expect to be." Sexually involved adolescents of all ages are sometimes beset by guilt feelings, though less often than were their elders. Admits Ellen Sims, a Tenafly girl of 15 who says she has turned celibate after sleeping with three boys when she was in the eighth grade: "I was ashamed of myself. Sometimes I wish I didn't even know what I've done." Similarly, University of Pittsburgh Junior Kathy Farnsworth confesses that "I know sex isn't dirty. It's fun. But I always have this nagging thing from my parents in my head. They'd kill me if they knew, and I've never been able to have an orgasm." Occasionally the pangs of old-fashioned conscience are so strong that a student drops out of school and requires months of therapy before he is able to resolve the conflict between his "liberated" behavior and the standards, acquired from his parents, that he still unconsciously accepts.

Experts also detect a frequent sense of shame and incompetence at not enjoying sex more. "A great many young people who come into the office these days are definitely doing it more and enjoying it less," says Psychiatrist Holmes. According to Simon and Gagnon, sexual puritanism has been replaced by sexual utopianism. "The kid who worries that he has debased himself is replaced by the kid who worries that he isn't making sex a spectacular event."

Infidelity creates additional problems, warns Columbia University Psychiatrist Joel Moskowitz. "A couple agree that each can go out with anyone. The girl says, 'So-and-so turns me on; I'm going to spend the night with him.' Despite the contract they've made, the boy is inevitably enraged, because he feels it's understood that such things hurt him." When the hurt is great enough to end the affair, the trauma for both may approach that of divorce, or worse. One college student asked his high school girl friend to live in his room with him, and then watched despairingly as she fell in love with his roommate, and, overcome with grief and confusion, tried to commit suicide.

Cool Sex

To lay and professional observers alike, one of the most distressing aspects of teen sex is its frequent shallowness, particularly when the participants are still in high school. At that stage, Simon and Gagnon report, it is often the least popular students who engage in sex—and who find, especially if they are girls, that their sexual behavior brings only a shady sort of popularity and more unhappiness. Wisconsin Psychiatrist Seymour Halleck ascribes a "bland, mechanistic quality" to some youthful relationships, and Beverly Hills Psychoanalyst Ralph Greenson observes that, "instant warmth and instant sex make for puny love, cool sex."

His words seem to fit the experience of Judy Wilson. Recalling the day she lost her virginity in her own bedroom at the age of 17, she says blithely: "One afternoon it just happened. Then we went downstairs and told my younger sister because we thought she'd be excited. We said, 'Guess what. We just made love.' And she said, 'Oh, wow. How was it?' And we said, 'Fine.' Then we went out on the roof and she took pictures of us."

But among more mature young people, shallowness is anything but the rule. "Our kids are actually retrieving sexuality from shallowness," insists Sex Counselor Mary Calderone. "They are moving away from the kind of trivialization we associated with the Harvard-Yale games in the '20s when the object was to get drunk and lay a lot of girls." Los Angeles Gynecologist J. Robert Bragonier agrees: "Kids aren't looking for the perfect marriage, but they're idealistic about finding a loving relationship." Sarrel adds that he finds most student liaisons "more meaningful than the typical marriage in sharing, trusting and sexual responsibility."

Epitomizing this free but deep relationship is the experience of Yale Students Rachel Lieber and Jonathan Weltzer. Recently she wrote about it for a forthcoming book: "We had always assumed we'd marry eventually. We had lived together for two years and were growing closer . . . On our wedding night, Jonathan and I lay in bed, letting all the feelings well up around us and bathe our skins in warmth as the words we had said during the ceremony started coming back. We mixed our faces in each other's hair, and we looked at each other for a long time. So we spent our wedding night, not as virgins, but very close."

Informal liaisons often mature into marriage, and when they do, Yale's Coffin has found, many areas of the relationship are apt to be sounder than in less tested unions. This is especially true now that unmarried sex has largely lost its stigma. As Coffin explains, "The danger of premarital sex while it was *verboten* was that it covered up a multitude of gaps. A girl had to believe she was in love because, she told herself, she wouldn't otherwise go to bed. As a result, the real relationship never got fully explored."

Many psychiatrists have come to agree that the new openness has much to recommend it. One of these is Graham Blaine, until recently chief psychiatrist of the Harvard health services. In 1963, Blaine wrote that "college administrations should stand by the old morality" and decried relaxed dormitory rules that allowed girls to visit boys' rooms till 7 p.m. In 1971 he switched sides. "I have been convinced by the young that the new relationships are a noble experiment that should be allowed to run its course."

Today Blaine elaborates: "I thought we college psychiatrists would see a lot more emotional problems. I was wrong; most students are not being hurt. The pendulum should be allowed to swing." It will swing back—at least part way back—he predicts, as it did after the easygoing days of the English Restoration. "It's much more in keeping with human nature to make sex a private thing and to have some elements of exclusivity." Mrs. Callahan, speaking to student audiences, has found on campuses "a new puritanism or perhaps a lingering puritanism," and she usually gets a smiling response when she calls on her listeners to "join the chastity underground."

Yes or No

Whether or not the chastity underground is the wave of the future, as Mrs. Callahan hopes, some youths, at least, appear to be searching for firmer guidelines. "Sometimes I wish I were a Victorian lady with everything laid out clearly for me," admits Sarah Warren. Warns Coffin: "It's much easier to make authority your truth than truth your authority."

At Yale, the Sarrels, who had dropped a lecture on morals, were asked by the students to add one on sexual values and decision-making. But to search for guidelines is not necessarily to find them. Most of the proliferating courses, clinics and handbooks detail, meticulously, the biology of intercourse, contraception, pregnancy and abortion; few do more than suggest the emotional complexities of sex. For instance, *The Student Guide to Sex on Campus* (New American Library; $1), written by Yale students with the help of the Sarrels, has this to say on the subject of "Intercourse—Deciding Yes or No":

"When a relationship is probably not permanent, but still very meaningful, it is more difficult to decide confidently . . . There is so much freedom . . . The decision is all yours, and can be very scary . . . No one should have intercourse just because they can't think of any reason *not* to. The first year in college can create confusion about sexual values. Your family seems very far away, and their ideas about almost everything are challenged by what you see and hear . . . Girls who have intercourse just to get rid of their virginity usually seem to find it not a pleasurable or fulfilling experience."

Sense of Trust

In personal counseling sessions, the Sarrels offer psychological support for students who would rather not rush things, telling them that "it's just as O.K. not to have sex as it is to have it." "People need to unfold sexually," Sarrel

believes, and there is no way to speed the process. What is right may vary with a student's stage of emotional development. "A freshman may need to express rebellion and independence from his family and may use sex to do it." That is acceptable, Sarrel believes, as long as the student understands his motives: "We don't worry too much about the freshman who's going to bed with someone. We worry about the freshman who's just going to bed and thinks it's love." For an older student, intercourse may be right only if the lovers are intimate emotionally. How to judge? One crucial sign of intimacy is "a sense of trust and comfort. If you find you're not telling each other certain kinds of things, it's not a very trusting relationship."

Apparently this kind of advice is what the students want. Sarrel has been dubbed "the Charlie Reich of sex counseling" by an irreverent observer, and like the author of *The Greening of America*, he is very popular: 300 men and women crowd into his weekly lectures at Yale, and more than 1,000 other colleges have asked for outlines of his course. For good reason. The Sarrels' careful counseling has cut the VD and unwanted pregnancy rate at Yale to nearly zero.

But what about ethical questions? For those who are not guided by their families or their religion, Sarrel's system—and the whole body of "situation ethics"—fails to offer much support for making a decision. Years ago William Butler Yeats wrote a poem about the problem:

> I whispered, "I am too young."
> And then, "I am old enough";
> Wherefore I threw a penny
> To find out if I might love.

How did the toss come out? Yeats, unsurprisingly, gave himself a clear go-ahead, ending his poem:

> Ah penny, brown penny, brown
>   penny,
> One cannot begin it too soon.

Nowadays a great many adolescents, like Yeats, seem to be simply tossing a coin, and singing the same refrain.

An 18-Year-Old Looks Back on Life

Joyce Maynard

Ms Maynard is a student at Yale. When she wrote this article, she was a freshman. In the meantime this perceptive essay has been published by Doubleday under the title Looking Back: A Chronicle of Growing Up Old in the Sixties *(1973).*

Every generation thinks it's special—my grandparents because they remember horses and buggies, my parents because of the Depression. The over-30's are special because they knew the Red Scare of Korea, Chuck Berry and beatniks. My older sister is special because she belonged to the first generation of teen-agers (before that, people in their teens were *adolescents*), when being a teen-ager was still fun. And I—I am 18, caught in the middle. Mine is the generation of unfulfilled expectations. "When you're older," my mother promised, "you can wear lipstick." But when the time came, of course, lipstick wasn't being worn. "When we're big, we'll dance like that," my friends and I whispered, watching Chubby Checker twist on "American Bandstand." But we inherited no dance steps, ours was a limp, formless shrug to watered-down music that rarely made the feet tap. "Just wait till we can vote," I said, bursting with 10-year-old fervor, ready to fast, freeze, march and die for peace and freedom as Joan Baez, barefoot, sang "We Shall Overcome." Well, now we can vote, and we're old enough to attend rallies and knock on doors and wave placards, and suddenly it doesn't seem to matter any more.

My generation is special because of what we missed rather than what we got, because in a certain sense we are the first and the last. The first to take technology for granted. (What was a space shot to us, except an hour cut from Social Studies to gather before a TV in the gym as Cape Canaveral counted down?) The first to grow up with TV. My sister was 8 when we got our set, so to her it seemed magic and always somewhat foreign. She had known books already and would never really replace them. But for me, the TV set was, like the kitchen sink and the telephone, a fact of life.

We inherited a previous generation's hand-me-downs and took in the seams, turned up the hems, to make our new fashions. We took drugs from the college kids and made them a high-school commonplace. We got the Beatles, but not those lovable look-alikes in matching suits with barber cuts and songs that made you want to cry. They came to us like a bad joke—aged, bearded, discordant. And we inherited the Vietnam war just after the crest of the wave—too late to burn draft cards and too early not to be drafted. The boys of 1953—my year—will be the last to go.

So where are we now? Generalizing is dangerous. Call us the apathetic generation and we will become that. Say times are changing, nobody cares about prom queens and getting into the college of his choice any more—say that (because it sounds good, it indicates a trend, gives a symmetry to history) and you make a movement and a unit out of a generation unified only in its common fragmentation. If there is a reason why we are where we are, it comes from where we have been.

Like overanxious patients in analysis, we treasure the traumas of our childhood. Ours was more traumatic than most. The Kennedy assassination has become our myth: Talk to us for an evening or two—about movies or summer jobs or Nixon's trip to China or the weather—and the subject will come up ("Where were *you* when you heard?"), as if having lived through Jackie and the red roses, John-John's salute and Oswald's on-camera murder justifies our disenchantment.

We haven't all emerged the same, of course, because our lives were lived in high-school corridors and drive-in hamburger joints as well as in the pages of *Time* and *Life*, and the images on the TV screen. National events and personal memory blur so that, for me, Nov. 22, 1963, was a birthday party that had to be called off and Armstrong's moonwalk [sic] was my first full can of beer. If you want to know who we are now; if you wonder how we'll vote, or whether we will, or whether, 10 years from now, we'll end up just like all those other generations that thought they were special—with 2.2 kids and a house in Connecticut—if that's what you're wondering, look to the past because, whether we should blame it or not, we do.

I didn't know till years later that they called it the Cuban Missile Crisis. But I remember Castro. (We called him Castor Oil and were awed by his beard—beards were rare in those days.) We might not have worried so much (what would the Communists want with our small New Hampshire town?) except that we lived 10 miles from an air base. Planes buzzed around us like mosquitoes that summer. People talked about fallout shelters in their basements and one family on our street packed their car to go to the mountains. I couldn't understand that. If everybody was going to die, I certainly didn't want to stick around, with my hair falling out and—later—a plague of thalidomide-type babies. I wanted to go quickly, with my family.

Dying didn't bother me so much—I'd never known anyone who died, and death was unreal, fascinating. (I wanted Doctor Kildare to have more terminal cancer patients and fewer love affairs.) What bothered me was the business of immortality. Sometimes, the growing-up sort of concepts germinate slowly, but the full impact

of death hit me like a bomb, in the night. Not only would my body be gone—that I could take—but I would cease to think. That I would no longer be a participant I had realized before; now I saw that I wouldn't even be an observer. What especially alarmed me about The Bomb (always singular like, a few years later, The Pill) was the possibility of total obliteration. All traces of me would be destroyed. There would be no grave and, if there were, no one left to visit it.

Newly philosophical, I pondered the universe. If the earth was in the solar system and the solar system was in the galaxy and the galaxy was in the universe, what was the universe in? And if the sun was just a dot—the head of a pin—what was I? We visited a planetarium that year, in third grade, and saw a dramatization of the sun exploding. Somehow the image of that orange ball zooming toward us merged with my image of The Bomb. The effect was devastating, and for the first time in my life—except for Easter Sundays, when I wished I went to church so I could have a fancy new dress like my Catholic and Protestant friends—I longed for religion.

I was 8 when Joan Baez entered our lives, with long, black, beatnik hair and a dress made out of a burlap bag. When we got her first record (we called her Joan *Baze* then—soon she was simply Joan) we listened all day, to "All My Trials" and "Silver Dagger" and "Wildwood Flower." My sister grew her hair and started wearing sandals, making pilgrimages to Harvard Square. I took up the guitar. We loved her voice and her songs but, even more, we loved the idea of Joan, like the 15th-century Girl of Orleans, burning at society's stake, marching along or singing, solitary, in a prison cell to protest segregation. She was the champion of nonconformity and so—like thousands of others—we joined the masses of her fans.

I knew she must but somehow I could never imagine Jackie Kennedy going to the bathroom. She was too cool and poised and perfect. We had a book about her, filled with color pictures of Jackie painting, in a spotless yellow linen dress, Jackie on the beach with Caroline and John-John, Jackie riding elephants in India and

Jackie, in a long white gown, greeting Khrushchev like Snow White welcoming one of the seven dwarfs. (No, I wasn't betraying Joan in my adoration. Joan was beautiful but human, like us; Jackie was magic.) When, years later, she married Rumpelstiltskin, I felt like a child discovering, in his father's drawer, the Santa Claus suit. And, later still, reading some Ladies' Home Journal exposé ("Jacqueline Onassis's secretary tells all . . .") I felt almost sick. After the first few pages I put the magazine down. I wasn't interested in the fragments, only in the fact that the glass had broken.

They told us constantly that Oyster River Elementary School was one of the best in the state, but the state was New Hampshire, and that was like calling a mound of earth a peak because it rose up from the Sahara Desert. One fact of New Hampshire politics I learned early: We had no broad-based tax. No sales or income tax, because the anti-Federalist farmers and the shoe-factory workers who feared the Reds and creeping Socialism acquired their political philosophy from William Loeb's Manchester Union Leader. We in Durham, where the state university stands, were a specially hated target, a pocket of liberals filling the minds of New Hampshire's young with high-falutin, intellectual garbage. And that was why the archaic New Hampshire Legislature always cut the university budget in half, and why my family had only one car, second-hand, (my father taught English at the university). And The Union Leader was the reason, finally, why any man who wanted to be elected Governor had better pledge himself against the sales tax, so schools were supported by local property taxes and the sweepstakes, which meant that they weren't supported very well. So Oyster River was not a very good school.

But in all the bleakness—the annual memorizing of Kilmer's "Trees," the punishment administered by banging guilty heads on hard oak desks—we had one fine, fancy new gimmick that followed us from fourth grade through eighth. It was a white cardboard box of folders, condensed two-page stories about dinosaurs and earthquakes and Seeing-Eye dogs, with questions at the end. The folders were called Power Builders

and they were leveled according to color—red, blue, yellow, orange, brown—all the way up to the dreamed-for, cheated-for purple. Power Builders came with their own answer keys, the idea being that you moved at your own rate and—we heard it a hundred times—that when you cheated, you only cheated yourself. The whole program was called SRA and there were a dozen other abbreviations, TTUM, FSU, PQB—all having to do with formulas that had reduced reading to a science.

We had Listening Skill Builders, too—more reader-digested minimodules of information, read aloud to us while we sat, poised stiffly in our chairs, trying frantically to remember the five steps (SRQPT? VWCNB? XUSLIN?) to Better Listening Comprehension. A Listening Skill Test would come later, to catch the mental wanderers, the doodlers, the deaf.

I—and most of the others in the Purple group —solved the problem by tucking an answer key into my Power Builder and writing down the answers (making an occasional error for credibility) without reading the story or the questions. By sixth grade, a whole group of us had been promoted to a special reading group and sent to an independent study-conference unit (nothing was a *room* any more) where we copied answer keys, five at a time, and then told dirty jokes.

SRA took over reading the way New Math took over arithmetic. By seventh grade, there was a special Developmental Reading class. (Mental reading, we called it.) The classroom was filled with audio-visual aids, phonetics charts, reading laboratories. Once a week, the teacher plugged in the speed-reading machine that projected a story on the board, one phrase at a time, faster and faster. Get a piece of dust in your eye—blink—and you were lost.

There were no books in the Developmental Reading room—the lab. Even in English class we escaped books easily. The project of the year was to portray a famous author (one of the 100 greatest of all time). I was Louisa May Alcott, and my best friend was Robert McCloskey, the man who wrote "Make Way for Ducklings." For this we put on skits, cut out pictures from magazines and, at the end of the year, dressed up. (I wore a long nightgown with my hair in a bun and got A-plus; my friend came as a duck.) I have never read a book by Louisa May Alcott. I don't think I read a book all that year. All through high school, in fact, I read little except for magazines. Though I've started reading seriously now, in college, I still find myself drawn in bookstores to the bright covers and shiny, power-builder look. My eyes have been trained to skip non-essentials (adjectives, adverbs) and dart straight to the meaty phrases. (TVPQM.) But—perhaps in defiance of that whirring black rate-builder projector—it takes me three hours to read 100 pages.

If I had spent at the piano the hours I gave to television, on all those afternoons when I came home from school, I would be an accomplished pianist now. Or if I'd danced, or read, or painted. . . . But I turned on the set instead, every day, almost, every year, and sank into an old green easy chair, smothered in quilts, with a bag of Fritos beside me and a glass of milk to wash them down, facing life and death with Dr. Kildare, laughing at Danny Thomas, whispering the answers—out loud sometimes—with "Password" and "To Tell the Truth." Looking back over all those afternoons, I try to convince myself they weren't wasted. I must have learned something; I must, at least, have changed.

What I learned was certainly not what TV tried to teach me. From the reams of trivia collected over years of quiz shows, I remember only the questions, never the answers. I loved "Leave It to Beaver" for the messes Beaver got into, not for the inevitable lecture from Dad at the end of each show. I saw every episode two or three times, witnessed Beaver's aging, his legs getting longer and his voice lower, only to start all over again with young Beaver every fall. (Someone told me recently that the boy who played Beaver Cleaver died in Vietnam. The news was a shock—I kept coming back to it for days until another distressed Beaver fan wrote to tell me that it wasn't true after all.)

I got so I could predict punch lines and endings, not really knowing whether I'd seen the episode before or only watched one like it. There was the bowling-ball routine, for instance:

Lucy, Dobie Gillis, Pete and Gladys—they all used it. Somebody would get his finger stuck in a bowling ball (Lucy later updated the gimmick using Liz Taylor's ring) and then they'd have to go to a wedding or give a speech at the P.-T.A. or have the boss to dinner, concealing one hand all the while. We weren't supposed to ask questions like "Why don't they just tell the truth?" These shows were built on deviousness, on the longest distance between two points, and on a kind of symmetry which decrees that no loose ends shall be left untied, no lingering doubts allowed. (The Surgeon General is off the track in worrying about TV violence, I think. I grew up in the days before lawmen became peacemakers. What carries over is not the gunfights but the memory that everything always turned out all right.) Optimism shone through all those half hours I spent in the dark shadows of the TV room—out of evil shall come good.

Most of all, the situation comedies steeped me in American culture. I emerged from years of TV viewing indifferent to the museums of France, the architecture of Italy, the literature of England. A perversely homebound American, I pick up paperbacks in bookstores, checking before I buy to see if the characters have foreign names, whether the action takes place in London or New York. Vulgarity and banality fascinate me. More intellectual friends (who watch no TV) can't understand what I see in "My Three Sons." "Nothing happens," they say. "The characters are dull, plastic, faceless. Every show is the same." I guess that's why I watch them—boring repetition is, itself, a rhythm—a steady pulse of flashing Coca-Cola signs, McDonald's Golden Arches and Howard Johnson roofs.

I don't watch TV as an anthropologist, rising loftily above my subject to analyze. Neither do I watch, as some kids now tune in to reruns of "The Lone Ranger" and "Superman" (in the same spirit they enjoy comic books and pop art) for their camp. I watch in earnest. How can I do anything else? Five thousand hours of my life have gone into this box.

There were almost no blacks in our school. They were Negroes then; the word *black* was hard to say at first. *Negro* got hard to say for a while too, so I said nothing at all and was embarrassed. If you had asked me, at 9, to describe Cassius Clay, I would have taken great, liberal pains to be color-blind, mentioning height, build, eye color and shoe size, disregarding skin. I knew black people only from newspapers and the TV screen—picket lines, National Guardsmen at the doors of schools. (There were few black actors on TV then, except for Jack Benny's Rochester.) It was easy, in 1963, to embrace the Negro cause. Later, faced with cold stares from an all-black table in the cafeteria or heckled by a Panther selling newspapers, I first became aware of the fact that maybe the little old lady didn't want to be helped across the street. My visions of black-and-white-together look to me now like shots from "To Sir With Love." If a black is friendly to me, I wonder, as other blacks might, if he's a sellout.

I had no desire to scream or cry or throw jelly beans when I first saw the Beatles on the Ed Sullivan Show. An eighth-grader would have been old enough to revert to childhood, but I was too young to act anything but old. So mostly we laughed at them. We were in fifth grade, the year of rationality, the calm before the storm. We still screamed when the boys came near us (which they rarely did) and said they had cooties. Barbie dolls tempted us. That was the year when I got my first Barbie. Perhaps they were produced earlier, but they didn't reach New Hampshire till late that fall, and the stores were always sold out. So at the close of our doll-playing careers there was a sudden dramatic switch from lumpy, round-bellied Betsy Wetsys and stiff-legged little-girl dolls to slim, curvy Barbie, just 11 inches tall, with a huge, expensive wardrobe that included a filmy black negligee and a mouth that made her look as if she'd just swallowed a lemon.

Barbie wasn't just a toy, but a way of living that moved us suddenly from tea parties to dates with Ken at the Soda Shoppe. Our short careers with Barbie, before junior high sent her to the attic, built up our expectations for teen-age life before we had developed the sophistication to go along with them. Children today are accustomed to having a tantalizing youth culture all around them. (They play with Barbie in the nursery school.) For us, it broke like a cloudburst, without preparation. Caught in the deluge, we were torn—wanting to run for shelter but tempted, also, to sing in the rain.

To me, a 10-year-old sixth-grader in 1964, the Goldwater-Johnson election year was a drama, a six-month basketball playoff game, more action-packed than movies or TV. For all the wrong reasons I loved politics and plunged into the campaign fight. Shivering in the October winds outside a supermarket ("Hello, would you like some L.B.J. matches?"), Youth for Johnson tried hard to believe in the man with the 10-gallon hat. We were eager for a hero (we'd lost ours just 11 months before) and willing to trust. Government deceit was not yet taken for granted—maybe because we were more naive but also because the country was. Later, the war that never ended and the C.I.A. and the Pentagon Papers and I.T.T. would shake us, but in those days, when a man said, "My fellow Americans . . . ," we listened.

At school, I was a flaming liberal, holding lunchroom debates and setting up a 10-year-old's dichotomies: If you were for Johnson, you were "for" the Negroes, if you were for Goldwater, you were against them. Equally earnest Republicans would expound the domino theory and I would waver in spite of myself (what they said sounded logical), knowing there was a fallacy somewhere but saying only, "If my father was here, he'd explain it. . . ."

A friend and I set up a campaign headquarters at school, under a huge "All the Way With L.B.J." sign. (The tough kids snickered at that— "all the way" was reserved for the behavior of fast girls in the janitor's closet at dances.) The pleasure we got from our L.B.J. headquarters and its neat stacks of buttons and pamphlets was much the same as the pleasure I got, five years later, manning the "Support your Junior Prom" bake-sale table in the lobby at school. I liked playing store, no matter what the goods.

And I believed, then, in the power of dissent and the possibility for change. I wrote protest songs filled with bloody babies and starving

Negroes, to the tune of "America the Beautiful." I marched through the streets of town, a tall candle flickering in my hand, surrounded by college kids with love beads and placards (what they said seems mild and polite now). I remember it was all so beautiful I cried, but when I try to recapture the feeling, nothing comes. Like a sharp pain or the taste of peach ice cream on a hot July day, the sensation lasts only as long as the stimulus.

Ask us whose face is on the $5 bill and we may not know the answer. But nearly everyone my age remembers a cover of *Life* magazine that came out in the spring of 1965, part of a series of photographs that enter my dreams and my nightmares still. They were the first shots ever taken of an unborn fetus, curled up tightly in a sack of veins and membranes, with blue fingernails and almost transparent skin that made the pictures look like double exposures. More than the moon photographs a few years later, that grotesque figure fascinated me as the map of a new territory. It was often that way with photographs in *Life*—the issue that reported on the "In Cold Blood" murders; a single picture of a boy falling from an airplane and another of a woman who had lost 200 pounds. (I remember the faces of victims and killers from seven or eight years ago, while the endless issues on Rome and nature studies are entirely lost.)

Photographs are the illustrations for a decade of experiences. Just as, when we think of *Alice in Wonderland*, we all see Tenniel's drawings, and when we think of the Cowardly Lion, we all see Bert Lahr, so, when we think of Lyndon Johnson's airborne swearing-in as President in 1963, we have a common image furnished by magazines, and when we think of fetuses, now, those cabbages we were supposed to have come from and smiling, golden-haired cherubs have been replaced forever by the cover of *Life*. Having had so many pictures to grow up with, we share a common visual idiom and have far less room for personal vision. The movie versions of books decide for us what our heroes and villains will look like, and we are powerless to change the camera's decree. So, while I was stunned and fascinated by that eerie fetus

(where is he now, I wonder, and are those pictures in his family album?) I'm saddened too, knowing what it did to me. If I were asked to pinpoint major moments in my growing up, experiences that changed me, the sight of that photograph would be one.

Eighth grade was groovy. When I think of 1966, I see pink and orange stripes and wild purple paisleys and black and white vibrating to make the head ache. We were too young for drugs (they hadn't reached the junior high yet) but we didn't need them. Our world was psychedelic, our clothes and our make-up and our jewelry and our hair styles were trips in themselves. It was the year of the gimmick, and what mattered was being noticed, which meant being wild and mod and having the shortest skirt and the whitest Yardley Slicker lips and the dangliest earrings. (We all pierced our ears that year. You can tell the girls of 1966—they're the ones with not-quite-healed-over holes in their ears.)

I've kept my *Seventeen* magazines from junior high: vinyl skirts, paper dresses, Op and Pop, Sassoon haircuts, Patty Duke curls and body painting. My own clothes that year would have glowed in the dark. I remember one, a poor-boy top and mod Carnaby Street hat, a silver microskirt and purple stockings. (Pantyhose hadn't been invented yet; among our other distinctions, call us the last generation to wear garter belts. I recall an agonizing seventh-period math class in which, 10 minutes before the bell rang, my front and back garters came simultaneously undone.)

It was as if we'd just discovered color, and all the shiny, sterile things machines made possible for us. Now we cultivate the natural, homemade look, with earthy colors and frayed, lumpy macrame sashes that no one would mistake for store-bought. But back then we tried to look like spacemen, distorting natural forms. Nature wasn't a vanishing treasure to us yet—it was a barrier to be overcome. The highest compliment, the ultimate adjective, was *unreal*.

I can understand the Jesus freaks turning, dope-muddled, to a life of self-denial and asceticism. The excesses of eighth-grade psychedelia left me feeling the same way and I turned, in 1967, to God. To the church, at least, anxious to wash away the bad aftertaste of too many Cokes and too much eye shadow. The church I chose, the only one conceivable for a confirmed atheist, wasn't really a church at all, but a dark gray building that housed the Unitarian Fellowship. They were an earnest, liberal-minded, socially-conscious congregation numbering 35 or 40. If I had been looking for spirituality, I knocked at the wrong door; the Unitarians were rationalists—scientists, mostly, whose programs would be slide shows of plant life in North Africa or discussions of migratory labor problems. We believed in our fellow man.

We tried Bible-reading in my Liberal Religious Youth group, sitting on orange crates in a circle of four but in that mildewed attic room, the Old Testament held no power. We gave up on Genesis and rapped, instead, with a casual college student who started class saying, "Man, do I have a hangover." We tried singing: one soprano, two tenors, and a tone-deaf alto, draped in shabby black robes designed for taller worshipers. After a couple of weeks of singing we switched, wisely, to what Unitarians do best, to the subjects suited to orange crates. We found a cause.

We discovered the Welfare Mothers of America—one Welfare Mother in particular. She was an angry, militant mother of eight (no husband in the picture) who wanted to go to the national conference in Tennessee and needed someone to foot the bill. I don't know who told us about Mrs. Mahoney, or her about us. In one excited Sunday meeting, anyway, the four of us voted to pay her way and, never having earned $4 without spending it, never having met Peg Mahoney, we called the state office of the Unitarian Church and arranged for a $200 loan. Then we made lists, allocated jobs, formed committees (as well as committees can be formed, with an active membership of four and a half dozen others who preferred to sleep in on Sundays). We would hold a spaghetti supper, all proceeds to go to the Mahoney fund.

We never heard what happened at the welfare conference—in fact, we never heard from our welfare mother again. She disappeared, with the red-plaid suitcase I lent her for the journey and the new hat we saw her off in. Our $200 debt lingered on through not one but three spaghetti suppers, during which I discovered that there's more to Italian-style, fund-raising dinners than red-and-white-checked tablecloths and Segovia records. Every supper began with five or six helpers; as more and more customers arrived, though, fewer and fewer L.R.Y.-ers stayed on to help. By 10 o'clock, when the last walnut-sized meatball had been cooked and the last pot of spaghetti drained, there would be two of us left in our tomato-spotted red aprons, while all around, religious youth high on red wine sprawled and hiccupped on the kitchen floor, staggering nervously to the door, every few minutes, to make sure their parents weren't around. I never again felt the same about group activity—united we stand, and that wonderful feeling I used to get at Pete Seeger concerts, singing "This Land is Your Land"—that if we worked together, nothing was impossible.

After the debt was paid I left L.R.Y., which had just discovered sensitivity training. Now the group held weekly, nonverbal communication sessions, with lots of hugging and feeling that boosted attendance to triple what it had been in our old save-the-world days. It seemed that everybody's favorite topic was himself.

Marijuana and the class of '71 moved through high school together. When we came in, as freshmen, drugs were still strange and new; marijuana was smoked only by a few marginal figures while those in the mainstream guzzled beer. It was called pot then—the words grass and dope came later; hash and acid and pills were almost unheard of. By my sophomore year, lots of the seniors and even a few younger kids were trying it. By the time I was a junior—in 1969—grass was no longer reserved for the hippies; basketball players and cheerleaders and boys with crewcuts and boys in black-leather jackets all smoked. And with senior year—maybe because of the nostalgia craze—there was an odd liquor revival. In my last month of school, a major bust led to the suspension of half a dozen boys. They were high on beer.

Now people are saying that the drug era is winding down. (It's those statisticians with their graphs again, charting social phenomena like the rise and fall of hemlines.) I doubt if it's real, this abandonment of marijuana. But the frenzy is gone, certainly, the excitement and the fear of getting caught and the worry of where to get good stuff. What's happened to dope is what happens to a new record: you play it constantly, full volume, at first. Then, as you get to know the songs, you play them less often, not because you're tired of them exactly, but just because you know them. They're with you always, but quietly, in your head.

My position was a difficult one, all through those four years when grass took root in Oyster River High. I was on the side of all those things that went along with smoking dope—the clothes, the music, the books, the candidates. More and more of my friends smoked, and many people weren't completely my friends, I think, because I didn't. Drugs took on a disproportionate importance. Why was it I could spend half a dozen evenings with someone without his ever asking me what I thought of Beethoven or Picasso but always, in the first half hour, he'd ask whether I smoked?

It became—like hair length and record collection—a symbol for who you were, and you couldn't be all the other things—progressive and creative and free-thinking—without taking that crumpled roll of dry, brown vegetation and holding it to your lips. You are what you eat—or what you smoke, or what you don't smoke. And when you say "like—you know," you're speaking the code, and suddenly the music of the Grateful Dead and the poetry of Bob Dylan and the general brilliance of Ken Kesey all belong to you as if, in those three fuzzy, mumbled words, you'd created art yourself and uttered the wisdom of the universe.

In my junior year I had English and algebra and French and art and history, but what I really had was fun. It was a year when I didn't give a thought to welfare mothers or war or peace or brotherhood; the big questions in my life were whether to cut my hair and what the theme of the Junior Prom should be. (I left my hair long. We decided on a castle.) Looking back on a year of sitting around just talking and drinking beer and driving around drinking beer and dancing and drinking beer and just drinking beer, I can say, "Ah yes, the post-Woodstock disenchantment; the post-Chicago, postelection apathy; the rootlessness of a generation whose leaders had all been killed . . ."

But if that's what it was, we certainly didn't know it. Our lives were dominated by parties and pranks and dances and soccer games. (We won the state championship that year. Riding home in a streamer-trailing yellow bus, cheering "We're Number One," it never occurred to us that so were 49 other schools in 49 other states.) It was a time straight out of the goldfish-swallowing thirties, with a difference. We knew just enough to feel guilty, like trick-or-treaters nervously passing a ghost with a UNICEF box in his hand. We didn't feel bad enough not to build a 20-foot cardboard-and-crepe-paper castle, but we knew enough to realize, as we ripped it down the next morning, Grecian curls unwinding limply down our backs, that silver-painted cardboard and tissue-paper carnations weren't biodegradable.

I had never taken Women's Liberation very seriously. Partly it was the looks of the movement that bothered me. I believed in all the right things, but just as my social conscience evaporated at the prospect of roughing it in some tiny village with the Peace Corps, so my feminist notions disappeared at the thought of giving up eye liner (just when I'd discovered it). Media-vulnerable, I wanted to be on the side of the beautiful, graceful people, and Women's Libbers seemed—except for Gloria Steinem, who was just emerging—plain and graceless. Women's Lib was still new and foreign, suggesting—to kids at an age of still-undefined sexuality—things like lesbianism and bisexuality. (We hadn't mastered one—how could we cope with the possibility of two?)

Besides, male chauvinism had no reality for me. In my family—two girls and two girl-loving parents—females occupied a privileged position. My mother and sister and I had no trouble getting equal status in our household. At school, too, girls seemed never to be discriminated against. (I wonder if I'd see things differently, going back there now.) Our class was run mostly by girls. The boys played soccer and sometimes held office on the student council—amiable figureheads—but it was the girls whose names filled the honor roll and the girls who ran class meetings. While I would never be Homecoming Sweetheart—I knew that—I had power in the school.

Then suddenly everything changed. A nearby boys' prep school announced that it would admit girls as day students. So at 17, in my senior year, I left Oyster River High for Phillips Exeter Academy.

The new world wasn't quite as I'd imagined. Exeter was a boys' school (*"Huc venite pueri, ut viri sitis"*) in which girls were an afterthought. We were so few that, to many, we appeared unapproachable. Like the Exeter blacks, the Exeter girls moved in gangs across the campus, ate together at all-girl tables and fled, after classes, to the isolated study areas allotted to them. The flight of the girls angered me; I felt newly militant, determined not to be intimidated by all those suits and ties and all the ivy-covered education. I wasn't just me anymore, but a symbol of my sex who had to prove, to 800 boys used to weekend girls at mixers, that I could hold my own. I found myself the only girl in every class—turned to, occasionally, by a faculty member accustomed to man-talk, and asked to give "the female point of view."

It makes one suspicious, paranoid. Why was I never asked to give the Scorpio's viewpoint, the myopic's, the half-Jewish, right-handed, New Hampshire resident's? Was being female my most significant feature? The subject of coeducation gets boring after a while. I wanted to talk about a book I'd read (having just discovered that reading could be fun) or a play I was in— and then somebody would ask the inevitable "What's it like to be a girl at Exeter?"

I became a compulsive overachiever, joining clubs and falling asleep at the typewriter in the hope of battering down doors I was used to having open, at my old school, where they knew me. Here someone else was the newspaper editor, the yearbook boss, the actor, the writer. I was the girl. All of first semester I approached

school like a warrior on the offensive, a self-proclaimed outsider. Then, in the ceasefire over Christmas, I went to a hometown New Year's Eve party with the people I'd been romanticizing all that fall when I was surrounded by lawyers' sons. The conversation back home was of soccer games I hadn't been to and a graduation I wouldn't be marching in. The school had gone on without me; I was a preppie.

Something strange got into the boys at Exeter that year as if, along with the legendary saltpeter, something like lust for the country was being sprinkled into the nightly mashed potatoes. It wasn't just the overalls (with a tie on top to meet the dress code) or the country music that came humming out of every dorm. Exonians—Jonathan Jrs. and Carter 3d's, Latin scholars and mathematicians with 800's on their college boards—were suddenly announcing to the college-placement counselor that no, they didn't want a Harvard interview, not now or ever. Hampshire, maybe, (that's the place where you can go and study Eastern religion or dulcimer-making). But many weren't applying any place—they were going to study weaving in Norway, to be shepherds in the Alps, deckhands on a fishing boat or—most often—farmers. After the first ecological fury died down, after Ehrlich's "Population Bomb" exploded, that's what we were left with. Prep school boys felt it more than most, perhaps, because they, more than most, had worked their minds at the expense of their hands. And now, their heads full of theorems and declensions, they wanted to get back to the basics—to the simple, honest, uncluttered life where manure was cow s——, not bovine waste.

Exeter's return to the soil took the form of the farm project, a group of boys who got together, sold a few stocks, bought a red pick-up truck and proposed, for a spring project, that they work a plot of school-owned land a few miles out of town. The country kids I went to Oyster River with, grown up now and working in the shoe factory or married—they would have been amused at the farming fairy tale. In March, before the ice thawed, the harvest was already being planned. The faculty objected and the project died, and most—not all—went on to college in the fall. (They talk now, from a safe distance, about the irrelevance of Spenser and the smell of country soil and fresh-cut hay.) A friend who really did go on to farming came to visit me at school this fall. He looked out of place in the dorm; he put his boots up on my desk and then remembered he had cow dung on the soles. He laughed when I reminded him about the farm project. It's best they never really tried, I think. That way, in 10 years, when they're brokers, they'll still have the dream: tomatoes big as pumpkins, pumpkins big as suns and corn that's never known the touch of blight.

Gene McCarthy must have encountered blizzards in 1968, and mill towns like Berlin, N. H.—where I went to campaign for George McGovern last February—must have smelled just as bad as they do now. But back in '68 those things made the fight even more rewarding, because in suffering for your candidate and your dreams, you were demonstrating love. But now, in 1972, there's nothing fun about air so smelly you buy perfume to hold under your nose, or snow falling so thick you can't make out the words on the Yorty billboard right in front of you. No one feels moved to build snowmen.

Campaigning in New Hampshire was work. Magazines and newspapers blame the absence of youth excitement on McGovern and say he lacks charisma—he isn't a poet and his bumper stickers aren't daisy shaped. But I think the difference in 1972 lies in the canvassers; this year's crusaders seem joyless, humorless. A high-school junior stuffing envelopes at campaign headquarters told me that when she was young—what is she now? —she was a Socialist. Another group of students left, after an hour of knocking on doors, to go snowmobiling. Somebody else, getting on the bus for home, said, "This makes the fifth weekend I've worked for the campaign," and I was suddenly struck by the fact that we'd all been compiling similar figures—how many miles we'd walked, how many houses we'd visited. In 1968 we believed, and so we shivered; in 1972, we shivered so that we might believe.

Our candidate this year is no less believable, but our idealism has soured and our motives have gotten less noble. We went to Berlin—many of us—so we could say "I canvassed in New Hampshire," the way high-school kids join clubs so they can write "I'm a member of the Latin Club" on their college applications. The students for McGovern whom I worked with were engaged in a business deal, trading frost-bitten fingers for guilt-free consciences; 1968's dreams and abstractions just don't hold up on a bill of sale.

The freshman women's dorm at Yale has no house mother. We have no check-in hours or drinking rules or punishments for having boys in our rooms past midnight. A guard sits by the door to offer, as they assured us at the beginning of the year, physical—not moral—protection. All of which makes it easy for many girls who feel, after high-school curfews and dating regulations, suddenly liberated. (The first week of school last fall, many girls stayed out all night, every night, displaying next morning the circles under their eyes the way some girls show off engagement rings.)

We all received the *Sex at Yale* book, a thick, black pamphlet filled with charts and diagrams and a lengthy discussion of contraceptive methods. And at the first women's assembly, the discussion moved quickly from course-signing-up procedures to gynecology, where it stayed for much of the evening. Somebody raised her hand to ask where she could fill her pill prescription, someone else wanted to know about abortions. There was no standing in the middle any more— you had to either take out a pen and paper and write down the phone numbers they gave out or stare stonily ahead, implying that those were numbers *you* certainly wouldn't be needing. From then on it seemed the line had been drawn.

But of course the problem is that no lines, no barriers, exist. Where, five years ago a girl's decisions were made for her (she had to be in at 12 and, if she was found—in—with her boyfriend . . .); today the decision rests with her alone. She is surrounded by knowledgeable, sexually experienced girls and if *she* isn't willing to sleep with her boyfriend, somebody else will. It's peer-group pressure, 1972 style—the embarrassment of virginity.

Everyone is raised on nursery rhymes and nonsense stories. But it used to be that when you grew up, the nonsense disappeared. Not for us—it is at the core of our music and literature and art and, in fact, of our lives. Like characters in an Ionesco play, we take absurdity unblinking. In a world where military officials tell us "We had to destroy the village in order to save it," Dylan lyrics make an odd kind of sense. They aren't meant to be understood; they don't jar our sensibilities because we're used to *non sequiturs.* We don't take anything too seriously these days. (Was it a thousand earthquake victims or a million? Does it matter?) The casual butcher's-operation in the film "M*A*S*H" and the comedy in Vonnegut and the album cover showing John and Yoko, bareback, are all part of the new absurdity. The days of the Little Moron joke and the elephant joke and the knock-knock joke are gone. It sounds melodramatic, but the joke these days is life.

You're not supposed to care too much any more. Reactions have been scaled down from screaming and jelly-bean-throwing to nodding your head and maybe—if the music really gets to you (and music's the only thing that does any more)—tapping a finger. We need a passion transfusion, a shot of energy in the veins. It's what I'm most impatient with, in my generation—this languid, I-don't-give-a-s——-ism that stems in part, at least, from a culture of put-ons in which any serious expression of emotion is branded sentimental and old-fashioned. The fact that we set such a premium on being cool reveals a lot about my generation; the idea is not to care. You can hear it in the speech of college students today: cultivated monotones, low volume, punctuated with four-letter words that come off sounding only bland. I feel it most of all on Saturday morning, when the sun is shining and the crocuses are about to bloom and, walking through the corridors of my dorm, I see there isn't anyone awake.

I'm basically an optimist. Somehow, no matter what the latest population figures say, I feel everything will work out—just like on TV. I may doubt man's fundamental goodness, but I believe in his power to survive. I say, sometimes,

that I wonder if we'll be around in 30 years, but then I forget myself and speak of "when I'm 50. . . ." Death has touched me now—from Vietnam and Biafra and a car accident that makes me buckle my seat belt—but like negative numbers and the sound of a dog whistle (too high-pitched for human ears), it's not a concept I can comprehend. I feel immortal while all the signs around me proclaim that I'm not.

We feel cheated, many of us—the crop of 1953—which is why we complain about inheriting problems we didn't cause. (Childhood notions of justice, reinforced by Perry Mason, linger on. Why should I clean up someone else's mess? Who can I blame?) We're excited also, of course: I can't wait to see how things turn out. But I wish I weren't quite so involved. I wish it weren't my life that's being turned into a suspense thriller.

When my friends and I were little, we had big plans. I would be a famous actress and singer, dancing on the side. I would paint my own sets and compose my own music, writing the script and the lyrics and reviewing the performance for *The New York Times.* I would marry and have three children (they don't allow us dreams like that any more) and we would live, rich and famous, (donating lots to charity, of course, and periodically adopting orphans), in a house we designed ourselves. When I was older I had visions of good works. I saw myself in South American rain forests and African deserts, feeding the hungry and healing the sick, with an obsessive selflessness, I see now, as selfish, in the end, as my original plans for stardom.

Now my goal is simpler. I want to be happy. And I want comfort—nice clothes, a nice house, good music and good food, and the feeling that I'm doing some little thing that matters. I'll vote and I'll give to charity, but I won't give myself. I feel a sudden desire to buy land—not a lot, not as a business investment, but just a small plot of earth so that whatever they do to the country I'll have a place where I can go—a kind of fallout shelter, I guess. As some people prepare for their old age, so I prepare for my 20's. A little house, a comfortable chair, peace and quiet—retirement sounds tempting.

9 WOMEN'S RIGHTS—NOW AND FOREVER?

A Woman Anthropologist Offers a Solution to the Woman Problem

Sheila K. Johnson

From *The New York Times Magazine* (August 27, 1972), 7, 31, 32–35, 37–39. © 1972 by The New York Times Company. Reprinted by permission.

In addition to her anthropological work, Ms Johnson has written Idle Haven: Community Building Among the Working-Class Retired *(1971), a study of elderly people who live in mobile-home parks.*

The first time I ever stood up in front of a class to lecture about anthropology was several years ago at San Francisco State College. It was not long after the campus had been seriously disrupted by Black Panthers and others trying to "reconstitute" the college, and some of my fellow teachers were worried that I, as a novice, might be "hassled" by revolutionaries. I was a little nervous about this myself, but I delivered a wholly uneventful first lecture describing the topics I planned to cover: marriage, the family, kinship, social organization—in other words, the stock-in-trade of any basic course in social anthropology. No Panthers raised their fists; no Maoists heckled me. At the end of my lecture, however, a very sweet-faced, long-haired boy came up to the podium and demanded, with unmistakable iciness, "Mrs. Johnson, are you planning to teach this course from a heterosex-

ual point of view? Because, you see, I'm gay, and I want to know how you're going to relate this material to my life-style."

I tried to reassure my student, who turned out to be the head of the campus branch of the Gay Liberation Front, that anthropology had a good deal to say about homosexuality in various societies and that I thought I could relate it to his life-style. At the same time, I had to admit that I had no intention of teaching the course from either a heterosexual or a homosexual point of view. I believed social science could and ought to be dispassionate in matters of sex as well as politics. In fact, my student's inquiry as to the sexual nature of my approach drove home to me the folly of trying to teach courses from *any* specialized point of view, black, Chicano, native American, Women's Lib or whatever. Such partisan approaches to knowledge remind me of Robert Benchley's famous solution to a Harvard international-law exam when, having been asked to discuss the Newfoundland fisheries dispute between the United States and Great Britain and knowing nothing about it, he decided to answer the question from the point of view of the fish.

All this is by way of saying that when it comes to discussing the role of women in our own society, I do so not from the standpoint of a woman but as an anthropologist. Anthropology, which includes both the physical and the social study of man (or, as the old schoolroom joke has it, "of man . . . embracing woman") has contributed at least two major insights concerning sex roles. One is that men and women *are* different, physiologically, endocrinologically and, as a result, perhaps also psychologically. (A female anthropology professor of mine once said, half jokingly, that she was convinced all women were psychotic at least once a month—which drew appreciative laughter from most of the women in the room and rather blank stares from the young men.) The other is that all known societies assign certain tasks on the basis of the distinction between the sexes. The jobs that are considered appropriate to males and females may differ greatly from group to group: in one society, men may be the weavers and potters, whereas in another, women perform these tasks. However, there also appear to be certain broad cultural regularities in the division of labor between the sexes that build directly upon physiological differences. Women, if they are engaged in food gathering or food production, are usually assigned the lighter tasks and tasks that keep them close to home, where they are also the chief caretakers of young children. Men are usually assigned the heavier and more dangerous tasks, such as hunting, housebuilding and fighting on behalf of the community.

Now, if one accepts these two insights (or, if one prefers, premises) that there *are* inborn sexual differences and that *all* cultures pattern roles on the basis of sex—then why has the role of women in our own society become such an issue all of a sudden? Why are so many women in the United States and, to a lesser extent, in Western Europe and other industrialized countries, arguing that men are oppressors and they are the oppressed?

To begin with, the traditional division of labor between the sexes in primitive societies has been radically altered in industrial societies by modern technology. Once upon a time, it may

have made sense for men to hunt buffalo or wildebeest because they were brawnier than women, and for women to be tied to babytending because they had milk-giving breasts. But modern technology has largely freed us from these considerations: a woman can drive a pickup truck with power steering as readily as a man, and a man is as capable of filling and heating a formula bottle as a woman.

A second reason present-day women have become dissatisfied with the traditional roles stems from a combination of increased longevity and reduced fertility. The life expectancy of women in the United States today is 74, and the birthrate has recently fallen to 2.136 children per family. American women are also tending to marry young—their average age at marriage is 20.8—and to have their children early and closely spaced. An average woman who marries at 21 and has her first child at 23 may have her second (and last) at 25. She will thus be only 30 years old when her youngest child enters kindergarten, leaving her partly bereft of her role as a full-time mother, and she will be between 42 and 45 years old when her last child leaves the nest entirely, either to enter college or marriage, or both.

These demographic facts have a great deal to do with the increasing numbers of middle-aged women who want to finish their educations or find work outside the home. Some sociologists also think that they may help to explain the increasing number of divorces among middle-aged couples. As little as 50 years ago, a woman could expect to be widowed before her last child had married and left home. Today, although a married woman who lives to be 74 can expect to be a widow for at least 10 years (men have shorter life expectancies and women usually marry older men) she and her husband are nevertheless faced with some 20 years together as a couple after they have finished raising their children. If the marriage is not a happy one, or if the partners have simply grown apart, divorce becomes the increasingly common solution—with the usual side effect that the woman will, at least for a time, want a job.

A third reason sometimes cited for increased

dissatisfaction of women with their traditional roles is that housework has become less time-consuming, therefore less important, therefore less fulfilling than it once was. Even if being a mother were still a major role for women, so the argument goes, the tasks associated with raising children and running a house have been greatly simplified by a variety of gadgets and services. A housewife is no longer obliged to make soap, bake bread, can vegetables, spin, weave and make the family's clothes. On the other hand, a housewife no longer has servants or female relatives (or even older children) to help, and labor-saving devices still require someone to operate them. Women's Lib itself seems to vacillate between the view that housework has shrunk in scope and is therefore unsatisfying and the view that it remains one of the last vestiges of the 18-hour day.

The truth lies somewhere in the middle. It has been estimated that the average American woman devotes 60 or more hours a week to household maintenance, purely aside from the time she spends with her husband and children. At the same time, the role of a modern house-wife is far from being as one-dimensional and stultifying as Women's Lib often makes it out to be. In a recent study entitled "Occupation: Housewife," sociologist Helena Z. Lopata analyzes the relationships that a housewife maintains—with her husband, children, parents, in-laws, friends, neighbors, repairmen, shop clerks, children's teachers, children's friends, doctors, and so forth—until the mind grows dizzy with the complexity of it all. And, indeed, many busy housewives find that their lives are a good deal more varied than their husbands' working day.

Moreover, as modern technology has simplified certain aspects of housekeeping, it has also made possible the creative elaboration of other aspects. For example, the advent of frozen foods, which has made it unnecessary for a wife to cook full-fledged meals every single day, has gone hand-in-hand with the burgeoning interest in gourmet cooking. And with the disappearance of the *need* to make all of a family's clothing, many women have turned to knitting, crocheting, and needlework as hobbies. To deride such pursuits as time-killers—as many ardent feminists do—is to overlook the fact that for many women they are a source of genuine satisfaction and pride. After all, long before Julia Child became an author and a TV celebrity, she was, quite simply, a housewife whose hobby was gourmet cooking.

The fourth explanation often cited for the dissatisfactions of women is the nature of the prestige system. In very small, primitive tribes there is virtual equality among all adult members. One man may have more prestige because he is a good hunter; one woman may have more prestige because she has born many healthy children. But in general the sexes are equally respected within the framework of their respective competences. In more complex but still pre-industrial societies there are major prestige differences, but these may be ascribed to people at birth, some being born into noble or highcaste families and others as serfs. Both men and women alike are subject to this prestige system, and a woman may even have a slightly better chance than a man of improving her lot, since in highly stratified societies hypergamy—the marriage of a lower-class or lower-caste woman to a man of a higher social group—is common. The reverse (hypogamy) is rare because with marriage a woman and her future offspring take on the social position of the husband, and so an upper-class woman marrying a lower-class man reduces her position as well as that of her children. In industrial societies, although there are vestiges of this older, inherited prestige system ("first" families and the like) the basic class distinctions are determined by the amount of education, the type of job (professional, white-collar, blue-collar) and the amount of money that a *man* has. Just as in the preindustrial societies, a woman derives her status first from her father and then from the man she marries; and just as in these more traditional societies, she can rise in status by marrying "upward"—the chorus girl who nabs herself a millionaire. What seems to rankle with many women today is that their own position in society has remained derivative and ascribed to them by virtue of their birth or marriage, whereas a man's status is something that he can affect by his own achievements.

Now, it is true many women are not in the least anxious to enter the marketplace on their own merits. The wife of a high-powered industrialist or a famous surgeon is usually only too happy to accept the social position and income that go with her husband's job, in exchange for raising the children, running the home and entertaining mutual friends. Moreover, many wives become deeply involved in their husbands' careers either in a purely emotional way or in actual fact, as with politicians' or diplomats' wives, thus satisfying their own ambitions vicariously. However, there are certain psychological risks involved in doing this. What if the husband decides, in midcareer, to dump his wife in favor of a nubile secretary? Or what if, because of overstriving, he drops dead of a heart attack at 45? The middle-aged, college-educated former wife of a businessman—even if he leaves her with a handsome alimony or insurance check—is suddenly cast adrift. She has lost not only her husband but also her identity. And this is something about which Women's Lib is quite properly concerned.

How, then, might one go about altering the present, unsatisfying status of women in our society? One solution, sometimes dreamed about by men, would be a blissful return to the *status quo ante*—to the time when men were men and women knew their place. I do not know of any serious advocates of this solution or, at least, of anyone who can explain how to go about turning back the social clocks. The physical changes that industrial society has wrought in the lives of women are simply too great not to produce some parallel adjustments in the way their roles are conceived.

A second possible solution is one that I call "male-oriented," because it is based on the assumption that the male role in our society is the more valuable and the more desirable. One would think that such an approach would strike women as outrageously sexist—rather like Henry Higgins asking, "Why can't a woman be more like a man?" But, strange to say, many women today ardently embrace this point of view. Even

Margaret Mead in her pioneering study *Male and Female* ultimately opts for the male-oriented solution. After describing both the physiological development of the two sexes and the ways in which various societies go on to define the scope of male and female adult roles, she nevertheless concludes with a plea for greater female access to traditionally male-defined roles in our own society. As Diana Trilling has pointed out, in a sensitive and too-little-known essay, "Dr. Mead would . . . seem to share with our society its low estimate of the female role. And when she asks that each sex be indulged in its special work aptitudes, she is not restoring to women their lost pride in their female function. She is merely attempting to minimize the contradictions between her case for sexual differentiation and her true feminist preference."

Basically, the male-oriented solution calls for all women to enter the labor force just as men do and for children to be raised in nurseries. However, unless sex-typing in jobs also disappears (part of a more radical proposal that I call the "androgynous solution," which I shall consider in a moment) it seems likely that such nurseries would, in fact, be largely staffed with women. This is precisely what happened in Israel with the formation of the *kibbutzim*. Designed in part to liberate women and put them on an equal footing with men, the *kibbutzim* nevertheless ended up assigning the heavier work in the fields and orchards to men and leaving most of the jobs in the laundries, kitchens and children's houses in the hands of women. The reasons for this were not at all sexist but had to do with practical matters such as physical stamina and the desire of nursing mothers to work near the infants' house, where they could nurse their children every few hours.

Even given such differential job allocations, proponents of the male-oriented solution insist that women will be happier working outside of the home because they will be cooking, ironing or caring for children as professionals rather than as mere housewives. However, it strikes me as equally possible that at least some women will find 9-to-5 child care or 9-to-5 jobs of any sort more stultifying than the greater variety of chores and freedom from scheduling they enjoy at home.

The whole problem of boring unfulfilling jobs currently held by men is ducked by the male-oriented solution. Feminists, when they lobby for greater access to male occupations, always seem to cast their argument in terms of highly visible, satisfying careers, such as those of doctors, lawyers, university professors or journalists. They never stop to consider that for every one such job there are at least 10 which consist of working on an assembly line, driving a truck or bus, or clerking in a store. Just as not every man either aspires to or can qualify for a profession, neither does every woman. Many who are being urged to, and often do, enter the labor force do so as typists, salesgirls and waitresses. Whether they take such jobs in order to fulfill themselves or merely for the extra money is something only they could answer, but I suspect it is the latter.

Some sociologists have suggested that the whole feminist thrust toward male roles is misguided because we are moving into a postindustrial society in which *all* work will be highly mechanized and alienating. In such a world, it is argued, the entire puritan ethic will have to be abandoned. Men, while their jobs may be routine and dull, will have an increasingly shorter work week, and they will develop their self-image not in terms of their work but in terms of the way they use their leisure time (woodworking, civic responsibilities, stamp collecting, whatever) precisely as most women do today. It may be that the present-day female role, with its greater flexibility, will prove to be the model for both male and female roles in the future; and I often think, when I hear feminists argue the "male-oriented" position, of James Baldwin's crack about black-and-white integration: "Do I really *want* to be integrated into a burning house?"

At the same time, I would not want to push this argument all the way into what I call the "female-oriented" solution, which basically proposes not that women should act more like men but that men should act more like women. Men should stop being chauvinistic pigs, give rein to their nurtural impulses, take half-time or unde-

manding jobs and become involved with caring for their children and homes. I do not know of any social scientist who has seriously proposed this solution, but it is, in fact, the life-style adopted by many young college-educated (or college-dropout) couples. Whether this life-style is merely a temporary or a youthful phenomenon remains to be seen. But it may be just close enough to the high-leisure, low-job-involvement ethic that has been predicted for the future to remain viable. I suspect, however, that it will be the life-style of blue-collar and lower-echelon white-collar workers; I do not think it will work for the professions.

Even, or perhaps particularly, in a highly automated society, there will still be jobs requiring long periods of training and specialized skills. The female-oriented solution ignores the fact that once people have been so extensively and expensively trained, it is not sensible to use them on a less than full-time basis. Jobs which require such training are also likely to have very high rewards—financially and emotionally. Many sociological studies have demonstrated that executives, doctors and other professionals work many more hours a day than men who punch a time clock, and they do so voluntarily, because they are stimulated by the work itself.

It is the nature of these high-status jobs that makes it impractical for men to fill them on a half-time or on-again-off-again basis; and this is also why, with these particular jobs, there is often great resistance to opening them up to women. It is not, I think, that male doctors, lawyers, scientists and journalists doubt that females can make excellent colleagues (there are already too many women in each of these fields to make a viable argument). But professional men *do* want the same criteria applied to women that are applied to them, and they want to have the same expectations of women in their field that they do of men. This is why, for example, there is great resistance in medical schools to adjusting internships so that women internes can care for their children. If you want to be a doctor, the attitude seems to be, you should get used to long and difficult hours just as male doctors do. For the same sort of reasons, major companies are reluctant to promote women to high executive positions because they doubt that most women are really prepared to undertake everything that goes with such jobs: extensive travel, evening and weekend work and often the necessity of moving. It is useless to argue, as some feminists do, that not all male executives are willing to pay this price either. It is true that some men are not, but they usually find this reflected in their promotions and paychecks.

What I am saying is that I do not find either the male-oriented or the female-oriented position wholly satisfactory as a model to which both sexes should aspire. I do not find the vision of a society in which all men and women have full-time jobs entirely credible, nor can I envision a society where all men and women have part-time or intermittent jobs. I think society needs both sorts of life-styles, and I think it is not entirely accidental that one has become associated with the female sex and the other with the male sex. It would be possible to break this association, however, and this brings us to the fourth solution, the androgynous solution, which takes its name from an important article by the sociologist Alice S. Rossi. It is basically the position of many members of Women's Lib writing today. They argue that the physiological differences between men and women are minimal or nonexistent, and that sex roles are a cultural product "inappropriate to the kind of world we live in in the second half of the twentieth century." The old distinctions between masculine and feminine should be abandoned, and children of both sexes should be raised precisely the same way, to have the same expectations and the same goals.

It is enough to make a Frenchman weep, and perhaps some women too. The women who espouse the androgynous solution point, correctly, to the fact that Americans already train female children in highly inconsistent ways. They urge their girls to excel in school and go to college, and yet they expect these same girls somehow to abandon their academic interests and become pliable wives. Supporters of the androgynous solution also point out that sex-

linked occupations (nurses are female, doctors are male; secretaries are female, executives are male) are largely traditional. In newer occupations, such as computer programing or being a laboratory technician, the sex barriers are either nonexistent or much less rigid. Yet I wonder whether the solution to these inconsistencies is to do away with sex roles altogether. I am inclined to agree with Margaret Mead that there may well be certain jobs that are more congenial to one sex than the other, and I would hate to see such human potential denied simply in the name of a programmatic conviction that equality means similarity.

Finally, therefore, I want to offer my own solution to the woman problem, although since I am a social analyst rather than an advocate, it is a statement more of where we are today than where I think we ought to be going. I call it the "alternative life-styles" solution. The United States is already a pluralistic society in terms of its ethnic groups, its religious groups, its regions, and the types of life-styles that go with these various groupings. Why not accept a pluralistic view of male and female roles as well? According to this view, women who want careers should have them (and get equal pay with men for the work they choose to do), and women who want to stay at home should do so (and not be despised for it). Men who want to continue being aggressive, male chauvinist pigs should feel free to do so (not least because there are some women who are wildly attracted to this type of behavior), but men who want to give rein to their passive impulses should also be encouraged (since there are plenty of women who like that sort of man too). Under this live-and-let-live rubric it should even be possible for society to accommodate itself comfortably to those women who prefer the company of other women, and to men who prefer other men.

I realize that this laissez-faire approach is too noncombative to please most ardent feminists. And it can be faulted by them for failing to take adequate account of the dead weight of tradition: What about those professions that women are genuinely prevented from entering? What about those jobs that a woman can get only by being *twice* as good as the nearest competing man? I am probably too sanguine about these problems because my own field, anthropology, has never discriminated against women. Any list of prominent anthropologists would have to include such names as Ruth Benedict, Margaret Mead, Cora du Bois, Hortense Powdermaker, Lucy Mair, Monica Wilson, Florence Kluckhohn, Dorothy Lee, Elizabeth Colson, and many more.

So I have been lucky, and, indeed, for women whose interests lie in male-dominated fields, the road may be much harder. The answer, I think, lies in legislation to insure nondiscriminatory hiring and equal pay for women. The answer does *not* lie in the promotion of quotas: the notion that because women represent 51 percent of the population they must have close to that number in all occupations, political bodies and private clubs. If the foregoing analysis has any validity at all it should have established that (1) some occupations will continue to attract more males and others to attract more females because of certain sexually determined psychological predispositions (women make better kindergarten teachers than men), and (2) not all women will *want* to enter the 9-to-5 rat race. The beauty of a pluralistic approach is that it frees men and women from rigidly sex-defined roles without either destroying the distinction between the sexes or casting them in new, equally rigid sex roles.

Even if pluralism in male and female roles becomes an entirely accepted fact, it will not be without its cost. When there are no longer any absolute cultural values to guide men and women in how they should shape their lives, it takes a good deal of individualism and strength of character to map a course of one's own. The costs, even for an outwardly successful individual, may be self-doubt and perpetual tension. One reason for the tension is that, with every individual free to "do his own thing," there is no one else to blame if one makes a bad choice. For example, one of the dilemmas created by effective birth-control methods (backstopped by the availability of safe abortions) is that a woman—

or a couple—must actively decide to have children. Even to abdicate that decision (to "let nature take its course" or to "take a chance") is to choose, when alternatives are available. Many women find this an acutely uncomfortable position to be in. It is, after all, much easier to say that you never managed to finish college because the babies started coming. It is even relatively easy, given a little help from Women's Lib organizations, to argue that you cannot finish college now because the Administration refuses to establish child-care centers. What is hard is to choose among available—and sometimes competing—alternatives.

I do not mean to imply that maternity and a career are necessarily alternative choices (although for some women they unquestionably are). Certainly, the shortened period of the mother role, in the context of a woman's entire life-span, means that other meaningful substitutes must be found. Whether they are to be continuous or discontinuous, paid or unpaid, careers or avocations, is, I think, an open question. Grandma Moses managed to start a quite amazing career as a painter in her late 70's, and I will always remember an art teacher of mine who argued that Grandma Moses would have been ruined had she ever taken lessons or, for that matter, set brush to canvas any sooner than she did. She was, in an extreme way, a late bloomer.

I myself had a solution to women's roles all worked out when I was 4 years old. When one of my mother's friends asked me what I wanted to be when I grew up, I said I wanted to be a ballerina and a fishwife. (I should perhaps explain that I grew up in Holland, where the women who sold fresh herring on the streets wore wonderfully voluminous costumes and white, starched butterfly caps anchored to their foreheads with gold-filigree hat pins.) When my mother's friend, somewhat startled, asked me how I planned to combine these two professions, I explained that I would be a ballerina until I got too old to dance, and *then* I would become a fishwife. It didn't quite work out that way, but I still think it's not a bad solution.

An Intelligent Woman's (or Man's) Guide
to the Woman Problem

I have listed these books and articles in the order of their publication because this reveals the rather peculiar cyclical nature of works dealing with the "woman problem." Perhaps, like the poor, it is something we always have with us and it merely floats into our collective consciousness about once per decade. The best books from the late nineteen-forties and early fifties are Mead's and de Beauvoir's, although Mead should be read in conjunction with the Trilling essay. The best works from the sixties are by Friedan and Rossi; and the best from the early seventies are by Lopata and Epstein—Lopata's book being a fine sociological analysis of what is entailed in being a housewife, and Epstein's an equally fine sociological analysis of the complex of roles that a professional woman who is also a housewife undertakes. It should also be noted that all of the titles here (and not by any special design) are by women. So perhaps things are not quite as bad as some of the ladies seem to think.

Margaret Mead, *Male and Female*, Dell and Apollo paperbacks. First published by William Morrow & Co., 1949.

Simone de Beauvoir, *The Second Sex*, Bantam Books. First published in French by Gallimard, 1949, and in English by Alfred A. Knopf, 1953.

Diana Trilling, "Men, Women and Sex," in *Claremont Essays*, Harcourt Brace Jovanovich, 1964. First published in *The Partisan Review*, April 1950.

Betty Friedan, *The Feminine Mystique*, Dell paperback. First published by W. W. Norton & Company, in 1963.

Alice S. Rossi, "Equality Between the Sexes: An Immodest Proposal," in Rose Laub Coser, ed., *Life Cycle and Achievement in America*, Harper Torchbooks. First published in Daedalus, 93 (1964).

Cynthia Fuchs Epstein, *Woman's Place*, University of California Press paperback. First published by the University of California Press, 1970.

Helena Z. Lopata. *Occupation: Housewife*, Oxford University Press paperback. First published by Oxford University Press, 1971.

10 THE GAY WORLD— OUT OF THE CLOSET?

The Homosexual:
Newly Visible, Newly Understood

Time Magazine

From *Time Magazine* (October 31, 1969), 56, 61–62, 64–67. Reprinted by permission from *Time, The Weekly Newsmagazine*; copyright Time Inc.

An exclusive formal ball will mark Halloween in San Francisco this week. In couturier gowns and elaborately confected masquerades, the couples will whisk around the floor until 2 a.m., while judges award prizes for the best costumes and the participants elect an "Empress." By then the swirling belles will sound more and more deep-voiced, and in the early morning hours dark stubble will sprout irrepressibly through their Pan-Cake Make-Up. The celebrators are all homosexuals, and each year since 1962 the crowd at the annual "Beaux Arts Ball" has grown larger. Halloween is traditionally boys' night out, and similar events will take place in Los Angeles, New York, Houston, and St. Louis.

Though they still seem fairly bizarre to most Americans, homosexuals have never been so visible, vocal or closely scrutinized by research. They throw public parties, frequent exclusively "gay" bars (70 in San Francisco alone), and figure sympathetically as the subjects of books, plays, and films. Encouraged by the national climate of openness about sex of all kinds and the spirit of protest, male and female inverts have been organizing to claim civil rights for themselves as an aggrieved minority.

POLITICAL PRESSURE

Their new militancy makes other citizens edgy, and it can be shrill. Hurling rocks and bottles and wielding a parking meter that had been wrenched out of the sidewalk, homosexuals rioted last summer in New York's Greenwich Village after police closed one of the city's 50 all-gay bars and clubs on an alleged liquor law violation. Pressure from militant self-styled "homophiles" has forced political candidates' views about homosexuality into recent election campaigns in New York, San Francisco, and Los Angeles. Homosexuals have picketed businesses, the White House, and the Pentagon, demanding an end to job discrimination and the right to serve in the Army without a dishonorable discharge if their background is discovered.

Some 50 homophile organizations have announced their existence in cities across the country and on at least eight campuses. Best known are the Mattachine societies (named for sixteenth century Spanish masked court jesters), and the Daughters of Bilitis (after French Poet Pierre Louÿs' *The Songs of Bilitis*, a nineteenth century series of lyrics glorifying lesbian love). W. Dorr Legg, educational director at Los Angeles' 17-year-old ONE, Inc., claims, "I won't be happy until all churches give homosexual dances and parents are sitting in the balcony saying 'Don't John and Henry look cute dancing together?'" Radical groups such as the Gay Liberation Front chant "Gay power" and "Gay is good" and turgidly call for "the Revolution of Free and Frequent Polysexuality."

Last week's report to the National Institute of Mental Health urged legalization of private homosexual acts between adults who agree to them.[1] It was the latest sign that the militants are finding grudging tolerance and some support in the "straight" community. The Federal Appeals Court in Washington, D.C., for example, has responded to a recent case by declaring that a governmental agency could not dismiss an employee without first proving that his homosexuality would palpably interfere with the efficiency of the agency's operations. *The New York Times*, which for years shied from the word homosexual, in June permitted a homosexual writing under his own name, Freelance Critic Donn Teal, to contribute an article on "gay" themes in theater. In large cities, homosexuals have reached tacit agreements with police that give them the *de facto* right to their own social life.

Homosexual organizations across the country run discussion groups and record hops. A San Francisco group known as S.I.R. (Society for Individual Rights) organizes ice-skating parties, chess clubs and bowling leagues. Nor is it necessary for a homosexual to join a homophile organization to enjoy a full social life: homosexuals often are the parlor darlings of wealthy ladies ("fag hags"). Marriage in these circles can involve a homosexual and a busy career woman who coolly take the vows for companionship—

and so that they can pool their incomes and tax benefits for a glittering round of entertaining.

SEDUCTION AND SODOMY

Homosexuals with growing frequency have sought the anonymity and comparative permissiveness of big cities. It is this concentration of homosexuals in urban neighborhoods rather than any real growth in their relative numbers that has increased their visibility and made possible their assertiveness. According to the Kinsey reports, still the basic source for statistics on the subject, 10 percent of American men have long periods of more or less exclusive homosexuality; only 4 percent (2 percent of women) are exclusively homosexual all their lives. These may be inflated figures, but most experts think that the proportion of homosexuals in the U.S. adult population has not changed drastically since Kinsey did his survey, giving the country currently about 2,600,000 men and 1,400,000 women who are exclusively homosexual. Despite popular belief, these numbers are not substantially increased by seduction: most experts now believe that an individual's sex drives are firmly fixed in childhood.

Inevitably, the homosexual life has attracted eager entrepreneurs. A firm in Great Neck, N.Y., runs a computer-dating service for homosexuals; San Francisco's Adonis bookstore has some 360 different magazines on display that carry everything from lascivious photos of nude men to reports on the homophile movement and lovelorn advice by "Madame Soto-Voce." Police and homosexuals agree that operating a gay bar is still an occupation that often appeals to Mafiosi. In New York City, sleazy movie houses along Broadway now match their traditional offerings of cheesecake with "beefcake."

Off-Broadway producers have found that homosexuals will flock to plays about themselves. Yet most dramas about deviates are written for heterosexual audiences. The New York stage [has recently offered] John Osborne's *A Patriot for Me*, Mart Crowley's *The Boys in the Band* and John Herbert's *Fortune and Men's Eyes*, a 1967 drama about prison life. Revived

---

[1] Three dissenting members of the study group shied away from making policy recommendations, claiming that the issues were moral and not scientific in nature.

... in a new production, it has been rewritten so that a scene of forcible sodomy that used to take place out of the audience's sight is now grimly visible (though simulated). In movies, too, homosexuality is the vogue: *Staircase*, starring Rex Harrison and Richard Burton, *Midnight Cowboy*, and Fellini's *Satyricon*. On the lesbian side there are *The Fox*, *Thérèse and Isabelle*, and *The Killing of Sister George*.

The quality of these works ranges from excellent to nauseating. But it is a fact that treatment of the theme has changed. "Homosexuality used to be a sensational gimmick," says Playwright Crowley. "The big revelation in the third act was that the guy was homosexual, and then he had to go off-stage and blow his brains out. It was associated with sin, and there had to be retribution." These days a movie or play can end, as *Staircase* does, with a homosexual couple still together or, as *Boys in the Band* winds up, with two squabbling male lovers trying desperately to save their relationship. Beyond that, the homosexual is a special kind of anti-hero; his emergence on center stage reflects the same sympathy for outsiders that has transformed oddballs and criminals from enemies into heroic rebels against society in such films as *Bonnie and Clyde* and *Alice's Restaurant*.

Is there a homosexual conspiracy afoot to dominate the arts and other fields? Sometimes it seems that way. The presence of talented homosexuals in the field of classical music, among composers, performers, conductors, and management, has sometimes led to charges by disappointed outsiders that the music world is a closed circle. The same applies to the theater, the art world, painting, dance, fashion, hairdressing, and interior design, where a kind of "homintern" exists: a gay boss will often use his influence to help gay friends. The process is not unlike the ethnic favoritism that prevails in some companies and in big-city political machines; with a special sulky twist, it can be vicious to outsiders. Yet homosexual influence has probably been exaggerated. The homosexual cannot go too far in foisting off on others his own preferences; the public that buys the tickets or the clothes is overwhelmingly heterosexual. Genuine talent is in such demand that entrepreneurs who pass it by on the grounds of sex preference alone may well suffer a flop or other damage to their own reputations.

THE DARK SIDE OF LOVE

Discrimination aside, what about the more indirect propagation of homosexual points of view? Homosexual taste can fall into a particular kind of self-indulgence as the homosexual revenges himself on a hostile world by writing grotesque exaggerations of straight customs, concentrates on superficial stylistic furbelows or develops a "campy" fetish for old movies. Somerset Maugham once said of the homosexual artist that "with his keen insight and quick sensibility, he can pierce the depths, but in his innate frivolity he fetches up from them not a priceless jewel but a tinsel ornament."

In many cases, including Maugham's own, that is an exaggeration. Indeed the talented homosexual's role as an outsider, far from disqualifying him from commenting on life, may often sharpen his insight and esthetic sensibility. From Sappho to Colette to Oscar Wilde and James Baldwin, homosexual authors have memorably celebrated love—and not always in homosexual terms. For example, W. H. Auden's *Lullaby*—"Lay your sleeping head, my love/Human on my faithless arm"—must rank as one of the twentieth century's most exquisite love lyrics.

In recent years, writes Critic Benjamin DeMott, "the most intense accounts of domestic life and problems, as well as the few unembarrassedly passionate love poems, have been the work of writers who are not heterosexual ... Tennessee Williams, Edward Albee, Allen Ginsberg, Jean Genet, and Auden. They have a steady consciousness of a dark side of love that is neither homo- nor heterosexual but simply human." *The New York Times* Drama Critic Clive Barnes muses, "Creativity might be a sort of psychic disturbance itself, mightn't it? Artists are not particularly happy people anyway."

Despite the homosexual's position in the arts,

it is easy to overestimate the acceptance he has achieved elsewhere. Most straight Americans still regard the invert with a mixture of revulsion and apprehension, to which some authorities have given the special diagnostic name of homosexual panic. A Louis Harris poll released last week reported that 63 percent of the nation consider homosexuals "harmful to American life," and even the most tolerant parents nervously watch their children for real or imagined signs of homosexuality, breathing sighs of relief when their boy or girl finally begins dating the opposite sex.

Such homophobia is based on understandable instincts among straight people, but it also involves innumerable misconceptions and oversimplifications. The worst of these may well be that all homosexuals are alike. In fact, recent research has uncovered a large variation among homosexual types. With some overlap, they include:

The Blatant Homosexual

Chaucer's Pardoner in *The Canterbury Tales* had a voice "small as a goat's. He had no beard nor ever would have, his face was as smooth as if lately shaven; I trow he were a mare or a gelding." This is the eunuch-like caricature of femininity that most people associate with homosexuality. In the 1960s he may be the catty hairdresser or the lisping, limp-wristed interior decorator. His lesbian counterpart is the "butch," the girl who is aggressively masculine to the point of trying to look like a man. Blatants also include "leather boys," who advertise their sadomasochism by wearing leather jackets and chains, and certain transvestites, or "Tvs." (Other transvestites are not homosexuals at all and, while they enjoy dressing in female clothing, may also have women as sex partners.)

Actually, such stereotype "queers" are a distinct minority. Paul Gebhard, director of Alfred Kinsey's Institute for Sex Research, estimates that only around 10 percent of all homosexuals are immediately recognizable. Blatants often draw sneers from other homosexuals, and in fact many of them are only going through a phase.

Having recently "come out"—admitted their condition and joined the homosexual world—they feel insecure in their new roles and try to re-create their personalities from scratch. Behaving the way they think gay people are supposed to behave, they too temporarily fall victim to the myth.

The Secret Lifer

The other 90 percent of the nation's committed inverts are hidden from all but their friends, lovers, and occasionally, psychiatrists. Their wrists are rigid, their "s's" well formed; they prefer subdued clothes and close-cropped hair, and these days may dress more conservatively than flamboyant straights. Many wear wedding rings and have wives, children and employers who never know. They range across all classes, all races, all occupations. To lead their double lives these full or part-time homosexuals must "pass" as straight, and most are extremely skilled at camouflage. They can cynically tell—or at least smile at—jokes about "queers"; they fake enjoyment when their boss throws a stag party with nude movies.

The Desperate

Members of this group are likely to haunt public toilets ("tearooms") or Turkish baths. They may be pathologically driven to sex but emotionally unable to face the slightest strains of sustaining a serious human relationship, or they may be married men who hope to conceal their need by making their contacts as anonymous as possible.

The Adjusted

By contrast, they lead relatively conventional lives. They have a regular circle of friends and hold jobs, much like Los Angeles Businessman "Charles Eliott" or Manhattan Secretary "Rachel Porter," described on pages 116–17. Their social lives generally begin at the gay bars or in rounds of private parties. Often they try to settle down with a regular lover, and although these liaisons are generally short-lived among men, some develop into so-called "gay marriages," like the 14-year union between Poets Allen Ginsberg and Peter Orlovsky.

The Bisexual

Many married homosexuals are merely engaging in "alibi sex," faking enjoyment of intercourse with their wives. Some researchers, however, have found a number of men and women who have a definite preference for their own sex but engage in occasional activity with the opposite sex and enjoy it. The description of Julius Caesar's protean sex life probably contained a core of fact: "He was every man's wife and every woman's husband." (Caesar's wife was a different case.)

The Situational-Experimental

He is a man who engages in homosexual acts without any deep homosexual motivation. The two Kinsey reports found that almost 40 percent of white American males and 13 percent of females have some overt sexual experience to orgasm with a person of their own sex between adolescence and old age. Yet a careful analysis of the figures shows that most of these experiences are only temporary deviations. In prisons and occasionally in the armed forces,[2] for example, no women are available. Thus the men frequently turn to homosexual contacts, some in order to reassert their masculinity and recapture a feeling of dominance.

The homosexual subculture, a semipublic world, is, without question, shallow and unstable. Researchers now think that these qualities, while inherent in many homosexuals, are also induced and inflamed by social pressures. The notion that homosexuals cause crime is a homophobic myth: studies of sex offenders show that homosexuals are no more likely to molest young children than are heterosexuals. Homosexuals are more likely to be victims of crime: Sociologists John Gagnon, of the State

[2] As Winston Churchill said of the traditions of the Royal Navy just before World War I: "What are they? Rum, sodomy and the lash."

University of New York at Stony Brook, and William Simon, of the Illinois Institute of Juvenile Research, in a recent survey of homosexuals found that only 10 percent of them had ever been arrested; by contrast, 10 percent had been blackmailed and over 25 percent had been robbed, frequently after being attacked and beaten.

Insecurity and promiscuity go hand in hand. One man told U.C.L.A. Researcher Evelyn Hooker that he had had relations with 1,500 different partners during a 15-year span. Since homosexual couples cannot comfortably meet in mixed company, the gay bars become impersonal "meat racks"—not unlike "swinger" bars for heterosexual singles—whose common denominator is little more than sex. Keeping a gay marriage together requires unusual determination, since the partners have no legal contract to stay together for worse or better; there are no children to focus the couple's concern.

The strain of the covert life shows clearly in brittle homosexual humor, which swings between a defensive mockery of the outside world and a self-hating scorn for the gay one. Recent research projects at the Indiana sex research institute and elsewhere have sought out homosexuals who are not troubled enough to come to psychiatrists and social workers and have found them no worse adjusted than many heterosexuals. Nonetheless, when 300 New York homosexuals were polled several years ago, only 2 percent said that they would want a son of theirs to be a homosexual. Homophile activists contend that there would be more happy homosexuals if society were more compassionate; still, for the time being at least, there is a savage ring of truth to the now famous line from *The Boys in the Band:* "Show me a happy homosexual, and I'll show you a gay corpse."

HOW AND WHY?

What leads to homosexuality? No one knows for sure, and many of the explanations seem overly simple and unnecessarily doctrinaire. Sociologist Gagnon says: "We may eventually conclude that there are as many causes for homosexuality as there are for mental retardation—and as many kinds of it." The only thing most experts agree on is that homosexuality is not a result of any kinky gene or hormone predispositions—at least none that can be detected by present techniques. Male and female homosexuals do not constitute a "third sex"; biologically, they are full men and women.

The reason that the invert's sex behavior is not dictated by his anatomy is related to a remarkable finding of sex researchers: no one becomes fully male or female automatically. The diverse psychological components of masculinity and femininity—"gender role identity"—are learned. Gender is like language, says Johns Hopkins University Medical Psychologist John Money: "Genetics ordains only that language can develop, not whether it will be Nahuatl, Arabic, or English."

This does not mean that homosexuality is latent in all mature humans, as has been widely believed from a misreading of Freud. In American culture, sex roles are most powerfully determined in the home, and at such a young age (generally in the first few years of life) that the psychological identity of most homosexuals—like that of most heterosexuals—is set before they know it. In the case of homosexuality, parents with emotional problems can be a powerful cause, leaving their child without a solid identification with the parent of the same sex and with deeply divided feelings for the parent of the opposite sex. In an exhaustive study of homosexuals in therapy, a group of researchers headed by Psychoanalyst Irving Bieber observed that a large number of homosexuals came from families where the father was either hostile, aloof or ineffectual and where the mother was close-binding and inappropriately intimate (CBI in scientific jargon). Bieber's wife, Psychologist Toby Bieber, has found many of the same patterns in the parents of lesbians, although in reverse.

Yet scientists have begun to realize that the homosexual hang-up is not exclusively home-made. For one thing, social pressures can unbalance parents' child-raising practices. Marvin Opler, an anthropologist trained in psychoanalysis who teaches at the State University of New York at Buffalo, says that Western culture generally, and the U.S. in particular, puts such a high premium on male competition and dominance that men easily become afraid that they are not measuring up, and take out their frustrations by being hostile to their sons.

The accepted notion that boys and girls should ignore each other until puberty and then concentrate heavily on dating can also distort parental attitudes. If a mother catches a little boy playing doctor with a little girl under the porch and tells him he has been bad, says Gebhard, she may be subtly telling him that sex with girls is bad: "Anything that discourages heterosexuality encourages homosexuality." If an uptight parent or teacher catches an impressionable adolescent boy in sexual experiments with other boys and leaps to the conclusion that he is a homosexual, the scoldings he gets may make him freeze up with girls in another way. He may start to think that if everyone considers him a homosexual, he must be one. Many schools compound the problem by enshrining the supermale and overemphasizing sports. The inevitable peer group yelling "Sissy!" at the drop of a fly ball can also start the long and complicated process by which a boy can come to think of himself as "different."

So potent is the power of suggestion, says Psychologist Evelyn Hooker, that one male need never have been sexually aroused by another to begin thinking of himself as gay. The unathletic, small, physically attractive youth is particularly prone to being singled out for "sissyhood," and authorities agree that it is this social selection rather than anything genetic that makes homosexuality somewhat more common among so-called "pretty boys."

Most experts agree that a child will not become a homosexual unless he undergoes many emotionally disturbing experiences during the course of several years. A boy who likes dolls or engages in occasional homosexual experiments is not necessarily "queer": such activities are often a normal part of growing up. On the other hand, a child who becomes preoccupied with such interests or is constantly ill at ease with the opposite sex obviously needs some form of psychiatric counseling. While only about one-third of confirmed adult inverts can be helped to change, therapists agree that a much larger number of "prehomosexual" children can be treated successfully.

CHANGING SEXUAL ROLES

A more elusive question is whether or to what extent homosexuality and acceptance of it may be symptoms of social decline. For varying reasons, homosexual relations have been condoned and at times even encouraged among certain males in many primitive societies that anthropologists have studied. However, few scholars have been able to determine that homosexuality had any effect on the functioning of those cultures. At their fullest flowering, the Persian, Greek, Roman and Moslem civilizations permitted a measure of homosexuality; as they decayed, it became more prevalent. Sexual deviance of every variety was common during the Nazis' virulent and corrupt rule of Germany.

Homosexuality was also common in Elizabethan England's atmosphere of wholesale permissiveness. Yet the era not only produced one of the most robust literary and intellectual outpourings the world has ever known but also laid the groundwork for Britain's later imperial primacy—during which time homosexuality became increasingly stigmatized.

In the U.S. today, homosexuality has scarcely reached the proportions of a symptom of widespread decadence (though visitors sometimes wonder as they observe the lounging male whores on New York's Third Avenue or encounter male couples embracing effusively in public parks). Still, the acceptance or rejection of homosexuality does raise questions about the moral values of the society: its hedonism, its concern with individual "identity." The current conceptions of what causes homosexuality also pose a fundamental challenge to traditional ideas about the proper role to be played by all men and women. In recent years, Americans have learned that a man need not be a Met pitcher or suburban Don Juan to be masculine: the most virile male might well be a choreographer or a far-out artist. Similarly, as more and more women become dissatisfied with their traditional roles, Americans may better understand that a female can hold a highly competitive job—or drive a truck—without being forced to sacrifice her sexuality or the satisfactions of child rearing. A nation that softens the long and rigid separation of roles for men and women is also less likely to condemn the homosexual and confine him to a netherworld existence.

MORALITY AND TOLERANCE

The case for greater tolerance of homosexuals is simple. Undue discrimination wastes talents that might be working for society. Police harassment, which still lingers in many cities and more small towns, despite a growing live-and-let-live attitude, wastes manpower and creates unnecessary suffering. The laws against homosexual acts also suggest that the nation cares more about enforcing private morality than it does about preventing violent crime. To be sure, it is likely that a more permissive atmosphere might convince many people, particularly adolescents, that a homosexual urge need not be resisted since the condition would, after all, be "respectable." On the other hand, greater tolerance might mitigate extreme fear of not being able to live up to exaggerated standards of heterosexual performance—and might thus reduce the number of committed homosexuals.

A violently argued issue these days is whether the confirmed homosexual is mentally ill. Psychoanalysts insist that homosexuality is a form of sickness; most homosexuals and many experts counter that the medical concept only removes the already fading stigma of sin, and replaces it with the charge—even more pejorative nowadays—that homosexuality is pathological. The answers will importantly influence society's underlying attitude (see TIME *symposium*). While homosexuality is a serious and sometimes crippling maladjustment, research has made clear that it is no longer necessary or morally justifiable to treat all inverts as outcasts. The challenge to American society is simultaneously to devise civilized ways of discouraging the condition and to alleviate the anguish of those who cannot be helped, or do not wish to be.

A Discussion: Are Homosexuals Sick?

One of the crucial issues in the public discussion about homosexuality is whether or not the condition is a mental illness. To try to find out, Time *asked eight experts on homosexuality—including two admitted homosexuals—to discuss the subject at a symposium in New York City. The participants: Robin Fox, British-born anthropologist at Rutgers University; John Gagnon, sociologist at the State University of New York; Lionel Tiger, a Canadian sociologist also at Rutgers; Wardell Pomeroy, a psychologist who co-authored the Kinsey reports on men and on women and who is now a psychotherapist; Dr. Charles Socarides, a psychoanalyst who has seen scores of homosexuals in therapy and is associate clinical professor of psychiatry at Albert Einstein College of Medicine in The Bronx; the Rev. Robert Weeks, an Episcopal priest who has arranged for the meetings of a homosexual discussion group to take place at his Manhattan church; Dick Leitsch, a homosexual who is executive director of the Mattachine Society of New York; and Franklin Kameny, an astronomer and homosexual who is founder-president of the Mattachine Society of Washington.*

Kameny. All the homosexuals whom you have explored in depth were patients or others in clinical circumstances. So how do you know that all the ones who wouldn't come near you are sick and suffer from severe anxieties?

Socarides. We do hear, from people who are in treatment, about their friends in homosexual life and some of these also come to us. They see around them a complete disaster to their lives. They see that the most meaningful human relationship is denied them—the male-female relationship.

Tiger. There is a lack of a tragic sense here. All people have problems. I have all kinds of anxieties; everybody I know has anxieties. Some of them are severe; some of them are not severe. Often they are severe at different stages of the life cycle and for different reasons. To pick on homosexuals in this particular way, as on Communists or Moslems in another, is to shortchange their option for their own personal destiny.

Socarides. By God, they should live in the homosexual world if they want to! No one is arguing that point; no one is trying to say that a homosexual should be forced to seek help. Everybody is now saying that the homosexual needs compassion and understanding, the way the neurotic does or anybody else suffering from any illness. That is true. I agree with that.

Weeks. I think that historically the church has had a very hypocritical view of homosexuality. Instead of accepting the totality of sexuality, the church is still a little uncomfortable with the total sexual response; it still insists that people conform to a certain type of sexual behavior.

Fox. I was talking to a very pretty American girl recently who said that her first reaction to European males was one of considerable shock because the kind of touching behavior, the kind of behavior between males, was something that she would have been horrified to see in the men she had grown up with. This strikes me as a very American attitude, because of its rigidity, because of its absolute exclusiveness, because of its treatment of this as something horrible and beyond the pale.

Gagnon. There is no explanation for this attitude unless you want to take Ken Tynan's explanation, which is that people think that people ought to be alike, and anyone who didn't get wife, have spear and carry shield was bad juju, and you threw him out of the crowd.

Leitsch. It has always struck me that one of the primary reasons for the American attitude toward homosexuality is that we are so close to our agrarian background. When America was first settled, we had a hell of a big country to fill up, and we had to fill it up in a hurry. We have never been big enough to be decadent before.

Fox. Yes, America has to learn to be decadent gracefully, I think.

Weeks. I just finished counseling a person who was addicted to the men's room in Grand Central Station. He knows he is going to get busted by the cops; yet he has to go there every day. I think I did succeed in getting him to cease going to the Grand Central men's room, perhaps in favor of gay bars. This is a tremendous therapeutic gain for this particular man. But he is sick; he does need help. However, I don't think Dr. Socarides is talking about people like another acquaintance of mine, a man who has been "married" to another homosexual for fifteen years. Both of them are very happy and very much in love. They asked me to bless their marriage, and I am going to do it.

Pomeroy. I think they are beautiful. I don't think they are sick at all.

Socarides. In medicine we are taught that sickness is the failure of function. For example, a gall bladder is pathological precisely when it ceases to function or its functioning is impaired. A human being is sick when he fails to function in his appropriate gender identity, which is appropriate to his anatomy. A homosexual who has no other choice is sick in this particular way. Is the man who goes to the "tearooms" any more or less sick that the two men in this "married" relationship? No. I think they are all the same. However, I think that perhaps the element of masochism or self-punitive behavior is greater in the man who will go openly, publicly, and endanger himself in this particular way.

Fox. You seem to say that the anxieties provoke a homosexual into seeking a partner of the same sex. Isn't it possible that he prefers such a partner, and that this provokes anxieties?

Socarides. If his actions are a matter of preference, then he would not be considered a true obligatory homosexual.

Gagnon. I am troubled here by the sense of intel-lectual and historical narrowness. We should not get hung up on the twentieth century nuclear family as the natural order of man, living in the suburbs and having three kids, or on the kind of Viennese-Jewish comparison that Freud really created. All of a sudden, I find a new penisology—that somehow the shape of the penis and of the vagina dictate the shape of human character. I have a minimum definition of mental health. You don't end up in a psychiatrist's office or in the hands of the police, you stay out of jail, you keep a job, you pay your taxes, and you don't worry people too much. That is called mental health. Nobody ever gets out of it alive. There is no way to succeed.

Socarides. It is a very bitter definition. Freud's test was a person's ability to have a healthy sexual relationship with a person of the opposite sex and to enjoy his work.

Fox. A psychoanalyst says that we are destined to heterosexual union, and anything that deviates from this must by definition be sick. This is nonsense even in animal terms. Animal communities can tolerate quite a lot of homosexual relationships. The beautiful paradigm of this is geese. Two male geese can form a bond that is exactly like the bond between males and females. They function as a male-female pair; and geese, as far as I can see, are a very successful species.

So far as the two "married" individuals are concerned, they are engaged in what to them is a meaningful and satisfying relationship. What I would define as a sick person in sexual terms would be someone who could not go through the full sequence of sexual activity, from seeing and admiring to following, speaking, touching, and genital contact. A rapist, a person who makes obscene telephone calls—these seem to me sick people, and I don't think it matters a damn whether the other person is of the same sex or not.

Socarides. The homosexuals who come to our offices tell us: "We are alone, we are despairing, we cannot join the homosexual society—this would be giving up. We like what they are doing, but we will not join in terms of calling ourselves normal. We are giving up our heritage, our very lives. We know how we suffer. Only you will know how we suffer, because we will tell only you how we suffer." As a physician, I am bothered by this, because I deal with the suffering of human beings.

Pomeroy. I am not speaking facetiously, but I think

it would be best to say that all homosexuals are sick, that all heterosexuals are sick, that the population is sick. Let us get rid of this term and look at people as people. I have heard psychiatrists perfectly soberly say that 95 percent of all the population in the U.S. is mentally ill.

Gagnon. The issue is that the society can afford it and the homosexuals cannot. The society can afford 4 percent of its population to be homosexuals and treat them as it wishes, as it does the 10 percent who are black. The homosexual pays a terrible price for the way the society runs itself. This is central to the daily life of the homosexual. Can he get a job? Can he do this? Can he do that? If we took the law off the books tomorrow, the homosexual would still pay a very high price.

Kameny. One of the major problems we have to face is the consequences of these attitudes, which are poisonous to the individual's self-esteem and self-confidence. The individual is brainwashed into a sense of his own inferiority, just as other minorities are. When we are told "You are sick," and "You are mentally ill," that finishes the destruction.

Pomeroy. If I were to base my judgment of homosexuals, both male and female, on the people who come to me in my practice, I think I would agree that they are sick, that they are upset in many, many different ways. But I had 20 years of research experience prior to this, in which I found literally hundreds of people who would never go to a therapist. They don't want help. They are happy homosexuals.

Socarides. I guess some of you feel that obligatory homosexuality should be proposed as a normal form of sexuality to all individuals. I think that this would be a disaster. A little boy might go next door to the Y and an older man might say to him, "Look, this is normal, my son. Just join me in this." If you sell this bill of goods to the nation, you are doing irreparable harm, and there will be a tremendous backlash against the homosexual.

Fox. I went through the English school system, which everybody knows is a homosexual system in the very fullest sense. Speaking as an obligatory heterosexual on behalf of myself and the other 90 percent, we went through it, we enjoyed it, we came out the other end, and we are fine. Some people have strayed about somewhere in the middle. This notion, therefore, that if you catch somebody and tell him that homosexuality is normal and practice it with him, he is necessarily going to get stuck in it, is absolutely nonsense. And I cite my three daughters as evidence.

Socarides. The only place to get the material that will tell us the truth about what the homosexual suffers is in-depth analysis. Sociologists, anthropologists, even psychologists do not tell us what is going on in the basic psyche of the homosexual. I believe we should change the laws. I believe that homosexuals have been persecuted. The homosexual must be seen as a full-fledged citizen in a free society and must be given all the rights and prerogatives that all other citizens enjoy, neither more nor less. I think, however, that we must do one other thing. It must be declared that homosexuality is a form of emotional illness, which can be treated, that these people can be helped.

Kameny. With that, you will surely destroy us.

Four Lives in the Gay World

The personal experiences related below are those of a male homosexual, a lesbian and a girl who calls herself bisexual, and a former homosexual who has undergone extensive psychotherapy. In otherwise candid interviews with Time *correspondents, all four requested that they be identified by pseudonyms.*

Charles Eliott, 40, owns a successful business in Los Angeles. In the den of his $60,000 house he has a bronze profile of Abe Lincoln on the wall and a copy of *Playboy* on the coffee table. Wearing faded chinos and a button-down Oxford shirt, he looks far more subdued than the average Hollywood male; he might be the happily married coach of a college basketball team —and a thoroughgoing heterosexual. In fact, his male lover for the past three months has been a 21-year-old college student. He says: "I live in a completely gay world. My lawyer is gay, my doctor is gay, my dentist is gay, my banker is gay. The only person who is not gay is my housekeeper, and sometimes I wonder how he puts up with us."

Eliott has never been to an analyst; introspection is not his forte. Why did he become homosexual? "Well, my mother was an alcoholic; my brother and I ate alone every night. I was the person who always went to the circus with the chauffeur. But I wouldn't say I was exactly sad as a child; I was rather outward-going." He went to prep school at Hotchkiss, and on to Yale. There he discovered his homosexual tendencies.

Eliott returned home to Chicago to run the family business; to maintain his status in the community, he married. It lasted five months. After the divorce he married again, this time for two years: "She began to notice that I didn't enjoy sex, and that finally broke it up. I don't think she knows even today that I am a homosexual."

It took ten years to make Eliott give up his double life in Chicago for the uninhibited world of Los Angeles. He avoids the gay bars, instead throws catered parties around his pool. "I suppose most of my neighbors know," he says. "When you have 100 men over to your house for cocktails, people are going to suspect something. Now that I no longer try to cope with the straight world, I feel much happier."

"If Katie were a man, I would marry her and be faithful to her the rest of my life." So vows Rachel Porter, 21, who is slightly plump, wears her blond hair in a pert pixy cut, and works as a secretary in a Manhattan publishing firm. Rachel has been seeing Katie Burns, a tall, strikingly handsome private secretary in a large corporation, for three years now, and sharing an apartment with her for three months. Yet Rachel's feelings are mixed. "I don't really say to this day that I am a lesbian," she says. "I'm bisexual. My interests are definitely guys, and eventually I'd like to have a child or two, probably out of wedlock." Katie, by contrast, in the past three years has given up dates with men.

Rachel grew up in the large family of a plumber who was too poor to send her to college. "I probably wouldn't know that a good relationship was possible if it wasn't for my mother and father. I was pretty much of a loner, and to this day I do horrible things like going to the movies alone. I never had a crush on a girl;

I had an affair with a boy behind my parents' back when I was 18."

Rachel met Katie shortly after that affair ended. "Gradually there was definitely a growing feeling," she recalls. "When I realized it, I was *very* upset. I didn't want to be gay. When I first went to a psychologist, I thought, 'Gee, I'm such a creep!' I thought that being in love with a girl made me a boy. He told me that I most certainly was not a boy. I couldn't erase the fact that I loved another woman, but I began thinking that as long as I was a woman too, things couldn't be all that bad."

Rachel and Katie have both told their parents about their relationship. "Our mothers both said, 'You're my daughter and I love you anyway,'" says Rachel. They refuse to live an exclusively gay life and engage in tennis, horseback riding and softball games with a circle of many straight friends (who also know the nature of their relationship). Muses Rachel: "Do I see myself living with Katie the rest of my life? Off and on, yes. I will probably date, because it's nice to get involved with other people, but that's difficult to work out. I certainly don't think our relationship ought to be exclusive. All I know is that life ought to be loving."

What was it like to be gay? "There were peaks and valleys of despair," says Tom Kramer, 28, a tall New York City public relations man who was a practicing homosexual until 2½ years ago. "Throughout high school and college, I would try to put it out of my mind. I had sissified gestures, and when I was with people I would concentrate on not using them. I would constantly think they were talking about my homosexuality behind my back. In my homosexual contacts, I'd try to be surreptitious, not telling my name or what kind of work I did. When I read about somebody being a pervert, it was like a slap in the face—my God, that's what *I* am!"

Two years after college, and weighed down with feelings of hopelessness, Tom heard that therapy was possible for homosexuals and went into treatment with an analyst. His prognosis was good: unlike many homosexuals, he desperately wanted to change. Twice a week for two years he discussed his past: the disciplinarian father who said Tom should have got straight A's when he got only A-minuses; the mother who made Tom her favorite. Gradually, Tom says, "I learned that my homosexuality was a way of handling anxiety. Some men drink. My way was homosexuality."

The process went slowly. Strengthened by insights gained in treatment, at one point Tom finally brought himself to kiss a girl good night—and became so terrified that he "cruised" on the way home for a homosexual partner. Two and a half years ago, however, he had his last male assignation, and several months later he "met a wonderful girl. We dated steadily. We had an affair. It was the first time I had had actual intercourse, and it was the happiest moment of my life." Six months ago, he and the girl were married.

Tom is still in analysis, attempting to cope with problems stemming from the same fears that led to his homosexuality. But he is self-confident about sex. "Women arouse me now," he says. "It's a total reversal." He has discussed his therapy with homosexual friends and urged them to attempt the same thing —so far without success. Ironically, though he is no longer attracted to them sexually, Tom says: "I like men better now than I did before. I'm no longer afraid of them."

Queer-Baiting for Faith, Fun, and Profit

David Brudnoy

From *The Alternative* (February, 1973), 8–12. Reprinted with permission, *The Alternative* Magazine, Bloomington, Indiana, copyright 1973.

David Brudnoy is a TV commentator, film critic of National Review, *a free-lance writer and lecturer, and a newspaper columnist. His most recent publication is* The Conservative Alternative *(1973).*

"Then the Lord rained on Sodom and Gomorrah brimstone and fire from out of heaven; and He overthrew those cities and all the valley and all the inhabitants of the cities." Thus did God deal with the Sodomites, who had come to Lot's house demanding that he surrender his two visitors, who turned out to be disguised angels. "Where are the men who came to you tonight? Bring them out to us, that we may know them," said the lecherous men of Sodom. But "Lot went out the door to the men, shut the door after him and said, 'I beg you, my brothers, do not act so wickedly. Behold, I have two daughters who have not known man; let me bring them out to you, and do to them as you please; only do nothing to these men, for they have come under the shelter of my roof.' "

From this story in Genesis 19 it is obvious that homosexuality was a serious offense in Biblical times. And as Women's Liberationists might point out, the Sodom story also makes apparent the abysmal devaluation of women in the ethics of the ancient Hebrews. Lot valued the dignity of his male guests more highly than that of his female children. When the men of Sodom were entrapped by God's plainclothesmen, the rain of fire commenced. While the episode in Sodom is the earliest account of the entrapment of homosexuals, and the remarks in Genesis the first explicit condemnation of homosexuality, that occasion was not the last of either. The town itself, however, gave its name to the generic term used in the West to describe most forms of homosexual activity, and some types of other sex activity: sodomy.

When we reflect on the tolerance granted to sexual heterodoxy in many eastern lands— among the Arabs, the ancient Chinese, the medieval Japanese, and others—we recognize that it is primarily in western societies that homosexuality is considered a major problem.

God in His wisdom added other warnings to

the rather plain lesson in Genesis. In Leviticus 18:22-23, for instance, He said: "You shall not lie with a man as with a woman; it is an abomination. If a man lies with a male as with a woman, both of them have committed an abomination; they shall be put to death, their blood is upon them." Judges 1:22-30 has a similar message. I Kings 22:46 tells how Jehosaphat took the rest of the Sodomites out of the land; II Kings 23:7 again talks of the Sodomites. Romans 1:27 teaches that God punished men who left "the natural use of the woman, burned in their lust one toward another." Paul's epistle to the Corinthians (I, 6:9) says: "Know ye not that the unrighteous shall not inherit the kingdom of God? Be not deceived: neither fornicators, nor idolaters, nor adulterers, nor effeminates, nor abusers of themselves with mankind. . . ." Paul's epistle to Timothy (1:10) refers to "them that defile themselves with mankind. . . ."

God says nothing about female homosexuality. Woman is thought fit to be offered to Lot's neighbors, but unsuited to be considered in this regard; so says the Bible by omission and implication. How very much like the God of the Bible was Queen Victoria, who, when shown an anti-homosexuality bill prepared in Parliament containing a provision mentioning lesbians, refused to believe that such people existed. And so, like many other Christian nations, Britain emulated the Bible and proscribed only male homosexuality.

The Roman Catholic Church until the late Middle Ages opposed homosexuality not only (or even primarily) because it was abnormal or unnatural, but also because it satisfied carnal lust and yielded bodily pleasure. The Church fathers condemned sexual pleasure, glorifying the ascetic ideal derived from Platonism, which had crept into Christianity via Saint Paul. They glorified the activities of those mountain and desert hermits such as Saint Simon Stylites, who utterly refused to see any woman, even his pleading, wailing mother. Simon was a hero, not incidentally because he avoided *all* sex.

" 'Tis better to marry than to burn," said Paul, who thought remaining pure was even better. Pursuit of the ascetic ideal, which resulted in misogyny, might conceivably have led to an acceptance of homosexuality as a convenient, if unworthy, alternative—but it did not. By the tenth century, woman's subjection as a chattel-slave was virtually complete; and even when the notions of courtly, chivalric love took their place in western Christianity, it was not a breakthrough for women, who found their pedestals rather cold and not very much fun, or for homosexuals, who were still anathema.

The European Middle Ages were in many ways far less grim than the designation "Dark Ages" would have us believe, but the standard picture of those years as unenlightened derives at least partly from fact. As a symbol of darkness, the concept of witchcraft, and as a phenomenon, the Inquisition, give adequate testimony to that picture. Witches were supposed to have a characteristic passion for carnality, that is, for sex not aiming at procreation but at pleasure. The Devil, with whom witches satisfied their cravings by rather torrid copulation, was thought to have a forked penis for penetration at once vaginally and anally.

During the centuries of witch-hunting, the Church agglutinated the two notions of religious deviance and sexual offense; heresy and homosexuality became one and the same. During the Middle Ages, writes Edward Westermark in his *Origin and Development of the Moral Ideal*, "heretics were accused of unnatural vice (homosexuality) as a matter of course. . . . In medieval laws sodomy was also repeatedly mentioned together with heresy, and the punishment was the same for both." In thirteenth-century Spain, the penalty for homosexuality was castration and execution by stoning. In 1479, Ferdinand and Isabella, those noted humanitarian rulers of Castile and Aragon, the patrons of Columbus and the expellers of the Jews from Spain, changed that to "burning alive and confiscation." Earlier, Pope Nicholas V had empowered the Inquisition to deal with homosexuality and in 1451 it was made the subject of a special inquest. Twelve homosexuals were burnt in that year alone. Thus, the Spanish Inquisition found the time and energy to burn homosexuals as well as religious heretics.

By 1640, homosexuals in Portugal were by

statute treated like heretics; their punishment was "relaxation" (burning) or "scourging" (flogging), and the galleys. As late as 1723, a homosexual in Lisbon was scourged and sentenced to ten years as a galley slave. In Valencia, homosexuals were regularly given up to the flames, although homosexual priests, oddly enough, were treated more leniently than laymen. In Spain from 1780 to 1820, one hundred homosexuals came before the Valencia Tribunal.

English-speaking nations also neatly connected heresy and homosexuality through a single word used for both: buggery. The word is derived from the medieval Latin *Bugarus* and *Bulgarus*, meaning a Bulgarian, because the Bulgarians were considered religiously heretical. To be stigmatized as a heretic or bugger in fourteenth-century England was to be cast out of society. The sin of heresy eclipsed all contradictory, personal characteristics, just as the teachings of God and the Church eclipsed all contradictory empirical observations. To be a heretic meant to worship the devil; to be a witch meant to sleep with the devil; and to be a bugger meant—well, the inference is clear.

The case is often made for active homosexuality among the ancients. But the argument from history is tricky, and no clear-cut conclusions can easily be drawn. Evidently, homosexual *feelings* were considered acceptable and apparently, the Greeks and Romans did practice homosexuality to some degree. But the *laws* were often harsh, homosexual acts often specifically proscribed. As we all know, the gap between law and practice is frequently wide. Herodotus (I, 135) tells us that "the Persians, taught by the Greeks, learned to sleep with boys." Atheneus (XIII, 81) says: "Sophocles loved boys, as Euripides loved women." Plutarch writes in the *Life of Lycurgus:* "Their lovers and favorers, too, had a share in the young boy's honor or disgrace. One was fined by the magistrates because the lad he loved cried out effeminately as he was fighting." It still remains, however, a matter of academic controversy as to just how much homosexuality was tolerated in Greece and Rome, although the record is less ambiguous for various times and places in the East.

Make of all this what we will; we cannot accurately determine much about anti-homosexuality by studying the ancients. The Judeo-Christian experiences offer much more in the way of solid evidence. The Bible explicitly condemned homosexuality; the Jews condemned it in practice; the Christians followed the Jews. I am unqualified to make *ex cathedra* pronouncements about the underlying causes for anti-homosexual attitudes. But I would hazard a guess and suggest, with the libertarian Theodore Schroeder (1864–1953), that Judeo-Christian sex-suppression may result from unresolved sexual cravings, and that erotic hallucinations which produce fear and shame and modesty are historically most often tamed by rigorous suppression of eroticism. According to this hypothesis, the results of such sex-suppression have been the Churchmen's celibacy, the traditional prohibitions against birth control (which enables people to enjoy sex without procreating), and the medieval hysteria about sexual unorthodoxy, among others.

The medieval attitude, which, as Thomas Szasz points out in *The Manufacture of Madness,* made homosexuality a twin of witchcraft, lasted up to the twentieth century in western countries. As short a time ago as 1895, Oscar Wilde was ruined. Wilde's *De Profundis,* an extended love letter to his "Bosie," Lord Alfred Douglass, shows how the most civilized western nation, traditionally most tolerant of dissenters, dealt with the unfortunate pederast Wilde. We might also look into the varied career of the late Senator Joseph McCarthy, who, among his unfortunate activities, traded on the public fear of sexual deviation by hinting at links between queerness and Redness. Since the common feeling as late as the 1950s in this country was that homosexuals were totally wicked, the association of sexual and political deviation came easily.

And it works in reverse. If Communists are the modern secular incarnations of the Devil, then they too are without redeeming features; they too must be completely bad; they must be homosexuals. Furthermore, it works from still another side, the Communist side. In Red nations today, the two most heinous crimes, punished with almost equal ferocity, are political deviation and homosexuality.

Nothing gets closer to the heart of American society's problem of accommodating tradition to radical innovation, and nothing unnerves Middle America more—or more thoroughly stimulates the imagination of the so-called New Left—than things sexual. Those in the "middle" can grin and bear a Black Power movement, or put up with an Indian seizure of Alcatraz, or even contemplate the consequences of eighteen-year-olds voting. But an assault on traditional, sexual values is intolerable. The championing of Women's Liberation and Gay Liberation by leftists is but a manifestation of their own judgment that many of the sexual aspects of our culture are in need of re-evaluation, that precisely such an evaluation will be violently resisted by non-leftists, and that therefore there is much political capital to be gained by exploiting such movements.

Most Americans have only so much compassion and only so much ability to understand those perceived to be radically different. Not enough, for instance, to seriously accept the homosexuals' demands for complete equality—not only under law, but in attitudes as well. The Left, alone among Americans as a sociopolitical "type," has shown that an improved attitude toward homosexuals is possible for non-gays. To my knowledge, the Socialist Workers' party is the only American non-homosexual political group to declare its sympathy with the goals of Gay Liberation. Of course, some on the Left are like those mentioned in Merle Miller's famous *New York Times Magazine* article in 1970, those for whom a "faggot is that homosexual gentleman who's just left the room." Nevertheless, the major stumbling-blocks to homosexual liberation come not from the Left, but from conservatives and liberals.

In fact, the rejection of homosexuals is currently expressed through a set of twin attitudes: from the conservatives, hostility; and from the liberals, condescending "tolerance."

Vehement essays in the magazines, pamphlets, and newsletters of the extreme Right, of course,

reflect the most uncompromising and relentlessly antagonistic attitudes toward the "morally degenerate" homosexuals. However, these opinions represent a mentality alien to responsible conservatism. Such material is a Left-liberal caricature of the Right and those of the responsible Right disdain it.

More disturbing are the articles or asides which touch on sex matters from this point of view in the better conservative journals. I recollect, as an instance, an article a few years ago by Will Herberg in the most respected popular conservative journal, *National Review;* though *National Review* did publish early in 1972, to its great credit, a quite humane article on a homosexual lounge at Columbia University by the young novelist, D. Keith Mano. Unfortunately, the article by Dr. Herberg speaks, I believe, more for the conservative position today than does Mr. Mano's.

Briefly stated, Dr. Herberg's "Case for Heterosexuality" was this: 1) "Homosexuality (is) a perversion in the individual . . . and a source of corruption in society." 2) The Bible condemns homosexuality as "aberrant," instructing Dr. Herberg that if a man is "homosexual, he is deviant, he is 'sick,' he is pathological." 3) "Natural Law" proclaims the family to be the "basic cell of society" and heterosexuality the "normative structure of being." 4) History shows that the Greeks did not approve of it. 5) Freud, "the most telling witness," called homosexuality a "perversion." 6) Although the author "does not want to heap abuse upon the homosexual, who is often more to be pitied than blamed, or to reproach him for his aberrancy," he does just that, lapsing into the *ad personam* mode: "pathological, deviant, sickness, sin, vice, perversion" are words he employs while not heaping abuse. 7) The author wants no criminal sanctions against adult homosexual acts, but he lures us into the shadowy world of homosexual seducers of minors, for whom he craves punishment. 8) Homosexuality must "constitute an impediment to certain kinds of employment," because homosexuals are "undesirable" in certain fields. (9 His scorn is reserved for the "homosexual who flaunts his perversion and even makes it into a badge of distinction." To deserve Dr. Herberg's "sympathy and help," the homosexual must "recognize his own abnormality as a sickness, albeit incurable" (sic).

The other approach, condescending tolerance, differs specifically from Herberg's in stressing the idea of "sickness" almost to the exclusion of other aspects. Once considered the most heinous of crimes, homosexuality, as Dr. Szasz imaginatively points out, is now considered a form of mental illness by American psychiatric opinion, which is the brainchild of the liberal mentality. I exempt from that generalization Sigmund Freud and some of his followers.

Freud referred to the *"unhonored* title of perversion," not "unhonorable," meaning perhaps that he doubted the value judgment of those who despised homosexuality. In his famous "Letter to an American Mother" (April, 1935), Freud noted that "homosexuality is nothing to be ashamed of, no vice, no degradation, it cannot be classified as an illness. . . . It is a great injustice to persecute homosexuality and a crime and cruelty too." Freud's most explicit remark on homosexuality is reported in Joseph Wortis' book, *Fragments of an Analysis with Freud:* "No psychoanalyst has ever claimed," Freud is quoted as saying, "that homosexuals cannot be perfectly decent people. Psychoanalysis does not undertake to judge people in any case. I don't understand . . . how you can concern yourself with such purely conventional problems, what is a neurosis and what is not a neurosis, what is pathological or not pathological—all mere words—fights about words."

Freud's view has not predominated in American psychiatric circles, however; here, the dominant view is that homosexuality is a disease to be treated and cured. For instance, among the most knowledgeable and humane of liberal psychologists was Robert Lindner, who wrote in *Must You Conform?:* "Homosexuality is a form of rebellion against society [which Lindner in other areas heartily approved, calling it "creative protest, productive revolt"] which can be treated and should be treated and hence eradicated." Dr. Lindner saw the sex-repression of contemporary American society as the fruit of

centuries of such repression, and he recognized that "our society's attitude toward sex is a travesty on human nature; inhibiting and repressing all forms of natural sexual appetites." But homosexuality, the late Dr. Lindner told us accurately, is widely detested, not a happy part of our culture; so it must be considered a disease and eradicated accordingly.

Long ago, Dante's *Divine Comedy* placed inverts in the most scorching part of Hell. And Andre Gide, in *Corydon* (1911), reminded us that homosexuals have often been victims, but few have been martyrs, because most recant under fire. Then Albert Ellis, one of the most fashionable of all psychoanalysts practicing today, takes a leaf from Dante and confirms Gide by writing in his *American Sexual Tragedy* that there is nothing wrong with homosexuality as long as it is not exclusive homosexuality. "It is clear that an exclusive homosexual is neurotically afraid of heterosexuality, or is fearfully fixated on a homosexual level of behavior, or is obsessed with the idea of homosexuality, or is compulsively attached to homosexual activity, or is otherwise neurotically (or perhaps psychotically) homosexual." In other words, one may like it, but to be stuck on it is "abnormal or deviant." He does say the same thing about "exclusive heterosexuality" and reminds us of the inanity of statutory prohibitions against sodomy. And he tells us with considerable feeling that, when solicited by other males, many men will physically beat their homosexual petitioners because "the assailants are . . . unwilling to face, and so emotionally disturbed by, their own underlying homosexual tendencies." Ellis' insistence on defining "sick" as exclusivity and "healthy" as bi-sexuality might give us pause.

Fundamentally, the modern psychiatric therapist confuses the social role of "disease" and the medical definition of the word. Here again, Dr. Szasz is a most helpful guide to understanding. It is the psychiatrist's purpose in life to practice therapy, to correct, to treat. And so homosexuality becomes a "mental disease," the new twin of witchcraft (in Schroeder's term), and no more real than witchcraft because both exist in the mind of the believer and not in the object of study. The overriding tendency of modern psychiatry, its constant critic Szasz shows, is to brand as sick that which is merely unconventional. Thus, the question of whether or not homosexuality is an illness is in part a pseudo-problem. Clearly it is not a disease like diabetes—diagnosable, with visible physical symptoms, and treatable. And just as clearly it is not a "mental illness," in the sense in which we should use the term. It is, in relation to what is considered normal, simply a "deviation."

To be stigmatized as a heretic or bugger in the fourteenth century was to be cast out of society. At present, to be so stigmatized is to be thrown out of society and, were it up to those doing the name-calling, into the clutches of the $50-an-hour headshrinker. Homosexuals are a group of medically stigmatized and socially disparaged individuals; to call them mentally ill is to hide that fact, and to give people an opportunity for smug, condescending tolerance.

As Dr. Szasz writes: "So long as men can denounce each other as mentally sick (homosexual, addicted, insane, and so fourth)—so that the madman can always be considered the Other, never the Self—mental illness will remain an easily exploitable concept, and Coercive Psychiatry a flourishing institution." In legal courts today, instead of sentencing a homosexual to prison, a humane, liberal judge will often let the homosexual go, on condition that he seek psychiatric "help."

One might consult Dr. Karl Menninger's *The Vital Balance* in addition to Szasz's book. Menninger, widely recognized as the most liberal and progressive modern psychiatrist, sees homosexuality as a symptom of illness which *must* be treated. A homosexual who fails to realize that he is "sick," writes Dr. Menninger, is only "rationalizing." In his "Introduction to The Wolfenden Report," Dr. Menninger even writes that "prostitution and homosexuality rank high in the kingdom of evils." Of this, "there is no question."

In sum, psychiatric opinion about homosexuals is not a strictly scientific proposition, but a social prejudice masquerading as medicine. It is

as if homosexuality were equivalent to measles, and measles the same as leprosy, and leprosy identical to murder. Certainly there are homosexuals who think they are sick. And it is their right, perhaps their obligation to themselves, to see a psychiatrist if *they* believe they are sick. But most homosexuals do not think that, though our liberals would have us believe it is so because the homosexuals cannot recognize their own illness. It reminds me of Dr. Benjamin Rush, the father of American psychiatry. Jefferson's friend Rush felt that Negroes were suffering from congenital leprosy, and with time, treatment, and luck, they would get back to their "natural whiteness." How little things change among psychiatrists. And how little things change in the minds of authoritarians: The National Socialists had their final solution to the Jewish Problem—the ovens; the modern totalitarians of psychiatry have their final solution to the homosexual matter:—enforced therapy.

As Szasz insists, the homosexual is the model psychiatric scapegoat. Abby Mann exaggerates, but nevertheless makes a telling point: "It's easier to be accepted by our society as a murderer than as a homosexual." Our society dreads homosexuality with the same intensity as the theological societies of old dreaded heresy and witchcraft. Homosexuality is considered a crime by many moderns and a disease by most. There is scant chance of escape. The laws of all but five states prohibit homosexual behavior in much the same way as the laws of fifteenth-century Spain prohibited the practice of the Jewish faith. The results are analogous: in Spain, Jews practiced secretly (the Judaizers) and kept their faith; in America, homosexuals "practice" homosexuality, the laws notwithstanding.

Even the Negro is better off. Victimized in the past, and sometimes now, the Negro is today recognized as a fully human being with an unconditional "right" to his brown skin. The homosexual, however, has neither this status nor the right to his sexual proclivities and practices; he is a defective object, a man "afflicted" with a disease to which, as Szasz puts it, he has no more right than the heterosexual has to being cursed with the Black Plague. He, like the Jew in anti-Semitic medieval Europe, is denied recognition as a human being in his authentic identity and selfhood—and for the same reasons: each undermines the beliefs and values of the dominant group.

The homosexual is blackmail-prone, hence "unsuitable" for certain positions. Furthermore, he is in hot water if he tries to emigrate to America. By virtue of a 1967 decision of the Warren Supreme Court, a homosexual applicant for citizenship may be excluded by the government because, as the Court reminds us in citing the Chinese Exclusion Case of 1889, the "Congress has plenary power to make rules for the admission of aliens and to exclude those who possess those characteristics which Congress has forbidden." Previously, the Court and Congress expressed their biases against colored peoples, anarchists, and the like. Yesterday's coolie immigrant is today's homosexual seeking entry into this country. In the specific case under discussion, that of Michael Clive Boutilier in 1967, psychiatric evidence was required in court, and the psychiatrist felt no duty to protect his subject's privacy. The state's interest took precedence. So Mr. Boutilier, a Canadian resident in the United States from 1955, who applied for citizenship in 1963, and whose record showed a sodomy arrest in New York in 1959, was banished.

The Boutilier precedent stands at the high court level although various recent lower court rulings are reopening the matter. A person acknowledged as a homosexual, in any case, can at present be denied citizenship. Were Congress to pass a statute barring from immigration persons afflicted with the mental disease called "Witchcraft," we would be vastly amused. But the mental disease called homosexuality, the mental disease created by liberal psychiatry, is today's witchcraft, and the flames have been replaced by compulsory servitude on the couch or in a mental hospital. God tested the men of Sodom and sent two angels in the form of attractive men. And Uncle Sam tests his people too, in similar ways. God, knowing nothing of modern psychiatry, smote the Sodomites. Uncle

Sam is a lay analyst, however, and so his punishment is liberal and humane: compulsory submission to treatment.

When New York's Governor Nelson Rockefeller advocated the enforced mental hospitalization of drug addicts, and both former Justice Abe Fortas and Justice William O. Douglas suggested the same, might we not worry about the day when some zealous liberal will suggest the same for homosexuals? So long as the concept of the "psychopathic personality" is afloat—so long as the 1189 psychiatrists who responded to Ralph Ginzburg's questionnaire in 1964, for his *Fact* magazine, and, without so much as five-minutes' consultation with the Senator from Arizona, branded Barry Goldwater a psychopathic personality, are considered other than unethical quacks—just so long will the liberal mentality have at its disposal a tool to use against their sick homosexual brethren.

To say, as some do, that many homosexuals have risen high in science, government, the arts, live good lives, and so forth, is irrelevant. Spanish Jews were expelled in 1492 though they had risen high in Spain. German Jews were exterminated in the hundreds of thousands, although they were a vital part of the German people. Negroes have lived blameless lives—and been lynched. It is fruitless to observe that the homosexual population is by and large decent, even beneficial to America, so long as the device of the shrill cry "Mental Illness!" is still in working order. Scapegoats do not suffer because they have committed evil acts, but because they are seen as "enemies within." As Sartre put it: "The homosexual must remain an object, a flower, an insect, an inhabitant of ancient Sodom or the planet Uranus, an automaton that hops about in the limelight, anything you like except my fellowman, except my image, except myself. For a choice must be made: If every man is all of man, this black sheep must be only a pebble or must be *me*."

Dr. Szasz writes: "It is nothing less than obscene to talk about the homosexual as a sick person whom we are trying to help so long as, by treating him as a defective thing, we demonstrate through our actions that what we want him to be is useful, rather than annoying, an *object for us*, and that what we will not tolerate is his wanting to be an authentic *person for himself*." The brilliant psychoanalyst-sociologist Ernest van den Haag asserts: "Prohibition of homosexuality is not needed to protect society. . . . I do not believe that homosexuality as such can or need be treated." The pain and sorrow many homosexuals endure is more a reflection of societal sexism, and the double-life that many gay people live out of fear of ostracism or punishment, than a function of "unnaturalness."

When our legislators and judges discriminate against homosexuals in the belief that they are applying the findings of modern liberal psychiatric science to the making of policy for the nation's welfare, they make a monstrous blunder. This is a kind of medical witch-hunting, doctors persecuting patients for their alleged medical heresies. Quotes Szasz: "Thus has the physician replaced the priest, and the patient the witch, in the drama of society's perpetual struggle to destroy precisely those human characteristics that, by differentiating men from their fellows, identify persons as individuals rather than as members of the herd."

To argue as some conservatives do is to be needlessly harsh to a group hounded for millennia, and to "conserve" only the depressing and repressing legacies of our less happy past. To argue in the rhetoric of liberal psychiatry is equally grim, in fact more so, since the liberal argument is the dominant mode of expressing antihomosexuality.

Even the manifestations of our currently most fashionable cultural form, the film, contribute to this morass. The homosexual is served ill by such travesties as *The Boys in the Band* and *Some of My Best Friends Are. . .* , which may be a homosexual's nightmare, and, for the liberal pursuer of the "in" and the "kicky," a dream come true; liberals can find so much to *sympathize* with. A way of ridiculing the homosexual, such condescension is also a way to rake in the bread, to profit indirectly from homosexuality's unpleasant situation in society. In his movie *The Damned*, Visconti equates Nazism

with Sexual Decadence, arm-chair Krafft-Ebing, nothing more. Many other films suggest the same thing. And we find similar approaches in other media. Examples are many, but one might do. In *Esquire* magazine, Malcolm Muggeridge, that journal's urbane, witty book reviewer, managed some time ago to rub Oscar Wilde's nose again in his mess. Wilde was described by Muggeridge, wholly gratuitously, as "this overweight, overblown, over-articulate sodomite," after which the article went further down-hill.

Those opposed to queer-baiting can take little comfort from the 1971 court ruling in Dallas that said Texas's sodomy statute is an unconstitutional invasion of privacy. The ruling left a loophole, which Dallas and Houston quickly filled, as will other cities, allowing the cities themselves to prohibit sodomy in public places, and to define "public place" so broadly that only the bedroom is out of bounds.

Nor, after looking at copies of the major homosexual journal, the Los Angeles *Advocate*, can one feel very sanguine about the manifestations of the so-called "new homosexuality." Despite its virtues, the *Advocate* confirms much of what antihomosexual thinkers say, providing its own bludgeon with which queer-baiters can whonk homosexuals on the head. Gay Liberation, as the *Advocate* pictures it, manifests here and there the whining, self-pitying, special-pleading of inferior creatures begging to be thought equal, on the one hand, and, on the other, represents nothing so much as blatant, teasing, titillating cutesyness and sex come-ons, which will repel those who already think homosexuals are evil, and will evoke a chord of condescending sympathy from those who think homosexuals are sick.

Blatancy for blatancy's sake will lead to little but more repression and tension. If the American homosexual revolution succeeds, it must do so without rending the fabric of the dominant heterosexual society. It must get the aid of those conservatives who mean what they preach about liberty and individual freedom, about doing one's own thing. It must get the help of those liberals who talk endlessly about opening society, about bringing about conditions wherein true equality is possible. But it will not gain this support if it ties itself to ludicrous forms of outrageous behavior. Nor will it gain such support if it marries itself to a host of destructive movements such as the residue of the Bomber Left.

Gide wrote in *Corydon:* "In homosexuality as in heterosexuality, there are all shades and degrees, from Platonic love to lust, from self-denial to sadism, from healthy joy to moroseness, from natural development to all the refinements of vice." And if Gide's words represent special pleading from an acknowledged homosexual, so be it. The conservative must speak and act for himself, the radical for himself, the Chicano and Negro and Indian for himself, the woman for herself; so must the homosexual, aided by those heterosexuals of all persuasions politically, who do not feel threatened by the subject and can see the injustice of what is yet done to gays in our country. Honest, non-aggressive pride in being what one is has usually been considered admirable, in theory at least, by American conservatives and liberals alike; and it is part of the rhetoric of the radical Left, perhaps the most honest part of that rhetoric.

Many questions remain as to homosexuality's "cause"; these I cannot deal with for lack of special training. And what of the law? Should the laws in a decent society interfere with private, consentual sexual activities in private by mature individuals? Does society gain or lose more when such sex laws as do exist in most of our fifty states are relaxed? Where do the individual's rights and those of society conflict, and how do we resolve those conflicts?

By writing this article in *The Alternative*, with its particular readership of largely younger people—conservatives, liberals, libertarians—I have hoped to bring some measure of understanding to an abysmal historical and contemporary situation, and to encourage some discussion and perhaps some degree of improvement in the attitudes of my fellows. I offer here no answers to many pertinent questions, having intended primarily to show how harshly homosexuals have been treated in western history and how awkward is their lot today. The question of what to do now is hardly irrelevant to those who are concerned with the enhancement of individual liberties within the context of a viable, cohesive society. That question may perhaps be peripheral just now, given the more pressing plights of our society at present. Peripheral, possibly, but certainly not lacking in importance.

11 BLACK RIGHTS— STILL RIGHT ON?

The Failure of Black Separatism

Bayard Rustin

From *Harper's Magazine* (January, 1970), 25–32, 34. Copyright © 1971, by Minneapolis Star and Tribune Co. Reprinted by permission of the author.

Bayard Rustin is a civil rights activist, field secretary of the Congress for Racial Equality, organizer of the March on Washington (1963), and is Executive Director of A. Philip Randolph Institute. Besides being the author of Down the Line *(1971), he has contributed many articles on civil rights.*

We are living in an age of revolution—or so they tell us. The children of the affluent classes pay homage to their parents' values by rejecting them; this, they say, is a youth revolution. The discussion and display of sexuality increases—actors disrobe on stage, young women very nearly do on the street—and so we are in the midst of a sexual revolution. Tastes in music and clothing change, and each new fashion too is revolutionary. With every new social phenomenon now being dubbed a "revolution," the term has in fact become nothing more than a slogan which serves to take our minds off an unpleasant reality. For if we were not careful, we might easily forget that there is a conservative in the White House, that our country is racially polarized as never before, and that the forces of liberalism are in disarray. Whatever there is of revolution today, in any meaningful sense of the term, is coming from the Right.

But we are also told—and with far greater urgency and frequency—that there is a black revolution. If by revolution we mean a radical escalation of black aspirations and demands, this is surely the case. There is a new assertion of pride in the Negro race and its cultural heritage, and although the past summer was marked by the lack of any major disruptions, there is among blacks a tendency more pronounced than at any time in Negro history to engage in violence and the rhetoric of violence. Yet if we look closely at the situation of Negroes today, we find that there has been not the least revolutionary reallocation of political or economic power. There is, to be sure, an increase in the number of black elected officials throughout the United States and particularly in the South, but this has largely been the result of the 1965 Voting Rights Act, which was passed before the "revolution" reached its height and the renewal of which the present Administration has not advocated with any noticeable enthusiasm. Some reallocation of political power has indeed taken place since the Presidential election of 1964, but generally its beneficiaries have been the Republicans and the anti-Negro forces. Nor does this particular trend show much sign of abating. Nixon's attempt to reverse the liberal direction of the Supreme Court has just begun. Moreover, in the 1970 Senate elections, 25 of the 34 seats to be contested were originally won by the Democrats in the great liberal surge of 1964, when the political picture was quite different from that of today. And if the Democrats only break even in 1970, the Republicans will control the Senate for the first time since 1954. A major defeat would leave the Democrats weaker than they have been at any time since the conservative days of the 1920s.

There has been, it is true, some moderate improvement in the economic condition of Negroes, but by no stretch of the imagination could it be called revolutionary. According to Andrew Brimmer of the Federal Reserve System, the median family income of Negroes between 1965 and 1967 rose from 54 percent to 59 percent of that for white families. Much of that gain reflected a decrease in the rate of Negro unemployment. But between February and June of 1969, Negro unemployment rose again by 1.3 percent and should continue to rise as Nixon presses his crusade against inflation. The Council of Economic Advisers reports that in the past eight years the federal government has spent $10.3 billion on metropolitan problems while it has spent $39.9 billion on agriculture, not to mention, of course, $507.2 billion for defense. In the area of housing, for instance, New York City needs at the present time as many new subsidized apartments—780,000—as the federal housing program has constructed *nationally* in its entire thirty-four years. The appropriations for model cities, rent supplements, the Job Corps, the Neighborhood Youth Corps, and other programs have been drastically reduced, and the Office of Economic Opportunity is being transformed into a research agency. Nixon's welfare and revenue-sharing proposals, in addition to being economically stringent, so that they will have little or no effect on the condition of the Northern urban poor, are politically and philosophically conservative.

Any appearance that we are in the grip of a black revolution, then, is deceptive. The problem is not whether black aspirations are outpacing America's ability to respond but whether they have outpaced her willingness to do so. Lately it has been taken almost as axiomatic that with every increase in Negro demands, there must be a corresponding intensification of white resistance. This proposition implies that only black complacency can prevent racial polarization, that any political action by Negroes must of necessity produce a reaction. But such a notion ignores entirely the question of what *kind* of political action, guided by what *kind* of political strategy. One can almost assert as a law of American politics that if Negroes engage in violence as a tactic they will be met with repression, that if they follow a strategy of racial separatism they will be isolated, and that if they engage in antidemocratic activity, out of the deluded wish to skirt the democratic process, they will provoke a reaction. To the misguided, violence, separatism, and minority ultimatums may seem revolutionary, but in reality they issue only from the desperate strivings of the impotent. Certainly such tactics are not designed to enhance the achievement of progressive social change. Recent American political history has proved this point time and again with brutal clarity.

The irony of the revolutionary rhetoric uttered in behalf of Negroes is that it has helped in fact to promote conservatism. On the other hand, of course, the reverse is also true: the failure of America to respond to the demands of Negroes has fostered in the minds of the latter a sense of futility and has thus seemed to legitimize a strategy of withdrawal and violence. Other things have been operating as well. The fifteen years since *Brown* v. *Topeka* have been for Negroes a period of enormous dislocation. The modernization of farming in the South forced hundreds of thousands of Negroes to migrate to the North where they were confronted by a second technological affliction, automation. Without jobs, living in cities equipped to serve neither their material nor spiritual needs, these modern-day immigrants responded to their brutal new world with despair and hostility. The civil rights movement created an even more fundamental social dislocation, for it destroyed not simply the legal structure of segregation but also the psychological assumptions of racism. Young Negroes who matured during this period witnessed a basic challenge to the system of values and social relations which had presumed the inferiority of the Negro. They have totally rejected this system, but in doing so have often substituted for it an exaggerated and distorted perception both of themselves and of the society. As if to obliterate the trace of racial shame that might be lurking in their souls they have embraced racial chauvinism. And as if in reply to past exclusions (and often in response to present insecurities), they have created their own pattern of exclusiveness.

The various frustrations and upheavals experienced recently by the Negro community accounts in large part for the present political orientation of some of its most vocal members: seeing their immediate self-interest more in the terms of emotional release than in those of economic and political advancement. One is supposed to think black, dress black, eat black, and buy black without reference to the question of what such a program actually contributes to advancing the cause of social justice. Since real victories are thought to be unattainable, issues become important in so far as they can provide symbolic victories. Dramatic confrontations are staged which serve as outlets for radical energy but which in no way further the achievement of radical social goals. So that, for instance, members of the black community are mobilized to pursue the "victory" of halting construction of a state office building in Harlem, even though it is hard to see what actual economic or social benefit will be conferred on the impoverished residents of that community by their success in doing so.

Such actions constitute a politics of escape rooted in hopelessness and further reinforced by government inaction. Deracinated liberals may romanticize this politics, nihilistic New Leftists may imitate it, but it is ordinary Negroes who will be the victims of its powerlessness to work any genuine change in their condition.

The call for Black Power is now over three years old, yet to this day no one knows what Black Power is supposed to mean and therefore how its proponents are to unite and rally behind it. If one is a member of CORE, Black Power posits the need for a separate black economy based upon traditional forms of capitalist relations. For SNCC the term refers to a politically united black community. US would emphasize the unity of black culture, while the Black Panthers wish to impose upon black nationalism the philosophies of Marx, Lenin, Stalin, and Chairman Mao. Nor do these exhaust all the possible shades and gradations of meaning. If there is one common theme uniting the various demands for Black Power, it is simply that blacks must be guided in their actions by a consciousness of themselves as a separate race.

Now, philosophies of racial solidarity have never been unduly concerned with the realities that operate outside the category of race. The adherents of those philosophies are generally romantics, steeped in the traditions of their own particular clans and preoccupied with the simple biological verities of blood and racial survival. Almost invariably their rallying cry is racial self-determination, and they tend to ignore those aspects of the material world which point up divisions within the racially defined group.

But the world of black Americans is full of divisions. Only the most supine of optimists would dream of building a political movement without reference to them. Indeed, nothing better illustrates the existence of such divisions within the black community than the fact that the separatists themselves represent a distinct minority among Negroes. No reliable poll has ever identified more than 15 percent of Negroes as separatists; usually the percentage is a good deal lower. Nor, as I have already indicated, are the separatists unified among themselves, the differences among them at times being so intense as to lead to violent conflict. The notion of the undifferentiated black community is the intellectual creation of both whites—liberals as well as racists to whom all Negroes are the same —and of certain small groups of blacks who illegitimately claim to speak for the majority.

The fact is that like every other racial or ethnic group in America, Negroes are divided by age, class, and geography. Young Negroes are at least as hostile toward their elders as white New Leftists are toward their liberal parents. They are in addition separated by vast gaps in experience, Northern from Southern, urban from rural. And even more profound are the disparities in wealth among them. In contrast to the white community, where the spread of income has in recent years remained unchanged or has narrowed slightly, economic differentials among blacks have increased. In 1965, for example, the wealthiest 5 percent of white and non-white families each received 15.5 percent of the total income in their respective communities. In 1967, however, the percentage of white income received by the top 5 percent of white families had dropped to 14.9 percent while among non-whites the share of income of the top 5 percent of the families had risen to 17.5 percent. This trend probably reflects the new opportunities which are available to black professionals in industry, government, and academia, but have not touched the condition of lower-class and lower-middle-class Negroes.

To Negroes for whom race is the major criterion, however, divisions by wealth and status are irrelevant. Consider, for instance, the proposals for black economic advancement put forth by the various groups of black nationalists. These proposals are all remarkably similar. For regardless of one's particular persuasion—whether a revolutionary or a cultural nationalist or an unabashed black capitalist—once one confines one's analysis to the ghetto, no proposal can extend beyond a strategy for ghetto development and black enterprise. This explains in part the recent popularity of black capitalism and, to a lesser degree, black cooperatives: once both the economic strategy and goal are defined in terms of black self-determination, there is simply not much else available in the way of ideas.

There are other reasons for the popularity of black capitalism, reasons having to do with material and psychological self-interest. E. Franklin Frazier has written that Negro business is "a social myth" first formulated toward the end of the nineteenth century when the legal structure of segregation was established and

Negro hopes for equality destroyed. History has often shown us that oppression can sometimes lead to a rationalization of the unjust conditions on the part of the oppressed and following on this, to an opportunistic competition among them for whatever meager advantages are available. This is, according to Frazier, exactly what happened among American Negroes. The myth of Negro business was created and tied to a belief in the possibility of a separate Negro economy. "Of course," wrote Frazier, "behind the idea of the separate Negro economy is the hope of the black bourgeoisie that they will have the monopoly of the Negro market." He added that they also desire "a privileged status within the isolated Negro community."

Nor are certain Negro businessmen the only ones who stand to gain from a black economy protected by the tariff of separatism. There are also those among the white upper class for whom such an arrangement is at least as beneficial. In the first place, self-help projects for the ghetto, of which black capitalism is but one variety, are inexpensive. They involve no large-scale redistribution of resources, no "inflationary" government expenditures, and above all, no responsibility on the part of whites. These same upper-class whites may have been major exploiters of black workers in the past, they may have been responsible for policies which helped to create ghetto poverty, but now, under the new dispensations of black separatism, they are being asked to do little more by way of reparation than provide a bit of seed money for a few small ghetto enterprises.

Moreover, a separate black economy appears to offer hope for what Roy Innis has called "a new social contract." According to Innis's theory, the black community is essentially a colony ruled by outsiders; there can be no peace between the colony and the "mother country" until the former is ruled by some of its own. When the colony is finally "liberated" in this way, all conflicts can be resolved through negotiation between the black ruling class and the white ruling class. Any difficulties within the black community, that is, would become the responsibility of the black elite. But since self-determination in the ghetto, necessitating as it would the expansion of a propertied black middle class, offers the advantage of social stability, such difficulties would be minimal. How could many whites fail to grasp the obvious benefit to themselves in a program that promises social peace without the social inconvenience of integration and especially without the burden of a huge expenditure of money? Even if one were to accept the colonial analogy—and it is in many ways an uninformed and extremely foolish one—the strategy implied by it is fatuous and unworkable. Most of the experiments in black capitalism thus far have been total failures. As, given the odds, they should continue to be. For one thing, small businesses owned and run by blacks will, exactly like their white counterparts, suffer a high rate of failure. In fact, they will face even greater problems than white small businesses because they will be operating in predominantly low income areas where the clientele will be poor, the crime rate and taxes high, and the cost of land, labor, and insurance expensive. They will have to charge higher prices than the large chains, a circumstance against which "Buy Black" campaigns will in the long or even the short run have little force. On the other hand, to create large-scale black industry in the ghetto is unthinkable. The capital is not available, and even if it were, there is no vacant land. In Los Angeles, for example, the area in which four-fifths of the Negroes and Mexican-Americans live contains only 0.5 percent of all the vacant land in the city, and the problem is similar elsewhere. Overcrowding is severe enough in the ghetto without building up any industry there.

Another current axiom of black self-determination is the necessity for community control. Questions of ideology aside, black community control is as futile a program as black capitalism. Assuming that there were a cohesive, clearly identifiable black community (which, judging by the factionalism in neighborhoods like Harlem and Ocean Hill-Brownsville, is a far from safe assumption), and assuming that the community were empowered to control the ghetto, it would still find itself without the money needed in order to be socially creative. The ghetto would

still be faced with the same poverty, deteriorated housing, unemployment, terrible health services, and inferior schools—and this time perhaps with the exacerbation of their being entailed in local struggles for power. Furthermore, the control would ultimately be illusory and would do no more than provide psychological comfort to those who exercise it. For in a complex technological society there is no such thing as an autonomous community within a large metropolitan area. Neighborhoods, particularly poor neighborhoods, will remain dependent upon outside suppliers for manufactured goods, transportation, utilities, and other services. There is, for instance, unemployment in the ghetto while the vast majority of new jobs are being created in the suburbs. If black people are to have access to those jobs, there must be a metropolitan transportation system that can carry them to the suburbs cheaply and quickly. Control over the ghetto cannot build such a system nor can it provide jobs within the ghetto.

The truth of the matter is that community control as an idea is provincial and as a program is extremely conservative. It appears radical to some people because it has become the demand around which the frustrations of the Negro community have coalesced. In terms of its capacity to deal with the social and economic causes of black unrest, however, its potential is strikingly limited. The call for community control in fact represents an adjustment to inequality rather than a protest against it. Fundamentally, it is a demand for a change in the racial composition of the personnel who administer community institutions: that is, for schools, institutions of public and social service, and political organizations—as all of these are presently constituted—to be put into the keeping of a new class of black officials. Thus in a very real sense, the notion of community control bespeaks a fervent hope that the poverty-stricken ghetto, once thought to be a social problem crying for rectification, might now be deemed a social good worthy of acceptance. Hosea Williams of SCLC, speaking once of community control, unwittingly revealed the way in which passionate self-assertion can be a mask for accommodation:

"I'm now at the position Booker T. Washington was about sixty or seventy years ago," Williams said. "I say to my brothers, 'Cast down your buckets where you are'—and that means there in the slums and ghettos."

There is indeed profound truth in the observation that people who seek social change will, in the absence of real substantive victories, often seize upon stylistic substitutes as an outlet for their frustrations.

A case in point is the relation of Negroes to the trade-union movement. In their study *The Black Worker*, published in 1930, Sterling D. Spero and Abram L. Harris describe the resistance to separatism among economically satisfied workers during the heyday of Marcus Garvey:

> . . . *spokesmen of the Garvey movement went among the faction-torn workers preaching the doctrine of race consciousness. Despite the fact the Garveyism won a following everywhere at this time, the Negro longshoremen of Philadelphia were deaf to its pleas, for their labor movement had won them industrial equality such as colored workers nowhere else in the industry enjoyed.*

The inverse relation of black separatism and antiunionism to the quality of employment available to Negroes holds true today also. In the May 1969 UAW elections, for example, black candidates won the presidency and vice-presidency of a number of locals. Some of the most interesting election victories were won at the Chrysler Eldon Gear and Axle Local 961 and at Dodge #3 in Hamtramek where the separatist Eldon Revolutionary Union Movement (ELRUM) and Dodge Revolutionary Union Movement (DRUM) have been active. At both locals the DRUM and ELRUM candidates were handily defeated by black trade unionists who campaigned on a program of militant integrationism and economic justice.

This is not to say that there are not problems within the unions which have given impetus to the separatist movements. There are, but in the past decade unions have taken significant steps toward eliminating discrimination against Negroes. As Peter Henle, the chief economist of the Bureau of Labor Statistics, has observed:

> *Action has been taken to eliminate barriers to admission, abolish discrimination in hiring practices, and negotiate changes in seniority arrangements which had been blocking Negro advances to higher-paying jobs. At the same time, unions have given strong support to governmental efforts in this same direction.*

Certainly a good deal is left to be done in this regard, but just as certainly the only effective pressure on the unions is that which can be brought by blacks pressing for a greater role *within* the trade-union movement. Not only is separatism not a feasible program, but its major effect will be to injure black workers economically by undermining the strength of their union. It is here that ignorance of the economic dimension of racial injustice is most dangerous, for a Negro, whether he be labeled a moderate or a militant, has but two alternatives open to him. If he defines the problem as primarily one of race, he will inevitably find himself the ally of the white capitalist against the white worker. But if, though always conscious of the play of racial discrimination, he defines the problem as one of poverty, he will be aligned with the white worker against management. If he chooses the former alternative, he will become no more than a pawn in the game of divide-and-conquer played by, and for the benefit of, management —the result of which will hardly be self-determination but rather the depression of wages for all workers. This path was followed by the "moderate" Booker T. Washington who disliked unions because they were "founded on a sort of enmity to the man by whom he [the Negro] is employed" and by the "militant" Marcus Garvey who wrote:

> *It seems strange and a paradox, but the only convenient friend the Negro worker or laborer has in America at the present*

time is the white capitalist. The capitalist being selfish—seeking only the largest profit out of labor—is willing and glad to use Negro labor wherever possible on a scale reasonably below the standard union wage . . . but if the Negro unionizes himself to the level of the white worker, the choice and preference of employment is given to the white worker.

And it is being followed today by CORE, which collaborated with the National Right to Work Committee in setting up the Black Workers Alliance.

If the Negro chooses to follow the path of interracial alliances on the basis of class, as almost two million have done today, he can achieve a certain degree of economic dignity, which in turn offers a genuine, if not the only, opportunity for self-determination. It was this course which A. Philip Randolph chose in his long struggle to build a Negro-labor alliance, and it was also chosen by the black sanitation workers of Memphis, Tennessee, and the black hospital workers of Charleston, South Carolina.

Not that I mean here to exonerate the unions of their responsibility for discrimination. Nevertheless, it is essential to deal with the situation of the black worker in terms of American economic reality. And as long as the structure of this reality is determined by the competing institutions of capital and labor (or government and labor, as in the growing public sector of the economy), Negroes must place themselves on one side or the other. The idea of racial self-determination within this context is a delusion.

There are, to be sure, sources beyond that of economic discrimination for black separatism within the unions. DRUM, ELRUM, and similar groups are composed primarily of young Negroes who, like whites their age, are not as loyal to the union as are older members, and who are also affected by the new militancy which is now pervasive among black youth generally. This militancy has today found its most potent form of expression on campus, particularly in the predominantly white universities outside of the South. The confusion which the movement for programs in black studies has created on campus almost defies description. The extremes in absurdity were reached this past academic year at Cornell, where, on the one hand, enraged black students were demanding a program in black studies which included Course 300c, Physical Education: "Theory and practice in the use of small arms and hand combat. Discussion sessions in the proper use of force," and where, on the other hand, a masochistic and pusillanimous university president placed his airplane at the disposal of two black students so that they could go to New York City and purchase, with $2,000 in university funds, some bongo drums for Malcolm X Day. The foolishness of the students was surpassed only by the public-relations manipulativeness of the president.

The real tragedy of the dispute over black studies is that whatever truly creative opportunities such a program could offer have been either ignored or destroyed. There is, first, the opportunity for a vastly expanded scholastic inquiry into the contribution of Negroes to the American experience. The history of the black man in America has been scandalously distorted in the past, and as a field of study it has been relegated to a second-class status, isolated from the main themes of American history and omitted in the historical education of American youth. Yet now black students are preparing to repeat the errors of their white predecessors. They are proposing to study black history in isolation from the mainstream of American history; they are demanding separate black-studies programs that will not be open to whites, who could benefit at least as much as they from a knowledge of Negro history; and they hope to permit only blacks (and perhaps some whites who toe the line) to teach in these programs. Unwittingly they are conceding what racist whites all along have professed to believe, namely that black history is irrelevant to American history.

In other ways black students have displayed contempt for black studies as an academic discipline. Many of them, in fact, view black studies as not an academic subject at all, but as an ideological and political one. They propose to use black-studies programs to create a mythologized history and a system of assertive ideas that will facilitate the political mobilization of the black community. In addition, they hope to educate a cadre of activists whose present training is conceived of as a preparation for organizational work in the ghetto. The Cornell students made this very clear when they defined the purpose of black-studies programs as enabling "black people to use the knowledge gained in the classroom and the community to formulate new ideologies and philosophies which will contribute to the development of the black nation."

Thus faculty members will be chosen on the basis of race, ideological purity, and political commitment—not academic competence. Under such conditions, few qualified black professors will want to teach in black-studies programs, not simply because their academic freedom will be curtailed by their obligation to adhere to the revolutionary "line" of the moment, but because their professional status will be threatened by their association with programs of such inferior quality.

Black students are also forsaking the opportunity to get an education. They appear to be giving little thought to the problem of teaching or learning those technical skills that all students must acquire if they are to be effective in their careers. We have here simply another example of the pursuit of symbolic victory where a real victory seems too difficult to achieve. It is easier for a student to alter his behavior and appearance than to improve the quality of his mind. If engineering requires too much concentration, then why not a course in soul music? If Plato is both "irrelevant" and difficult, the student can read Malcolm X instead. Class will be a soothing, comfortable experience, somewhat like watching television. Moreover, one's image will be militant and, therefore, acceptable by current college standards. Yet one will have learned nothing, and the fragile sense of security developed in the protective environment of college will be cracked when exposed to the reality of competition in the world.

Nelson Taylor, a young Negro graduate of Morehouse College, recently observed that many black students "feel it is useless to try to compete. In order to avoid this competition, they build themselves a little cave to hide in." This "little cave," he added, is black studies. Furthermore, black students are encouraged in this escapism by guilt-ridden New Leftists and faculty members who despise themselves and their advantaged lives and enjoy seeing young Negroes reject "white middle class values" and disrupt the university. They are encouraged by university administrators who prefer political accommodation to an effort at serious education. But beyond the momentary titillation some may experience from being the center of attention, it is difficult to see how Negroes can in the end benefit from being patronized and manipulated in this way. Ultimately, their only permanent satisfaction can come from the certainty that they have acquired the technical and intellectual skills that will enable them upon graduation to perform significant jobs competently and with confidence. If they fail to acquire these skills, their frustration will persist and find expression in ever-newer forms of antisocial and self-destructive behavior.

The conflict over black studies, as over other issues, raises the question of the function in general served by black protest today. Some black demands, such as that for a larger university enrollment of minority students, are entirely legitimate; but the major purpose of the protest through which these demands are pressed would seem to be not so much to pursue an end as to establish in the minds of the protesters, as well as in the minds of whites, the reality of their rebellion. Protest, therefore, becomes an end in itself and not a means toward social change. In this sense, the black rebellion is an enormously *expressive* phenomenon which is releasing the pent-up resentments of generations of oppressed Negroes. But expressiveness that is oblivious to political reality and not structured by instrumental goals is mere bombast.

James Forman's *Black Manifesto*, for instance, provides a nearly perfect sample of this kind of bombast combined with positive delusions of grandeur. "We shall liberate all the people in the U.S.," the introduction to the *Manifesto* declares, "and we will be instrumental in the liberation of colored people the world around. . . . We are the most humane people within the U.S. . . . Racism in the U.S. is so pervasive in the mentality of whites that only an armed, well-disciplined, black-controlled government can insure the stamping out of racism in this country. . . . We say think in terms of the total control of the U.S."

One might never imagine from reading the *Manifesto* that Forman's organization, the National Black Economic Development Conference, is politically powerless, or that the institution it has chosen for assault is not the government or the corporations, but the church. Indeed, the exaggeration of language in the *Black Manifesto* is directly proportional to the isolation and impotence of those who drafted it. And their actual achievements provide an accurate measure of their strength. Three billion dollars in reparations was demanded—and $20,000 received. More important, the effect of this demand upon the Protestant churches has been to precipitate among them a conservative reaction against the activities of the liberal national denominations and the National Council of Churches. Forman's failure, of course, was to be expected: the only effect of an attack upon so organizationally diffuse and nonpolitical an institution as the church can be the deflection of pressure away from the society's major political and economic institutions and consequently, the weakening of the black movement for equality.[1]

The possibility that his *Manifesto* might have exactly the opposite effect from that intended, however, was clearly not a problem to Forman, because the demands he was making upon white people were more moral than political or economic. His concern was to purge white guilt far more than to seek social justice for Negroes. It was in part for this reason that he chose to direct his attack at the church, which, as the institutional embodiment of our society's religious pretensions, is vulnerable to moral condemnation.

Yet there is something corrupting in the wholesale release of aggressive moral energy, particularly when it is in response to the demand for reparations for blacks. The difficulty is not only that as a purely racial demand its effect must be to isolate blacks from the white poor with whom they have common economic interests. The call for three billion dollars in reparations demeans the integrity of blacks and exploits the self-demeaning guilt of whites. It is insulting to Negroes to offer them reparations for past generations of suffering, as if the balance of an irreparable past could be set straight with a handout. In a recent poll, *Newsweek* reported that "today's proud Negroes, by an overwhelming 84 to 10 percent, reject the idea of preferential treatment in hiring or college admissions in reparation for past injustices." There are few controversial issues that can call forth greater uniformity of opinion than this in the Negro community.

I also question both the efficacy and the social utility of an attack that impels the attacked to applaud and debase themselves. I am not certain whether or not self-flagellation can have a beneficial effect on the sinner (I tend to doubt that it can), but I am absolutely certain it can never produce anything politically creative. It will not improve the lot of the unemployed and the ill-housed. On the other hand, it could well happen that the guilty party, in order to lighten his uncomfortable moral burden, will finally begin to rationalize his sins and affirm them as virtues. And by such a process, today's ally can become tomorrow's enemy. Lasting political alliances are not built on the shifting sands of moral suasion.

On his part, the breast-beating white makes the same error as the Negro who swears that "black is beautiful." Both are seeking refuge in

---

[1] Forman is not the only militant today who fancies that his essentially reformist program is revolutionary. Eldridge Cleaver has written that capitalists regard the Black Panther Breakfast for Children program (which the Panthers claim feeds 10,000 children) "as a threat, as cutting into the goods that are under their control." He also noted that it "liberates" black children from going to school hungry each morning. I wonder if he would also find public-school lunch programs liberating.

psychological solutions to social questions. And both are reluctant to confront the real cause of racial injustice, which is not bad attitudes but bad social conditions. The Negro creates a new psychology to avoid the reality of social stagnation, and the white—be he ever so liberal—professes his guilt precisely so as to create the illusion of social change, all the while preserving his economic advantages.

The response of guilt and pity to social problems is by no means new. It is, in fact, as old as man's capacity to rationalize or his reluctance to make real sacrifices for his fellow man. Two hundred years ago, Samuel Johnson, in an exchange with Boswell, analyzed the phenomenon of sentimentality:

> Boswell: "I have often blamed myself, Sir, for not feeling for others, as sensibly as many say they do."
> Johnson: "Sir, don't be duped by them any more. You will find these very feeling people are not very ready to do you good. They pay you by feeling."

Today, payments from the rich to the poor take the form of "Giving a Damn" or some other kind of moral philanthropy. At the same time, of course, some of those who so passionately "Give a Damn" are likely to argue that full employment is inflationary.

We are living in a time of great social confusion—not only about the strategies we must adopt but about the very goals these strategies are to bring us to. Only recently whites and Negroes of good will were pretty much in agreement that racial and economic justice required an end to segregation and the expansion of the role of the federal government. Now it is a mark of "advancement," not only among "progressive" whites but among the black militants as well, to believe that integration is passé. Unintentionally (or as the Marxists used to say, objectively), they are lending aid and comfort to traditional segregationists like Senators Eastland and Thurmond. Another "advanced" idea is the notion that government has gotten too big and

that what is needed to make the society more humane and livable is an enormous new move toward local participation and decentralization. One cannot question the value or importance of democratic participation in the government, but just as misplaced sympathy for Negroes is being put to use by segregationists, the liberal preoccupation with localism is serving the cause of conservatism. Two years of liberal encomiums to decentralization have intellectually legitimized the concept, if not the name, of states' rights and have set the stage for the widespread acceptance of Nixon's "New Federalism."

The new anti-integrationism and localism may have been motivated by sincere moral conviction, but hardly by intelligent political thinking. It should be obvious that what is needed today more than ever is a political strategy that offers the real possibility of economically uplifting millions of impoverished individuals, black and white. Such a strategy must of necessity give low priority to the various forms of economic and psychological experimentation that I have discussed, which at best deal with issues peripheral to the central problem and at worst embody a frenetic escapism. These experiments are based on the assumption that the black community can be transformed from within when, in fact, any such transformation must depend on structural changes in the entire society. Negro poverty, for example, will not be eliminated in the absence of a total war on poverty. We need therefore, a new national economic polity. We also need new policies in housing, education, and health care which can deal with these problems as they relate to Negroes within the context of a national solution. A successful strategy, therefore, must rest upon an identification of those central institutions which, if altered sufficiently, would transform the social and economic relations in our society; and it must provide a politically viable means of achieving such an alteration.

Surely the church is not a central institution in this sense. Nor is Roy Innis's notion of dealing with the banking establishment a useful one. For the banks will find no extra profit—quite the contrary—in the kind of fundamental structural change in society that is required.[2]

Moreover, the recent flurry of excitement over the role of private industry in the slums seems to have subsided. A study done for the Urban Coalition has called the National Alliance of Businessmen's claim to have hired more than 100,000 hard-core unemployed a "phony numbers game." Normal hiring as the result of expansion or turnover was in some cases counted as recruitment. Where hard-core workers have been hired and trained, according to the study, "The primary motivation . . . is the need for new sources of workers in a tight labor market. If and when the need for workers slackens, so will industry's performance." This has already occurred. The *Wall Street Journal* reported in July of 1969 that the Ford Motor Company, once praised for its social commitment, was forced to trim back production earlier in the year and in the process "quietly closed its two inner-city hiring centers in Detroit and even laid off some of the former hard-cores it had only recently hired." There have been similar retrenchments by other large companies as the result of a slackening in economic growth, grumblings from stockholders, and the realization by corporate executives that altruism does not make for high profits. Yet even if private industry were fully committed to attack the problem of unemployment, it is not in an ideal position to do so. Private enterprise, for example, accounted for only one out of every ten new jobs created in the economy between 1950 and 1960. Most of the remainder were created as the result of expansion of public employment.

While the church, private enterprise, and other institutions can, if properly motivated, play an important role, finally it is the trade-union movement and the Democratic party which offer the greatest leverage to the black

struggle. The serious objective of Negroes must be to strengthen and liberalize these. The trade-union movement is essential to the black struggle because it is the only institution in the society capable of organizing the working poor, so many of whom are Negroes. It is only through an organized movement that these workers, who are now condemned to the margin of the economy, can achieve a measure of dignity and economic security. I must confess I find it difficult to understand the prejudice against the labor movement currently fashionable among so many liberals. These people, somehow for reasons of their own, seem to believe that white workers are affluent members of the Establishment (a rather questionable belief, to put it mildly, especially when held by people earning over $25,000 a year) and are now trying to keep the Negroes down. The only grain of truth here is that there *is* competition between black and white workers which derives from a scarcity of jobs and resources. But rather than propose an expansion of those resources, our stylish liberals underwrite that competition by endorsing the myth that the unions are the worst enemy of the Negro.

In fact it is the program of the labor movement that represents a genuine means for reducing racial competition and hostility. Not out of a greater tenderness of feeling for black suffering —but that is just the point. Unions organize workers on the basis of common economic interests, not by virtue of racial affinity. Labor's legislative program for full employment, housing, urban reconstruction, tax reform, improved health care, and expanded educational opportunities is designed specifically to aid both whites and blacks in the lower- and lower-middle classes where the potential for racial polarization is most severe. And only a program of this kind can deal simultaneously and creatively with the interrelated problems of black rage and white fear. It does not placate black rage at the expense of whites, thereby increasing white fear and political reaction. Nor does it exploit white fear by repressing blacks. Either of these courses strengthens the demagogues among both races

[2] Innis's demand that the white banks deposit $6 billion in black banks as reparations for past injustices should meet with even less success than Forman's ill-fated enterprise. At least Forman had the benefit of the white churchman's guilt, an emotion not known to be popular among bankers.

who prey upon frustration and racial antago-
nism. Both of them help to strengthen conservative forces—the forces that stand to benefit from
the fact that hostility between black and white
workers keeps them from uniting effectively
around issues of common economic interest.

President Nixon is in the White House today
largely because of this hostility; and the strategy
advocated by many liberals to build a "new
coalition" of the affluent, the young, and the
dispossessed is designed to keep him there. The
difficulty with this proposed new coalition is
not only that its constituents comprise a distinct
minority of the population, but that its affluent
and youthful members—regardless of the
momentary direction of their rhetoric—are
hardly the undisputed friends of the poor.
Recent Harris polls, in fact, have shown that
Nixon is most popular among the college educated and the young. Perhaps they were
attracted by his style or the minimal concessions
he has made on Vietnam, but certainly their
approval cannot be based upon his accomplishments in the areas of civil rights and economic
justice.

If the Republican ascendancy is to be but a
passing phenomenon, it must once more come
to be clearly understood among those who favor
social progress that the Democratic party is still
the only mass-based political organization in the
country with the potential to become a majority
movement for social change. And anything calling itself by the name of political activity must
be concerned with building precisely such a
majority movement. In addition, Negroes must
abandon once and for all the false assumption
that as 10 percent of the population they can by
themselves effect basic changes in the structure
of American life. They must, in other words,
accept the necessity of coalition politics. As a
result of our fascination with novelty and with
the "new" revolutionary forces that have

emerged in recent years, it seems to some the
height of conservatism to propose a strategy that
was effective in the past. Yet the political reality
is that without a coalition of Negroes and other
minorities with the trade-union movement and
with liberal groups, the shift of power to the
Right will persist and the democratic Left in
America will have to content itself with a well-
nigh permanent minority status.

The bitterness of many young Negroes today
has led them to be unsympathetic to a program
based on the principles of trade unionism and
electoral politics. Their protest represents a
refusal to accept the condition of inequality,
and in that sense it is part of the long, and I
think, magnificent black struggle for freedom.
But with no comprehensive strategy to replace
the one I have suggested, their protest, though
militant in rhetoric and intention may be reac-
tionary in effect.

The strategy I have outlined must stand or fall
by its capacity to achieve political and economic
results. It is not intended to provide some new
wave of intellectual excitement. It is not
intended to suggest a new style of life or a
means to personal salvation for disaffected
members of the middle class. Nor is either of
these the proper role of politics. My strategy is
not meant to appeal to the fears of threatened
whites, though it would calm those fears and
increase the likelihood that some day we shall
have a truly integrated society. It is not meant
to serve as an outlet for the terrible frustrations
of Negroes, though it would reduce those frustrations and point a way to dignity for an
oppressed people. It is simply a vehicle by which
the wealth of this nation can be redistributed
and some of its more grievous social problems
solved. This in itself would be quite enough to
be getting on with. In fact, if I may risk a slight
exaggeration, by normal standards of human
society I think it would constitute a revolution.

12 JUSTICE AND PRISONS— WHICH COMES FIRST?

Of Prisons, Asylums, and Other Decaying Institutions

David J. Rothman

From *The Public Interest*, No. 26 (Winter 1972), 3–17. Copyright © by National Affairs Inc., 1972. Reprinted by permission of the publisher and the author.

Professor Rothman is Professor of American History at Columbia University and is a specialist in social history.

Over the course of the past several decades, without clear theoretical justification or even a high degree of self-consciousness, we have been completing a revolution in the treatment of the insane, the criminal, the orphaned, the delinquent, and the poor. Whereas once we relied almost exclusively upon incarceration to treat or punish these classes of people, we now frame and administer many programs that maintain them within the community or at least remove them as quickly as possible from institutions. Policy makers in each of these areas interpret their own measures as specific responses to internal developments—an advance in drug therapy or a dissatisfaction with prevailing penitentiary conditions—not as part of a general anti-institutional movement. But such a movement exists, and it must be seen in a comprehensive way if it is ever to be understood.

The basic statistics are, themselves, most striking. Since 1955 the annual number of inmates in the nation's mental hospitals has been falling. New York state institutions, for example, held 93,000 patients in 1955; in 1966, their number dropped to 82,765, and in 1970 to 64,239. A similar decline has occurred in correctional institutions. In 1940, 131.7 prisoners per 100,000 of the population served time in federal or state penitentiaries; in 1965, the number fell to 109.6 per 100,000, and this without a concomitant drop in the number of crimes committed or criminals convicted. Dramatic changes have also affected the young. The orphan asylum has almost disappeared, and the juvenile correction center has also declined in use. As for the poor, the almshouse or traditional poorhouse is no longer a specter in their lives.

Obviously, no one would be foolish enough to predict that within the next 20 or 30 years incarcerating institutions will disappear. Some 400,000 adults and juveniles remain in correctional institutions, and a similar number fill mental hospitals. Nevertheless, when our current practices are viewed within historical perspective, the degree to which we have moved away from the incarcerative mode of coping with these social problems is clear enough. We are witnessing nothing less than the end of one era in social reform and the beginning of another.

THE MOVEMENT FOR INCARCERATION

Institutionalization of "problem people" in the United States originated in the opening decades of the nineteenth century. Prior to that, colonial communities, particularly the more settled ones along the seaboard, relied upon very different mechanisms of control. Their level of expectations was very low; they did not expect to eliminate poverty or to reform the criminal. Rather, the colonists devoted their energies to differentiating carefully between neighbor and stranger. Typically, they provided assistance to the resident within his household or that of a friend—and they banished the troublesome outsider. A neighbor's poverty was not suspect—clergymen, after all, preached regularly on the virtue of charity, making little effort to distinguish the worthy from the unworthy poor. (As one cleric put it, "What if God were to refuse his mercy to those of us who do not deserve it?") Local ne'er-do-wells were fined or whipped or shamed before their neighbors through such devices as the stocks. Outsiders on the other hand, whether honest and poor or petty criminals, were sent on their way as quickly as possible, often with a whipping to insure their continuing absence.

When these responses proved inadequate, as they often did—residents might not correct their ways or strangers might persist in returning—the community had recourse to the gallows. The frequency with which eighteenth-century magistrates sentenced offenders to capital punishment testified to the fragility of the system. But almost nowhere did the colonists incarcerate the deviant or the dependent. Jails held only prisoners awaiting trial, not those convicted of a crime; and the few towns that erected almshouses used them only in exceptional cases—for the sailor so ill that he could not be moved, or the resident so incapacitated that no neighbor would care for him.

Beginning in the 1820s the perspective on both poverty and crime underwent a major shift. The relatively passive attitudes of the eighteenth century gave way to a new, energetic program, as Americans became convinced that poverty and crime, as well as insanity and delinquency, could be eliminated from the New World. Crime, it was decided, did not reflect the innate depravity of man but the temptations at loose in the society. Insanity was not the work of the devil, but the product of a deleterious environment. Poverty was not inevitable, but rather reflected the inadequacies of existing social arrangements. These interpretations revealed not only an Enlightenment optimism about the perfectability of human nature, but a nagging fear that American society, with its unprecedented geographic and social mobility, was so open and fragmented that stability and cohesion could not be maintained unless reforms were instituted. An odd marriage of ideas occurred in the young republic. The optimism of an environmentalist doctrine joined a basic concern that American society was in a state of imbalance—though the majority were coping well enough, a minority seemed unable to confront the challenges of American life. The result was a widespread belief that insanity could be cured in the New World because its causes were rooted in a social order that encouraged limitless ambition and disrespect for traditional opinions and practices. The criminal, too, could be reformed, once he was removed from a setting in which gambling halls and dens of iniquity corrupted him. Poverty would also be eliminated as soon as the poor were taught to resist the temptations at loose in a free community.

Starting from these premises, reformers moved quickly and enthusiastically to a new program: the construction of asylums—new "environments"—for the deviant and dependent. Between 1820 and 1840 penitentiaries spread through the country, and the states constructed insane asylums. Concomitantly, they built orphan asylums, houses of refuge (for juvenile delinquents), and almshouses. The walls that surrounded these structures were intended not only to confine the deviant and dependent but also to exclude the community—for, in origin, incarceration was a semi-utopian venture. Superintendents aimed to establish a corruption-free environment which would compensate for the irregularities and temptations existing in the larger, more turbulent society. Thus the bywords of all Jacksonian institutions became order and routine, discipline and regularity, steady work and steady habits. The inmates would be provided with a new spiritual armor, so that upon release they would go forth shielded from temptations and corruptions.

MODELS OF REFORM

In fact, the initial organization of the asylums closely approximated the reformers' designs. The institutions consistently isolated the inmates from the community. Wardens sharply limited the number of letters and visits a prisoner could receive and prohibited the circulation of periodicals and newspapers. Insane asylum superintendents instructed relatives to remove the sick patient from the family and bring him to the institution as soon after the onset of the disease as possible, and then not to visit or to write him frequently. Many child-care institutions insisted that the parents abdicate all rights to their children.

The asylums' internal organization put a premium on bell-ringing punctuality and a precise routine. Regimentation became the standard style of prison life in the popular Auburn plan, where the inmates remained isolated in individual cells during the night and worked in congregate shops during the day. Convicts did not walk from place to place, but went in lock step, a curious American invention that combined a march and shuffle. A military precision marked other aspects of their lives. At the sound of a morning bell, keepers opened the cells, prisoners stepped onto the deck, lock-stepped into the yard, washed their pails and utensils, marched to breakfast, and then, when the bell rang, stood, and marched to the workshops where they remained till the next signal.

The new world set before the insane was similar in many respects. The essential ingredient in "moral treatment" was to bring discipline and regularity into chaotic lives without exciting frenetic reaction. In the well-ordered asylum, declared Issac Ray, a prominent nineteenth-century psychiatrist, "quiet, silence, regular routine, would take the place of restlessness, noise, and fitful activity." One of his colleagues noted that in the asylum "the hours for rising, dressing, and washing, for meals, labor, occupation, amusement . . . should be regulated by the most *perfect precision.*" This style reappeared in the first houses of refuge. One official boasted that "a month's stay in the company with boys accustomed to systematic discipline and obedience, with a sense that there is no escape from order and regularity, generally converts the most wayward into good pupils." And a visitor to a Long Island orphan asylum was struck by the military exercises that the children followed, ostensibly "as a useful means of forming habits of order." She added that it was supposed to be "beautiful to see them pray; for at the first tip of the whistle, they all dropped to their knees. . . . Everything moves by machinery."

Under these routines American asylums became world famous as models of progressive social reform. Tocqueville and Beaumont and a host of European visitors traveled here to examine our penitentiaries, and the verdicts were almost always favorable. Americans themselves were not reluctant to boast of the glories of their insane asylums or of their almshouses. The reformers' rhetoric and these accolades from distinguished visitors sanctioned the new program, and few contemporaries objected to it. On the contrary, incarceration became the first resort as psychiatrists rushed to put patients behind walls, and judges, with little hesitation, meted out long sentences for convicted criminals. Legislators kept commitment laws as simple as possible, reluctant to erect legal barriers between the insane and the asylum, or between the delinquent and the reformatory. With the promise of rehabilitation by incarceration so grand, safeguards were clearly irrelevant.

FROM REHABILITATION TO CUSTODY

Unfortunately, the promise turned out to be hollow, and by 1870 the asylums exhibited all their modern ills. They were overcrowded and in sad disrepair, without internal discipline, disorderly, enervating, monotonous, and cruel. Their preoccupation was with custody and security, not rehabilitation. And yet they lasted, maintaining through the nineteenth century their monopoly over corrections and treatment.

Both the failure and the persistence of the asylums had common causes. The environmental theories of the founders helped at once to promote and disguise the shift from rehabilitation to custody. Superintendent after superintendent succumbed to the notion that in administering a holding operation he was still promoting rehabilitation. The first proponents had so enthusiastically praised the benefits of incarceration that their successors could smugly assume that just keeping the inmates behind walls accomplished much good. Regardless of the degree of overcrowding, or the extent of corruption, or the absence of supervision, officials could still self-righteously declare that institutionalization was therapeutic.

Another critical element in both the asylums' failure and persistence was the ethnic and class composition of the inmates. By 1870, and increasingly thereafter, the lower classes and the immigrants filled the penitentiaries and mental hospitals. First it was the Irish, then the Eastern Europeans, and later the blacks. Incarceration thus became identified in the public mind as the particular fate of the outsider. To the middle and upper classes, the inmate was an outcast even before entering his ward or cell. Since institutionalization served marginal people, the conditions could be no worse than the inmates. In essence, the promise of reform had built up the asylums and the functionalism of custody perpetuated them.

THE NEW REFORM MOVEMENT

The Progressive era marked a dividing point in public policy, giving the initial thrust to new,

non-institutional programs. Change was uneven and selective, affecting some areas more quickly than others. Nevertheless, between 1890 and 1920 care and correction of the deviant and dependent began to shift away from incarceration. The changes were most popular and complete where citizens' suspicions and fears were least intense. The first caretaker institutions to decline in importance were orphan asylums, replaced by foster homes and liberalized adoption proceedings. Public and private benevolent societies that in the nineteenth century had devoted their funds to administering child-care institutions transformed themselves into placing-out and adoption agencies. Simultaneously, innovations in public welfare programs decreased reliance on the almshouse, at least for some groups. State aid that allowed widowed mothers to care for their dependent children at home was first enacted in Illinois in 1911 and then spread quickly through densely populated and industrial states. No longer would these women be dispatched to an almshouse and their dependents to an orphan asylum.

New Deal legislation furthered these trends. The Social Security Act of 1935 eliminated incarceration for other segments of the poor, keeping the aged and the able-bodied unemployed out of the almshouse. The law expressly prohibited federal grants to states to expand their almshouses, and refused to match state funds that went to the support of persons institutionalized. Incarceration had been the mainstay of public relief for over one hundred years, and the abolition of this policy was no mean feat.

In the first decades of the twentieth century, state mental hospitals also began to decline in importance. Between 1920 and 1940, outpatient facilities for the mentally ill—caring for the patient during the day and returning him home at night—opened in several metropolitan centers. In the post-World War II period the program grew increasingly popular, particularly after the passage of the Community Mental Health Act of 1963, under which the federal government matches state funds for constructing community mental health facilities. As a result, institutionalization in large state mental hospitals has steadily dropped, so that patients discharged now outnumber patients admitted. Indeed, the principles of anti-institutionalism are now so widely accepted that the mental health literature is beginning to focus on the administrative question of how best to convert custodial institutions into community outpatient centers.

Other types of custodial institutions are also gradually disappearing. It was the pride of Jacksonian reformers to construct asylums for retarded and defective children, and many of those structures lasted into this century. Physicians and administrators, however, are now eager to abandon this approach and to end the isolation of these children. They organize special public school curriculums that enable many of these youngsters to live at home; and where residential treatment is necessary, they design small structures in the community, not large, isolated ones in a country location.

In this same spirit, states are experimenting with incentives to encourage not just foster care, but adoption for orphaned and illegitimate children. Traditionally, the foster home received compensation for its effort but the adoptive one did not. Convinced that many foster families would prefer to adopt their child but cannot afford to give up the stipends they receive, officials are offering payments, based on need, to adopting parents as well. The motive is clear; the closer the surrogate family approximates the normal one, the less it resembles an institution, the better. In fact, the spread of contraceptive knowledge together with liberalization of the abortion laws makes it not unlikely that child asylums, and perhaps even adoption, will disappear within the next two decades.

THE DECLINE OF THE PRISON

Although prison walls still impose themselves massively upon the public eye, in this field too we have decreased our reliance upon incarceration. Correctional institutions have lost their nineteenth-century monopoly. Since 1961 the percentage of the population in prisons has declined annually. The most important procedure effecting this change is probation. In 1965, 53 percent of all offenders were out in the community under the periodic supervision of a probation officer. By 1975, according to the estimates of an advisory committee to the President's Commission on Law Enforcement and the Administration of Justice, the proportion will rise to 58 percent. The most dramatic increases have been among juvenile offenders. In 1965 only 18 percent of convicted delinquents served in correctional institutions, while 64 percent were on probation. Among adult offenders, 39 percent of those convicted of a crime were institutionalized, while 49 percent (including, to be sure, misdemeanants) were on probation.

The other major alternative to prolonged incarceration is parole, whereby a convict having completed some fraction of his sentence is discharged from prison and obliged to report regularly to a corrections officer. Although the idea of parole is not new—it was advocated by many prison experts as early as the 1870s—it has been extensively used only in the post-1930 period. Reliance on parole, it is true, varies enormously from state to state. In New Hampshire and Washington, practically every convict leaves the state prison before completing his formal sentence; in Oklahoma, Wyoming, and South Dakota, less than 20 percent of the inmates enjoy this privilege. Still, by 1965, 18 percent of all juvenile delinquents and 12 percent of adult offenders were on parole. Among all convicts serving in American prisons in 1964, fully 65 percent won release under this program.

Several states are also experimenting with new programs to decrease the distance between correction programs and the community. The publicity given these procedures to date outweighs their actual importance, but they all look to the same anti-institutional goal. One such effort is work release, whereby the offender leaves the prison in the morning, works at his job in the community, and then returns to confinement at night. One warden regards this innovation as "revolutionary, not evolutionary. It's going to change," he predicts, "about all of penology." For the moment, however, work release has been authorized in some 24 states and for the federal corrections systems. Important programs operate in Wisconsin, California, Minnesota, and North Carolina; in Wisconsin, for example, it affected 30 percent of the misdemeanants in 1956, and 48 percent in 1964. And, at present, some five percent of all federal offenders come under it. But the scope of work release is limited, typically not covering those convicted of crimes of violence or of a morals charge, or those believed to be part of an organized crime syndicate. Some preliminary evaluations also suggest that the arrangement is expensive and cumbersome to administer. Nevertheless, some states are trying to extend the program to cover felons, and they also report a significant drop in such incarceration-related costs as welfare payments to convicts' families.

LEGAL REFORM

These developments have stimulated and in turn been furthered by an important series of legal actions intended to reduce dependence on incarceration. The most notable advances have occurred in the field of juvenile detention. In the *Gault* decision (1967) the Supreme Court brought some of the protections of "due process" to the juvenile courts. While the requirements that the Court insisted upon were by no means negligible—notification of charges and the right to confront witnesses—it is not only for procedural reasons that the case stands out; for the *Gault* decision was premised upon a disillusionment with incarceration. Underlying the majority opinion, written by Justice Fortas, was the belief that the juvenile institution was totally inadequate to the job of reformation. As Justice Black insisted in a concurring opinion, "It is in all but name a penitentiary." And since the disposition of a juvenile case might well result in confining the offender to an essentially penal institution, the justices wanted the trial proceedings to protect the defendants' rights. A similar reason appeared in the Court's decision in the *Winship* case. In an earlier day, magistrates assumed that a reformatory would accomplish some good and were therefore content to incarcerate delinquents on the basis of the "pre-

ponderance of the evidence." Now, far less enthusiastic about these institutions, the Court ruled that juvenile convictions had to meet the standard of "beyond a reasonable doubt."

Public interest law firms and reform organizations have also launched major campaigns to extend legal protections to prison inmates and to reduce the disabilities convicts suffer after release. As a result of these efforts, lower courts have ruled that solitary confinement for juveniles violates their constitutional right against cruel and unusual punishment. They have also extended this reasoning to prohibit the use of "strip cells," in which the convict must crouch naked in a space so designed that he can neither stand nor sit down. Recent state penal codes have begun to expand convicts' procedural rights, and the courts, most notably and recently in the *Landman* decision, have also insisted on expanding the prerogatives and protection due the convict. In *Landman*, the federal district court forbade the Virginia state penitentiary system from any longer imposing a bread and water diet, from using chains or tape or tear gas except in an immediate emergency, from using physical force as a punishment; it also demanded minimum due process protections before a convict lost "good time" (that would shorten his sentence), or suffered any deprivation of his normal prison privileges (such as loss of exercise or communication with other inmates). Suits now pending are also contesting the constitutionality of prohibiting ex-convicts from obtaining trucker's or chauffer's licenses and the restrictions on parolees' rights of association and travel. Thus, one detects not only a closing of the gap between the legal rights of citizens and those of inmates, but the beginnings of a series of changes that will make the prison system as we know it increasingly unworkable.

Another major concern of these reformers is the liberalization of bail. One of their goals is to insure that bail itself will not be set excessively high, and that bonds are not difficult to obtain. But they are also experimenting with methods that eliminate bail altogether, allowing many of those awaiting trial to go free on their own recognizance. Since city detention centers and jails are filled with arrestees waiting their turns on crowded court calendars, this innovation would dramatically reduce the numbers incarcerated. One pilot project by the Vera Institute revealed that, in New York City, with careful field work the percentage of those arrested on minor offenses who can be sent home without bail is substantial, and only a few of them will fail to appear at trial (4.6 percent of some 37,000 cases). Moreover, these procedures saved the city some $2.5 million in police and court costs. With such results it is no wonder that the Institute is trying to expand the program to persons caught committing petty crimes, a step that would further decrease the numbers incarcerated and save additional funds.

AVOIDING NEW ILLUSIONS

Thus, over the past several decades public officials and private organizations have energetically and successfully attempted to reduce reliance upon incarceration. They have done so with considerable enthusiasm—one doesn't achieve sweeping reforms of this kind without enthusiasm. However, there is the danger that this enthusiasm could lead to exaggerated expectations and, eventually, public disillusionment.

One of the first tasks confronting the various proponents of anti-institutional measures is a clear and level-headed definition of expectations and purposes. In the Progressive era, when many of these plans were first devised, the reform rhetoric promised breathtaking success. Advocates shared not only a disgust with the custodial practices of large state institutions but a generally unqualified faith that the deviant and dependent, if left in the community under proper supervision, would quickly undergo rehabilitation. Incarcerating these classes, the reformers insisted, had the effect of confirming their antisocial impulses. Keeping them within society would break the pattern and promote normal behavior. But this is probably to promise too much. More important, it focuses attention on the wrong things. We do not yet know whether the anti-incarceration movement will be any more effective than the original proincarceration movement—equally idealistic and enthusiastic—in effecting "cures." But there are other and very powerful arguments in its favor.

To begin with, there is the fact that many of the institutions functioning today, particularly correctional ones, are simply a national scandal, a shame to the society. They brutalize the inmates, humiliate them, and educate them in the ways of crime. Moreover, an impressive sociological literature, exemplified in the writings of Erving Goffman and Gresham Sykes, convincingly demonstrates that these characteristics are inherent in institutions, which by their very nature are infantalizing or corrupting. Moreover, while incarceration does exclude the deviant from the community for a period of time, eventually he is released; so unless one is prepared to lock up the criminal and throw away the key, institutionalization does not offer permanent security. And while public opinion may be growing tougher on the offender, we have not yet reached, and in all likelihood we are not going to reach the point where life sentences for robbers, burglars, car thieves, and embezzlers will seem like an equitable solution.

Institutionalization is also incredibly expensive. To confine 201,220 criminals in state institutions in 1965 cost $384,980,648; to administer probation programs for slightly more than twice that number of people cost $60 million. Somehow, it would seem, the vast sums expended on institutionalization could be better spent.

THE LESSON OF ATTICA

But perhaps the most compelling reason for experimenting with anti-institutional programs is that the penitentiary has actually lost much, if not all, of its legitimacy in our society. It is not just academic students of criminal incarceration who despair of the penal system. Those in charge of the prisons, from wardens and corrections commissioners to state legislators, also share an incredibly high degree of self-doubt, ambivalence, dismay, and even guilt over prison operations. They are no longer secure in what they are doing. The depth and impact of these attitudes emerged with striking clarity and force in the recent events at Attica. Given the history of prison administration in this country, what is surprising and unusual about this revolt is not that it was suppressed harshly, but that several days were spent in negotiation. Attica was not our first prison riot; all through the 1920s and 1930s bloody revolts broke out, only to be repressed immediately, even at the cost of some hostages' lives. Why was Attica different? Why were negotiators flown in, an ad hoc committee formed, proposals and counterproposals exchanged? Why did this prison riot come to resemble so closely the student uprising and the university administration's response at Columbia in 1968?

The most obvious answer, that many hostages' lives were at stake, is altogether inadequate. It is a clear rule of prison guard life, one that is conveyed immediately to recruits, that guards are not ransomable. Should one or more of them be taken hostage, no bargain will be struck for their release. The maxim is not as coldhearted as one might first think. On the contrary, it assumes that once convicts understand that guards are not ransomable, they will have no reason—except for pure revenge—to take them as hostages. And, in fact, events have usually borne out the shrewdness of this calculation: For all the brutality of the prison system, guards have not often been the victims of the prisoners' anger or desperation. Then why did not officials in New York stand by this rule, move in quickly at Attica to regain control, and rationalize the entire operation as necessary to protect guards' lives everywhere?

The failure to act immediately and with confidence points directly to the prison's loss of legitimacy. Both the inmates and their keepers shared an attitude that Attica was in a fundamental way out of step with American society. Most of the convicts' demands were not obviously unreasonable in the light of public opinion today: better pay for their work, better communications with their families, rights to law books and counsel. Most citizens were probably surprised to learn that these privileges were not already established. Commissioner Oswald himself had promised Attica inmates just before the riot that these changes were long overdue and would soon be enacted. How could he then act with sure and fast resolve to repress harshly a revolt when many of its aims were conceded to be sensible and appropriate and long overdue? It is one thing to sacrifice guards' lives for a system that has a sense of its own purpose; it is quite another to sacrifice them when the system is full of self-doubts. So Oswald negotiated, brought in outsiders, and tried to bargain. In the end it did not work, perhaps because not enough time was allowed, perhaps because compromise is impossible in such a charged situation. The revolt was suppressed, with a rage and force that in part reflects the urge to obliterate the questions and the ambivalence. Still, from Attica we have learned that we cannot administer penal institutions that we no longer believe in.

From Attica we have also learned how impossible it is to administer existing prisons when inmates withold their compliance. The internal organization of penitentiaries today is an irrational mix of old rules, some relaxed, others enforced. Whereas once all prisoners spent their time isolated in a cell, now they mingle freely in the yard, communicate with each other, and move about. As a result, the cooperation of hundreds of prisoners is necessary to the smooth running of the institution. The ratio of guards to inmates is generally low; officers are able to prevent mass break-outs but are not able to prevent takeovers. As events at Attica demonstrated clearly, a group acting in concert has great power to disrupt the normal routine. Moreover, the likelihood of similar actions recurring seems very high. For one, prisoners are certain to sense the steady loss of legitimacy of incarcerating institutions in our society. For another, the convicts in state institutions are bound to be more homogeneous in terms of class (lower), color (black), crime (violent), and politics (radical). As white embezzlers or blacks guilty of property offenses increasingly go out on probation or enter minimum-security prison farms, the possibilities for uprisings by those remaining in penitentiaries increases. To be sure, the state might respond to this crisis by building bigger and internally more secure prisons; we do have the managerial ability to structure settings where 20 guards can keep 1,000 men captive. But this response will probably not get very far. The courts, given their due process inclinations, will not allow such prisons, and wardens do not seem to have the inclination to administration.

A NEW CALCULUS

The implication of this state of affairs makes clear that we must experiment with alternatives. Incarceration is at once inhumane by current standards, destructive of inmates, incredibly expensive, and increasingly losing its legitimacy. Our institutions of incarceration are nineteenth-century anachronisms, out of step with the other American institutions of the 1970s. This marked discrepancy among our social institutions cannot continue for very long without provoking crises more disastrous than Attica. It is time for a new calculus and a new strategy.

The dilemma we now face may enable us to progress in ways that might have been impossible in calmer times. For we no longer need to demonstrate that innovations will accomplish such grandiose goals as solving the problem of crime or reforming the deviant. Such goals are, of course, desirable. But the plain fact of the matter is that we have not yet been able to invent techniques or procedures to achieve them. The record on criminal reform, past and present, is dismal—if by reform one means transforming criminals into law-abiding citizens. That existing prisons do not rehabilitate anybody, or produce lower rates of crime, or decrease recidivism, is beyond dispute. Would newer programs like increased staff for probation, or half-way houses, or intensive prison counseling, or liberalized bail accomplish these ends? Probably not. Research findings on the effectiveness of these procedures demonstrate all too unanimously that no one procedure has a better effect in reforming the criminal or lowering recidivism rates than any other. Social science has not reached the point of being able to fulfill these aims.

Yet if we look to more simple and realizable goals, if we employ such criteria as the degree of humanity and cruelty, or the levels of financial cost, or the kinds of structures we want to live with in a democratic society, we may fare a good deal better. In essence, if we recognize that we face a choice among evils, we may do more to ameliorate existing conditions than if we cling to fanciful notions of reform.

These considerations are immediately relevant to policy decisions we now confront. Ought we to build new and better equipped prisons, with better lighting, larger cells, more schoolrooms and workshops? Ought we at the same time to construct max-max security prisons, ostensibly to bring more intensive treatment to the hard-core recidivist, while allowing inmates in other institutions to gain greater freedom of action (a plan now under consideration in New York State)? Those pressing for these modifications invariably cloak their arguments in the garb of reform: The hard-core recidivist will receive far more personal attention than before; he will be able to visit a prison psychiatrist for counseling and have the benefit of individual instruction; in new and more commodious prisons inmates will live more comfortably, master a trade, and return, without anger or frustration, to the community as diligent, law-abiding citizens. One suspects, with much justification, that this rhetoric is really an after-the-fact rationalization for a more straightforward urge to get tough with the criminal. But even in its own terms, the program is foolhardy. One psychiatrist per maximum security prison (as in the New York plan) is not going to rehabilitate anybody; indeed, given the state of the art, even 20 or 30 of them could not do the job. Nor are workshops and classrooms automatically going to turn convicts into respectable citizens. In the name of such illusory goals we ought not to invest thousands of dollars in prison structures. At best, these changes would be temporary and shaky supports for an already crumbling system. Ultimately, when their goals prove illusory, as they surely will, we will be back where we started with brutal, expensive, and increasingly illegitimate institutions.

Instead let us invest these funds in broadening probation, parole, bail, and half-way houses—not because they offer a hope of redeeming the criminal, or of ridding our society of crime, but because (a) they will do no worse than our present system in terms of prevention, and (b) the price we pay for them, in terms of human and financial and social costs, will be considerably lower. The sums saved on institutional expenditures could well be used to underwrite a national crime insurance program to compensate victims (a procedure already in limited operation in six states), or perhaps to increase the number of policemen on the beat. It might prove necessary to administer a few maximum security prisons for recidivists, rapists, and murderers—but they would function admittedly as places of last resort, without any pretense of reform.

There is no magical plan for prison reform that can promise to reduce the number of criminals or the number of crimes. We know of no correction system that can deliver on such a promise. But that is no reason to continue to suffer our present arrangements. If we scale down our expectations and rely upon such basic standards as human decency and economic costs, we will be in a better position to consider the merits of innovation and decarceration.

If Every Criminal Knew He Would Be Punished If Caught . . .

James Q. Wilson

From *The New York Times Magazine* (January 28, 1973), 9, 44, 52–56.
Copyright © 1973 by The New York Times Company. Reprinted by permission.

Professor Wilson teaches government at Harvard University, edited Metropolitan Enigma, *and, in addition to his journal articles, has written* Varieties of Police Behavior *(1968) and* Amateur Democrat: Club Politics in Three Cities *(1962).*

The proposals by Gov. Nelson Rockefeller for high mandatory minimum sentences for drug dealers, the recent study released by U. S. Attorney Whitney North Seymour on disparities in sentences among judges and continued rumors of judicial corruption in various places are symptomatic of rising popular concern over the relationship between public safety and judicial behavior. The criminal-court judges are well on their way to becoming the objects of the same intense scrutiny once reserved for the police, but with one important difference. The police always had many vocal supporters; the judges are likely to have none.

The police spend most of their time dealing with people in need of help; the judges spend most of theirs dealing with accused criminals. If the police fail, their friends can claim it was because they were too few in number, too weak in authority, too exposed to danger, or too lacking in support. If the judges fail, they cannot so easily claim these excuses.

But "fail" at what? The function of the police is to prevent crime, catch criminals, preserve order and render aid. What is the function of the courts? In theory it is to determine the guilt or innocence of the accused. In fact, it is to decide what to do with persons whose guilt or innocence is not at issue. Our judiciary is organized around the assumption that its theoretical function is its actual one—hence the emphasis on the adversary system, the rules of evidence and the procedures and standards for testimony. In some jurisdictions, especially small ones with relatively few cases, the courts indeed act as theory would have it, and in all jurisdictions, even the big and busy ones, the courts will act that way some of the time. But most of the time, for most of the cases in our busier courts, the important decision concerns the sentence, not conviction or acquittal. In Manhattan, for example, only 3 percent of the 13,555 persons indicted between July, 1963, and July, 1966, were convicted after a trial; almost 80 percent pleaded guilty. Even in one middle-sized, nonmetropolitan county in Wisconsin, 94 percent of the convictions were the result of a plea of guilty, and it made little difference whether the offender had a lawyer or not.

Everyone involved in the criminal justice system knows this, and increasingly the public at large is aware of it—or at least is aware that Perry Mason-style courtroom drama is found only on television, not in courtrooms. But despite this knowledge, very little has been done to equip the courts to perform their essential function well. Indeed, there has been very little serious public discussion of what we even mean by a "good" or "bad" sentence. And only by deciding that question can we begin to think seriously about what other reforms are necessary in the criminal courts.

For example, one way of defining a good sentence is to say it is that disposition that minimizes the chance of a given offender's repeating his crime. Under that definition, we would not only expect but want to have disparities in sentences—one armed robber getting five years in prison and another getting probation—provided only that we had good reason to believe that each sentence was appropriate to each criminal's prospects for rehabilitation. On the other hand, if we believe that a good sentence is one which deters others from committing a crime, then we might wish to impose the same penalty on per-

sons with very different prospects for rehabilitation and to make that penalty sufficiently severe to discourage potential criminals, especially those who believe they might be regarded as good bets for rehabilitative—which is to say, lenient—treatment.

A crucial question in deciding what is a good sentence, then, is what effect on actual or potential offenders any given sentence will have. It is not the only crucial question: We also want, or ought to want, sentences to give appropriate expression to our moral concern over the nature of the offense and to conform to our standards of humane conduct. But these latter standards, though inevitably matters of controversy, are ones which even if met would still leave a substantial zone of discretion to the judge.

Persons will differ over how they would resolve these issues, but whatever definition of a good sentence one adopts, it is unlikely that it will be descriptive of what is in fact happening in our criminal courts today. It is not too much to say that many sentences being administered are, in the strict sense, irrational—that is, there is no coherent goal toward which they are directed.

For example, Prof. Martin A. Levin of Brandeis University found in a study of the Pittsburgh Common Pleas Court in 1966 that well over half the white males convicted of burglary, grand larceny, indecent assault or possession of narcotics, *and who had a prior record* were placed on probation; nearly half of the two-time losers convicted of aggravated assault were placed on probation, as were more than one-fourth of those convicted of robbery. In Wisconsin, Dean V. Babst and John W. Mannering found that 63 percent of the adult males convicted of a felony during 1954—59 who had previously been convicted of another felony were placed on probation, and 41 percent of those with two or more felony convictions were given probation for the subsequent offense.

The judges did not seem to operate on either the deterence or the rehabilitation theory of sentencing—the low proportion of jail sentences for persons convicted of serious crimes who had prior convictions suggests that the judges did not believe jail had a deterrent effect, and the fact that the men were convicted after an earlier offense implies that for them, at least, there had been no rehabilitation.

The treatment of persons in organized crime is even harder to reconcile with some theory of justice. Between 1963 and 1969, the number of persons arrested in New York State on felony narcotics charges (these typically were dealers, not merely users) increased by more than 700 percent, and the number convicted more than tripled. But the number going to state prison remained unchanged and thus the proportion going to prison fell from 68 percent of those convicted to less than 23 percent. Being essentially businessmen (and businesswomen), members of organized crime are probably less likely than youthful brawlers or addict thieves to be likely prospects for rehabilitation: They are acting, not out of passion or compulsion, but out of calculation. And in many jurisdictions those who can calculate best have seen the costs of their criminal ventures decline and the profits boom.

In Boston, the average penalty in heroin cases fell during the sixties—at the very time heroin abuse was rising. Between 1963 and 1970, the proportion of heroin cases before the Suffolk County (Boston) district and superior courts resulting in prison sentences fell from almost half to about one-tenth; meanwhile, the estimated number of heroin users rose from fewer than 1,000 to almost 6,000. This pattern of sentencing can be explained by neither a deterrence nor a rehabilitation philosophy: Obviously the decrease in penalties did not deter heroin dealers, and the absence during most of this time of any treatment-alternative to prison for heroin users meant that rehabilitation, if it were to occur at all, would have to occur spontaneously (which, of course, it did not).

The reasons for the sentencing patterns in many courts have little or nothing to do with achieving some general social objective, but a great deal to do with the immediate problems and idiosyncratic beliefs of the judges. A few sentences can be explained by corruption, many more by the growing belief among some judges that since prisons apparently do not rehabilitate, it is wrong to send criminals to them, and most of all by the overwhelming need in busy jurisdictions to clear crowded court dockets.

When thousands of felony cases must be settled each year in a court, there are overpowering pressures to settle them on the basis of plea bargaining in order to avoid the time and expense of a trial. The defendant is offered a reduced charge or a lighter sentence in exchange for a plea of guilty. Though congested dockets are not the only reason for this practice, an increase in congestion increases the incentives for such bargaining and thus may increase the proportion of lighter sentences. For those who believe in the deterrence theory of sentencing, it is a grim irony: The more crime increases, the more the pressure on court calendars, and the greater the chances that the response to the crime increase will be a sentence decrease.

But the use of probation and suspended sentences also reflects the belief of growing numbers of judges that the purpose of prisons is to rehabilitate, that the prisons have failed in this assignment and that a criminal left out of prison has at least as good a chance, and perhaps a better chance, to stop stealing as one sent away. And there is some evidence to support this point of view. In a recent review of the studies of persons on probation, Professor Levin concluded that they "all indicate that offenders who have received probation generally have significantly lower rates of recidivism [i.e., are less likely to be arrested for, or convicted of, a subsequent offense than those who have been incarcerated.]" Furthermore, of those who are incarcerated, those receiving shorter sentences are somewhat less likely to become repeaters than those who have received longer sentences.

Perhaps the most comprehensive of these studies is one completed in California in 1970 by Ronald H. Beattie and Charles K. Bridges. It found that almost two-thirds of those offenders placed on probation had, one year later, no known subsequent arrest, while less than half of those sent to prison had been equally successful.

These differences in "success" persisted even when one took into account the sex, age, race, offense and prior record of the offender.

One rejoinder to the apparent policy implications of such studies is obvious, and Levin has made it: Naturally probationers succeeded more than did prisoners—they were selected for probation precisely because the judges thought they *would* succeed. Putting more offenders now sent to prison on probation would not necessarily lead to better results; it would simply put the poorer risks on the street with a consequent increase in the over-all failure rate of probationers. If probation success rates now appear good, it is only because judges are good at guessing who will be successful.

In fact, in New York, where the proportion of juveniles on probation has been going up, a *New York Times* survey published last September suggests that the failure rate has also been going up. And it might be going up even more if we knew for certain how many persons on probation were actually breaking the law, but we don't—we know only how many are *caught* breaking the law, and that is probably only a small fraction of the total.

There have been very few efforts to put probation to the crucial test by assigning offenders randomly to probation and prison and then comparing the results. Perhaps the best known of these is the Community Treatment Program in California. After the most dangerous or serious of a group of first offenders were screened out and sent to an institution, the remainder were assigned randomly to probation or to a regular juvenile detention facility. Those on probation received intensive counseling. Two years later, the failure (i.e., reconviction) rate of those sent to regular institutions was 61 percent (about the average for most studies of this kind), while the rate for those undergoing special probation was only 38 percent.

The California experiment has been cited in countless reports on correctional reform and was urged as one possible model by President Johnson's Commission on Law Enforcement and Administration of Justice. Promising as this approach seems to be, no one is yet sure of its general applicability. In the first place, it was used only on young first offenders, not on habitual criminals; second, most of the subjects were white—no one knows if the same techniques would work with blacks; third, probation that involves intensive counseling and group-therapy programs run by specially skilled personnel may be hard to duplicate on a large scale for tens of thousands of probationers; and, finally, it is possible that the counselors may have chosen to overlook behavior by the offenders that would have constituted technical violations of the terms of probation under normal circumstances, thereby keeping the recidivism rate lower than it otherwise would have been.

In any event, most judges do not have a Community Treatment Program to which they can sentence offenders. In most courts, the practical choices are between routine probation (that involves few services) and jail or prisons with varying degrees of security and amenity. And here the evidence seems quite clear: In general, different kinds of institutions do not make any appreciable difference in the prospects of rehabilitation. R. G. Hood published in 1967 a review of the leading studies on the effects of prison and probation, and little has happened since—with the possible exception of highly experimental efforts such as the California program—that would change his conclusion: "Overall results are not much different as between different treatments." Specifically, recidivism is about the same whether the prison sentence is short or long, whether the prison itself is "open" (i.e., more permissive or "therapeutic") or "closed," or whether a probation officer has a relatively large or a relatively small caseload.

The reason for these discouraging results is not hard to find. On the whole, it is the *characteristics of the offender* more than the characteristics of the program that affect the likelihood of recidivism. Age, race, prior criminal record, the presence or absence of a narcotic habit and similar matters turn out to be among the best predictors of whether or not an offender will continue to break the law.

In crime, as in education, we are slowly learning about the limits of public policy. Just as the Coleman Report on equal opportunity in education revealed that existing differences in school programs have little measureable effect on educational achievement, studies of recidivism reveal that most existing differences in correctional programs have only modest (if any) measureable effects on criminal rehabilitation.

But we seem to draw different conclusions from these reports. Few persons are proposing that we close down the schools on the grounds that they are frightfully expensive and ineffective in reducing intellectual inequalities. Many people are proposing that we close down the prisons on the grounds that they are frightfully expensive and ineffective in reducing recidivism rates. Students have rioted in the schools, and the response has been that schools must be bigger and better. Prisoners have rioted in jails, and the response (from the same people) is that jails should be smaller and fewer.

The plight of the criminal-court judge is obvious. Should he sentence a person to an institution that does not have a demonstrable effect on his criminality, or place him on probation not knowing whether that will have any effect either? Even more important, should he take into account the characteristics of the offender in deciding on his prospects for rehabilitation, giving those with the best prospects (as predicted from his age, sex, race and prior record) the shortest sentences and those with the worst prospects the longest ones?

A moment's thought on such issues leads one squarely into the philosophical problem with the rehabilitation theory of sentencing. If rehabilitation is the object, and if there is little or no evidence that available correctional systems will produce much rehabilitation, why should any offender be sent to any institution? But to turn them free on the grounds that society does not know how to make them better is to fail to protect society from those crimes they may commit again and to violate society's moral concern for criminality and thus to undermine society's conception of what constitutes proper conduct.

Furthermore, if rehabilitation is the goal, and persons differ in their capacity to be rehabilitated, then two persons who have committed precisely the same crime under precisely the same circumstances might receive very different sentences, thereby violating the offenders' and our sense of justice. The indeterminate sentence, widely used in many states, is expressive of the rehabilitation ideal: A convict will be released from an institution, not at the end of a fixed period, but when someone (a parole board, a sentencing board) decides he is "ready" to be released. Rigorously applied on the basis of existing evidence about what factors are associated with recidivism, this would mean that if two persons together rob a liquor store, the one who is a young black male from a broken family with little education and a record of drug abuse will be kept in prison indefinitely, while an older white male from an intact family with a high school diploma and no drug experience will be released almost immediately. Not only the young black male, but most fair-minded observers, would regard that outcome as profoundly unjust.

Now suppose we abandon entirely the rehabilitation theory of sentencing and corrections—not the *effort* to rehabilitate, just the theory that the governing purpose of the enterprise is to rehabilitate. We could continue experiments with new correctional and therapeutic procedures, expanding them when the evidence warrants. If existing correctional programs do not differ in their rehabilitative potential, we could support those that are least costly and most humane (while still providing reasonable security) and phase out those that are most costly and inhumane. But we would not do any of these things on the mistaken notion that we were thereby reducing recidivism.

Instead, we would view the correctional system as having a very different function—namely, to isolate and to punish. It is a measure of our confusion that such a statement will strike many enlightened readers today as cruel, even barbaric. It is not. It is merely a recognition that society at a minimum must be able to protect itself from dangerous offenders and to impose some costs (other than the stigma and inconvenience of an arrest and court appearance) on criminal acts; it is also a frank admission that society really does not know how to do much else.

The purpose of isolating—or, more accurately, closely supervising—offenders is obvious: Whatever they may do when they are released, they cannot harm society while confined or closely supervised. The purpose of punishment is two-fold: retribution for a wrongful act, and deterrence for would-be offenders. It is precisely on the latter point that many judges today will object. Not only do prisons not reform, it is argued, they do not deter. Clearly the prospect of prison does not deter the man imprisoned. But does it deter the man not imprisoned?

Over the last few years, several efforts have been made to assess the deterrent effect of sentences. These efforts are not immune to criticism: They are based on police reports of crimes committed (which are in error to some degree), they are based on comparing sentencing behavior among states (which are very large units within which much variation no doubt occurs), and they are not experimental studies (that is, they do not show what happens when one deliberately changes the pattern of sentencing while holding everything else constant). Nonetheless, since all the studies come more or less to the same conclusion, and since the statistical techniques used make it very unlikely that the results could be due to chance, the general thrust of these studies is revealing.

The best summary and reanalysis of them is in a paper by George E. Antunes of Rice University and A. Lee Hunt of the University of Houston, delivered last fall at the meeting of the American Political Science Association. They found that the *certainty* of punishment has a significant deterrent effect on crime rates, while the *severity* of punishment has a deterrent effect only on murder.

"Certainty" was measured by dividing the number of persons sent to prison in each state for a given crime in a given year by the number of those crimes reported to the police in that state in the preceding years. The larger the pro-portion of reported crimes resulting in imprisonment, the greater the certainty of punishment. "Severity" was the median length of a prison sentence (in months or years) imposed in a given state for a given crime. The longer the sentence, the more severe it is (capital punishment was ignored in these studies).

A judge reading these studies might agree with the results but explain them differently. Low conviction rates do not cause high crime rates, he might argue; rather, high crime rates lead to low conviction rates because they produce crowded court calendars which can only be cleared by giving offenders suspended sentences in exchange for guilty pleas. There may be some truth in that explanation, or possibly both explanations are true.

In short, while the evidence that penalties deter some crimes is not conclusive, it is certainly suggestive. What is remarkable is that so few knowledgeable persons, especially among the ranks of many professional students of crime, are even willing to entertain the possibility that penalties make a difference. We have become so preoccupied with dealing with the causes of the crime (whether the causes are thought to be social conditions or police inadequacies) that we have almost succeeded in persuading ourselves that criminals are radically different from ordinary people—that they are utterly indifferent to the costs and rewards of their activities, and are responding only to deep passions, fleeting impulses or uncontrollable social forces.

There is scarcely any evidence to support the proposition that would-be criminals are indifferent to the risks associated with a proposed course of action. Criminals may be willing to run *greater* risks (or they may have a weaker sense of morality) than the average middle-class citizen, but if the expected cost of crime goes up without a corresponding increase in the expected benefits, then the would-be criminal should—unless he or she is among that small fraction of criminals who are in fact utterly irrational—engage in less crime just as the average citizen will be less likely to take a job as a day laborer if the earnings from that occupation, relative to those from other occupations, go down.

Some preliminary studies by Gordon Tullock, Isaac Ehrlich, Gary Becker and others suggest that much of the crime that occurs can be explained by a simple economic theory—namely, crime pays. If they are correct, the wonder is not that there is a lot of crime, but that all of us are not criminals.

Most of us are prepared to accept the notion that the effective application of penalties, even rather modest ones, will deter certain forms of behavior. Everyone who has traveled to Los Angeles from the East Coast observes with awe the extent to which routine traffic laws, including those against jaywalking, are obeyed. The explanation is obvious: For decades, the police have enforced those laws with sufficient vigor to make the average Angeleno feel that the risks of breaking the law are sufficiently great, and the costs of observing the law sufficiently small, to make it worthwhile to obey. The enforcement of laws against driving while intoxicated in Scandinavia has apparently reduced substantially the number of persons who drive after drinking. The passing of bad checks in various states was found in one study to be related to the vigor of enforcement efforts.

But while most of us are prepared to concede all this, many of us are reluctant to apply the same analysis to more serious forms of crime— apparently on the unstated assumption that traffic laws, jaywalking ordinances and bad-check statutes are primarily enforced against middle-class people who are more "rational" than the lower-class people who commit "real" crimes. In fact there probably are differences between social classes having to do with the taste for risk, but while that may mean that there will always be absolute differences in the crime rate among classes, it does not mean that changes in the size of the risk will produce no change in the rate of crime.

Other critics of these studies will argue that they neglect the importance of severe penalties. Among these would presumably be Governor Rockefeller. While I am skeptical about his proposal for mandatory life sentences for drug deal-

ers, one must nevertheless concede that in any rational system of criminal justice it will always be necessary to have *some* very severe penalties, even *if they* have no deterrent effect on crime. In the first place, the moral horror of certain offenses is such that society would not—and probably should not—tolerate the imposition of small penalties even if larger ones do not increase the deterrent effect. As the English legal philosopher James Fitzjames Stephens observed in the nineteenth century, if murder could be prevented by a fine of 1 shilling, we could not without doing violence to the moral bonds of society settle for a 1-shilling fine for murderers.

In the second place, there must always be a penalty that can be imposed on persons who, while serving the maximum existing penalty, commit another crime—for example, a convict serving a long prison sentence who kills a prison guard. Some ultimate penalty must always exist to help protect innocent persons from criminals who "have nothing to lose." Third, the threat of severe penalties is an important resource for investigators seeking to obtain criminal informers. If those who inform on a ring of heroin dealers risk death, while those who deal in heroin risk only one year in prison, scarcely anybody will become a police informer—avoiding a one-year sentence is not worth the chance of assassination. But if the sentence they avoid is 5 or 10 years, many more pushers will be willing to run at least a reasonable risk of being murdered.

Finally, it is possible that in particular cases very severe penalties *are* a deterrent, though statistically, severity is related only to the deterrence of murder.

But even if all of these arguments are correct, there are at least two considerations that should lead us to conclude that severity in penalties cannot be the norm. First, except in unusual cases, severity is probably subject to rapidly diminishing returns. The difference between a one-year and a five-year sentence is likely to appear very great to a convict, but the difference between a 20-year and a 25-year sentence (or even a 30-year sentence) is likely to appear rather small. Second, the more severe the penalty, the more unlikely that it will be imposed. To insure a conviction, to avoid an expensive trial, to reduce the chances of reversal on appeal, and to give expression to their own views of benevolence, prosecutors and judges will try to get a guilty plea, and all they can offer in return is a lesser sentence. The more severe the sentence, the greater the bargaining power of the accused, and the greater the likelihood he will be charged with a lesser offense. Extremely long mandatory minimum sentences do not always strengthen the hand of society; they often strengthen the hand of the criminal instead.

If this analysis is correct, what does it imply for the criminal court system? In an *ideal* world, it would imply something like the following:

First, the court system would be organized around the primary task of sentencing, not around the largely mythic task of determining guilt. Hearings and trials under strict standards of due process would still be held, of course, where the issue of guilt is in doubt but (again, in the ideal world) this would occupy only a fraction of the courts' resources and perhaps be handled by judges who specialized in that work.

Second, the sentencing process would be placed under central management with uniform standards enforced by a presiding officer and applied under his direction.

Third, every conviction for a non-trivial offense would entail a penalty that involved a deprivation of liberty, even if brief. For many offenses, the minimum sentence might be as low as one week, and even that might be served on weekends. For most offenses, the average sentence would be relatively short—perhaps no more than six months or a year—*but it would be invariably applied.* Only the most serious offenses would result in long penalties.

Fourth, "deprivation of liberty" need not, and usually would not, entail confinement in a conventional prison. *After* the deprivation of liberty is decided upon, a decision would be made as to whether it would involve confinement at night and on weekends, while allowing a person to work during the day; enrollment in a closely supervised community-based treatment program; referral to a narcotics treatment program, or

confinement in a well-guarded prison. Judgment as to the *form* the deprivation would take would be based on the need to protect society and on the prospects for rehabilitation of the offender. But the prospects for rehabilitation should not be allowed to govern the length of the sentence, nor whether there should be some deprivation of liberty: To permit the former would be unjust to the offender, to permit the latter would be unjust to society. Conventional probation—releasing an offender on the understanding that occasionally he would visit his probation officer—would be virtually abolished.

Fifth, conviction for a subsequent offense would invariably result in an increased deprivation of liberty. If the second offense were minor, the magnitude of the increase would be minor. The central point is that *something would be done.*

But of course nothing will be done. The proposal is hopelessly utopian. It will be opposed by judges unwilling to surrender their authority to do as they please. It will be opposed by legislators who would feel that it is morally necessary (or, more likely, politically expedient) to pass bills requiring massive sentences that experience shows are rarely imposed. It will be opposed by taxpayers' groups that do not wish to foot the bill for the substantial additional expenditures required for new correctional facilities and more court and correctional personnel. It will be opposed by community associations and block clubs which are all in favor of imposing criminal penalties, so long as the institutions in which they are imposed are not situated in their neighborhoods. It will be opposed by those who feel that punishment does not work, or that, whether it works or not, it is wrong to apply it to criminals until society itself has been punished for "producing" criminals. It will be opposed by many police officers who think that long sentences are better than short ones, not recognizing that the actual choice today is between long sentences and no sentences, and that the latter is the norm.

And even if the opposition of these groups could be overcome, there would be problems in administering the new system. If every offender knew that *some* penalty would befall him, he might have less incentive to plead guilty, and thus would demand a trial, thereby changing the mythic function of the courts into the real one and so paralyzing them. (In fact, I would guess that many offenders would prefer the certainty of a relatively short sentence to the cost of a trial and the possibility of a longer or more confining sentence which might result from revelations during the trial of the full range of evidence against him and of the nature of his character.)

We shall never try the proposal because we are divided between a majority that believes crime is a serious problem but thinks the solution is to be found in more police, more arrests or more rehabilitation; and a minority that feels crime is either not a grave problem, or is the symptom of something more important, or is beyond the reach of society at all. And in between are those who, whatever their feelings, seek to maintain the existing institution of criminal justice, secure from fundamental change.

Delta Prison

John T. Fargason, Jr.

From *The American Scholar* V. 40, No. 4, (Autumn 1971), 667–671. Copyright © 1971 by the United Chapters of Phi Beta Kappa. Reprinted by permission of the publishers and author.

Mr. Fargason, on parole from the Mississippi State Penitentiary, is a graduate of the University of Virginia and is a cotton planter in the Mississippi Delta.

"Where we goin', you reckon?" asked a worried boy, sitting in the back of the closed hospital van. There were seventeen of us, six to a side on benches and five who stood and kept their balance by pressing their hands against the roof. Heavy wire mesh separated us from the two trusties up front, the driver and the guard.

"Who gives a goddam, jest so we're gittin' away from that stinkin' hospital!" answered the man beside him. We were all new men, and, upon entering the front gate of the prison, had been sent directly to the hospital for routine processing. This consisted of a physical examination, which was to be expected, and of having our heads shaved to the skull, which came as a

humiliating surprise to many of us. It was the first of many such surprises. The ward where we were kept was filthy and depressing, a zoo-like cage with bars and a zoo-like smell. The attitude of the staff was antagonistic and hostile, and after five days we were glad to get away, yet fearful in our ignorance of what was to come.

"We're goin' to the Reception Center at Camp Nine," volunteered another man. "I hear they'll keep us there about a month, long enough to ask a bunch of dumb-ass questions. Then after the nut doctors have decided we're all underprivileged boys who need rehabilitatin', we'll be sent to the long-line to chop cotton come next summer."

"How in hell you know all that, for God's sake?"

"I'm a parole violator. They didn't have all this kind of crap when I was here before. When we come in we jest went straight to whatever camp needed men. That's why I got to do it now with you guys. Biggest bunch of garbage I ever heard of."

Camp Nine is situated on a gravel road, well away from the main headquarters of Parchman. Like all but a few of the camps, it consists of a one-story, red brick building containing two cages, one on either side of an entrance hall, followed by a mess hall and a kitchen. At this camp, however, the mess hall had been converted into a group of offices for the rehabilitation counselors and psychologists. A shed had been constructed off the kitchen, and it was here that the inmates were fed. It was unheated and, in February, very uncomfortable. There were three long plank tables with benches attached to each side, at which we ate. If too many men sat on one side, the table tipped over.

The cage I occupied measured about fifty feet each way. To accommodate the influx of new prisoners, it was necessary that the double-decker bunks be pushed together, and lined against all four walls. The center of the room was filled with single cots jammed against one another but with narrow aisles kept open so men could get around without walking on each other's beds. High on one wall was a television set, which stayed turned on as long as there was a program to watch. This room was my home for a month. Prisoners stayed as long as the staff needed them for processing, and our population was always changing as the interviewers completed their work.

The first time I entered the cage I had not taken more than five steps when a short, squat man came up to me and stuck out his hand. "My name's Frank Rodgers, Mr. MacDonough. I been readin' about your case in the papers. Good to meet you! You made out better than me; I got life for doin' the exact same thing you done." The man who spoke was older than I was, and rather fat. He was bald-headed and tired-looking, but he was friendly and I tried to return the broad smile he greeted me with; I did not quite manage it. It had grown dark outside, and when the lights of the cage came on, the men inside seemed to grow louder in their talk. I attempted to relax some of the tension that plagued me.

The crowded room made me think of a box full of snakes.

"Good to meet you, Frank," I said. "My name's MacDonald. You spell it with an a-l-d. But it is kind of like MacDonough. Where's an empty bed?"

He showed me one, the lower half of one of the double-deckers. The men on either side of me had been here before.

"This your first fall, ain't it?" asked one, whose name I learned was Freddie. I nodded that it was. "Well, you're lucky in one way, that you ain't no young punk. Maybe you won't have to worry so much about gettin' corn-holed."

His words stunned me, and I lay there on the bunk unable to speak. Corn-holed! I had, of course, read of such things happening in prison. I had discussed it a little in jail with one of the trusties there. So. Here it was. I prayed to God that I would not be subjected to such an outrage, that I would never have to witness it. I knew my own nature and that I could not submit to such a thing, no matter what the consequences might be. I feared and dreaded violence, but I knew, too, how far I could be pushed. Later, in the pale glow of the dim light that burned perpetually at the top of the cage, I looked around at the restless forms surrounding me. My God, I thought, they all seem so young.

A few days later I sat in a straight-backed chair in one of the interviewing offices and stared across a desk at a pleasant-faced young man, a staff member. "How in hell do we rehabilitate you?" he asked, half to himself. I did not attempt to offer a suggestion. "We don't see many college graduates in here. And, of course, we know your history, that you aren't a criminal or habitually inclined toward trouble. It's a damn shame you have to be here, but you do, so you might as well face it. Adjusting to Parchman isn't going to be easy; we are aware of what you are going through right now."

This statement surprised me; I had thought I was to be treated simply as another number. But still I remained silent, waiting for him to go on.

"I'd like to see you use your knowledge of farming while you're here, but I understand the superintendent has other ideas, and he's the boss. My father is the animal husbandman on this plantation. I sure would like to see you go to work for him. I think you and he would get along fine."

"Why do you think so?" I asked. "I don't know anything about livestock. I'm a cotton farmer."

"I realize that, but it wouldn't take you long to catch on. Mainly though, I was thinking it would be nice if you could work with a man who doesn't find it necessary to use four-letter words every other breath. He's a rare individual in this place. And my old man never cusses."

I had to smile at this. "You know, mine doesn't either," I said. "But if cussing is all I have to put up with, I'll survive."

"Sure you will." The counselor stood up and held out his hand. "You're gonna make it okay. I'll keep in touch."

I had had the complete course; tests in educational development, aptitude, psychological tests, an I.Q. test, were all shoved at me. It took days, for there were days in between tests when I did nothing but sit in the cage and worry. The reality of things began to gnaw at my insides, and for the first time in my life I realized the feeling of a cold, hard knot in the pit of my stomach. I dreaded the loss of my wife and child, yet could no longer avoid facing the truth that I had lost them. I was afraid, deathly afraid, of what was to come next in this prison. I worried about time, nine years of it, exactly like the present, filled with nothingness. And as I worried, I created a new terror: that I would not be able to absorb what was to come, and would eventually, little by little, crumble into pieces.

I tried to control this reaction, but anxiety and fear and hopelessness kept creeping into my brain. No matter how hard I tried to occupy myself in reading, in conversation and in the always available TV, I would find myself slipping back into a dreamlike world of total and absolute misery.

"Say, John, you sure do write fast. I watched you write that letter last night, and it didn't take you no time a'tall to fill up the whole page." The speaker was my aisle partner, although there

was no aisle between us. He slept on the opposite side of me from the one Freddie slept on.

"Thanks, but I've had plenty of experience writing letters over the years," I said to him.

"I was jes' wonderin', would you min' puttin' the ad-dress on mine for me?" said the convict.

"I'll be glad to, but you can do it yourself; I saw you writing a letter too."

"Aw hell, I know, but I can't write pretty like you, and I'd be ashamed for the sergeant to see my han' writin' on a envelope. Mainly though, I jes' hate for the other guys to see it. Look, my han' writin' looks like a little kid's." It did, too, and it was easy to see how much trouble he had had getting his letter done. His hands had rarely held a pencil. He told me the last letter he had written was ten years ago, from Parchman. "I even learned what little bit I do know about readin' and writin' here in the penitentiary. My aisle partner at Camp Five learnt me."

I took his envelope and began to address it in the approved fashion, with the inmate's name, number and camp in the upper left-hand corner. "What's your full name?" I asked.

"Red Morrison. I mean, J. T. Morrison," he told me.

When I had finished addressing the envelope I asked him, out of curiosity and by way of conversation, what he had done in the free world. "I was a tractor driver, heavy equipment operator, stuff like that," he said. "But I got busted for bein' a small-time thief, an' for bein' stupid. I found out how much these farm chemicals was worth, and I just couldn't resist makin' off with a few dozen cans from a warehouse one night. They would have let me off even then, but later I got caught with some tools in the trunk of my car that they said was good for burgalizin' places. So here I am, again, and I could kick my own ass! I shore got better things to do with my time that set here another three years. I got four little bitty kids."

Red told me later that this was to be his last time in prison, that he had made up his mind to that. He was right; it was his last time.

Two years later Red became eligible for parole and was turned down at his hearing, "set off" a year because of his prior conviction (and lack of influence). Less than a month after that a trusty guard dashed into the hall at Red's camp one night, pointed a pistol at his stomach, and shot him dead. Red Morrison was the night "hall shooter," a trusty himself by then, and no one ever learned why he died, for he was surprised by his assailant and made no move to interfere with him. The killer was "running," making an escape, and we convicts surmised that Red simply happened to get in the way. His wife came and brought his oldest boy to claim the body, and his death was mentioned in the *Tupelo Journal*, once. The trusty who killed him got an extra year for manslaughter when they caught him, but I think he beat the charge later on.

As the days passsed, the men I came to the reception center with began to disappear. Old Frank Rodgers was transferred to Camp Four, a unit for the old, crippled, permanently ill white inmates. Freddie Wilkins and Red Morrison were sent to their old camp, Five. Each time a prisoner left I wondered what would happen to me when it came my turn to go.

One night a prisoner named Wall came and sat beside me on my bed. "Say, John, you might ought to ask that sergeant to let you outta here for a little while. I been watchin' you for two or three days now, and you're goin' downhill fast, whether you know it or not. You ain't said nothin' to anybody since day before yesterday."

I thought for a moment, and realized the man was right; I had been in a nightmare world of my own, consisting of endless years of sitting in a cage. There was no relief, no future, and no hope. Gradually, I seemed to step outside myself, and my mind separated itself from my body. I am coming unglued, I thought. I don't want to fall apart, but in spite of myself, I am doing just that. There is no way I can make it in this place. No way at all.

"Wall," I said, "I'm scared to ask that man for anything. I don't even want him to know I'm here."

"Well, you can jes' bet your ass he knows, so don't worry about that. How long since you had

any sleep, anyway? Every time I look over toward your bunk at night, I see a cigarette glowin' in the dark."

"Too long, I suppose. I don't know how long it's been. I just want them to leave me alone."

For five months I had held up. I had withstood the blows one by one as they fell; I had been staggered time and again. But I had managed to keep my head, under pressure, and although at times I saw no end to it, I never lost control. The night it all began should have been enough to drive me out of my mind, but it did not, not even when I came back to reality in the jail cell and realized that I had shot and probably killed someone. Nor did it when he died and my world fell to pieces. The months in the mental ward, wondering if I were really crazy, the pressure of waiting, isolated from others, for trial, should have been too much to bear, yet I bore it all. I do not know how, for each day I was surprised that I had survived another one and had, for a while longer, kept my sanity.

Now, here in this filthy, ancient cage, I felt myself slipping inch by inch, day by day. I saw only one thing, a fantasy of nine interminable years of endless, unrelieved hell. And so at last, I was going under.

Wall kept at me and finally persuaded me that even if it did no good, I should go to the window and ask to speak to the sergeant. It was not hard to do, physically, for the man sat at a desk in the hall and was within earshot all the time. I gathered up what courage I could and asked to be let out just for a few minutes.

The sergeant looked up. "What the hell for?" he demanded.

"My nerves, sergeant. I just don't see how I can take it any more in here without flying all to pieces."

"Say, ain't you MacDonald?" he asked.

"Yes."

He got himself up from his chair, telling me as he did so to meet him at the cage door, which the hall boy came to unlock. He had been taking it all in.

"Come on out and go out on the front porch for a little while. It'll do you good to get some fresh air. Say, ain't Rafferty your lawyer?"

I said that he was and walked out the front door of the camp, being careful to stay well within the gun line on the porch. So that was it, I thought. Now I see what Jack meant when he said having the lieutenant governor for an attorney would be a help. This guy thinks I'm some kind of political force. My God!

The sergeant went a step further than letting me out for some air; he even took me to the hospital for some tranquilizers which I got from my friend, Luther Jones, the Negro convict doctor.

This incident gave me an insight into the hold that politics had on the penitentiary. I did not know it at the time, but virtually every employee here owed his job to some form of political influence. Most of the officials in the low echelon bracket did not have much pull; their jobs were not sought after as a rule, but they were the best these people could get. Their positions were insecure, their pay was miserably low. And as a result, their qualifications were nil. Almost to a man, they had come here only when there was no place else to go, for they had failed at everything they had ever tried.

I got the pills on a Saturday, and that night I had a good sleep for the first time in days. The next morning we went to the church service and joined the Negro prisoners to sing, "Amazing Grace, how sweet the sound, that saved a wretch like me . . ."

"Look out on that feller from Clarksdale! Yeah, you. Th'ow your stuff in this here box. An' git ready to go." The hall boy issued a minimum of instructions, but there was no mistaking his meaning; I was moving to a camp at last.

There were two of us, and we were told to get in the back of the sergeant's pickup truck with our cardboard boxes of belongings. "Where you reckon we're goin'?" asked my companion.

"God, I don't know, and I don't really care, just so we go somewhere away from that god-dam reception center," I said. "I have had just about enough of that place."

We pulled into a neat-looking, white-painted camp with a chain link fence surrounding it. "Okay, Scott. This here's your new home. Git out," said the sergeant as he swung down from the driver's seat.

"Me too, Sarge?" I asked.

"Naw, this here's Camp Six. You go to Seven."

Seven! I had heard of it. The prison nut house. Oh God, I thought, will this nightmare never end?

Camp Seven is also known as the M.S.P. Adjustment Center. It was created in an effort to stave off complete mental and emotional breakdowns among convicts who were unable to accept prison environment. Before its inception mentally ill inmates were simply branded as troublemakers, and treated accordingly. If they failed to respond to a period of confinement in the maximum security unit, accompanied by appropriate treatment, including beatings, purging with water hoses, milk of magnesia forced down their throats, cold water dousings and starvation, they were eventually either transferred to the state hospital for the insane or they died. Camp Seven was supposed to cut down on some of this.

The day I arrived at Seven it was freezing, and I wore a canvas billed cap of the type that ties under the chin. I walked into the hall with the old sergeant, stared at the new one, and heard his words of greeting. "Take off that goddam cap when you come in the hall!"

I grabbed at it; the chin strap was still tied. Attempting to untie the string, I only got it hopelessly snarled into a hard knot.

"Good God," said my new warden. "Git on in the cage."

The hall boy swung the wooden door wide, and as I stepped in, I heard him close it and snap the lock. I never got used to that sound.

The Politics of Criminal Justice

Richard H. Kuh

Reprinted from *The New Leader* (January 8, 1973), 7–12. Copyright © 1973 by The American Labor Conference on International Affairs, Inc.

Mr. Kuh, formerly an assistant district attorney and assistant to Frank S. Hogan (New York County Prosecutor), is a member of the law firm of Kuh, Goldman, Cooperman, and Levitt. He has been active in trying to upgrade the criminal courts.

Of the three branches of American government, the judiciary has the greatest mystique. Presidents, governors and legislators must cater to their constituencies—by kissing babies, pumping hands, donning hard hats, eating knishes or hot dogs while smiling interminably—and we are not surprised to see them at work in shirt-sleeves. But our image of the judge—always austerely robed, the flag at his right hand, a state seal of heavenly reminder ("In God We Trust") carved into the wall behind him—places him above the mundane let alone the political.

Moreover, judges literally perform their functions from an eminence: They sit higher than the rest of us behind a polished wooden altar called the "bench," and they are set further apart by the physical presence known as the "bar." This elevation may have its source not only in the tradition of English courts, but in our early religious training. The Biblical judges were sages, wise men; they spoke in thunder and lightning; God-anointed, they were larger than life, leaders of the sorely tried flock of Abraham, Isaac, and Jacob.

Even local part-time justices of the peace are reverentially called "Your Honor"; junketing British lawyers deferentially address American judges as "Your Lordship." And like kings, judges perform their official duties in "court" and are surrounded by hosts of sycophants:

robing clerks, bailiffs, *confidential* attendants, aides, secretaries, correctional personnel, clerks. Although genuflection is not a feature of our courts, as it is in England, all must rise upon His Honor's coming in and going out, cued by the banging, clanging, or oyezing of the appropriate bailiff. After several years of such day-to-day adulation, the most self-effacing of humans is apt to regard his views as quasi-holy writ. Indeed, the late Supreme Court Justice Felix Frankfurter often cautioned, in the language of Oliver Cromwell (*neither* of these gentlemen having themselves epitomized humility), "I beseech you, in the bowels of Christ, think it possible you may be mistaken."

But who are our city and state judicial Olympians? A *New York Times* story announcing a new crop of judges offers a fair cross section: "A Queens man recommended by the John V. Lindsay Association . . . and the brother of the Bronx District Attorney were among 10 new judges sworn in yesterday by Mayor Lindsay. Two of the three Bronx appointees were recommended by the Bronx Democratic organization, and one of the two Brooklyn appointees by the Brooklyn Democratic organization."

The group was reasonably representative of those who serve on the bench in most cities across the nation. Scratch a judge and, in all probability, beneath you will find a former city councilman, state senator or assemblyman, a local political leader or a leader's spouse, a commissioner or deputy, a judge's aide or similar official. In England, political activity of any sort is almost certain disqualification for judicial robes; in the U.S., it is the surest path to the bench. Relatively rarely is an American judge recruited from the ranks of notable barristers or top-ranking legal scholars.

The results, interestingly, are not *all* bad. The political system produces an occasional Benjamin Cardozo (that thoughtful, kind, and classically articulate jurist was the son of an old-time Tammany politico). In addition, the street wisdom politicians are likely to bring to the bench embraces realities that are useful in dealing with the men who appear before them. Still, the best that can be said for the justices politics provides is that, as in most lines of work, the overwhelming majority of them are mediocre. In other words, they are a far, far cry from the Olympians implied by the courts' panoply, substantiating the frequently heard charge that much is rotten about the selection of judges.

(I am not referring here to the persistent, but unproven, rumor that judgeships may be bought in New York City and elsewhere with sizable cash contributions to political leaders. Since few designees have been noted for their opulence, it would seem unlikely that they had the supposedly requisite $50-100 thousand lying idly about.)

Basic to the rottenness of political recruitment is the unhappy fact that our ablest young people tend not to make long-term commitments to clubhouse politics. The sinews of local organizations are the tiresome tasks of doorbell ringing and envelope licking; the bone marrow is absolute, unquestioning loyalty to the club and its leader. For the lawyer whose skills are so limited that the job market may be somewhat barren, the clubhouse often represents the road to economic security. At the outset, the club may produce a ragtag of legal business: neighbors calling with problems. Then come more lucrative guardianships and other court assignments, from judges who have themselves traveled this route. Judicial clerkships are among the regular legal positions doled out to the faithful.

The young pol with polish, and a little neighborhood charisma, may receive his leader's blessing to run for the City Council, the State Assembly or Senate: The *quid pro quo* for this sponsorship is, of course, loyalty; criticism, cabals, opposition are not fondly regarded. (A man widely recognized as one of Brooklyn's ablest lawyers never got to don the judicial robe. Instead, he spent a lifetime as a respected assistant district attorney because, early in his career, he had the temerity to fight the county leader for political control. He lost, and the rest of his professional life was a dead end.)

The evils of the system were brought home to me in 1956, when I helped form a group of Greenwich Village volunteers for Adlai Stevenson (which subsequently became the insurgent Village Independent Democrats). A stalwart of Carmine De Sapio's Tamawa Democratic Club, a City Court judge wholly insensitive to the idealism that had brought us into the Stevenson fold, offered some friendly advice to the leaders of the new group. Straight-faced, with no hint of impropriety or embarrassment, he suggested that we abandon our efforts and link forces with the regulars (who were sitting out the Presidential race). Then, after years of doorbell ringing and praising the leader, we too might ultimately find ourselves on the path to success that our "counselor" was traveling. (The judge was later promoted to the State Supreme Court.)

Judgeships generally do not come quickly. They are the rewards for decades of day-in, day-out politics in elective office or in minor public service. Thus, by the time a judge is measured for the black robe and the relative tranquility it represents, habits of political obeisance have been so firmly ingrained as to need no reminders. This interferes directly with the judicial process.

To begin with, it has a distinct bearing upon judges' decisions. An outright rape of the law is uncommon, but a contested decision may go in one direction when the application of sounder legal principles would see it move in another. A lighter sentence than usual is sometimes imposed where the defendant, or his attorney, has the right political friends. Or a lesser plea is cajoled by the judge—probably without too much effort, for in most counties the prosecutor is a product of the same system.

Secondly, the quality of a judge's legal work is affected when his staff—especially the people theoretically responsible for helping him perform his official duties—has been politically recruited. The foremost qualification for the $22,450-a-year job of law secretary to a New York State Supreme Court justice is not an applicant's legal acumen, law school standing, distinction as a lawyer, or ability to express himself clearly; it is his political club and his leader's endorsement. New justices have been known to boast of retaining a veto power over the selection of their law assistants ("I told my leader he'd have to get me someone satisfactory to me"), but rare is the judge who has chosen his aides wholly on merit. Furthermore, many judicial staff members virtually disappear from the courthouse at primary and election times; they are busy working day and night at clubhouse politics, assuring the system's self-perpetuation.

There are also indirect ways that our judges manifest their political loyalties. Besides refraining from upsetting the status quo themselves (and certainly our appellate and administrative judges could take major steps to root out some of the rottenness), they are apt to be ill-tempered toward those who would lance the judiciary's pustules. When a senior, vastly experienced, New York City Legal Aid attorney colorfully put down appellate judges as "whores who had become madams," he was brought up on charges initiated by the appellate court.

The clamor for "more, more, more"—more judges and concomitant staffs, at great public expense, rather than increased efficiency in managing our courts—is eagerly joined by our judges. It serves the double purpose of expiating the guilt of an abysmally run judiciary and promising an ever-larger share of political plums. Symbolic of the political role judges retain are the dinners where their presence is the honey that attracts those flies of the bar and of the citizenry who enjoy greeting luminaries of the bench. Other overt political activities include participating in their own clubs' periodic fund-raising wing-dings, officiating at swearing-in ceremonies for their organizations' new officers, and openly aiding political cohorts campaigning for office.

Sub rosa, judges play loosely with the separation of powers fundamental to American government by counseling old fellow politicians in nonjudicial public office. This reached its peak —or nadir—at the U.S. Supreme Court level: Former Associate Justice Abe Fortas' activity as an advisor to President Lyndon B. Johnson was one of the reasons his nomination for Chief Justice was ultimately withdrawn. Parallel situations in local politics are considered perfectly normal.

Nor are they eradicated by "bi-partisan judicial selection," that much heralded panacea. If anything, the impact of political loyalties is intensified when both major parties (and sometimes the minor ones as well) nominate the same candidate: The electorate loses even the theoretical power of saying "No," and candidates for judgeships agreeable to leaders of mixed political stripe are likely to be those who have succeeded in not antagonizing or offending anyone.

"Resolved, that the appointive system of choosing judges is preferable to the elective," provides a hot topic for high school debates, but as for lessening the effect of the judges' political loyalties and indebtednesses, it offers no more than a Tweedledum-Tweedledee choice. New York City, for example, has a mixture of both systems: Supreme Court justices (the higher trial court) are elected, though vacancies are filled until the next general election by the Governor; Family Court and Criminal Court justices are appointed by the Mayor; Civil Court justices are elected, and vacancies are filled temporarily by the Mayor. There is no evidence that mayors and governors are any less political in choosing judges than are assembly district leaders. (For that matter, consider a President's appointments to the U.S. Supreme Court.)

Judicial screening committees have proven equally illusory in the drive for an improved judiciary. Most of them have been charged with recommending a handful of nominees for each vacancy. From this list the designating officials —a mayor exercising his appointive power, or a number of political leaders arranging a nomination—are supposed to make their choices. But some of the candidates are always politically palatable, for the screening committee members are invariably designated by, or with the approval of, those who do the final picking.

When slip-ups have occurred, both appointing and nominating officials have considered themselves free to ignore the recommendations of their own screening bodies. In 1969, this led Francis T. P. Plimpton, a former Ambassador to the United Nations and then president of the New York City Bar Association, to observe: "Unless screening committees or some other procedures for removing the selection of judges from unworthy hands are set up by law, preferably in the [State] Constitution, with enforceable sanctions, there is in my judgment little chance for improvement." Plimpton was bemoaning the system of selecting judges "by wheeling and dealing among the political bosses."

Judgeships being the Grail at the end of the politician's quest, and political loyalty being the sword, shield and armor advancing that quest, what is the impact of all this on the administration of urban criminal justice? About a year ago, New York's highly independent Police Commissioner, Patrick V. Murphy, told the city's bar that "the court system must accept the giant share of the blame for the continual rise in crime." It "has broken down" he charged. "Neither the innocent nor the guilty receive justice, for they are handled alike, mindlessly, randomly, hurriedly, blindly."

The courts have come to this low esteem in New York City largely because our judges have permitted them to drift. The interminable calendar delays, the prison riots, the high street violence—these require firm, purposeful handling, not the abdication of responsibility. Consider the following practices:

Plea Bargaining. Defendants today are seldom sentenced for the crimes they commit. Most of those involved in felony cases plead to and receive punishment for lesser transgressions. The relationship between the offense charged (and more-often-than-not committed) and that to which the accused may be encouraged to enter his "guilty" plea will vary with the strength of the prosecutor's proof, the circumstances sur-

rounding the crime, and the potential public danger shown by the defendant's prior criminal record (all legitimate considerations). It will vary as well with pressures to dispose of cases, the significance of *statistical* accomplishment to the prosecutor, the disposition of the assistant prosecutor who happens to be handling the particular case, and the initiative and diligence of the defense attorney (understandable, but nonetheless invalid considerations).

Most judges will not routinely participate in plea bargaining. By remaining aloof, they can elude criticism if a particular bargain backfires, since it was struck by the lawyers and the judicial role was simply one of passive acceptance.

Judges, however, *should* actively participate in the plea process. Being removed from the combatants' respective aggressive interests, they are in the best position to underscore the interests of justice, and to eliminate *ad hominem* factors. They can assure, on the one hand, that prosecutorial vindictiveness does not prevent a fair plea in a proper case, burdening the courts with a needless trial, and on the other, that a timorous prosecutor afraid of risking a loss in our adversary system does not "give away the courthouse" to a defendant who clearly threatens to be a future danger.

Ex parte meetings. The Canons of Judicial Ethics, simple rules setting forth minimum limitations upon the conduct of judges, specify in unmistakable language: "A judge should not permit private interviews, arguments or communications designed to influence his judicial action, where interests to be affected thereby are not represented before him. . . . Ordinarily all communications of counsel to the judge intended or calculated to influence action should be made known to opposing counsel."

In the criminal courts this canon is so vastly more honored in the breach than in the observance that, I venture, prosecutors and judges who have spent a lifetime handling criminal matters would register surprise on learning of its existence. This is not to suggest that they are unaware of strictures upon a judge's hearing from the defense *ex parte* (without the opposition being present). While not an unusual occurrence, when it comes to light—as allegedly happened in 1971 when a Supreme Court justice retired during hearings on his judicial fitness—it is recognized as improper. But the canon applies with equal force to *ex parte* meetings between *prosecutors* and judges.

The American Bar Association's Minimal Standards governing a prosecutor's conduct declare: "The prosecutor should not engage in unauthorized *ex parte* discussions with or submission of material to a judge relating to a particular case which is or may come before him. . . ." Yet there are judges who meet daily with assistant prosecutors whose cases are on trial before them; together they review the day's events and prepare for the morrow. It is also common for judges, faced with difficult legal questions during a trial, to summon appellate attorneys on the prosecutors' staffs for legal advice. The rationalization is that the attorneys who may have to fight in the higher courts to sustain convictions if they are returned should be consulted in advance about the legal questions likely to be raised upon such appeals. Even jury charges and proposed sentences are rehearsed by judges with prosecutors.

The Canons of Ethics and the Minimal Standards notwithstanding, judges—in court daily with the same group of prosecutors—often begin to see themselves as part of the prosecution team: They feel an obligation to be helpful to the "law and order" side of the bar. Of course, *ex parte* rehearsals and reviews can serve as a form of protection for the judge who is modest about his abilities, frequently with good reason. Forewarned as to what may be coming in the courtroom, and with his positions formulated extrajudicially, he is spared the embarrassment of truly *judging*.

My naïveté was first jolted shortly after graduating from law school. Working as a New York State special assistant attorney general investigating gambling and political corruption in Saratoga County, I got wind of the evening meetings between the special prosecutor and the judge assigned to the inquiry. Later, during my years in the New York City prosecutor's office, I learned that such meetings were a regular and unquestioned practice. And as a defense attorney, I have heard judges and prosecutors so freely refer to their *ex parte* conferences together that it was obvious they sensed no impropriety. In fact, when I have suggested as much, their cynical replies have insinuated that my boy scout training was going too far.

The rule against private meetings between the judge and either party to a litigated dispute is obviously sound: The courtroom can be of little value as a forum if the decisions have already been made elsewhere without equal benefit of argument from both the prosecution and the defense. "Truth," said Lord Eldon a century and a half ago, "is best discovered by powerful statements on both sides of the question."

Pretrial Motions. In 1923 Learned Hand noted that "indictments are calamities for honest men." With tens of thousands of indictments returned annually in New York City alone, it is evident that significant numbers of them should never have been voted, that many wrongly accuse innocent persons of criminal wrong-doing, and that some are likely to be calamitous for the accused. Imagine that a grand jury had unjustly charged you with felonies, and that those charges were given broad currency in the press. Quite apart from the high cost of lawyers and bail, and the time lost in court waiting out interminable adjournments before the trial that might clear you, what impact would the mere *existence* of these criminal charges have on your relationships with your employers, your friends, your family, not to mention your peace of mind?

Because an indictment can be catastrophic to one who is innocent, our civilized judicial system provides machinery for purging improper charges before trial. Judges are required to read the grand jury minutes and dismiss indictments when, even assuming the complete truthfulness of the witnesses, the evidence is insufficient to sustain criminal charges. Unfortunately, our judges do not regularly follow this procedure. Nor are they disposed to listen to significant argument or dismissal motions.

Frequently, even where a judge does agree to "hear" a pretrial dismissal motion, he is not the one who actually studies the legal papers both sides submit. In New York City's busy courts, "pools" of attorneys exist to rule on motions, both criminal and civil. They are truly the judges: anonymous, untitled, unrobed "law assistants," not high on the city's payroll. It is they who too often make the decisions and draft the opinions that appear over our judges' signatures.

Some pool attorneys are extremely knowledgeable, others are not. But virtually all of them receive—and retain—their jobs through their clubhouse activities or connections. Consequently, the guiding motto of these subalterns is not "Do Justice," but "Protect the Judge." The two are not synonymous. For the sake of protecting the judge, indictments that should be dismissed may be sustained. If a charge is dropped, the prosecutor can appeal, and the judge could be embarrassed; if the dismissal motion is denied, ordinarily no appeal will be allowed, for there is still a trial to be had.

Prosecutors usually have far greater access to press coverage than do defense counsel, too, and district attorneys have been known to blast judges discomfortingly for their temerity in dismissing indictments. Hence the law assistant's ingrained caution and political sense incline him toward nondismissal, saving critical action for the *trial* judge. The fact that an innocent man may have to suffer an indictment's awful cloud is of secondary importance. I am not saying that this always happens. Indictments are sometimes dismissed; and sometimes, for ignoble reasons, the ones that are dropped include entirely valid charges. The important point is that due to judicial neglect, too many persons are held for trial when the cases against them should not have survived the motion stage.

Court Administration. Bestowed as a reward for loyal party service, a place on the bench is seen as the most honorable sort of quasi-retirement. For those State Supreme Court justices who will so have it, the hours are short (roughly 10 A.M.-4 P.M. daily); the vacations are long (in some cases from July 4 until Labor Day, plus a week or two at Christmastime); the time off is abundant (all legal holidays, many days or at least afternoons immediately preceding them, frequent Friday afternoons, and various times to attend funerals of other judges, officials, and ex-officials); the staff is ample (a law assistant, a confidential assistant, a secretary, and miscellaneous court attendants); the pay is generous (more than $40,000 annually); and the perquisites are jolly (including a revered title and a special tab for one's car).

Most important of all, the ultimate responsibility, if a judge plays his cards wisely, is nil. In massive New York City there are so many judges, and they rotate their assignments so thoroughly (this is now being modified in civil cases), that what Judge Jones fails to clean up this month is casually left for Judge Smith the following month and may be passed on to Judge Brown the month thereafter, ad nauseum. The buck stops with no one. When a prison riot, a spate of irate news stories about court congestion, or a speech deploring injustice succeeds in provoking judicial comment, its substance is invariably: "Budget insufficiencies make the implementation of sound administrative measures impossible."

That is pure hokum. One need not be a highly trained management consultant to note the two faces of the same coin. On one side are the bankers' hours, the funeral directors' pace, the madhouse's inefficiencies, the jet setters' frequency of holidays. On the other are the interminable time pressures, the delays, congestion, overcrowding, and law assistants doing judges' work. Clearly, the yield per judge could be markedly increased.

Until a few years ago, for example, New York City's Criminal Court—which handles felony arraignments and misdemeanor dispositions, and processes over 100,000 defendants annually—was deeply mired. A new administrative judge was brought in who succeeded in straightening out the court without Parkinsonian manpower increases. His predecessor, a fine, warm and courteous gentleman, having proven a failure at running the lower court, was kicked upstairs to become administrative judge of the Supreme Court—then in bad shape although not in the *extremis* that the Criminal Court had been at his departure and that the higher court soon fell into. No face was lost, and no Supreme Court colleague had to fear the uncomfortable wrath of a determined new broom.

Despite new funds, the criminal sections of New York City's Supreme Court remain administrative nightmares; the added monies have simply been used to create additional "trial parts," even though the old ones have not been working full days and weeks. Unperturbed by a new "ready rule" that compels prosecutors to answer "ready for trial" once a case has aged six months, in most counties district attorneys continue to determine what cases will be tried, when, and before which judges by their control over court calendars. Judges persist in interrupting trials before them—keeping jurors, witnesses, and counsel waiting interminably—while they handle sentences and other calendar business that might be attended to, as in the Federal courts, in the early morning or late afternoon.

Presentence reports are routinely ordered, and the 6–8 weeks they require are permitted to delay sentencing, but once completed many judges do not take the time to read them. The court's sole concentrated doses of book work, ruling on motions, are bunched before a single judge who handles all motions for a month at one time (a minimum of several hundred decisions). Confronted with such a volume of cases, he could not possibly give proper attention to their prompt disposition, even if he were truly diligent and possessed the brain of a Holmes or a Brandeis. Plea bargains continue to be struck in the name of expediency, judges approving them with no knowledge of the defendant's background or prognosis for his future, and with little information about the particular crime to which the defendant is entering his reduced plea.

In Lewis Carroll's *Alice in Wonderland*, the solemn royal procession and the carrying of the King of Hearts' crown on a crimson velvet cushion did not render fair and just his Queen's incessant screaming of "Off with her head." Neither does the veneer of dignity provided by robed judges, flags, sacred mottos, attendants, high benches, and the rest, transmogrify into *justice* the daily charades acted out in our courts. There are a number of steps that could be taken to improve our criminal justice system:

1. Our highest appellate judges, those charged with the administration of the judiciary, should keep themselves directly informed of what is going on in the courts. The present sporadic day-tours of inspection cannot begin to provide a sense of their wheel-spinning and frustrations. In England, appellate judges periodically handle trial chores; were our key appellate judges to sit, say, one month a year in the courts, they would be better prepared to perform their administrative functions. Their power to remove judges, now scant indeed, should also be extended and far more liberally exercised: not merely for moral derelictions, but for laziness, excessive delegation of judicial responsibilities, continued political activities after ascension to the bench, employment of part-time help at full-time pay, and the like.

2. To stop the perpetual passing of the buck from judge to judge, current rotation policies should be terminated, along with the prosecutors' ability to choose particular judges for specific cases. In the Federal courts, criminal cases are ordinarily assigned by lot, and the same judge oversees a given case from the moment it enters the courts until it is disposed of. This curbs the tendency to adjourn unnecessarily, and it minimizes the practice of giving short shrift to motions. By handling all the dismissal, discovery, suppression, and exclusion motions involved, judges would become more familiar with the cases assigned to them; when "lesser pleas" were discussed, they would have a far better idea of their appropriateness. An additional benefit might be improved use of the court's "probation" facilities: Social histories (the so-called "prepleading reports") might more often be prepared *before* guilty pleas are entered.

3. Laws should be enacted against political activity by judges and their staffs. Further, criminal sanctions should be applied to full-time employes on the public payrolls who put in less than full working hours, and to their supervisors.

4. The press should recognize that what does not happen in the courts can be far more important, in the long run, than what does. Granted that trials have drama, they represent no more than about 5 percent of all felony cases. Detailed coverage of daily motion calendars when judges wave away argument, of the decision process carried on by unknown law clerks, of plea-bargaining conducted between counsel and ratified in semi-ignorance by judges, would do far more to improve the administration of criminal justice in most cities than any number of front-page spreads on sensational murder trials or alleged Black Panther plots.

5. Finally, and perhaps too idealistically, the selection of judges should be separated from party politics. Whether the process decided upon is an appointive or elective one, it should entail true searches for men whose legal talents alone make them worthy of a place on the bench.

If we are to refurbish our criminal justice system, we must penetrate beneath its trappings. And once we have chosen judges who are truly committed to judging, we must see to it that they remain dedicated acolytes at the altar of justice—even if this takes some seemingly unbecoming prodding.

13 SEX AND A PERMISSIVE SOCIETY—ALL THE WAY?

Sexuality in a Zero Growth Society

Alexander Comfort

From *Center Report* (December, 1972), 12–14. Reprinted, with permission, from the December 1972 issue of the *Center Report*, a publication of the Center for the Study of Democratic Institutions in Santa Barbara, California.

Dr. Comfort heads the Aging Research Institute, University College, London, and is a specialist in gerontology. His major contributions are The Powerhouse *(1944),* Aging, the Biology of Senescence *(1964), and* Nature and Human Nature *(1966). He edited* The Joy of Sex *(1972).*

We are on the verge, in developed countries, of a society in which zero population growth will be an overriding social objective. Few people will have more than two children, and many will have none. By the mid 2000s people will probably live and remain vigorous longer through the control of natural aging. It will be a new game with different rules. The concept of the family which will alter—and is already altering—is that which folklore still maintains as our ideal expectation—the exclusive, totally self-sufficient couple-relationship, involving the ideal surrender of identity and of personal selfhood, which excluded kin and only grudgingly included children. The expectation, implied in so many novels and films, was in fact only rarely fulfilled. Unlike the older pattern, where there were other and supporting satisfactions beside each other's company, it was often a neurotic

expectation. Young people today see this, and without diminishing their capacity for love, shy away from the idea of total self-surrender: "I am I and you are you, and neither of us is in this world to live up to the other's expectations . . . I love you, but in forty years we may be different people." This view, if not romantic, is at least realistic in terms of human experience.

Yet another change is that contraception has for the first time wholly separated the three human uses of sex—sex as parenthood, sex as total intimacy between two people ("relational" sex), and sex as physical play ("recreational" sex). "Morals," in their usual and sexual meaning, reflect in rules the culture's image of what the family should be. Religion, which in our culture traditionally rejects pleasure as a motive, has tried hard to fence in the use of recreational sex. Until lately it did this by asserting that reproduction was the only legitimate use of sexuality. With the growth of the image of the ideal couple, it changed its ground, rather behind the event, so that today, together with many of its later successors in psychiatry and counselling, it asserts that worthy sex can only be relational. There has been no time in human history when either of these valuations was wholly true,

169

though they have served in their time to reinforce the uses which that time made of the family. Even in the most strongly kin-based cultures, gaps were left for sexual activity which was not an expression either of a wish for children or of an all-embracing personal relationship. Such gaps concerned chiefly the male, who was often the legislator, and who claimed the right to experience sexual relations in a non-relational way, while excluding women from doing so, either by moral codes, or by the indoctrination of girls with the idea that relational sex is the sole kind of which women, as opposed to men, are capable.

The Pill has altered that. Secure from unwanted pregnancy, an increasing number of women have discovered that their capacity to experience sex at all three levels, either together or on different occasions and in different contexts, is as great as a man's, if not greater. The adult of today has all three options—sex as parenthood, sex as total relationship, and sex as physical pleasure accompanied by no more than affection. Older people looking at the young today realize increasingly how much the confusion between these modes, which they could not foresee, or even choose voluntarily between, has often complicated their lives; when play between boy and girl resulted in pregnancy and a forced marriage between mere acquaintances, when one partner misread the other's degree of involvement, or falsified his own selfishly to overcome reluctance.

Greater choice can bring greater problems and greater opportunities. It will bring problems in any event, and these can only be reduced by recognizing how great is the range of situations in which sex relations now take place, and learning to handle them to meet our own and our partner's needs. If we can do this, then the new freedom, though it now seems to be generating confusion, could reshape our living to meet the needs which were once met by the traditional human family pattern. We have dispensed with kin—to support us in life and look after us in old age. Consequently we are lonely, and we go to "sensitivity groups" to relearn how to treat people as people. The fantasy-concept of total

one-to-one sufficiency has let us down. Since sex is now divorced from parenthood, there are many more relationships into which it can enter if we choose.

All that can be certainly predicted for the future is that the variety of patterns will increase as individuals find the norm that suits them. For some, parenthood will still be the central satisfaction, carrying with it the obligation of giving the children the stability they require. For others sexuality will express total involvement with one person. For others, one or more primary relationships will be central, but will not exclude others, in which the recreational role of sex acts as a source of bonding to supply the range of relationships formerly met by kin—an old human pattern in which sexual contacts were permitted between a woman and all her husband's clan brothers, or a man and all his wife's titular sisters.

In the zero population growth world we are all "clan brothers" and will have to find ways of expressing the hippy ideal of universal kinship. For many of the young today, a wider range of permitted sexual relationships seems to express this ideal, and even the rather compulsive wife-swapping of middle-aged couples in urban America seems to be reaching towards the same solution. What is clear is that we cannot reimpose the old rigidities. In going forward to newer and more varied patterns, our sense of responsibility and our awareness of others is going to be severely tested if we are not to become still more confused and unhappy. If we pass the test, we may evolve into a universal human family in which all three types of sex have their place, in which we are all genuinely kin, and in which all but the most unrealistic inner needs can be met in one form or another.

Conventional morals are probably correct in asserting that all satisfactory sex is in some degree inherently relational—if it is satisfactory, and mutually so, a relation subsists. Only the wholly insensitive mate mechanically, even under the conditions of permitted non-discrimination which characterize a ritualized orgy. A society like ours, which has traditionally feared and rejected close personal contact, has also generated a mythology of all-or-none involvement which profoundly influences us to our hurt. Unable to exclude the recreational and the partly relational modes of sex, it has set about rejecting or falsifying them. Once rid of this ideology, it might find that the relation present in purely recreational or social sex is a uniquely effective tool in breaking down personal separateness—of which the proprietary notion of love is an offshoot—so that, for us as for many primitives, social sex comes to express and cement the equivalent of kinship through a general intimacy and non-defensiveness, reinforced by the very strong reward of realizing suppressed needs for variety and for acceptance.

Our society has moved illogically in this direction by virtually institutionalizing adultery: a growing number of spouses permit each other complete sexual liberty on the conditions that there shall be no "involvement" and that the extracurricular relations are not brought to their attention. It is beginning to institutionalize ritual spouse exchange. This is more honest, and a better bet anthropologically; non-involvement is, as it were, written in, the exchange is non-secret, and the partners, instead of excluding each other, share in the arrangement. How far conventional middle-class "swingers" profit emotionally in openness from their swinging is arguable—most studies suggest that they keep it in a watertight compartment and ritualize it as a sort of charismatic hobby or secret society, which embodies all current prejudices and does little to create any universal openness. At least, however, it marks the end, or the beginning of the end, of proprietary sexual attitudes. In part it has spread to the middle-aged from the young; older couples want to imitate their freedom without abandoning present attitudes. Unless the result disturbs children and leads to a backlash generation, the genuine insight present in "swinging" by the bored and the unrealized could expand into something far more like institutionalized sociosexual openness.

This process, so far as it has gone, would have been impossible without a gradual change in attitudes toward, and anxiety about, bisexuality. Mate-sharing, both psychoanalytically, and in primate ethology, reveals a surrogate sexual relation between males—expressed covertly so far in the gang night out and the attraction of the prostitute or "shared" woman, acceptable substitutes for overt male-male contacts because they are covert. The potential for more open bisexual contacts is greatly increased by two-couple activity. Men tend still to be disturbed by this, but women, who are in general less anxious about their bisexual potential, often embrace the opportunity with male encouragement. In fact, judging from primates, the state of sharing with another male, which reinforces individual dominance, could well help rather than hinder the heterosexuality of anxious people—dominance anxiety plays a large part in the suppression of heterosexual drives in most persons who regard themselves as constitutionally homosexual. Beside reinstating the kinship of men and women, a wider and opener use of sexuality is quite likely to reinstate, and reinforce, the kinship between men and men, which we now studiously avoid erotizing or expressing. In a fully erotized society, bisexuality, expressed or not, could cease to be a problem simply because social attitudes have changed.

Another important casualty of this process is likely to be sexual jealousy. Much argument has been devoted to discussing how far jealousy is a normal emotion, the counterpart of love, and how far it is a product of indoctrination. It would probably be true to say that in the traditional family jealousy was based on reproduction (knowing that my children are mine) and ideas of property, while in the romantic couple situation it is a product of the fear of rejection implicit in a surrender so alarmingly total. Modern attempts to transcend jealousy through wife-exchange or greater tolerance of affairs are often uncertain and anxious, but they have positive features—acceptance of a more realistic view of the needs of couples and individuals for variety, and recognition that the meeting of needs rather than their frustration is a gift which expresses love rather than devalues it, and strengthens the primary bond. (One need not be like the mischievous lovers of *"Les Liaisons Dangereuses"* to recognize this.) Such a recognition is important as marking the end of the mutual proprietorship, physical or emotional, which has so often characterized human sexual relationships in the past, and which modern woman, as well as modern man, rightly rejects as neurotic and immature. To our grandchildren, nineteenth century opera may be emotionally unintelligible.

Some will feel that the use of wider sex as a substitute for kinship devalues love and will leave us emotionally shallow. Others will see it as the defusing of a dangerous fantasy concerning the total nature of human love, which no society has enacted in fact or found satisfactory in the enactment, but which the folklore of the postkinship family has wished on us to our hurt. The relationships of the zero growth society will have to be relationships between whole, adult people, dependent on their own resources, not using kin, family and children as a bolthole or one another as climbingposts, but if this kind of adulthood can be attained at all widely (it will never be practicable for all) it could lead to relations far more supportive in a truly human sense than any we have so far known. Certainly none of the past fictions embodied in our stereotypes of male and female sex roles, of totally exclusive love, or even of central parenthood can readily persist unaltered.

We are not here talking about change which we can further or prevent, simply about changes which are now taking place. If we approach them on the basis of anxiety, past expectation and folklore they will only generate more of the anomie which we have now. The alternative is to see whether we can approach them with insight and compassion for one another.

Extension of survival into old age has already led to the concept of "two lifespans," with a second, adolescence-like identity crisis around the age of 40, when realized and unrealized goals are reassessed: the crisis may end in a resumption of established relationships, illness or depression, or a total recasting of relationships. The crisis is more prominent in men—their societal opportunity for a "new start," occupationally and sexually, is the greater—and it often leads to the starting of a second family with a younger partner. Women's opportunities are more cruelly circumscribed at this age—they tend to find themselves deserted, having "run out of" family and an established role. Any further extension of vigorous life through interference with aging might put them on a more equal footing with men; it will certainly increase the tendency for life-styles, and families, to be serial, so that each individual has the option of continuing in one pattern, or of entering a wholly different one, at the age when in the traditional family one was preparing for dependent senescence. The decline of the kinship family has born excessively hard on the old—dependency is rejected, and they become increasingly isolated in a forced "independence" which is worsened by the shortage of kin. Perhaps more than anyone they would benefit from a "spreading" of the couple-preoccupied family into something more like a tribe of friends.

I would expect accordingly to see a society in which pair relationships are still central, but initially less permanent, in which childbearing is seen as a special responsibility involving a special life style, and in which settled couples engage openly in a wide range of sexual relations with friends, with other couples, and with third parties as an expression of social intimacy, without prejudice to the primacy of their own relationship, and with no more, and probably less, permanent interchange than we see in the society of serial polygamy with adultery that now exists. Such a pattern is coming into existence in America, and is beginning to become explicit. Whether it will devalue relationships or only deprive them of neurotic compulsion will depend on the persons involved, the amount of support they receive from the social ethic, and the accuracy of the expectations with which they enter maturity. If these expectations become realistic, it will be the first time that a modern generation has been reared with confidence but without illusions.

The political implications of universalized kinship are interesting. Marcuse, in discussing the "erotization of relationships" as a political force was once challenged to "go erotize the state of Kansas." My suggestion is that this may in fact be happening. The family is in fact the microcosm of politics with a one to two generation timelag. Institutional politics today reflect combative paternalism, which had its family counterpart in the 1950s, and liberal politics the social expression of the ideal of individualist romantic love. It is possible to overstate the inherently revolutionary potential of "universal kinship," but if, as I suggest, it is explicitly erotized, it will find a counterpart socially in anarchic community action. How far it produces such action, and how far the nonpossessive individual and the anti-authoritarian society are products of the same change in social requirement it is hard to say. The acceptance of sensuality, and the widening of its focus to include not one but many others, would seem in itself to be an emotional technology capable of fitting well into the less compulsive and more gentle world view of the twenty-first as against the nineteenth and twentieth centuries. Marcuse is probably right in seeing justice, non-possession, non-exploitation, ecology and the wider erotization of relationships as possible correlates. We may have a rough few years ahead before this pattern emerges, but when and if it does, one could wish to live in those times.

Ethics and Unmarried Sex: Morals Re-examined

Joseph Fletcher

Professor Fletcher received his B.D. at the Berkeley Divinity School, has taught at the University of Cincinnati, the University of the South, and Clare College, Cambridge, and is now at the Harvard Episcopal Theological School. He has focused his attention on social ethics and has contributed Morals and Medicine *(1954),* Situation Ethics: The New Morality *(1966), and* Moral Responsibility *(1967) to explicate his ideas.*

Ever since birth control separated love-making and baby-making the resistance movement, principally in our Christian churches, has warned us that sooner or later "they" would be recommending it for "everybody"—even the unmarried. The time has come, *der Tag* is here.

Before World War II Lewis Terman predicted that premarital sex would be accepted in the near future. Now, in 1966, the press is picking up and publishing news that several universities and co-educational colleges are being faced with a policy question by their health services: Should unmarried students be informed, supplied and guided in the use of fertility control devices, upon request? Last year a report of the Group for the Advancement of Psychiatry, entitled *Sex and the College Student,* gave its support to the principle of privacy and accordingly challenged the theory that an institution of higher learning should try to be *in loco parentis.* The psychiatrists concluded that "sexual activity privately practiced with appropriate regard to the sensitivities of other people should not be the direct concern of the administration."

However, in this matter as in most, the usual distance between the conventional wisdom and critical reflection separates town and gown. Going to bed unwed is not regarded favorably in the sidewalk debate or at the coffee klatches after church. A Gallup Poll in October, 1965, showed that 74 percent of American adults disapproved of allowing college or university women to have oral contraceptives, or at least of *giving* them to them. This means, logically, an equal disapproval of making mechanical means such as diaphragms or intra-uterine devices available to undergraduates, as well as other nonsteroid pharmaceutical methods. Elements of psychodynamics and cultural taboo are strong in the general public's opposition. It is far from being simply an informed and critical opposition to a proposed ethical innovation. The "ancient good" is stubbornly grasped, no matter how "uncouth" it may be alleged to have become. Shakespeare put the grassroots temper very neatly in *The Tempest*, where he had Prospero warn Ferdinand,

If thou dost break her virgin knot before
All sanctimonius ceremonies may
With full and holy rite be minister'd,
No sweek aspersion shall the heavens let fall
To make this contract grow; but barren hate,
Sour-eyed disdain, and discord, shall bestrew
The union of your bed with weeds so loathly,
That you shall hate it both.

But Shakespeare did his thinking in a very different milieu. Approximately 40 percent of the sexually mature population are unmarried. Just in terms of statistical weight this shows, therefore, how many people are affected by our question, and we can also make a good guess as to the extent of the hypocrisy which surrounds it. Social competition penalizes early marriage, and the postponement required by a lengthening period of training for career roles and functions pushes marriage further and further away from the biological pressure following puberty. Physical maturity far outstrips our mental, cultural, and emotional development. It is said that menstruation in girls starts in this epoch on the average age of thirteen and a half years (13½) compared to seventeen (17) a century ago. No human culture in past history ever levied as much tension and strain on the human psychophysical structure as ours does. And since the Kinsey reports it is an open secret that male virility is greatest in the late teens—when young men used to marry and rear families. But now they go to high school and become college freshmen!

Just as Herman Kahn's *Thinking About the Unthinkable* has forced us to come to grips with such "unthinkable" possibilities as a nuclear decimation of people by the millions, so the "sexplosion" of the modern era is forcing us to do some thinking about the "unthinkable" in sex ethics. If we had to check off a point in modern times when the sex revolution started, first in practice but only slowly and reluctantly in thought, I would set it at World War I. Since then there has been a phenomenal increase of aphrodisiac literature, visual and verbal, as well as more informational materials. We have seen an unprecedented freedom of expression orally as well as in print, both in ordinary conversation and in the mass media which glamorize sex—the movies, television, radio, and slick paper magazines.

All of this reflects a new temper about sexual concerns. It is a new mental and emotional attitude, based on a new knowledge and a new frankness. Hollywood personalities are cultural heroes, and they lose none of their popularity or charismatic appeal when they openly engage in sexual adventures apart from the ring and the license. In the movie *The Sandpiper* even a minister is portrayed as improved and uplifted by a sex affair with an unmarried woman (played by the sexnik, Elizabeth Taylor). The radical psychic ambivalence of the old discredited antisexual tradition, in which women were seen as prostitutes (sexual and bad) or madonnas (angelic, nonsexual and pure), is not gone yet but its cure is well on the way.

In the great universities of our times, described by Clark Kerr as "multiversities," there is a pluralism or multiplicity of sexual practices and of ethical opinions. We have a sexual diversity which is in keeping with our principles of individual liberty and intellectual freedom. Some of us are quite archaic, some are extremely avant-garde; most of us are curious, critical, still cogitating. Undergraduates are often insecure in their sexual views and activities—as in most other areas of responsibility. They tend to despise the hypocrisy with which their elders deal with the "sex question" or evade it. Many of them, of course, profess to be far more confident in their pro-sex affirmations than they really are. In any case, the older generation has turned them loose, young men and women together in great co-educational communities, with only a few parietal rules to separate them. In the nineteenth century middle class parents protected their daughters' virginity with all kinds of chaperonage; in the mobile twentieth century they have turned it over to the boys and girls themselves.

In what follows we shall focus our attention sharply on one form of unmarried sex—*pre*marital. "Unmarried sex" is a term that covers a wide range of human and infrahuman sexuality, as we know. Homosexuality is a part of it, as well as ethical issues about noncoital sex problems such as abortion and sterilization. (For example, few states are as enlightened as North Carolina, which provides voluntary sterilizations and "pills" for unmarried mothers who request them.)

THE SITUATION

Back in 1960 Professor Leo Koch of the University of Illinois, a biologist, was fired for saying that it was ethically justifiable to approve of premarital intercourse. His offending statement was: "With modern contraceptives and medical advice readily available at the nearest drug store, or at least a family physician, there is no valid reason why sexual intercourse should not be condoned among those sufficiently mature to engage in it without social consequences and without violating their own codes of morality and ethics." With due regard for his three qualifying factors—maturity, social concern, and integrity—we can say that Professor Koch's position is the one at which this position essay will arrive. We shall try, incidentally, to demonstrate that the fear of honest discussion revealed by Koch's dismissal is at least not universal. (Professor Koch shared the earlier opinion of Professor George Murdock of Yale that premarital intercourse would prepare young people for more successful marriages. But this paper will not offer any analysis favoring or opposing the Murdock-Koch thesis about marriage preparation.)

The American Bar Association has lately urged the different states to review and revise their civil and criminal laws regulating sex acts. Few have done so—except for Illinois. Serious efforts are under way in California and New York in the face of strong opposition in the churches. A model code committee of the American Law Institute in 1956 reported out some important proposed changes in existing law, all in the direction of greater personal freedom sexually, and calling for a lowering of the age of consent to eliminate unjust convictions for statutory rape. Fornication is a criminal offense in thirty-six of our fifty states, the penalty running from $10.00 in Rhode Island to $500 plus two years in jail in Alaska. Fourteen states have no law against it, but in six of these States "cohabitation" (nonmarital intercourse consistently with the same person) is a criminal offense.

This is a typical anomaly of our sex laws. It makes the punishment for cohabitation heavier than for promiscuity, thus creating the absurd situation in which a measure of interpersonal commitment between such sexual partners is penalized and promiscuity or *casual* fornication is preferred! In Massachusetts, for example, the penalty for fornication is $30.00 or ninety days in jail, but for cohabitation it is $300 or as much as three years. While many states outlaw adultery, there are others that allow extramarital sex—as in wife swapping clubs. California is an example.

A great deal of both clinical and taxonomic evidence has been gathered showing that sexual activity, or at least sexual exploration, occurs before marriage—unrecognized by the conventional wisdom. The Kinsey findings were that 67 percent of college males are involved, 84 percent of males who go as far as high school, and 98 percent of those who only finish grade school. We can raise these figures for the intervening fifteen years or more, but very probably it is still true that there is a negative correlation between educational levels and nonmarital intercourse. With females the opposite is the case; the higher the school level the greater their frequency of fornication. College women rated 60 percent in Kinsey's studies (1953), but the rate was discernibly higher for 1966.

In recent years there has been a considerable black market in oral contraceptives. They can be had from "a man on the corner" or from drug stores that just don't ask for a prescription. Five million pills were hijacked in Philadelphia two years ago. Incidentally, local investigators have learned that more pills are sold in the vicinity of colleges than elsewhere. Doctors give unmarried girls and women prescriptions for them even when they do not personally approve of their patients' use of them. They rarely refuse them to applicants, and practically never when the young woman is engaged to be married. A year's prescription costs from $5.00 to $25.00 as the fee. In some college health services the medical staff make this distinction, giving to the engaged and refusing the unengaged. Soon we will have injections and vaccines which immunize against ovulation for several months at a time, making things easier than ever. It is even likely that a morning-after pill is coming, an abortifacient.

This will be a blessing because of the increase of unintended pregnancies and venereal diseases, due to the new sexual freedom. The Surgeon General has said that 1,400 get a venereal disease every day in the year. Syphilis increased by 200 percent from 1965 to 1966 among persons under twenty. The rate of illegitimate pregnancies among teenagers doubled from 1940 to 1961, and it quadrupled among women in the ages of twenty to twenty-five. The highest incidence of pregnancy is among those least promiscuous, i.e., those who are least competent sexually. Yet the risks do not deter them anymore. Fifty percent of teen-age girls who marry are pregnant; 80 percent of those who marry teen-age boys. It is estimated that nearly 200,000 teenagers are aborted every year.

Sociologists, psychologists, and psychiatrists give us many reasons for the spread of premarital sex. Popularity seeking, the need for a secure companion and dater, the prestige value of full sexual performance, the notion that it achieves personal self-identity, even—but rather rarely—the need for physical satisfaction, these are among the things most mentioned. It is probably still the case that the majority of young women and some young men ordinarily, except for an occasional lapse, stop short of coitus, practicing petting to the point of orgasm instead of actual intercourse. Yet from the moral standpoint it is doubtful that there is any real difference between a technical virgin and a person who goes "all the way." And as for the old double standard for masculine and feminine behavior, it is clearly on its way out in favor of a more honest and undiscriminatory sex ethic.

These changes in attitude are going on even among Christians. The Sycamore Community at Penn State made a survey anonymously of 150 men and women, mostly ministers or professors and their wives, and found that while 33 percent were opposed to premarital sex, 40 percent favored it selectively. Forty percent of their male respondents reported that they themselves engaged in it (a low percentage compared to the whole population), and 35 percent of the women so reported. Fifteen percent reported that they had or had had premarital coitus frequently or regularly. Of the married respondents 18 percent of the husbands and 15 percent of the wives reported extramarital sex acts, although one-third of them said they had petted short of coitus. Yet 40 percent felt it might be justifiable in certain situations.

In order, however, to get a sharp focus on the ethical problem and a possible solution, let us agree to stay with *pre*marital sex. And let us agree that this term covers both casual sexual congress and a more personalized experience with dating partners, "steadies," and a "shack up" friend.

THE PROBLEM

In terms of ethical analysis we have *two* problem areas. The first one is the problem of premarital sex for those whose moral standards are in the classical religious tradition, based on a faith commitment to a divine sanction—usually, in America, some persuasion or other of the Judaeo-Christian kind. The second area is the "secular" one, in which people's moral standards are broadly humanistic, based on a value commitment to human welfare and happiness. It is difficult, if not impossible, to say what proportion of our people falls in either area, but they exist certainly, and the "secular" area is growing all the time.

There is by no means a set or unchanging viewpoint in the religious camp. Some Christians are challenging the old morality of the marital monopoly of sex. The Sycamore report declares that "there are no distinctively Christian patterns of sexual behavior which can be characterized by the absence or presence of specific acts." Their report favors a more situational, less legalistic approach to sex ethics. "Let Christians," they say, "face squarely the fact that what the body of authoritative Christian thought passed off as God's revealed truth was in fact human error with a Pauline flavor. Let us remember this fact every time we hear a solemn assertion about this or that being God's will or *the* Christian ethic."

In contrast to situation ethics, or religious relativism, stands the legalistic ethics of universal absolutes (usually negatives and prohibitions), condemning every form of sexual expression except horizontal coitus eyeball-to-eyeball solely between the parties to a monagamous marriage contract. Thus one editorial writer in a semi-fundamentalist magazine said recently, and correctly enough, "The new moralists do not believe that the biblical moral laws are really given by God. Morals laws are not regarded as the products of revelation." A growing company of church people are challenging fixed moral principles or rules about sex or anything else.

The idea in the past has been that the ideal fulfillment of our sex potential lies in a monogamous marriage. But there is no reason to regard this ideal as a legal absolute. For example, if the sex ratio were to be overthrown by disaster, polygamy could well become the ideal or standard. Jesus showed more concern about pride and hypocrisy than about sex. In the story of the "Woman Taken in Adultery" her accusers were guiltier than she. Among the Seven Deadly Sins lust is listed but not sex, and lust can exist in marriage as well as out. But even so, lust is not so grave a sin as pride. As Dorothy Sayers points out scornfully, "A man may be greedy and selfish; spiteful, cruel, jealous and unjust; violent and brutal; grasping, unscrupulous and a liar; stubborn and arrogant; stupid, morose and dead to every noble instinct" and yet, if he practices his sinfulness within the marriage bond he is not thought by some Christians to be immoral!

The Bible clearly affirms sex as a high-order value, at the same time sanctioning marriage (although not always monogamy), but any claim that the Bible requires that sex be expressed solely within marriage is only an inference; there is nothing explicitly forbidding premarital acts. Only extramarital acts, i.e., adultery, is forbidden. Those Christians who are situational, refusing to absolutize any moral principle except "love thy neighbor," cannot absolutize St. Paul's one-flesh (*henosis*) theory of marriage in I Corinthians 6. Paul Ramsey of Princeton has tried to defend premarital intercourse by engaged couples on the ground that they become married thereby. But marriages are not made by the act itself; sexual congress does not create a marriage. Marriage is a mutual commitment, willed and purposed interpersonally.

Besides, all such "ontological" or "naturalistic" reasoning fails completely to meet the moral question of nonmarital sex acts between *un*engaged couples, since it presumably condemns them all universally as unjustifiable, simply because they are nonmarital. It is still the old marital monopoly theory, only one step relaxed.

The humanists in our "secular" society draw close to the nonlegalists, the nonabsolutists among Christians, when they choose concern for personal values as their ethical norm, for this is very close to the biblical "love thy neighbor as thyself." Professor Lester Kirkendall, in a privately circulated position paper, "Searching for the Roots of Moral Judgments," puts the humanist position well:

> The essence of morality lies in the quality of interrelationships which can be established among people. Moral conduct is that kind of behavior which enables people in their relationships with each other to experience a greater sense of trust and appreciation for others; which increases the capacity of people to work together; which reduces social distance and continually furthers one's outreach to other persons and groups; which increases one's sense of self-respect and produces a greater measure of personal harmony.
>
> Immoral behavior is just the converse. Behavior which creates distrust destroys appreciation for others, decreases the capacity for cooperation, lessens concern for others, causes persons or groups to shut themselves off or be shut off from others, and decreases an individual's sense of self-respect is immoral behavior.
>
> This is, of course, nothing new. The concept has been implicit in religions for ages. The injunction "love thy neighbor as thyself" is a case in point.

On this view sarcasm and graft are immoral but not sexual intercourse, unless it is malicious or callous or cruel. On this basis an act is not wrong because of the act itself but because of its *meaning*—its motive and message. Therefore, as Professor Kirkendall explains, the question "Should we ever spank a child?" can only be answered, "It depends upon the situation, on why it is done and how the child understands it."

In the same way, as a *Christian* humanist, Professor John Macmurray, declares, "The integrity of persons is inviolable. You shall not use a person for your own ends or indeed for any ends, individual or social. To use another person is to violate his personality by making an object of him; and in violating the integrity of another, you violate your own." Thus one of Kant's maxims, at least, has survived the ravages of time. And recalling Henry Miller's book titles, we might paraphrase Kant and Macmurray by saying, "The plexus of the sexus is the nexus."

Both religious and secular moralists in America's plural society need to remember that freedom *of* religion includes freedom *from* religion. There is no ethical basis for compelling noncreedalists to follow any creedal codes of behavior, Christian or non-Christian. A "sin" is an act against God's will, but if the agent does not believe in God he cannot commit sin; and even those who do believe in God disagree radically as to what God's will is. Speaking to the issue over birth control law, Cardinal Cushing of Boston says, "Catholics do not need the support of civil law to be faithful to their own religious convictions, and they do not need to impose their moral views on other members of society. . . ." What the Cardinal says about birth control applies just as much to premarital intercourse.

Harking back to the Group for the Advancement of Psychiatry report's support of sexual *laissez faire* on college campuses, we could offer an ethical proposition of our own: Nothing we do is truly moral unless we are free to do otherwise. We must be free to decide what to do before any of our actions even begins to be moral. No discipline but self-discipline has any moral significance. This applies to sex, politics, or anything else. A moral act is a free act, done because we want to do it.

Incidentally, but not insignificantly, let me

remark that this freedom, which is so essential to moral acts, can mean freedom *from* premarital sex as well as freedom for it. Not everybody would choose to engage in it. Some will not because it would endanger a precious relationship, interpersonally; some because it would endanger the sense of personal integrity. Value sentiments or "morals" may be changing (they *are* obviously), but we are still "living in the overlap" and a sensitive, imaginative person might both well and wisely decide against it. As Dr. Mary Calderone points out, very young men and women are not always motivated in the same way: "The girl plays at sex, for which she is not ready, because fundamentally what she wants is love; and the boy plays at love, for which he is not ready, because what he wants is sex."

Many will oppose premarital sex for reasons of the social welfare, others for relationship reasons, and some for simply egoistic reasons. We may rate these reasons differently in our ethical value systems, but the main point morally is to respect the freedom to choose. And short of coitus young couples can pet each other at all levels up to orgasm, just so they are honest enough to recognize that merely technical virgins are no better morally than those who go the whole way. In John Hersey's recent novel, the boy and girl go to bed finally but end up sleeping curled up at arm's length. It is ethically possible, that is to say, to be undecided, conflicted, and immobilized. What counts is being honest, and in some cases decision can be mistaken. Let honesty reign then too. Bryan Green, the evangelist, once said that the engaged but unmarried should thank God for the "experience" and ask his forgiveness for a lack of discipline.

THE SOLUTION

Just as there are two ethical orientations, theistic and humanistic, so there are two distinct questions to ask ourselves. One is: Should we prohibit and condemn premarital sex? The other is: Should we approve of it? To the first one I promptly reply in the negative. To the second I propose an equivocal answer, "Yes and no—depending on each particular situation." The most solid basis for any ethical approach is on the ground common to both the religiously oriented and the humanistically oriented—namely, the concern both feel for persons. They are alike *personalistically* oriented. For example, both Christians and non-Christians can accept the normative principle, "We ought to love people and use things; immorality only occurs when we love things and use people." They can agree also on a companion maxim: "We ought to love people, not rules or principles; what counts is not any hard and fast moral law but doing what we can for the good of others in every situation."

The first principle means that no sexual act is ethical if it hurts or exploits others. This is the difference between lust and love: lust treats a sexual partner as an object, love as a subject. Charity is more important than chastity, but there is no such thing as "free love." There must be some care and commitment in premarital sex acts or they are immoral. Hugh Hefner, the whipping boy of the stuffies, has readily acknowledged in *Playboy* that "personal" sex relations are to be preferred to impersonal. Even though he denies that mutual commitment needs to go to the radical lengths of marriage, he sees at least the difference between casual sex and actually callous congress.

The second principle is one of situation ethics—making a moral decision hang on the particular case. How, here and now, can I act with the most concern for the happiness and welfare of those involved—myself and others? Legalistic moralism, with its absolutes and universals, always thou-shalt-nots, cuts out the middle ground between being a virgin and a sexual profligate. This is an absurd failure to see that morality has to be acted out on a continuum of relativity, like life itself, from situation to situation.

The only independent variable is concern for people; love thy neighbor as thyself. Christians, whether legalistic or situational about their ethics, are agreed that the *ideal* sexually is the combination of marriage and sex. But the ideal gives no reason to demand that others should adopt that ideal or to try to impose it by law; nor is it even any reason to absolutize the ideal in practice for all Christians in all situations. Sex is not always wrong outside marriage, even for Christians; as St. Paul said, "I know . . . that nothing is unclean in itself." Another way to put it is to say that character shapes sex conduct, sex does not shape character.

As I proposed some years ago in a paper in *Law and Contemporary Problems*, the Duke University law journal, there are only three proper limitations to guide both the civil law and morality on sexual acts. No sexual act between persons competent to give mutual consent should be prohibited, except when it involves either the seduction of minors or an offense against the public order. These are the principles of the Wolfenden Report to the English Parliament, adopted by that body and endorsed by the Anglican and Roman Catholic archbishops. It is time we acknowledged the difference between "sins" (a private judgment) and "crimes" against the public conscience and social consensus.

Therefore, we can welcome the recent decision of the federal Department of Health, Education, and Welfare to provide birth control assistance to unmarried women who desire it. It is a policy which puts into effect the principles of the President's Health Message to Congress of March 1, 1966. If the motive is a truly moral one it will be concerned not only with relief budgets but with the welfare of the women and a concern to prevent unwanted babies. Why wait for even *one* illegitimate child to be born?

Dr. Ruth Adams, president of Wellesley College, has said that the college's role is to give information about birth control educationally but no medical assistance. Actually birth control for unmarried students, she thinks, is "the function of the student's private physician rather than the college." This is the strategy being followed by most universities and colleges—to separate knowledge and assistance, relegating to off-campus doctors the responsibility of protecting the unmarried from unwanted pregnancies. As a strategy it obviously avoids a clash with those who bitterly oppose sexual freedom; it is therefore primarily a public relations posture. It bows the neck to people whose attitude is that if premarital sex can't be prevented then the next best thing is to prvent tragic consequences—a curiously sadistic kind of pseudo-morality.

But surely this policy of information but no personal help is an ethical evasion by the universities. If they accept a flat fee for watching over the students' health, is not contraceptive care included? If college health services are able to prescribe treatment which is better than students can get in a drugstore, they *ought* to provide it. They should give *all* the medical service needed except what is too elaborate or technical for their facilities. Nobody is suggesting that pills or IUD's or diaphragms should be sold in the campus bookstore, but they ought to be regarded as a medical resource *owed* to the student as needed and requested. This is the opinion of most physicians on college health services, and I would support it for ethical reasons—chiefly out of respect for personal freedom.

14 EDUCATION— IS A NEW ORDER IN ORDER?

Changing Perspectives on Quality Education: The New Learners

K. Patricia Cross

From *Change* (February 1, 1973), 31–34. Reprinted by permission of the publisher and the author.

Dr. Cross is senior research psychologist and educator at the Center for Research and Development in Higher Education at the University of California, Berkeley, and is consultant to HEW's Fund for the Improvement of Post-Secondary Education. She is author of Beyond the Open Door *(1971).*

What is quality higher education? There was a time when people thought they knew. It was typified by bright students, a faculty distinguished in research and writing, and affluent and successful alumni.

To attain such heights a college selects students of known academic accomplishments, recruits faculty with big names and proven records, and assures itself of successful alumni through placing its sought-after seal of approval on its graduates. Somewhere between entrance and graduation it is assumed that students gain a "quality" education. But all we know for sure is that the best way to graduate a bright class is to admit a bright class.

Up until now higher education has been a low-risk venture. You get out about what you put in. So sure are people of this formula that most research and careful application of the findings reside in the admissions office—not in the classroom. Probably the closest thing to science in the practice of education lies in predicting the winners—and losers— of the academic race.

Despite all the hue and cry to the contrary, the science of academic prediction is decades ahead of the science of education and learning because in accuracy of prediction lies the promise of institutional success. But a new day is dawning. It looks very much as though quality education in the future will be measured in terms of value added, and that means we will have to look at the process of education itself— at what happens to the student between entrance and graduation.

A recent case study illustrates the issues involved in the transition from the relatively easy task of prediction and selection to the infinitely more difficult task of education. S. Resnik and B. Kaplan, the authors of an insightful and sympathetic analysis of the open-admissions policy at the City University of New York (CUNY), discovered to their "amazement," since they had "started out with an initial distrust of such tests," that the Cooperative English Test was uncannily predictive of student dropout and of independent teacher judgment about student performance. A very high percentage (fifty out of sixty) of students with low test scores "were dropped or left the program voluntarily during the first year, and most of the remaining ten left in the second year."

The findings illustrate the tension between the old and the new. The task of the old selective admissions approach was to find the most promising young people and to educate them for roles of leadership in the society. When technology was young and educational resources were scarce, it seemed logical and efficient for the growing nation to educate a cadre of elite leaders who would use their training and knowledge to raise the standard of living for everyone.

Now there seems to be an unending supply of the comforts and luxuries of technology. The problem for the future is not so much in the generation of new technology and new products as in better distribution systems, broader-based knowledge, and greater concern for individual development. The way to raise the standard of living for everyone is no longer to train leaders but but rather to educate the masses to their full humanity.

Certainly we will continue to educate leaders; we will always need intellectual leadership. But institutions like CUNY have taken on an additional and much more difficult assignment. The task of the new CUNY is not to predict who will fail, but to make life better for every student crossing its threshold.

The "amazing" success of the Cooperative English Test isn't so amazing after all. It shows two things. First, that failure on a traditional test predicted failure in the traditional curriculum with high accuracy. Second, that the traditional curriculum did not do anything to educate the nearly 100 percent of very low-scoring students who dropped out. The test, the curriculum, and faculty judgments about performance are all irrelevant to the task of improving life for everyone through education.

This change in philosophy about the purposes of college and who should attend will probably have more impact on educational methods and procedures than anything that has ever happened in higher education. Just as soon as a college agrees to do what it can for all comers, it forgoes the luxury of selecting students who fit its way of life, and it takes on the obligation of adapting itself to the needs of students.

That is where many colleges are today.

Thousands upon thousands of students who would never before have considered college are on our doorsteps, and we don't know how—or if—we can do anything to help them develop their talents to become happy and productive citizens. We face the task of gearing up to serve a new clientele.

The new clientele for higher education in the 1970s consists of everyone who wasn't there in the 1940s, 1950s, and 1960s. There are four distinctive but overlapping groups: (1) low academic achievers who are gaining entrance through open admissions; (2) adults and part-time learners who are gaining access through nontraditional alternatives; (3) ethnic minorities; and (4) women who are gaining admission through public conscience and Affirmative Action.

I have written extensively in *Beyond the Open Door* about low academic achievers as New Students in higher education. It is this group that epitomizes the problem of education beyond high school for the masses. It is not too difficult to accept adults—to deliver education in new ways, to credential adequate academic performance, and to permit part-time students to earn degrees. It is slow and sometimes traumatic but not impossible to abolish discrimination and grant ethnic minorities and women college degrees. But to deliberately set out to accept people who "can't do college work" as it is presently defined is an altogether different matter.

The greatest single barrier to college admission in the 1960s was not ethnic identity or socioeconomic status per se. Rather it was lack of demonstrated academic ability—as that ability is nurtured and measured in the schools.

Although black and brown and red students are overrepresented among this group of New

Students, a great disservice has been done to ethnic minorities in equating skin color with low academic achievement. Actually, most of the students flooding into colleges poorly prepared to undertake traditional college work are the white sons and daughters of blue-collar workers. Almost two thirds of the community colleges in this country report that less than 25 percent of the students enrolled in remedial courses are members of ethnic minorities. Numerically it is whites, not blacks, who have gained educational advantages through open admissions. But regardless of skin color, there is a powerful relationship between social class and academic achievement. Over two thirds of the lowest third of high school graduates are first-generation college students; their parents have never experienced college. So much ignorance of what college is all about among family and friends of entering college students will probably never be present again in this country. In California, for example, with its extensive development of public postsecondary education, 80 percent of the high school graduates are continuing their education, and they will be able to pass some firsthand experience on to their children.

It is not, however, the racial and socioeconomic characteristics of New Students that ought to concern educators most. Rather it is the pervasive experience of New Students with failure in the American school system. Most students who graduate from high school in the lowest academic third of the class have been poor students all of their young lives. Thus it is not surprising to find research that shows that they don't approach traditional college learning tasks with enthusiasm and confidence. . . . There is no reason to think that colleges will do a better job with these students than high schools have done as long as they use the same methods to teach the same materials. Research that repeats the tiresome statistics that a few (but not usually very many) "high-risk" students survive the first year of college should convince us that colleges are not making their adjustment to universal postsecondary education very smoothly.

We might do well to give up our preoccupation with correcting the "deficiencies" of New Students and concentrate instead on developing the new range of talents and interests that they bring to higher education. "College-level" work need not mean higher and higher levels of abstraction; it might well mean higher and higher standards of performance. In any event, our new educational purposes suggest that we begin with the student and help move him toward the development of his abilities. It does not suggest that we try to make him into a pale carbon copy of the academically elite leader of bygone days.

Under the new purposes of higher education adults too have a claim to education that helps them develop their abilities and fulfill their lives. They may not be young enough to meet the old criteria of furnishing fresh leadership to a growing technology, but they are able, eager, and interested students. In a research survey of the learning preferences and experiences of adults conducted for the Commission on Non-Traditional Study, sponsored by the College Board and Educational Testing Service, we found that 77 percent of the people between 18 and 60 in this country would like to learn more about something.

Although adults have been considerably more restrained about it than have some of the young people, it is quite apparent from the data that they too are demanding relevance in education. The message is clear that they want to learn how to *do* things—as opposed to how to think about things. Dedicated liberal arts advocates will be disappointed to learn that adult males are most interested in returning to school to improve their vocational and professional skills, whereas women are most interested in sewing, cooking, crafts, and gardening. And those interests are in the lead for college graduates as well as for the general population. Adult learning priorities seem to be dictated by the usefulness of the learning. Highest in priority are those skills that are needed by all adults in the course of daily living—vocational skills, investment, and home repair for men; home and family skills for women; sports and leisure-time activities for both men and women. Next in order comes learning that will foster personal development and community responsibility—humanities and the arts (especially for women) and public affairs and community problems. And finally at the bottom of the list of preferences, endorsed by fewer than 10 percent of the potential adult learners, are the basic academic tools of social, biological, and physical sciences and English language. Once again, college graduates aren't much more interested in learning more about these staples of academe than is the general public. The problem is not that the social and physical sciences are inherently dull or unimportant, but that they are taught as background for professional scholars—and not many of the new clientele have any interest in becoming professional scholars. The physical and social sciences, after all, form the backbone of the new curricula in ecology and urban studies that are extremely popular with young and old alike. But these courses of study have a problem-oriented focus. They are taught in order to solve problems—not to perpetuate the discipline into graduate school.

So adult learners do challenge the heart of higher education—the curriculum. But equally important—and more likely to succeed—is their challenge to the time and place requirements of traditional education. It is this battle that the nontraditional studies movement has taken on. No one can put forth a very strong argument that four years, chopped into 120 credit hours delivered to people who can present themselves physically in a room set aside for "classes," makes much sense as the major strategy of education. A concept of education for all the people requires new methods of delivery to take education into prisons, homes, and industrial plants. We need new measures of competency that acknowledge that what is learned rather than how it is learned is the true measure of education. And we need new flexibilities that can begin to make lifelong learning a reality.

More attention has been given to the educational needs of ethnic minorities and women than to other groups of new clientele. And yet their challenge to educational tradition as preserved by the academic disciplines and by institutional procedures is not nearly so great as that presented by New Students or adults. True, the demands for equality of educational opportunity on the part of ethnic minorities and women has struck a deep emotional response in the white, male-dominated system of higher education. Affirmative Action is a personal threat to ruling faculty, administrators, and students too. But minorities and women are not a threat to the content and form of traditional education except as they constitute highly visible segments of the New Student and adult populations.

It is hard to talk about curricular or classroom needs that are based on skin color or sex. But the assumption throughout this article has been that education is broadly interpreted to encompass the full development of individual potential. Given that interpretation, the educational problems of ethnic minorities and women are profound.

The influx of ethnic minorities and women into all segments of postsecondary education is increasing rapidly, as the Carnegie Commission report *American College and University Enrollment Trends in 1971* shows. In the single year from 1970 to 1971, the total undergraduate and graduate enrollment of women increased 5 percent (compared to a 3 percent increase for men). The increase for blacks was 17 percent and for those with Spanish surnames 19 percent. The most dramatic increases occurred where one might expect—in the previously closed graduate schools. Women made a 6 percent gain (compared with 4 percent for men), but blacks showed a 38 percent gain and those of Spanish descent a 31 percent increase. Spanish Americans are just beginning to get their message across with a force equal to that of the blacks. First-time graduate enrollments increased 36 percent for Spanish Americans, 11 percent for blacks, but only 5 percent for women.

As these data show, ethnic minorities, and to a lesser extent women, are assuredly part of the new clientele. Society looks to education to improve the lot of its citizenry, and the failure has been painful in the case of groups whose appearance marks them as targets for discrimination. As Martha Peterson, chairman of the American Council on Education, remarked recently,

"The shame of Affirmative Action is that HEW had to get into it at all."

The problems, however, are more than legal or even moral. Racial segregation on campus is a growing phenomenon that no one knows how to deal with (see *Time*, November 27, 1972, pages 44–45, and "The New Black Apartheid," *Change*, October 1972, page 8). Highly sensitized women and ethnic minorities are becoming increasingly aware that it is easier to deal with overt discrimination that can be fought head-on than it is to deal with covert and frequently unconscious discrimination on the part of well-meaning people.

The full meaning of universal postsecondary education has probably not been understood, and certainly not accepted, by the majority of people whose life work is education. The most common position among faculty who consider themselves enlightened is that higher education should be open to all those able and willing to do the work in the manner and form in which it is now offered. A second position is taken by a growing minority of misguided liberals who are willing to "lower the standards" of academic education in order to get credentials in the hands of the "disadvantaged" so that they can obtain the material and social benefits of society.

Neither position is adequate for these times. The purpose of education is not to certify (especially not falsely) nor is it to prepare a band of elite intellectual leaders (except perhaps in graduate education). It is to maximize the potential of each person to live a fulfilled and constructive life. And to accomplish that end, we need not lower standards. Quite the contrary, we should organize education around the premise that we must demand of each student the highest standards of performance in the utilization of his or her talents.

Subjective Sí! Objective No!

Robert Nisbet

From *The New York Times Book Review* (April 5, 1970), 1–2, 36–37, © 1970 by The New York Times Company. Reprinted by permission.

Along with his journal articles, Professor Nisbet has established his reputation in sociology with The Quest for Community *(1953),* Social Change and History *(1968),* The Social Bond *(1970),* The Social Philosopher: Community and Conflict in Western Thought *(1973). In addition to the University of Arizona, where he is presently teaching, he has taught at the University of California, Berkeley and Riverside, Columbia University, the University of Bologna, and Smith College.*

In a memorable address to his faculty colleagues at Harvard last spring (reprinted in part in the Winter issue of *The Public Interest*) the economic historian Alexander Gerschenkron likened the events there to those unfolded in the Hans Christian Andersen tale "The Most Unbelievable Thing."

A king once offered the hand of his daughter, the princess, to the man who could do the most unbelievable thing in the arts. There was great competition. At last it was decided that the most unbelievable thing among entries was a combined clock and calendar of ingenious design and surpassing beauty, the product of many years of work. Not only was the time given, the clock showed the ages back and forth into the past and future. And circling the clock were sculptured figures representing the greatest spiritual and cultural minds in the history of human society.

All assembled were agreed that this clock was without question the most unbelievable thing and that the hand of the princess must be given to the clock's handsome creator. But as judgment was about to be pronounced, a lowbrow competitor appeared, sledgehammer in hand. With a single blow he destroyed forever the marvelous clock. And everybody said, why, to destroy so beautiful a thing, this is surely the most unbelievable thing of all. And that was how the judges had to judge.

And, Mr. Gerschenkron concluded, in our own time of troubles the most unbelievable thing, surely, is not the fragile entity that is the university, product of centuries of love of learning for its own sake, but, rather, the acts of those, whether armed with student battering ram and torch or with faculty vote, who would seek to destroy the university in a matter of days.

Most of us would agree with Mr. Gerschenkron that this is indeed the most unbelievable thing at the present time. What, then, is the *next* most unbelievable thing? The answer is possibly not so clear. There must be many entries possible. But I will suggest one: the very recently begun, fast-accumulating nihilistic repudiation, in the social sciences of the ancient Western ideal of dispassionate reason, of objective inquiry, in the study of man and society.

I will come in a moment to a few of the symptoms of this ongoing repudiation of objectivity. First, though, it might be noted that as recently as 1960 had any social scientist been asked, "What is the most unbelievable thing?" he would undoubtedly have replied: "Why the fact that after many decades of effort by social scientists to achieve honored place in the community of science, we appear to be finally

there." Such a social scientist could have observed that the works of such twentieth-century titans as William I. Thomas, Edward Tolman, Joseph Schumpeter, A. L. Kroeber and V. O. Key—I limit myself to a few of the greater ones in this country—had at last taken effect. The august National Academy of Sciences was beginning to open its doors to social scientists as members; the physical and biological scientists on the campus had begun to make the possessive "our" include economists, sociologists, and political scientists. In a few places the hoary science requirement was being fulfilled by undergraduates with courses drawn from the social sciences. Surely, all of this would have seemed to any social scientist in 1960 as the most unbelievable thing.

But not in 1970. One is obliged by the evidence, I think, to conclude that the most unbelievable thing is the astonishing reversal of belief in the scientific, that is, the objective, the detached, the dispassionate character of the social sciences. What makes it unbelievable is that this reversal is to be found, not among physical scientists, government officials, or citizens. Not yet anyhow. Its locus is the social sciences themselves; more precisely, in the minds of a constantly increasing number of younger social scientists and among these most crucially, of students, graduate as well as undergraduate, in the social sciences.

What are the prime manifestations of this revolt against objectivity, this scuttling of the ideal of dispassionate reason in the study of man and society? I will limit myself to two or three of the more striking ones.

First, the declaration by self-styled *radical* social scientists that objectivity of inquiry is not even a proper end of the social sciences. From radical sociologist to radical political scientist to radical anthropologist, all across the spectrum of the social sciences, the refrain is the same: "Social scientists have heretofore sought to understand society. The point, however, is to destroy and then remake society." It is not, obviously, the mature Marx, who was capable of devoting himself for many years in the British Museum to the study of capitalism and society, but the youthful romantic Marx that these voices choose to echo. If anyone thinks I exaggerate the impact at the present time of the self-styled radical social scientist, I invite him to any annual meeting of one of the learned societies.

Let us look briefly at symptom number two. It is for me somewhat more chilling inasmuch as it makes inevitable a recollection of the Nazi Rosenberg and his efforts in the 1930s to deomonstrate differences between German or Aryan science on the one hand and Jewish or plutocratic science on the other. I refer here to widening belief at the present time to what can only be called *the necessary ethnic roots of science.*

It is being said, by white and black alike, chiefly with respect though to studies of blacks, chicanos, and other ethnic minorities, that it is not possible by any stretch of one's dedication to objectivity for the white to understand the black or the black to understand the white. There is black science and there is white science, and the twain shall never meet. More recently (and I can scarcely believe my eyes as I write the words) there have been intimations of a women's social science. As though one were dealing with public rest rooms.

How the gods must be laughing. We had no sooner started to erase (admittedly, *just* started) some of the more preposterous kinds of ethnic segregation in American society when there began—and began, let it be emphasized, among those forming the vanguard of reform—to be manifest a far more deadly type of segregation: deadly because it deals with the epistemological roots of the scientific study of man.

Let us concede immediately: One must be a Negro to understand what it is like being a Negro. The same is exactly true of being a Wasp, a Puerto Rican, a mountain climber, a college professor. It is impossible for men to understand women, and women men. All of this has been said a long time, and in the sense that is usually meant I am willing to stipulate that it will always be true; just as I am willing to trumpet the imperishable truth that no one—not my wife, children, lawyer, physician, least of all, friends—will ever understand me. No one to my

knowledge has ever challenged the existence in each of us, in each ethnic or cultural strain, of some doubtless forever unreachable essence. And, as the immortal Charlie Brown has concluded, it is probably good, all things considered, that this essence is unreachable.

But we are talking about science, not the metaphysics of identity or being. The movement I refer to among younger social scientists today is directed to the nature of science, *social science.* What used to be said by engineers, chemists, and the lay public is now being said by an ever widening group of social scientists themselves: particularly the younger ones. An objective understanding of social behavior is impossible; such understanding will always be limited by the political, or ethnic, or social and economic position one occupies in the social order. Its embedded values must become the values of the investigator and, hence, the bias of his conclusions. There is nothing that can be done about this.

Therefore it behooves us to abandon the vain pursuit of knowledge, objective knowledge, and to throw ourselves into action oriented toward values we can cherish. The remarkable study of conditions of classroom achievement in the schools completed a year or two ago by James Coleman, sociologist at Johns Hopkins University, cannot be believed because, first, Coleman is white and, second, his massive study was financed by the Federal Government. So runs the argument of what I can only think of as the most unbelievable thing today in the social sciences.

That it is hard to achieve objectivity, especially in the social sciences, admits of no doubt. The philosophical literature of the West is filled with notations of the idols of the mind—as they were called by Francis Bacon—that incessantly seek to engage our attention. I assume that not the most dedicated practitioner of science, even physical science, would cavil at this. In all scientific work, however good, there is no doubt some lingering element of personal predilection, some thrust that is rooted in bias.

But this said, is there, then, no significant difference between the gathering of ethnic data by an Otto Klineberg or a James Coleman, and the interpretation of these data, and the gathering and the interpretation of such data by a George Wallace? I assume all but the most hopelessly fanatical would say, yes, there is a difference. But, given the crisis of the times, the roles into which we are being forced by history and by the impending revolution, the difference is not worth emphasizing. Better, it is said, for the Klinebergs and the Colemans to abandon the idle conceit of a value-free science and to join directly the fight against George Wallace. It is quicker that way.

That it is also suicidal, on the evidence of history, seems not to enter the minds of the radical social scientists. Or if it does, it seems not to matter greatly. Without wanting to put too fine a point on the matter it is hard to resist the conclusion sometimes that this generation of the left has a rendezvous with suicide. Retreat to drugs, to sensitivity sessions, to illusory communitarianism, and to the calculatedly clownish behavior of the Chicago Seven would suggest it.

All that is beside the point. I am writing here about the revolt against objectivity I find everywhere in the country today, even among young social scientists who are not conspicuously left or conspicuously anything. There is nothing remarkable in preoccupation with objectivity. That is old. What is new is the profound difference one finds today in attitude toward the *ideal* of objectivity, toward the goal of protection from the ideals of the mind in one's work. *This* is the most unbelievable thing.

How unbelievable it is may perhaps be sensed from a reading of several very recently published books now on my desk. Here, for instance, is *Knowledge Into Action: Improving the Nation's Use of the Social Sciences.* It is the report of the Special Commission on the Social Sciences of the National Board, published by the National Science Foundation. It is excellent. The nihilistic movement I refer to is, however, making it seem as obsolete as one of those tracts written in the 1930s on planned economy. I cannot conquer the feeling, reading it, that the pious are converting the pious.

Here is Gunnar Myrdal, *Objectivity in Social Research.* With insight, wit, and elegance one of the towering social scientists of the age deals once again with what I called above the Baconian idols. But the waters of nihilism lap unfelt at his feet. His book would produce, not dissent, but yawning indifference in any audience of young social scientists today. Hearing his message, they would ignore it. Who needs it? He doesn't feel, he is white, he is nonpolitical, he doesn't *understand* man!

Or *Politics and the Social Sciences,* edited by Seymour Martin Lipset, one of the most creative sociologists of our time, contributed to by minds of the luster of Scott Greer, Giovanni Sartori, and Fred Greenstein. Mr. Lipset has brought together some splendid pieces on the relationships of the study of politics and the other social sciences. But I can find little if any evidence in the volume of recognition of that special form of nihilism that today spreads out from politically radical and ethnic sources.

And finally, here is *The Political Sciences: General Principles of Selection in Social Science and History* by the Australian, Hugh Stretton. It is a fascinating and in many ways original book even if the author does not seem to realize the overkill conferred so recently by time and events upon his academic argument. Mr. Stretton is as merciless and witty in his judgments as he is learned. I should wish to be spared the circle of Dante's hell to which Mr. Stretton has consigned functionalists, systems-makers, along with dust-bowl empiricists: and with their authors the tedious taxonomies and limping methodologies that have been passing themselves off for 20 years now as science. The howls and wails would be dreadful to have to listen to.

I rather suspect that Hugh Stretton is likely to become something of a hero in certain of the more literate quarters of the epistemological nihilism I write of in this essay. His learning is considerable, and he is a master of the one-two punch, setting his victim up with the faint jab of apparent praise, then coming through with a murderous right. But beyond this are the thrilling last lines of the book. The scientist's duty, Mr. Stretton writes, in today's conflict "goes beyond   discovering   and   understanding.   It becomes his business to win." That last sentence has the nice touch of the barricades seen from scholar's nest that can always be counted on to win applause in our day, no matter how badly the act has been going before. And, in Mr. Stretton's case, the act, I repeat, has been going well throughout.

As I say, I predict weeks, if not months, of magisterial status for this book in those quarters of the American academic left that ordinarily allow only days. Furthermore there is the proper element of Britannic establishment in the manner of Mr. Stretton's book that the American left invariably finds seductive even when the message is considerably to the political right of Mr. Stretton's.

But even Mr. Stretton—perhaps because he is at the University of Adelaide instead of Berkeley, Wisconsin, Brandeis, or Harvard—seems to me slightly archaic. His book and its message would have had more powerful impact a few years ago. The revolution of epistemological nihilism has left him, as well as others of its leaders, a mile or two behind.

No more than Gunnar Myrdal does he seem really aware of the recent, tempestlike ferocity of the movement that has been built around the slogan: *The scientist's business is to win*—that is, at the barricades, not in the laboratory or study. Mr. Stretton is anything but Auden's immured scholar of the 1930s "lecturing on navigation while the ship is going down." He is more nearly an elegant Bernarr McFadden preaching the gospel of fresh air as the hurricane gathers. I cannot conquer the feeling that though he will certainly enjoy brief heroic status in this country, he will yet become like certain refugees from Berkeley who, having sown the wind, avoided the whirlwind by retreating behind institute door or else snuggling under eastern ivy. Whirlwinds, alas, are no respecters of degrees—using that word in both its senses.

What the disciples of social-science-as-action can never seem to understand is that if action is the magic word, there are always others, less burdened by the trained incapacities of scholarship, who can act more swiftly. And ruthlessly. What the man of action looks to the scholar and

scientist for is knowledge, not barricade gymnastics. There is something about the cap-touching of graduate students and the genuflections of administrators' wives that unfits American university professors for the simple egalitarian civilities of the revolution.

All this would seem obvious enough; at least over Sunday morning coffee, if not Saturday night martinis. What we must ask, however, is, how is the revolution of nihilism in the social sciences at the present time to be explained? By the political objectives of the New Left, it has become fashionable to declare in academic circles—tenure circles—and by the stubborn unwillingness of members of the left to learn to become social scientists the way we did. Both explanations are variations on Original Sin. Let us look further into the matter, borrowing from the poet George Meredith: no villain need be; passions spin the plot; the wrong is mixed. Could we, the social scientists, have somehow betrayed ourselves during the past couple of decades by what is false within? Has there been anything resembling what Julien Benda called a *trahison des clercs*? I call to witness:

First, the special kind of hubris that attacked the social sciences in this country during the 1950s. With only the slenderest resources, they not only accepted invitations from all the men of power in Washington and elsewhere but actually started knocking on doors demanding invitations. Project Camelot, which can best be thought of as the social sciences' Black Sox scandal, was no doubt a fitting denouement. (A more or less clandestine "research" project based in Washington through which more or less clandestine investigation would be made in selected foreign countries of types of insurgency and counter-insurgency. Sponsored, and heavily financed by the U.S. Army, it was mercifully killed by Executive Order before it was more than barely launched.) But even after its odor spread internationally, few American social scientists got the point. The air filled quickly with imprecations of Congress, of the Executive Office, of the State Department, and other agencies in Washington for having saved the social sciences from even worse consequences of their appalling combination of naiveté and rapacity.

Second, the vastly greater affinity that built up throughout the 1950s and 1960s between the sciences generally (but not excluding the social sciences) and the military establishment. It is, especially for the social sciences, a strange affinity. Not strange economically. That's where the money is. But Willie Sutton's celebrated words fit the robbing of banks better than they do the image of the social sciences that continued to persist in the minds of the young. Even at this very moment it is necessary to go to Congress to find substantial opposition to the affinity between the Pentagon and the sciences, social included. The latter seem to find instant absolution by repeating a hundred times a day the words "pure," "basic," and "theoretical." Few if any social scientists (except, that is, for those of the political far left) do anything beyond that save to join committees to appoint committees to find proper terminology for converting rape into legitimate union. (Still, it's never clear just who is raping whom.)

Third, the whole emergence of the Higher Capitalism on the American campus during the 1950s. I'm not referring to the by-definition capitalist trustees. I have in mind the New Entrepreneurs of the sciences, social as well as physical, through which research started to become merchandised by the piece and the hour. In institute, bureau, and center instead of factory.

Hours 8 to 5, by appointment only. By the early 1960s there were as many institute and center directors on the American campus as there were officers in the old Mexican Army. They were doing good, of course, but also doing well. That is, until the revolt came and annual meetings became Bastilles stormed by disillusioned *sans-culottes.*

The physical sciences have been spared very much in the way of revolt, and heaven knows, they began the Higher Capitalism. But physical scientists have had more sense throughout than to spice their lectures to students with quotations from Rousseau, Marx, and Lenin. The social scientists thought they were being pious in so doing when in fact they were lighting matches before open kerosene. The combination of capitalist luxury in what the *Science* magazine reporter D. S. Greenberg irreverently calls the Institute for the Absorption of Federal Funds and the ritual radicalism of its owners was to prove by 1965 to be too explosive for further containment.

There are other reasons that might be offered here. These, however, will suffice to make clear that the revolution of nihilism presently attacking that most precious of intellectual ideals, objectivity, has roots beyond the commonly cited invincible ignorance of the revolutionaries. The wrong is indeed mixed. Though I persist in believing that there are villains.

Part 4

The Struggle For Self

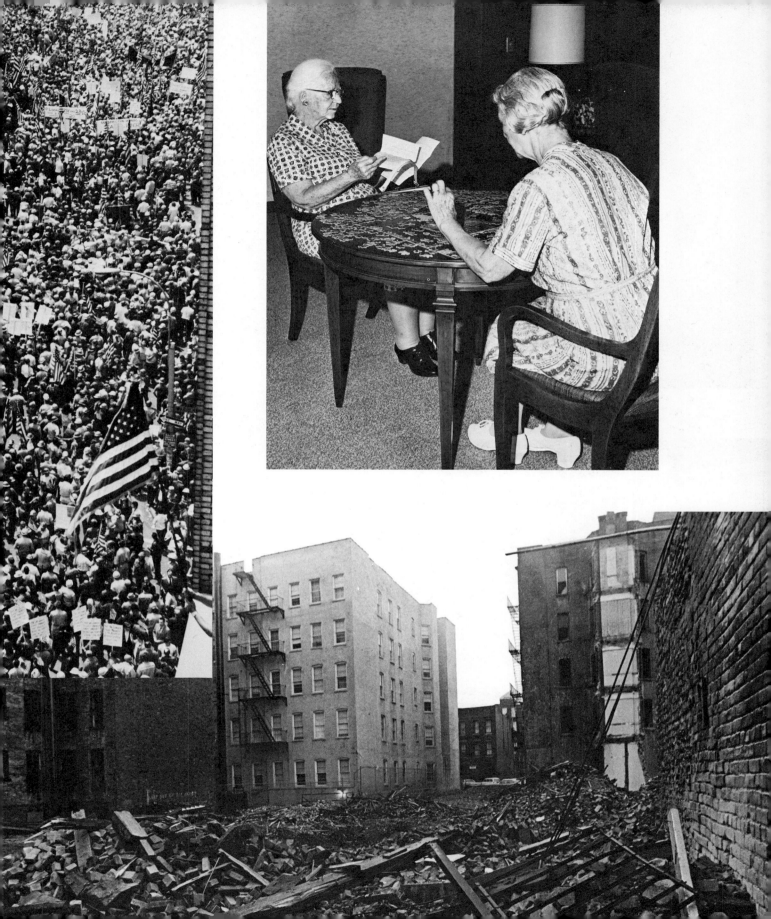

15 ALIENATION— IS ANYBODY LISTENING?

Youth, Change, and Violence

Kenneth Keniston

From *The American Scholar*, V. 37 (Spring, 1968), 227—245. Reprinted by permission of the author.

Professor Keniston is Director of the Behavorial Science Study Center at Yale. His speciality is clinical psychology. He has written The Uncommitted: Alienated Youth in American Society *(1965),* Young Radicals: Notes on Committed Youth *(1968), and* Youth and Dissent *(1971).*

We often feel that today's youth are somehow "different." There is something about today's world that seems to give the young a special restlessness, an increased impatience with the "hypocrisies" of the past, and yet an open gentleness and a searching honesty more intense than that of youth in the past. Much of what we see in today's students and nonstudents is of course familiar: to be young is in one sense always the same. But it is also new and different, as each generation confronts its unique historical position and role.

Yet we find it hard to define the difference. Partly the difficulty derives from the elusive nature of youth itself. Still this generation seems even more elusive than most—and that, too, may be one of the differences. Partly the problem stems from the sheer variety and number of "youth" in a society where youth is often protracted into the mid-twenties. No one characteri-

zation can be adequate to the drop-outs and stay-ins, hawks and doves, up-tights and cools, radicals and conservatives, heads and seekers that constitute American youth. But although we understand that the young are as various as the old in our complex society, the sense that they are different persists.

In giving today's American youth this special quality and mood, two movements have played a major role: the New Left and the hippies. Both groups are spontaneous creations of the young; both are in strong reaction to what Paul Goodman calls the Organized System; both seek alternatives to the institutions of middle-class life. Radicals and hippies are also different from each other in numerous ways, from psychodynamics to ideology. The hippie has dropped out of a society he considers irredeemable: his attention is riveted on interior change and the expansion of personal consciousness. The radical has not given up on this society: his efforts are aimed at changing and redeeming it. Furthermore, both "movements" together comprise but a few percent of their contemporaries. But, although neither hippies nor New Leftists are "representative" of their generation, together they are helping to give this generation its distinctive mood.

By examining the style of these young men and women, we come closer to understanding what makes their generation "different."

The Style of Post-Modern Youth

Today's youth is the first generation to grow up with "modern" parents; it is the first "post-modern" generation. This fact alone distinguishes it from previous generations and helps create a mood born out of modernity, affluence, rapid social change and violence. Despite the many pitfalls in the way of any effort to delineate a post-modern style, the effort seems worth making. For not only in America but in other nations, new styles of dissent and unrest have begun to appear, suggesting the slow emergence of youthful style that is a reflection of and reaction to the history of the past two decades.[1]

In emphasizing "style" rather than ideology, program or characteristics, I mean to suggest that the communalities in post-modern youth groups are to be found in the *way* they approach the world, rather than in their actual behavior, ideologies or goals. Indeed, the focus on process rather than program is itself a prime characteristic of the post-modern style, reflecting a world where flux is more obvious than fixed purpose. Post-modern youth, at least in America, is very much in process, unfinished in its development, psychologically open to a historically unpredictable future. In such a world, where ideologies come and go, and where revolutionary change is the rule, a style, a *way* of doing things, is more possible to identify than any fixed goals or constancies of behavior.

Fluidity, Flux, Movement. Post-modern youth display a special personal and psychological openness, flexibility and unfinishedness. Although many of today's youth have achieved a sense of inner identity, the term "identity" suggests a fixity, stability and "closure" that

[1] In the effort to delineate this style, I have been helped and influenced by Robert J. Lifton's concept of Protean Man. For a summary of his views, see *Partisan Review*, Winter 1968.

many of them are not willing to accept: with these young men and women, it is not always possible to speak of the "normal resolution" of identity issues. Our earlier fear of the ominous psychiatric implications of "prolonged adolescence" must now be qualified by an awareness that in post-modern youth many adolescent concerns and qualities persist long past the time when (according to the standards in earlier eras) they should have ended. Increasingly, post-modern youth are tied to social and historical changes that have not occurred, and that may never occur. Thus, psychological "closure," shutting doors and burning bridges, becomes impossible. The concepts of the personal future and the "life work" are ever more hazily defined; the effort to change oneself, redefine oneself, or reform oneself does not cease with the arrival of adulthood.

This fluidity and openness extends through all areas of life. Both hippie and New Left movements are nondogmatic, nonideological, and to a large extent hostile to doctrine and formula. In the New Left, the focus is on "tactics"; amongst hippies, on simple direct acts of love and communications. In neither group does one find clear-cut long-range plans, life patterns laid out in advance. The vision of the personal and collective future is blurred and vague: later adulthood is left deliberately open. In neither group is psychological development considered complete; in both groups, identity, like history, is fluid and indeterminate. In one sense, of course, identity development takes place; but, in another sense, identity is always undergoing transformations that parallel the transformations of the historical world.

Generational Identification. Post-modern youth views itself primarily as a part of a generation rather than an organization; they identify with their contemporaries as a group, rather than with elders; and they do not have clearly defined leaders and heroes. Their deepest collective identification is to their own group or "Movement"—a term that in its ambiguous meanings points not only to the fluidity and openness of post-modern youth, but to its physical mobility, and the absence of traditional patterns of leadership and emulation. Among young radicals, for example, the absence of heroes or older leaders is impressive: even those five years older are sometimes viewed with mild amusement or suspicion. And although post-modern youth is often widely read in the "literature" of the New Left or that of consciousness-expansion, no one person or set of people is central to their intellectual beliefs. Although they live together in groups, these groups are without clear leaders.

Identification with a generational movement, rather than a cross-generational organization or a nongenerational ideology, distinguishes post-modern youth from its parents and from the "previous" generation. In addition, it also creates "generational" distinctions involving five years and less. Within the New Left, clear lines are drawn between the "old New Left" (approximate age, thirty), the New Left (between twenty-two and twenty-eight) and the "new New Left" or "young kids" (under twenty-two). Generations, then, are separated by a very brief span; and the individual's own phase of youthful usefulness—for example, as an organizer—is limited to a relatively few years. Generations come and go quickly; whatever is to be accomplished must therefore be done soon.

Generational consciousness also entails a feeling of psychological disconnection from previous generations, their life situations and their ideologies. Among young radicals, there is a strong feeling that the older ideologies are exhausted or irrelevant, expressed in detached amusement at the doctrinaire disputes of the "old Left" and impatience with "old liberals." Among hippies, the irrelevance of the parental past is even greater: if there is any source of insight, it is the timeless tradition of the East, not the values of the previous generation in American society. But in both groups, the central values are those created in the present by the "Movement" itself.

Personalism. Both groups are highly personalistic in their styles of relationship. Among hippies, personalism usually entails privatism, a withdrawal from efforts to be involved in or to change the wider social world; among young radicals, personalism is joined with efforts to change the world. But despite this difference, both groups care most deeply about the creation of intimate, loving, open and trusting relationships between small groups of people. Writers who condemn the depersonalization of the modern world, who insist on "I-thou" relationships, or who expose the elements of anger, control and sadism in nonreciprocal relationships, find a ready audience in post-modern youth. The ultimate measure of man's life is the quality of his personal relationships; the greatest sin is to be unable to relate to others in a direct, face-to-face, one-to-one relationship.

The obverse of personalism is the discomfort created by any nonpersonal, "objectified," professionalized and, above all, exploitative relationship. Manipulation, power relationships, superordination, control and domination are at violent odds with the I-thou mystique. Failure to treat others as fully human, inability to enter into personal relationships with them, is viewed with dismay in others and with guilt in oneself. Even with opponents the goal is to establish intimate confrontations in which the issues can be discussed openly. When opponents refuse to "meet with" young radicals, this produces anger and frequently demonstrations. The reaction of the Harvard Students for a Democratic Society when Secretary McNamara did not meet with them to discuss American foreign policies is a case in point. Equally important, perhaps the most profound source of personal guilt among post-modern youth is the "hangups" that make intimacy and love difficult.

Nonasceticism. Post-modern youth is non-ascetic, expressive, and sexually free. The sexual openness of the hippie world has been much discussed and criticized in the mass media. One finds a similar sexual and expressive freedom among many young radicals, although it is less provocatively demonstrative. It is of continuing importance to these young men and women to overcome and move beyond inhibition and puritanism to a greater physical expressiveness, sexual freedom, capacity for intimacy, and ability to enjoy life.

In the era of the Pill, then, responsible sexual expression becomes increasingly possible outside of marriage, at the same time that sexuality becomes less laden with guilt, fear, and prohibition. As asceticism disappears, so does promiscuity: the personalism of post-modern youth requires that sexual expression must occur in the context of "meaningful" human relationships, of intimacy and mutuality. Marriage is increasingly seen as an institution for having children, but sexual relationships are viewed as the natural concomitant of close relationships between the sexes. What is important is not sexual activity itself, but the context in which it occurs. Sex is right and natural between people who are "good to each other," but sexual exploitation—failure to treat one's partner as a person—is strongly disapproved.

Inclusiveness. The search for personal and organizational inclusiveness is still another characteristic of post-modern youth. These young men and women attempt to include both within their personalities and within their movements every opposite, every possibility and every person, no matter how apparently alien. Psychologically, inclusiveness involves an effort to be open to every aspect of one's feelings, impulses and fantasies, to synthesize and integrate rather than repress and dissociate, not to reject or exclude any part of one's personality or potential. Interpersonally, inclusiveness means a capacity for involvement with, identification with and collaboration with those who are superficially alien: the peasant in Vietnam, the poor in America, the nonwhite, the deprived, and deformed. Indeed, so great is the pressure to include the alien, especially among hippies, that the apparently alien is often treated more favorably than the superficially similar: thus, the respect afforded to people and ideas that are distant and strange is sometimes not equally afforded those who are similar, be they one's parents or their middle-class values. One way of explaining the reaction of post-modern youth to the war in Vietnam is via the concept of inclu-

siveness: these young men and women react to events in Southeast Asia much as if they occurred in Newton, Massachusetts, Evanston, Illinois, Harlem, or Berkeley, California: they make little distinction in their reactions to their fellow Americans and those overseas.

One corollary of inclusiveness is intense internationalism. What matters to hippies or young radicals is not where a person comes from, but what kind of relationship is possible with him. The nationality of ideas matters little: Zen Buddhism, American pragmatism, French existentialism, Indian mysticism, or Yugoslav communism are accorded equal hearings. Interracialism is another corollary of inclusiveness: racial barriers are minimized or nonexistent, and the ultimate expressions of unity between the races, sexual relationships and marriage, are considered basically natural and normal, whatever the social problems they currently entail. In post-modern youth, then, identity and ideology are no longer parochial or national; increasingly, the reference group is the world, and the artificial subspeciation of the human species is broken down.

Antitechnologism. Post-modern youth has grave reservations about many of the technological aspects of the contemporary world. The depersonalization of life, commercialism, careerism and familism, the bureaucratization and complex organization of advanced nations—all seem intolerable to these young men and women, who seek to create new forms of association and action to oppose the technologism of our day. Bigness, impersonality, stratification, and hierarchy are rejected, as is any involvement with the furtherance of technological values. In reaction to these values, post-modern youth seeks simplicity, naturalness, personhood, and even voluntary poverty.

But a revolt against technologism is only possible, of course, in a technological society; and to be effective, it must inevitably exploit technology to overcome technologism. Thus in post-modern youth, the fruits of technology— synthetic hallucinogens in the hippie subculture, modern technology of communication among young radicals—and the affluence made possible by technological society are a precondition for a post-modern style. The demonstrative poverty of the hippie would be meaningless in a society where poverty is routine; for the radical to work for subsistence wages as a matter of choice is to *have* a choice not available in most parts of the world. Furthermore, to "organize" against the pernicious aspects of the technological era requires high skill in the use of modern technologies of organization: the long-distance telephone, the use of the mass media, high-speed travel, the mimeograph machine and so on. In the end, then, it is not the material but the spiritual consequences of technology that post-modern youth opposes: indeed, in the developing nations, those who exhibit a post-modern style may be in the vanguard of movements toward modernization. What *is* adamantly rejected is the contamination of life with the values of technological organization and production. It seems probable that a comparable rejection of the psychological consequences of current technology, coupled with the simultaneous ability to exploit that technology, characterizes all dissenting groups in all epochs.

Participation. Post-modern youth is committed to a search for new forms of groups, of organizations and of action where decision-making is collective, arguments are resolved by "talking them out," self-examination, interpersonal criticism and group decision-making are fused. The objective is to create new styles of life and new types of organization that humanize rather than dehumanize, that activate and strengthen the participants rather than undermining or weakening them. And the primary vehicle for such participation is the small, face-to-face primary group of peers.

The search for new participatory forms of organization and action can hardly be deemed successful as yet, especially in the New Left, where effectiveness in the wider social and political scene remains to be demonstrated. There are inherent differences between the often task-less, face-to-face group that is the basic form of organization for both hippies and radicals and the task-oriented organization—differences that make it difficult to achieve social effectiveness based solely on small primary groups. But there may yet evolve from the hippie "tribes," small Digger communities, and primary groups of the New Left, new forms of association in which self-criticism, awareness of group interaction, and the accomplishment of social and political goals go hand in hand. The effort to create groups in which individuals grow from their participation in the group extends far beyond the New Left and the hippie world; the same search is seen in the sidespread enthusiasm for "sensitivity training" groups and even in the increasing use of groups as a therapeutic instrument. Nor is this solely an American search: one sees a similar focuss, for example, in the Communist nations, with their emphasis on small groups that engage in the "struggle" of mutual criticism and self-criticism.

The search for effectiveness combined with participation has also led to the evolution of "new" styles of social and political action. The newness of such forms of political action as parades and demonstrations is open to some question; perhaps what is most new is the *style* in which old forms of social action are carried out. The most consistent effort is to force one's opponent into a personal confrontation with one's own point of view. Sit-ins, freedom rides, insistence upon discussions, silent and nonviolent demonstrations—all have a prime objective to "get through to" the other side, to force reflection, to bear witness to one's own principles, and to impress upon others the validity of these same principles. There is much that is old and familiar about this, although few of today's young radicals or hippies are ideologically committed to Gandhian views of nonviolence. Yet the underlying purpose of many of the emerging forms of social and political action, whether they be "human be-ins," "love-ins," peace marches or "teach-ins," has a new motive—hope that by expressing one's own principles, by "demonstrating" one's convictions, one can through sheer moral force win over one's opponents and lure them as well into participating with one's own values.

Antiacademicism. Among post-modern youth, one finds a virtually unanimous rejection of the "merely academic." This rejection is one manifestation of a wider insistence on the relevance, applicability and personal meaningfulness of knowledge. It would be wrong simply to label this trend "anti-intellectual," for many new radicals and not a few hippies are themselves highly intellectual people. What is demanded is that intelligence be engaged with the world, just as action should be informed by knowledge. In the New Left, at least amongst leaders, there is enormous respect for knowledge and information, and great impatience with those who act without understanding. Even amongst hippies, where the importance of knowledge and information is less stressed, it would be wrong simply to identify the rejection of the academic world and its values with a total rejection of intellect, knowledge, and wisdom.

To post-modern youth, then, most of what is taught in schools, colleges, and universities is largely irrelevant to living life in the last third of the twentieth century. Many academics are seen as direct or accidental apologists for the Organized System in the United States. Much of what they teach is considered simply unconnected to the experience of post-modern youth. New ways of learning are sought: ways that combine action with reflection upon action, ways that fuse engagement in the world with understanding of it. In an era of rapid change, the accrued wisdom of the past is cast into question, and youth seeks not only new knowledge, but new ways of learning and knowing.

Nonviolence. Finally, post-modern youth of all persuasions meets on the ground of nonviolence. For hippies, the avoidance of and calming of violence is a central objective, symbolized by gifts of flowers to policemen and the slogan, "Make love, not war." And although nonviolence as a philosophical principle has lost most of its power in the New Left, nonviolence as a psychological orientation is a crucial—perhaps *the* crucial—issue. The nonviolence of post-modern youth should not be confused with pacificism: these are not necessarily young men and women who believe in turning the other cheek or who are systematically opposed to fighting for what they believe in. But the basic style of both radicals and hippies is profoundly opposed to warfare, destruction and exploitation of man by man, and to violence whether on an interpersonal or an international scale. Even among those who do not consider nonviolence a good in itself, a psychological inoculation against violence, even a fear of it, is a unifying theme.

The Credibility Gap: Principle and Practice

In creating the style of today's youth, the massive and violent social changes of the past two decades have played a central role. Such social changes are not only distantly perceived by those who are growing up, but are immediately interwoven into the texture of their daily lives as they develop. The social changes of the post-war era affect the young in a variety of ways: in particular, they contribute to a special sensitivity to the discrepancy between principle and practice. For during this era of rapid social change the values most deeply embedded in the parental generation and expressed in their behavior in time of crisis are frequently very different from the more "modern" principles, ideals and values that this generation has professed and attempted to practice in bringing up its children. Filial perception of the discrepancy between practice and principle may help explain the very widespread sensitivity amongst post-modern youth to the "hypocrisy" of the previous generation.

The grandparents of today's twenty-year-olds were generally born at the end of the nineteenth century, and brought up during the pre-World War I years. Heirs of a Victorian tradition as yet unaffected by the value revolutions of the twentieth century, they reared their own children, the parents of today's youth, in families that emphasized respect, the control of impulse, obedience to authority, and the traditional "inner-directed" values of hard work, deferred gratification and self-restraint. Their children, born around the time of the First World War, were thus socialized in families that remained largely Victorian in outlook.

During their lifetimes, however, these parents (and in particular the most intelligent and advantaged among them) were exposed to a great variety of new values that often changed their nominal faiths. During their youths in the 1920s and 1930s, major changes in American behavior and American values took place. For example, the "emancipation of women" in the 1920s, marked by the achievement of suffrage for women, coincided with the last major change in actual sexual behavior in America: during this period, women began to become the equal partners of men, who no longer sought premarital sexual experience solely with women of a lower class. More important, the 1920s and the 1930s were an era when older Victorian values were challenged, attacked and all but discredited, especially in educated middle-class families. Young men and women who went to college during this period (as did most of the parents of those who can be termed "post-modern" today) were influenced outside their families by a variety of "progressive," "liberal," and even psychoanalytic ideas that contrasted sharply with the values of their childhood families. Moreover, during the 1930s, many of the parents of today's upper middle-class youth were exposed to or involved with the ideals of the New Deal, and sometimes to more radical interpretations of man, society, and history. Finally, in the 1940s and 1950s, when it came time to rear their own children, the parents of today's elite youth were strongly influenced by "permissive" views of child-rearing that again contrasted sharply with the techniques by which they themselves had been raised. Thus, many middle-class parents moved during their lifetime from the Victorian ethos in which they had been socialized to the less moralistic, more humanitarian, and more "expressive" values of their own adulthoods.

But major changes in values, when they occur in adult life, are likely to be far from complete. To have grown up in a family where unquestioning obedience to parents was expected, but to rear one's own children in an atmosphere of "democratic" permissiveness and self-determination—and never to revert to the practices of one's own childhood—requires a change of values more total and comprehensive than most adults can achieve. Furthermore, behavior that springs from values acquired in adulthood often appears somewhat forced, artificial or insincere to the sensitive observer. Children, clearly the most sensitive observers of their own parents, are likely to sense a discrepancy between their parents' avowed and consciously-held values and their "basic instincts" with regard to child-rearing. Furthermore, the parental tendency to "revert to form" is greatest in times of family crisis, which are of course the times that have the greatest effect upon children. No matter how "genuinely" parents held their "new" values, many of them inevitably found themselves falling back on the lessons of their own childhoods when the chips were down.

In a time of rapid social change, then, a special *credibility gap* is likely to open between the generations. Children are likely to perceive a considerable discrepancy between what their parents avow as their values and the actual assumptions from which parental behavior springs. In many middle-class teen-agers today, for example, the focal issue of adolescent rebellion against parents often seems to be just this discrepancy: the children arguing that their parents' endorsement of independence and self-determination for their children is "hypocritical" in that it does not correspond with the real behavior of the parents when their children actually seek independence. Similar perceptions of parental "hypocrisy" occur around racial matters: for example, there are many parents who in principle support racial and religious equality, but become violently upset when their children date someone from another race or religion. Around political activity similar issues arise. For example, many of the parents of today's youth espouse in principle the cause of political freedom, but are not involved themselves in politics and oppose their children's involvement lest they "jeopardize their record" or "ruin their later career."

Of course, no society ever fully lives up to its own professed ideals. In every society there is a gap between creedal values and actual practices, and in every society, the recognition of this gap constitutes a powerful motor for social change. But in most societies, especially when social change is slow and institutions are powerful and unchanging, there occurs what can be termed *institutionalization of hypocrisy.* Children and adolescents routinely learn when it is "reasonable" to expect that the values people profess will be implemented in their behavior, and when it is not reasonable. There develops an elaborate system of exegesis and commentary upon the society's creedal values, excluding certain people or situations from the full weight of these values, or "demonstrating" that apparent inconsistencies are not really inconsistencies at all. Thus, in almost all societies, a "sincere" man who "honestly" believes one set of values is frequently allowed to ignore them completely, for example, in the practice of his business, in his interpersonal relationships, in dealings with foreigners, in relationships to his children, and so on—all because these areas have been officially defined as exempt from the application of his creedal values.

In a time of rapid social change and value change, however, the institutionalization of hypocrisy seems to break down. "New" values have been in existence for so brief a period that the exemptions to them have not yet been defined, the situations to be excluded have not yet been determined, and the universal gap between principle and practice appears in all of its nakedness. Thus, the mere fact of a discrepancy between creedal values and practice is not at all unusual. But what is special about the present situation of rapid value change is, first, that parents themselves tend to have two conflicting sets of values, one related to the experience of their early childhood, the other to the ideologies and principles acquired in adulthood; and second, that no stable institutions or rules for defining hypocrisy out of existence have yet been fully evolved. In such a situation, children see the Emperor's nakedness with unusual clarity, recognizing the value conflict within their parents and perceiving clearly the hypocritical gap between creed and behavior.

This argument suggests that the post-modern youth may not be confronted with an "objective" gap between parental preaching and practice any greater than that of most generations. But they are confronted with an unusual internal ambivalence within the parental generation over the values that parents successfully inculcated in their children, and they are "deprived" of a system of social interpretation that rationalizes the discrepancy between creed and deed. It seems likely, then, that today's youth may simply be able to perceive the universal gulf between principle and practice more clearly than previous generations have done.

This points to one of the central characteristics of post-modern youth: they insist on taking seriously a great variety of political, personal, and social principles that "no one in his right mind" ever before thought of attempting to extend to such situations as dealings with strangers, relations between the races, or international politics. For example, peaceable openness has long been a creedal virtue in our society, but it has never been extended to foreigners, particularly with dark skins. Similarly, equality has long been preached, but the "American dilemma" has been resolved by a series of institutionalized hypocrisies that exempted Negroes from the application of this principle. Love has always been a central value in Christian society, but really to love one's enemies—to be generous to policemen, customers, criminals, servants, and foreigners—has been considered folly.

These speculations on the credibility gap between the generations in a time of rapid change may help explain two crucial facts about post-modern youth: first, they frequently come from highly principled families with whose principles they continue to agree; second, that they have the outrageous temerity to insist that individuals and societies live by the values they preach. And these speculations may also explain the frequent feeling of those who have worked intensively with student radicals or hippies that, apart from the "impracticality" of some of their views, these sometimes seem to be the only clear-eyed and sane people in a society and a world where most of us are still systematically blind to the traditional gap between personal principle and practice, national creed and policy, a gap that we may no longer be able to afford.

Violence: Sadism and Cataclysm

Those who are today in their early twenties were born near the end of World War II, the most violent and barbarous war in world history. The lasting imprint of that war can be summarized in the names of three towns: Auschwitz, Hiroshima, and Nuremberg. *Auschwitz* points to the possibility of a "civilized" nation embarking on a systematized, well-organized and scientific plan of exterminating an entire people. *Hiroshima* demonstrated how "clean," easy and impersonal cataclysm could be to those who perpetrate it, and how demonic, sadistic and brutal to those who experience it. And *Nuremberg* summarizes the principle that men have an accountability above obedience to national policy, a responsibility to conscience more primary even than fidelity to national law. These three lessons are the matrix for the growth of post-modern youth.

The terror of violence that has hung over all men and women since the Second World War has especially shaped the outlooks of today's youth. In the first memories of a group of young radicals, for example, one finds the following recollections: a dim recall of the end of World War II; childhood terror of the atomic bomb; witnessing the aftermath of a violent riot in the United States; being frightened by a picture of a tank riding over rubble; being violently jealous at the birth of a younger brother; taking part in "gruesome" fights in the school yard. Such memories mean many things, but in them, violence-in-the-world finds echo and counterpart in the violence of inner feelings. The term "violence" suggests both of these possibilities: the *psychological* violence of sadism, exploitation, and aggression, and the *historical* violence of war, cataclysm, and holocaust. In the lives of most of this generation, the threats of inner and outer violence are fused, each activating, exciting, and potentiating the other. To summarize a complex thesis into a few words: *the issue of violence is to this generation what the issue of sex was to the Victorian world.*

Stated differently, what is most deeply repressed, rejected, feared, controlled, and projected onto others by the post-modern generation is no longer their own sexuality. Sex, for most of this generation, is much freer, more open, less guilt- and anxiety-ridden. But violence, whether in one's self or in others, has assumed new prominence as the prime source of inner and outer terror. That this should be so in the modern world is readily understandable. Over all of us hangs the continual threat of a technological violence more meaningless, absurd, total, and unpremeditated than any ever imagined before. Individual life always resonates with historical change; history is not merely the backdrop for development, but its ground. To the grounded in the history of the past two decades is to have stood upon, to have experienced both directly and vicariously, violent upheaval, violent worldwide revolution, and the unrelenting possibility of worldwide destruction. To have been alive and aware in America during the past decade has been to be exposed to the assassination of a President and the televised murder of his murderer, to the well-publicized slaughter of Americans by their fellow countrymen, and to the recent violence in our cities. To have been a middle-class child in the past two decades is to have watched daily the violence of television, both as it reports the bloodshed and turmoil of the American and non-American world, and as it skillfully elaborates and externalizes in repetitive dramas the potential for violence within each of us.

It therefore requires no assumption of an increase in biological aggression to account for the salience of the issue of violence for post-modern youth. The capacity for rage, spite, and aggression is part of our endowment as human beings: it is a constant potential of human nature. But during the past two decades—indeed, starting before the Second World War—we have witnessed violence and imagined violence on a scale more frightening than ever before. Like the angry child who fears that his rage will itself destroy those around him, we have become vastly more sensitive to and fearful of our inner angers, for we live in a world where even the mildest irritation, multiplied a billionfold by modern technology, might destroy all civilization. The fact of violent upheaval and the possibility of cataclysm has been literally brought into our living rooms during the past twenty years: it has been interwoven with the development of a whole generation.

It should not surprise us, then, that the issue of violence is a focal concern for those of contemporary youth with the greatest historical consciousness. The hippie slogan "Make love, not war" expresses their sentiment, albeit in a form that the "realist" of previous generations might deem sentimental or romantic. Although few young radicals would agree with the wording of this statement, the underlying sentiment corresponds to their basic psychological orientation. For them, as for many others of their generation, the primary task is to develop new psychological, political, and international controls on violence. Indeed, many of the dilemmas of today's young radicals seem related to their extraordinarily zealous efforts to avoid any action or relationship in which inner or outer violence might be evoked. Distaste for violence animates the profound revulsion many of today's youth feel toward the war in Southeast Asia, just as it underlies a similar revulsion against the exploitation or control of man by man. The same psychological nonviolence is related to young radicals' avoidance of traditional leadership lest it lead to domination, to their emphasis on person-to-person participation and "confrontation," and even to their unwillingness to "play the media" in an attempt to gain political effectiveness. Even the search for forms of mass political action that avoid physical violence—a preference severely tested and somewhat undermined by the events of recent months—points to a considerable distaste for the direct expression of aggression.

I do not mean to suggest that post-modern youth contains a disproportionate number of tight-lipped pacifists or rage-filled deniers of their own inner angers. On the contrary, among today's youth, exuberance, passionateness, and zest are the rule rather than the exception. Nor are hippies and young radicals incapable of anger, rage, and resentment—especially when their principles are violated. But for many of these young men and women, the experiences of early life and the experience of the postwar world are joined in a special sensitivity to the issue of violence, whether in themselves or in others. This confluence of psychological and historical forces helps explain the intensity of their search for new forms of social organization and political action that avoid manipulation, domination, and control, just as it contributes to their widespread opposition to warfare of all kinds.

Yet the position of psychologically nonviolent youth in a violent world is difficult and paradoxical. On the one hand, he seeks to minimize violence, but on the other, his efforts often elicit violence from others. At the same time that he attempts to work to actualize his vision of a peaceful world, he must confront more directly and continually than do his peers the fact that the world is neither peaceful nor just. The frustration and discouragement of his work repetitively reawaken his anger, which must forever be rechanneled into peaceful paths. Since he continually confronts destructiveness and exploitation in the world, his own inevitable potential for destructiveness and exploitiveness inevitably arouses in him great guilt. The young men and women who make up the New Left in America, like other post-modern youth, have far less difficulty in living with their sexual natures than did their parents; but what they continue to find difficult to live with, what they still repress, avoid, and counteract is their own potential for violence. It remains to be seen whether, in the movement toward "resistance" and disruption of today's young radicals, their psychological nonviolence will continue to be reflected in their actions.

In pointing to the psychological dimension of the issue of violence, I do not mean to attribute causal primacy either to the experiences of early life or to their residues in adulthood. My thesis is rather that for those of this generation with the greatest historical awareness, the psychological and historical possibility of violence have come to potentiate each other. To repeat: witnessing the acting out of violence on a scale more gigantic than ever before, or imaginatively participating in the possibility of worldwide holocaust activates the fear of one's own violence; heightened awareness of one's inner potential for rage, anger, or destructiveness increases sensitivity to the possibility of violence in the world.

This same process of historical potentiation of inner violence has occurred, I believe, throughout the modern world, and brings with it not only the intensified efforts to curb violence we see in this small segment of post-modern youth, but other more frightening possibilities. Post-modern youth, to an unusual degree, remain open to and aware of their own angers and aggressions, and this awareness creates in them a sufficient understanding of inner violence to enable them to control it in themselves and oppose it in others. Most men and women, young or old, possess less insight: their inner sadism is pro-

jected onto others whom they thereafter loathe or abjectly serve; or, more disastrously, histori-cally-heightened inner violence is translated into outer aggression and murderousness, sanctioned by self-righteousness.

Thus, if the issue of violence plagues post-modern youth, it is not because these young men and women are more deeply rage-filled than most. On the contrary, it is because such young men and women have confronted this issue more squarely in themselves and in the world than have any but a handful of their fellows. If they have not yet found solutions, they have at least faced an issue so dangerous that most of us find it too painful even to acknowledge, and they have done so, most remarkably, without identifying with what they oppose. Their still-incomplete lives pose for us all the question on which our survival as individuals and as a world depends: Can we create formulations and forms to control historical and psychological violence before their fusion destroys us all?

16 DRUGS—REEFER MADNESS?

American Conservatives Should Revise Their Position on Marijuana

Richard C. Cowan

From *National Review* (December 8, 1972), 1344–1346. Reprinted by permission of the publisher of *National Review*. (The three articles that follow this were written in response to "American Conservatives Should Revise Their Position on Marijuana.")

Mr. Cowan is a charter member of YAF, active in the conservative movement, and supporter of the campaign to decriminalize the use of marijuana.

I am going to start with a few assertions of facts that, for all I know that they will be challenged, I consider to have been established by responsible scientific inquiry:

1. Marijuana is non-addictive—I use the word technically.

2. The use of marijuana does not in itself lead to the use of heroin.

3. No one has ever died from an overdose of marijuana.

4. Marijuana *used in moderation* causes no identified physical or mental problems for individuals who are otherwise healthy.

5. Marijuana does not induce criminal behavior or sexual aberration. In fact, it tends in most users to inhibit violence.

6. Marijuana *in moderate use* has little effect on the driving ability of experienced users of it—the contrast with socially equivalent alcohol consumption is to the disadvantage of alcohol.

7. Long-term abuse (gross overuse) should be assumed to be harmful but in fact there is as yet no conclusive evidence to that effect.

8. The moderate use of marijuana does not lead to changes in social behavior or to a loss of motivation. It may correspond with an observable change in people's lives but it is not the cause of that change.

9. Twenty-five million people use or have used marijuana. Marijuana is readily available today to anyone of minimum ingenuity who looks for it.

These assertions are of course contrary to what most agencies of the government have been telling us for the past forty years. (*National Review* has frequently ventilated the official line on marijuana.) Whether you doubt my assertions or not, please read *Marihuana Reconsidered* by Dr. Lester Grinspoon and *Marijuana, The New Prohibition* by John Kaplan. Both authors began their research, by their own admission, disposed in favor of the current legal proscriptions. Both came to the conclusion that our present laws are doing no good and a great deal of harm.

If you read those books and disagree, fine. But if you do not read them and you continue to support (or even if you fail to oppose) sending thousands of young people to prison, you are acquiescing in their punishment out of ignorance. A harsh statement, but true, I think.

It is my thesis that:

1. *Conservatives should support enlightened drug education.* Existing marijuana laws are destroying the credibility of drug education.

The key to education is credibility. Contrast the statements above with the postulates of the conventional government position. In deference to conventional notions about public enlightenment, I wish I could say that "recent discoveries" are responsible for such facts as are more commonly acknowledged nowadays concerning marijuana. In fact, many of them were available to anyone who cared to look into the matter even when the present laws were promulgated in the 1930s.

Accordingly, I ask you: If you are a young person who has found by experience—yours and your friends—that virtually everything you have been told about marijuana is totally untrue—wouldn't you question what they tell you about LSD, heroin, speed?

Drug abuse in our schools is a serious problem. Barbiturates and amphetamines and a variety of badly made, dangerously contaminated psychedelics are taking a fearful toll, even as parents and teachers rave along about marijuana. The point is *not* that the kids should be encouraged to use pot—certainly not; but that they should be told the truth about it.

The reasons why human beings should refrain from consuming drugs (including alcohol) during adolescence are undeniable. But the fact of it is that adolescents are going to drink the contraband beer, and smoke the contraband grass, and social reform should concern itself with the discrepancy between the law and the social usefulness of that law. The present laws, I maintain, not only have not worked, they are counterproductive.

2. *Conservatives should encourage a uniform respect for the law.* At present, 25 million people have, by common estimate, smoked marijuana at least once. Among college students—especially at the prestigious liberal-arts universities—a majority have smoked marijuana, according to the relevant polls, at least once. A significant minority of these take marijuana with some regularity, especially on weekends.

What is it that American conservatives favor? Search-and-destroy young Americans—one-eighth of the entire population—who experiment with the forbidden drug? Inasmuch as no one in sight appears to be in favor of busting the University of Illinois—or Yale—or Ole Miss—and sending all the malefactors to jail, just what do we conservatives propose?

We are, by the current standards, raising a generation of presumptive criminals—because we have so defined them. The situation is aggravated by the necessary use of undercover agents who regularly practice entrapment. How else does one enforce laws against victimless crimes, concerning which no one files a complaint?

But the story gets worse when the harshness of the penalties is considered. In general, the sale and possession of small quantities of marijuana have been punished more severely than crimes against person and property.

In my native Texas, for example, the average sentence for possession is nine years. At least one man is serving life for possession of a matchbox-full.

Long sentences are *still* being handed out in many states.

Arrests for possession of marijuana rose tenfold from 1965 to 1970, to more than 188 thousand. The FBI recorded a continued increase in drug crimes last year, and unless there is a (most unlikely) decline it is likely that as many as 250,000 young people will be arrested on possession charges this year.

The laws are themselves scientifically indefensible insofar as they proscribe marijuana as a "narcotic stimulant to the central nervous sytem." Marijuana is in fact not a narcotic, and narcotics are not in fact stimulants. They are depressants. For many years, under the Uniform Narcotic Drug Act, marijuana was legally classified as a narcotic; *not* because it had ever been supposed that such a classification was scientific, but because, as one legislator put it in 1932, "there is a universal antipathy to the use of narcotics"; and it was "antipathy," rather than understanding, that the law was intended to create. The distinction between marijuana and narcotics was restored by the Controlled Substances Act of 1970, but several states still persist in lumping them together, as do many citizens.

Would you respect a law that defined yogurt as a "vegetarian meat product"?

Laws should make sense, they should be uniformly enforced, they should carry a punishment in proportion to the damage done by the offender, and they should have the effect desired (in this case the discouragement of the use of marijuana). Our marijuana laws meet none of the above specifications, and while there are those who obey them, only fools respect them.

3. *Conservatives should recognize bureaucratic incompetence in whatever guise.*

Most government programs start when a politician discovers a "national disgrace." A new department is set up, billions are appropriated—and sure enough, the problem gets worse.

Marijuana was little known in the Thirties, until it was "discovered" by Harry Jacob Anslinger, the longtime head of the Narcotics Bureau. At that time there were perhaps as few as fifty thousand users, mostly blacks and Latin Americans, plus a few bohemians and hippies.

After 35 years of propaganda and repression, the drug has been introduced to 25 million people. As bureaucratic fiascos go, not bad.

It is incredible that conservatives should continue to support the bureaucratic mess that comprises the marijuana laws.

It is even more incredible that at a time when the crime rate soars, the hard-pressed police, courts, and prisons should be burdened with 25 million putative marijuana criminals.

Finally, it is puzzling—and frightening—to suppose that American conservatives sanction a tissue of laws the effect of which is to cast lackadaisical marijuana users—if they are so unlucky as to be a) caught, by b) the wrong people—into prisons which they share with men of tempered felonious disposition. The law defines them as criminals; the enforcement of the law makes them such.

4. *Conservative leadership is essential to an effective reform of the laws.*

If the present trend continues, the use of marijuana will soon approach market saturation and the use of it will level off. However, as more and more of the population become users—and users grow older—it will be increasingly rare for a jury to convict or a judge to sentence a defendant for possession or even sale of marijuana. While this may be an improvement from a humanitarian point of view, it leaves thousands of Americans rotting in jail for what millions on the outside are routinely doing.

For society as a whole it means widespread use of the drug without any objectively sanctioned controls on strength (how strong before it becomes hash?), quality (adulteration with opiates is routine), or distribution to minors. Continued outlawing will mean the growth of a large criminal industry analogous to the fabled bootleggers, and all the social ills that result from such a situation.

It will mean that it will not be possible to discourage by taxation the use of hashish (which is to marijuana roughly what 100 proof rum is to wine). And—worst of all—it will leave marijuana distribution in the same hands as methadone, LSD, barbiturates, amphetamines, and even heroin.

Finally, when legalization does come—say ten or fifteen years from now at the latest (assuming conservative opposition), or in five years (with conservative acquiescence)—patterns of use and distribution will have been set, and control will be increasingly difficult to enforce.

If on the other hand conservatives support the fight for legalization, we can have effective and humane laws that will succeed where the present system has so dismally failed—in keeping the drug from children; in making the vital distinctions. A prudent relaxation of the law will make possible some realistic restraints. Those substances which are now promiscuously forbidden will cease to be promiscuously consumed; as society distinguishes between pot and heroin, its children will be encouraged to learn the difference too. Moreover, gentler laws would soften the impact of their own violation: Under present laws, as has been pointed out, hard and soft drugs tend to circulate through the same channels; but under new laws, designed to regulate rather than to prohibit, even the younger teenager whose pot-smoking is still illicit, will tend to get it from an older brother or friend who has legal access (much as he now gets beer), instead of from the specialist in illegal drugs.

5. *Conservatives should take the lead in urging the decriminalization of individual use of marijuana.*

The marijuana laws have encouraged a disrespect for the laws; they have destroyed the credibility of government; and they have estranged the young.

The importance of marijuana to its youthful users is less the pleasure it gives the individual than the tribal value of it. The drug's use in the counterculture is analogous to the use of alcohol in the Establishment, as a social lubricant. Any attempt at interference with so fundamental a part of the new social life is doomed to failure in a free society.

6. *The notion that marijuana can, in and of itself, undermine the moral fabric of society is contrary to basic conservative philosophy.*

The notion that the use of marijuana is, or leads to, moral degeneracy is not sustained by any scientific investigation of the drug.

However, a moral society, like a moral individual (or a healthy individual for that matter) will use a drug: for recreation (alcohol); to alleviate pain (aspirin); to help him face and fulfill his obligations through crises (tranquilizers); but so long as the individual loves his family, his country and himself, he is going to use drugs to further his objectives, not to undermine them.

The superstition that cannabis is responsible for the muddlement of the student generation goes contrary to established conservative premises.

The hysterical myths about marijuana that have led conservatives to condone massive programs of social engineering, interference in the affairs of individuals, monstrous bureaucratic waste, the alienation of youth whom we struggle to attract to our institutions—are a great and current social menace.

7. *How do conservatives justify the hard data:* over 250,000 young people arrested every year (seventy thousand in California alone), tens of thousands put in jail or prison for long periods, lives disrupted and even ruined, families divided, records besmirched, a life of ostracism?

This is being done in our name?

I, for one, bitterly resent this; but, more, I fear its consequences. If the effect on individuals is tragic, the effect on society is disastrous—disastrous for our institutions, the rule of law, political stability, even public health. This is not being done by the enemy without, but by those to whom *we* have delegated the power and the authority to defend us. They have been a party to superstitions that are as false in content as they are in tone, but we cannot just blame them.

If now that we know that we have been deceived, now that the evidence is there for all to see, our jails full, our youth increasingly alienated and confused, if in the face of all this we do not *take the lead*, how are we conservatives going to speak to America, and how is our America going to speak to the world—of freedom and charity?

Commentary: What's the Rush?

James Burnham

From *National Review* (December 8, 1972), 1346–1348. Reprinted by permission of the publisher of *National Review*.

Mr. Burnham has been on the editorial board of National Review *since 1955. He was Professor of Philosophy at NYU from 1929 to 1953. His chief contributions are* The Managerial Revolution *(1941),* The Machiavellians *(1943),* Suicide of the West *(1964), and* The War We Are In *(1967).*

Mr. Cowan's hopped up prose leaves me feeling rather stoned, but I would not want my sluggish response to his mix of cliché ("drug abuse in our schools is a serious problem"), confusion ("marijuana does not lead to changes in social behavior. . . . It tends in most users to inhibit violence") and hyperbole ("thousands of Americans rotting in jail") to obscure my agreement with what I take to be one of his proposals. Luckily for all of us, it is possible to derive a true conclusion from faulty premises.

I agree, then, that possession of an amount of marijuana small enough to give presumptive indication that it is intended only for personal use should not of itself be a criminal offense, making the offender subject to a jail sentence. (I am not so sure whether it should stay on the books as a misdemeanor, subject, like parking beside a hydrant, to a fine.) My opinion here is independent of the question of marijuana's merits and demerits. Even if an individual's use of pot is a bad thing, it is not bad enough to motivate, in and by itself, making him a criminal. The punishment is out of proportion to the offense, and probably causes more damage than it cures. I believe, therefore, that laws should be modified, at least to the extent of decriminalizing personal possession of small amounts.

But I do feel Mr. Cowan paints too apocalyptic a picture even on this point. Some individuals have been jailed in some states of this country for such possession, but I have seen no statistics showing that "tens of thousands" have been "put in jail or prison for long periods." (For this offense hundreds of Americans have been put in jail or prison in *other* nations, in most of which laws against marijuana are stricter, and much more strictly enforced, than here—a fact the significance of which might be worth Mr. Cowan's pondering.) Moreover, I gather that laws against possession have been used rather like the income-tax law. That is, the real offense for which individuals are sent to jail is actually something else—not possession but pushing, or vandalism, rioting, trashing, serious vehicular offenses, etc. If pot is found on an individual involved in such activities, it offers a simple device for getting a conviction, much as the income-tax rap takes care of many gangsters. To juridical purists like Mr. Cowan this is in shocking disrespect of the law, but police and the courts would have an even harder time keeping us from reverting to the jungle without a few little angles of this sort. Still, I repeat: I am, on net, for decriminalization.

This, however, is the least of what Mr. Cowan is after. He wants us to believe a good many propositions about marijuana, and he wants not merely its decriminalization but its legalization under "realistic restraints." The effect of legalizing would be to make marijuana comparable to tobacco. Under suitable rules and regulations, disclosure requirements, quality standards and age restrictions, marijuana would be grown freely (doubtless subsidized in due course) and marijuana cigarettes (and other products) would be freely manufactured and sold. Brightly colored packages of Acapulco Golds, Tijuana

Clouds and Zen Sticks would join Camels and Marlboros in the vending machines. Newspapers, billboards and magazines—NR we may hope prominently among them—would carry many a new four-color invitation to Come to Zen Country, and Try a Cloud Trip. In fact, if Mr. Cowan's assertions about marijuana are true, its production and sale should be subject to considerably fewer regulations and restrictions than tobacco. In one paragraph he states that "The reasons why human beings should refrain from consuming drugs (including alcohol) during adolescence are undeniable," but he nowhere gives any reasons that might apply to marijuana.

I think it possible that legalization of marijuana will come, and I understand that the big tobacco companies are ready for M-Day, but it seems to me unnecessary to be in a rush about it. We don't really know enough yet about marijuana. Even if there is nothing wrong with it, its early legalization and public mass sale would be offensive to a big majority of the people of this country, which is surely a fact that conservatives ought to take into serious account. And there is something disturbing in the additional fact that cannabis and the cannabis rituals are non-Western in origin and tradition. The West's principal drug, indissolubly intertwining Western tradition, is alcohol.

What my own experience, observation, listening, and reading have suggested to me up to now about marijuana differs with various of Mr. Cowan's premises, though I have reached few hard and fast conclusions. From my list:

1. The occasional moderate use of marijuana seems to do no harm and can be enjoyable. (I wish Mr. Cowan weren't so all-fired solemn about pot. He never suggests that pot can be fun. Indeed, he dismisses any "pleasure it gives" in favor of its "tribal value.")

2. This business about pot's being "non-addictive" fails to impress me, even when someone adds, like Mr. Cowan, "I use the word technically." I know a dozen or two people, and there are hundreds of thousands in the country, who are hooked on high-calorie foods and who suffer frightful withdrawal agonies if the stuff is taken away from them. Few of them will ever succeed in laying off for good. But of course calories are "non-addictive in a technical sense." The human psyche is more intricate than mechanistic physiologists comprehend.

3. The question whether the use of marijuana leads to the use of hard drugs does not seem to have been put in a precise enough way to permit an answer. We do know that frequent use of marijuana is often one element, and chronologically an early element, in the syndrome that includes, chronologically later, the use of hard drugs, though it is also true that in many cases the use of marijuana is not correlated with the later use of hard drugs. Whether pot tends to "open the door" to hard drugs is an exceedingly difficult scientific problem, but the correlation is frequent enough to bring a legitimate qualm or two to parents watching a child take up pot.

4. As I have already noted, Mr. Cowan contradicts himself about whether marijuana leads to "changes in social behavior" when he writes that "it tends in most users to inhibit violence." (Many observers would equate "to inhibit violence" with the "loss of motivation" that Mr. Cowan denies.) Now the fact is that everybody with eyes in his head knows that frequent use of pot *does* bring changes in social behavior (just as everyone knows that heavy use on a particular occasion brings spectacular changes).

5. Research into the physiological effects of marijuana remains inconclusive. There is little indication so far of any appreciable effect from occasional moderate use. Some American researchers—with remarkable boldness considering the short and narrow scope of their investigations—have claimed there is no effect even from heavy long-term use. In England scientific opinion seems to be veering toward caution. Within the past year, a team of physiologists and neurologists have reported the possibility of brain damage from heavy use, and this autumn a meeting of pharmacological and forensic medicine specialists featured several reports on possible chemically induced damage to the organism.

6. Hashish, as Mr. Cowan recognizes, is merely strong pot. Hashish has been used widely and heavily in many nations, especially in the

Middle East: Egypt, Yemen, Iraq, India, for example, where there is a centuries-old social experience of cannabis. The hashish-using type of person is well known in all those countries, and hardly a model many Americans would like to adopt for the emulation of this country's youth. Again, cause, perhaps, for qualm.

These are among the considerations that prompt my query, What's The Rush? If the nation has struggled along for two hundred years without legal pot, it can doubtless survive without it a few years more. As with so many things, time may largely straighten out the pot problems without much crusading effort. In most states and most campuses there is little interference from the cops any longer with discreet and civil use of marijuana. Some states are softening their laws, and more will doubtless follow. Judges and prosecutors and cops are learning more about pot. And it is possible that the significance of the whole pot issue is diminishing through a familiar American process. Mr. Cowan may have jumped on yesterday's train. Pot—so at least it seems to me and a good many other observers—is going out of fashion. I know this is true at several schools with which I have direct acquaintance, and several college campuses. A Dartmouth colleague tells me that Dartmouth students have swung back to Dartmouth's traditional beer. In the West this year the most rapidly spreading campus organization is the Society for Creative Anachronism. Its local chapters take names from a past time or distant place (San Francisco = The Renaissance; Tucson with the University of Arizona campus = Tuscany). Activities include baking contests, costumed charades and poetry reading. Yes, of course; the Society began at Berkeley.

Commentary: Marijuana and the Counterculture

Jeffrey Hart

From *National Review* (December 8, 1972), 1346. Reprinted by permission of the publisher of *National Review*.

Mr. Hart is on the editorial board of National Review.

I have only a few things to add to the excellent—and generically conservative—analysis by James Burnham.

First of all, the argument (by no means settled) over whether or not marijuana is physically harmful does not seem important to me. Most things that are fun to do are harmful or dangerous: smoking, eating rich food, drinking, mountain climbing, playing football, and so forth. The things you like to do will probably kill you. That doesn't mean they should be illegal or even that you should stop doing them.

The case "against" marijuana (setting to one side the question of the role of law in the matter) seems to me to be cultural, or perhaps cultural-anthropological. Mr. Cowan touches upon this in his point number five. Marijuana is indeed an integral part of the counterculture of the 1960s, and I use the word integral advisedly. The *meaning* of marijuana—and, as I say, I care not a fig for its physical effects—has to do with this cultural symbolism. And though the laws may indeed be excessively harsh (Texas) or the regnant definition imprecise ("stimulant"), the *meaning* of those laws in the current historical circumstance is plain enough. They aim to lean on, to penalize the counterculture. They reflect the opinion, surely a majority one, that the counterculture, and its manners and morals, and all its works are *bad.* And though, as Mr. Cowan puts it, "the use of marijuana does not in itself lead to the use of heroin"; the marijuana milieu most assuredly does so lead.

Now I don't care much for all that "free society" rhetoric. No reference to marijuana occurs in the First Amendment. Mr. Cowan: "Any attempt at interference with so fundamental a part of the new social life is doomed to failure in a free society." Nonsense. Society "interferes" all along the line through laws, customs, sanctions, etc., in an attempt to preserve a variety of values, interferes successfully as well as unsuccessfully, and, from the point of view of *my* conservatism, interferes far too little: as in the case of pornography, for example. No society

can be "free" in the sense implicit in Mr. Cowan's sentence and still survive. As for the "new social life," *écrasez l'infâme.*

Of course the evangelical tone of Mr. Cowan's piece is something of a giveaway. There is an enormous surplus emotion operating here. If the Texas laws are out of line, take it up with the state legislature there. No doubt laws are harsh or anomalous here and there on various heterosexual acts, on double parking, on drinking, on fishing and hunting, on guns, on speeding, on divorce, and so on. I cannot see that the reform of the marijuana laws is a distinctively conservative issue. I would rate it, even conceding every one of Mr. Cowan's points—which I do not—304th on my scale of priorities, or perhaps lower.

Finally: marijuana became an *issue* during the 1960s with the rise of the counterculture. It will cease to be one about six months from now with the death of that counterculture.

The Spirit of the Law

William F. Buckley, Jr.

From *National Review* (December 8, 1972), 1346, 1366. Reprinted by permission of the publisher of *National Review.*

Mr. Buckley is editor-in-chief of National Review, *a syndicated newspaper columnist, "A Conservative Voice," and moderator of the TV program, "Firing Line." Since his first book,* God and Man at Yale *(1951), he has continued defending the conservative view in* Up from Liberalism *(1959),* Rumbles Left and Right *(1963),* The Jeweler's Eye *(1968), and* The Governor Listeth *(1970) and in numerous articles.*

It is easy to denigrate any cause by the technique of putting it alongside other, nobler, causes. Thus a decade or so back Mr. John Roche elegantly dismissed the fear of guilt by association as ranking, by his hierarchy of fears, between Fear #25 and Fear #27, the former being Mr. Roche's fear of college presidents, the latter his fear of being bitten to death by piranhas. The trouble with the technique is that it does not allow for latitudinarian preoccupation: with individuated preoccupation. Somewhere, somebody is being eaten by piranhas, or is in danger of being eaten by piranhas. I know Professor Hart both as a friend and as a craftsman, and he is altogether capable of spending a week trying to understand a single Canto of Ezra Pound, or perfecting a paragraph in one of his own books. I would never think to say to him that there are greater concerns in the world than the penetration of poetic marginalia, or graver causes than belletristic purity.

I do not see why we cannot proceed on the assumption that although the fear of marijuana, the need for marijuana, and the ignorance of marijuana, are neither a) the central concern of a balanced society; nor b) the most urgently needed social indulgence; nor c) the area of legislative concern about which there is the greatest ignorance—still I say: Cowan is entitled to his preoccupation, and I for one find his arguments not merely plausible, but overwhelming.

It is true, as Mr. Burnham points out, that the situation is in flux. But it is in flux because there is pressure brought to bear. It was in 1969 that Senator Barry Goldwater came out for the legalization, or more precisely, the decriminalization of pot. Senator Goldwater! Three years after he did so, a young man was raided in an upstate college in New York State, and was found to be in possession of marijuana. He resides now at Attica. Attica! Even if none of us were to bestir ourselves by a written paragraph or a spoken word in behalf of a reform in the draconian laws that govern the use of marijuana, probably common sense would assert itself, in due course, and the laws would be modified. But that kind of resignation is hardly consistent with the impera-

tives of a journal of opinion. Our responsibility is to move ahead of public opinion: indeed to influence public opinion. Mr. Cowan insists quite simply that there *are* no arguments, of any force or gravity, by which to justify the treatment routinely given to people who use marijuana here and there in the United States. I flatly agree with him.

While agreeing with Messrs. Burnham and Hart on the point that science is not only hubristic but childish when it says that the case for the innocence of pot is largely established. It is like the scientific law that declares a man to be under the influence of alcohol and therefore unfit to drive a car when his alcoholic content is .002—or whatever. This even though everybody knows—even Einstein must have known—the man who if he has .0000002 alcohol is a menace, vehicular and social; whereas there are those whose alcoholic content is usually .2, or whatever, and manage world wars and great speeches —if not quite adequate peace terms—altogether competently. Pot is a psychic poison to some people, and the hell with those who think otherwise: they are wrong.

Do we therefore legalize pot? Not, I should say, in the sense Mr. Burnham caricatures. But the President's Commission did not advocate a distinction that is purely idle when it recommended that pushers should be illegal, but consumers not so. Thus it was, mostly, under prohibition. Thus it is, by and large, with prostitution; and even with gambling. The gentle animadversions of the law are not useless. They do become, however, a great menace rather than a benefaction when they are taken too literally, and I understand this to be what Mr. Cowan is fighting to free us from, and I am on his side.

17 MARRIAGE AND FAMILY— TILL DEATH DO US PART?

The Fractured Family

Alvin Toffler

This selection is from Mr. Toffler's provocative book, Future Shock. *He is also the author of* The Culture Consumers *(1964) and has contributed to many magazines and journals. Besides his writing experience, he has been an associate editor of* Fortune *and on the faculty at the New School and Cornell University.*

The flood of novelty about to crash down upon us will spread from universities and research centers to factories and offices, from the marketplace and mass media into our social relationships, from the community into the home. Penetrating deep into our private lives, it will place absolutely unprecedented strains on the family itself.

The family has been called the "giant shock absorber" of society—the place to which the bruised and battered individual returns after doing battle with the world, the one stable point in an increasingly flux-filled environment. As the super-industrial revolution unfolds, this "shock absorber" will come in for some shocks of its own.

Social critics have a field day speculating about the family. The family is "near the point of complete extinction," says Ferdinand Lundberg, author of *The Coming World Transformation.* "The family is dead except for the first year or two of child raising," according to psychoanalyst William Wolf. "This will be its only function." Pessimists tell us the family is racing toward oblivion—but seldom tell us what will take its place.

Family optimists, in contrast, contend that the family, having existed all this time, will continue to exist. Some go so far as to argue that the family is in for a Golden Age. As leisure spreads, they theorize, families will spend more time together and will derive great satisfaction from joint activity. "The family that plays together, stays together," etc.

A more sophisticated view holds that the very turbulence of tomorrow will drive people deeper into their families. "People will marry for stable structure," says Dr. Irwin M. Greenberg, Professor of Psychiatry at the Albert Einstein College of Medicine. According to this view, the family serves as one's "portable roots," anchoring one against the storm of change. In short, the more transient and novel the environment, the more important the family will become.

It may be that both sides in this debate are wrong. For the future is more open than it might appear. The family may neither vanish *nor* enter upon a new Golden Age. It may—and this is far more likely—break up, shatter, only to come together again in weird and novel ways.

THE MYSTIQUE OF MOTHERHOOD

The most obviously upsetting force likely to strike the family in the decades immediately ahead will be the impact of the new birth technology. The ability to pre-set the sex of one's baby, or even to "program" its IQ, looks and personality traits, must now be regarded as a real possibility. Embryo implants, babies grown *in vitro*, the ability to swallow a pill and guarantee oneself twins or triplets, or, even more, the ability to walk into a "babytorium" and actually purchase embryos—all this reaches so far beyond any previous human experience that one needs to look at the future through the eyes of the poet or painter, rather than those of the sociologist or conventional philosopher.

It is regarded as somehow unscholarly, even frivolous, to discuss these matters. Yet advances in science and technology, or in reproductive biology alone, could, within a short time, smash all orthodox ideas about the family and its responsibilities. When babies can be grown in a laboratory jar what happens to the very notion of maternity? And what happens to the self-image of the female in societies which, since the very beginnings of man, have taught her that her primary mission is the propagation of and nurture of the race?

Few social scientists have begun as yet to concern themselves with such questions. One who has is psychiatrist Hyman G. Weitzen, director of Neuropsychiatric Service at Polyclinic Hospital in New York. The cycle of birth, Dr. Weitzen suggests, "fulfills for most women a major creative need . . . Most women are proud of their ability to bear children . . . The special aura that glorifies the pregnant woman has figured largely in the art and literature of both East and West."

What happens to the cult of motherhood, Weitzen asks, if "her offspring might literally not be hers, but that of a genetically 'superior' ovum, implanted in her womb from another woman, or even grown in a Petri dish?" If women are to be important at all, he suggests, it will no longer be because they alone can bear children. If nothing else, we are about to kill off the mystique of motherhood.

Not merely motherhood, but the concept of parenthood itself may be in for radical revision. Indeed, the day may soon dawn when it is possible for a child to have more than two biological parents. Dr. Beatrice Mintz, a developmental biologist at the Institute for Cancer Research in Philadelphia, has grown what are coming to be known as "multi-mice"—baby mice each of which has more than the usual number of parents. Embryos are taken from each of two pregnant mice. These embryos are placed in a laboratory dish and nurtured until they form a single growing mass. This is then implanted in the womb of a third female mouse. A baby is born that clearly shares the genetic characteristics of both sets of donors. Thus a typical multi-mouse, born of two pairs of parents, has white fur and whiskers on one side of its face, dark fur and whiskers on the other, with alternating bands of white and dark hair covering the rest of the body. Some 700 multi-mice bred in this fashion have already produced more than 35,000 offspring themselves. If multi-mouse is here, can "multi-man" be far behind?

Under such circumstances, what or who is a parent? When a woman bears in her uterus an embryo conceived in another woman's womb, who is the mother? And just exactly who is the father?

If a couple can actually purchase an embryo, then parenthood becomes a legal, not a biological matter. Unless such transactions are tightly controlled, one can imagine such grotesqueries as a couple buying an embryo, raising it *in vitro*, then buying another in the name of the first, as though for a trust fund. In that case, they might be regarded as legal "grandparents" before their first child is out of its infancy. We shall need a whole new vocabulary to describe kinship ties.

Furthermore, if embryos are for sale, can a corporation buy one? Can it buy ten thousand? Can it resell them? And if not a corporation, how about a noncommercial research laboratory? If we buy and sell living embryos, are we back to a new form of slavery? Such are the nightmarish questions soon to be debated by us. To continue to think of the family, therefore, in purely conventional terms is to defy all reason.

Faced by rapid social change and the staggering implications of the scientific revolution, super-industrial man may be forced to experiment with novel family forms. Innovative minorities can be expected to try out a colorful variety of family arrangements. They will begin by tinkering with existing forms.

THE STREAMLINED FAMILY

One simple thing they will do is streamline the family.

The typical pre-industrial family not only had a good many children, but numerous other dependents as well—grandparents, uncles, aunts, and cousins. Such "extended" families were well suited for survival in slow-paced agricultural societies. But such families are hard to transport or transplant. They are immobile.

Industrialism demanded masses of workers ready and able to move off the land in pursuit of jobs, and to move again whenever necessary. Thus the extended family gradually shed its excess weight and the so-called "nuclear" family emerged—a stripped-down, portable family unit consisting only of parents and a small set of children. This new style family, far more mobile than the traditional extended family, became the standard model in all the industrial countries.

Super-industrialism, however, the next stage of eco-technological development, requires even higher mobility. Thus we may expect many among the people of the future to carry the streamlining process a step further by remaining childless, cutting the family down to its most elemental components, a man and a woman. Two people, perhaps with matched careers, will prove more efficient at navigating through education and social shoals, through job changes and geographic relocations, than the ordinary child-cluttered family. Indeed, anthropologist Margaret Mead has pointed out that we may already be moving toward a system under which, as she puts it, "parenthood would be limited to a smaller number of families whose principal functions would be childrearing," leaving the rest of the population "free to function—for the first time in history—as individuals."

A compromise may be the postponement of children, rather than childlessness. Men and women today are often torn in conflict between a commitment to career and a commitment to children. In the future, many couples will sidestep this problem by deferring the entire task of raising children until after retirement.

This may strike people of the present as odd. Yet once childbearing is broken away from its biological base, nothing more than tradition suggests having children at an early age. Why not wait, and buy your embryos later, after your work career is over? Thus childlessness is likely to spread among young and middle-aged couples; sexagenarians who raise infants may be far more common. The post-retirement family could become a recognized social institution.

BIO-PARENTS AND PRO-PARENTS

If a smaller number of families raise children, however, why do the children have to be their own? Why not a system under which "professional parents" take on the childrearing function for others?

Raising children, after all, requires skills that are by no means universal. We don't let "just anyone" perform brain surgery or, for that matter, sell stocks and bonds. Even the lowest ranking civil servant is required to pass tests proving competence. Yet we allow virtually anyone, almost without regard for mental or moral qualification, to try his or her hand at raising young human beings, so long as these humans are biological offspring. Despite the increasing complexity of the task, parenthood remains the greatest single preserve of the amateur.

As the present system cracks and the super-industrial revolution rolls over us, as the armies of juvenile delinquents swell, as hundreds of thousands of youngsters flee their homes, and students rampage at universities in all the techno-societies, we can expect vociferous demands for an end to parental dilettantism.

There are far better ways to cope with the

problems of youth, but professional parenthood is certain to be proposed, if only because it fits so perfectly with the society's overall push toward specialization. Moreover, there is a powerful, pent-up demand for this social innovation. Even now millions of parents, given the opportunity, would happily relinquish their parental responsibilities—and not necessarily through irresponsibility or lack of love. Harried, frenzied, up against the wall, they have come to see themselves as inadequate to the tasks. Given affluence and the existence of specially-equipped and licensed professional parents, many of today's biological parents would not only gladly surrender their children to them, but would look upon it as an act of love, rather than rejection.

Parental professionals would not be therapists, but actual family units assigned to, and well paid for, rearing children. Such families might be multi-generational by design, offering children in them an opportunity to observe and learn from a variety of adult models, as was the case in the old farm homestead. With the adults paid to be professional parents, they would be freed of the occupational necessity to relocate repeatedly. Such families would take in new children as old ones "graduate" so that age-segregation would be minimized.

Thus newspapers of the future might well carry advertisements addressed to young married couples: "Why let parenthood tie you down? Let us raise your infant into a responsible, successful adult. Class A Pro-family offers: father age 39, mother, 36, grandmother, 67. Uncle and aunt, age 30, live in, hold part time local employment. Four-child-unit has opening for one, age 6–8. Regulated diet exceeds government standards. All adults certified in child development and management. Bio-parents permitted frequent visits. Telephone contact allowed. Child may spend summer vacation with bio-parents. Religion, art, music encouraged by special arrangement. Five year contract, minimum. Write for further details."

The "real" or "bio-parents" could, as the ad suggests, fill the role presently played by interested godparents, namely that of friendly and helpful outsiders. In such a way, the society could continue to breed a wide diversity of genetic types, yet turn the care of children over to mother-father groups who are equipped, both intellectually and emotionally, for the task of caring for kids.

COMMUNES AND HOMOSEXUAL DADDIES

Quite a different alternative lies in the communal family. As transience increases the loneliness and alienation in society, we can anticipate increasing experimentation with various forms of group marriage. The banding together of several adults and children into a single "family" provides a kind of insurance against isolation. Even if one or two members of the household leave, the remaining members have one another. Communes are springing up modeled after those described by psychologist B. F. Skinner in *Walden Two* and by novelist Robert Rimmer in *The Harrad Experiment and Proposition 31.* In the latter work, Rimmer seriously proposes the legalization of a "corporate family" in which from three to six adults adopt a single name, live and raise children in common, and legally incorporate to obtain certain economic and tax advantages.

According to some observers, there are already hundreds of open or covert communes dotting the American map. Not all, by any means, are composed of young people or hippies. Some are organized around specific goals—like the group, quietly financed by three East Coast colleges—which has taken as its function the task of counseling college freshmen, helping to orient them to campus life. The goals may be social, religious, political, even recreational. Thus we shall before long begin to see communal families of surfers dotting the beaches of California and Southern France, if they don't already. We shall see the emergence of communes based on political doctrines and religious faiths. In Denmark, a bill to legalize group marriage has already been introduced in the Folketing (Parliament). While passage is not imminent, the act of introduction is itself a significant symbol of change.

In Chicago, 250 adults and children already live together in "family-style monasticism" under the auspices of a new, fast-growing religious organization, the Ecumenical Institute. Members share the same quarters, cook and eat together, worship and tend children in common, and pool their incomes. At least 60,000 people have taken "EI" courses and similar communes have begun to spring up in Atlanta, Boston, Los Angeles and other cities. "A brand-new world is emerging," says Professor Joseph W. Mathews, leader of the Ecumenical Institute, "but people are still operating in terms of the old one. We seek to re-educate people and give them the tools to build a new social context."

Still another type of family unit likely to win adherents in the future might be called the "geriatric commune"—a group marriage of elderly people drawn together in a common search for companionship and assistance. Disengaged from the productive economy that makes mobility necessary, they will settle in a single place, band together, pool funds, collectively hire domestic or nursing help, and proceed—within limits—to have the "time of their lives."

Communalism runs counter to the pressure for ever greater geographical and social mobility generated by the thrust toward super-industrialism. It presupposes groups of people who "stay put." For this reason, communal experiments will first proliferate among those in the society who are free from the industrial discipline—the retired population, the young, the drop-outs, the students, as well as among self-employed professional and technical people. Later, when advanced technology and information systems make it possible for much of the work of society to be done at home via computer-telecommunication hookups, communalism will become feasible for larger numbers.

We shall, however, also see many more "family" units consisting of a single unmarried adult and one or more children. Nor will all of these adults be women. It is already possible in some places for unmarried men to adopt children. In 1965 in Oregon, for example, a thirty-eight-year-old musician named Tony Piazza became the first unmarried man in that state, and perhaps in the United States, to be granted the right to adopt a baby. Courts are more readily granting custody to divorced fathers, too. In London, photographer Michael Cooper, married at twenty and divorced soon after, won the right to raise his infant son, and expressed an interest in adopting other children. Observing that he did not particularly wish to remarry, but that he liked children, Cooper mused aloud: "I wish you could just ask beautiful women to have babies for you. Or any woman you liked, or who had something you admired. Ideally, I'd like a big house full of children—all different colors, shapes and sizes." Romantic? Unmanly? Perhaps. Yet attitudes like these will be widely held by men in the future.

Two pressures are even now softening up the culture, preparing it for acceptance of the idea of childrearing by men. First, adoptable children are in oversupply in some places. Thus, in California, disc jockeys blare commercials: "We have many wonderful babies of all races and nationalities waiting to bring love and happiness to the right families . . . Call the Los Angeles County Bureau of Adoption." At the same time, the mass media, in a strange non-conspiratorial fashion, appear to have decided simultaneously that men who raise children hold special interest for the public. Extremely popular television shows in recent seasons have glamorized womanless households in which men scrub floors, cook, and, most significantly, raise children. *My Three Sons*, *The Rifleman*, *Bonanza*, and *Bachelor Father* are four examples.

As homosexuality becomes more socially acceptable, we may even begin to find families based on homosexual "marriages" with the partners adopting children. Whether these children would be of the same or opposite sex remains to be seen. But the rapidity with which homosexuality is winning respectability in the techno-societies distinctly points in this direction. In Holland not long ago a Catholic priest "married" two homosexuals, explaining to critics that "they are among the faithful to be helped." England has rewritten its relevant legislation;

homosexual relations between consenting adults are no longer considered a crime. And in the United States a meeting of Episcopal clergymen concluded publicly that homosexuality might, under certain circumstances, be adjudged "good." The day may also come when a court decides that a couple of stable, well educated homosexuals might make decent "parents."

We might also see the gradual relaxation of bars against polygamy. Polygamous families exist even now, more widely than generally believed, in the midst of "normal" society. Writer Ben Merson, after visiting several such families in Utah where polygamy is still regarded as essential by certain Mormon fundamentalists, estimated that there are some 30,000 people living in underground family units of this type in the United States. As sexual attitudes loosen up, as property rights become less important because of rising affluence, the social repression of polygamy may come to be regarded as irrational. This shift may be facilitated by the very mobility that compels men to spend considerable time away from their present homes. The old male fantasy of the Captain's Paradise may become a reality for some, although it is likely that, under such circumstances, the wives left behind will demand extramarital sexual rights. Yesterday's "captain" would hardly consider this possibility. Tomorrow's may feel quite differently about it.

Still another family form is even now springing up in our midst, a novel childrearing unit that I call the "aggregate family"—a family based on relationships between divorced and remarried couples, in which all the children become part of "one big family." Though sociologists have paid little attention as yet to this phenomenon, it is already so prevalent that it formed the basis for a hilarious scene in a recent American movie entitled *Divorce American Style*. We may expect aggregate families to take on increasing importance in the decades ahead.

Childless marriage, professional parenthood, post-retirement childrearing, corporate families, communes, geriatric group marriages, homosexual family units, polygamy—these, then, are a few of the family forms and practices with which innovative minorities will experiment in the decades ahead. Not all of us, however, will be willing to participate in such experimentation. What of the majority?

THE ODDS AGAINST LOVE

Minorities experiment; majorities cling to the forms of the past. It is safe to say that large numbers of people will refuse to jettison the conventional idea of marriage or the familiar family forms. They will, no doubt, continue searching for happiness within the orthodox format. Yet, even they will be forced to innovate in the end, for the odds against success may prove overwhelming.

The orthodox format presupposes that two young people will "find" one another and marry. It presupposes that the two will fulfill certain psychological needs in one another, and that the two personalities will develop over the years, more or less in tandem, so that they continue to fulfill each other's needs. It further presupposes that this process will last "until death do us part."

These expectations are built deeply into our culture. It is no longer respectable, as it once was, to marry for anything but love. Love has changed from a peripheral concern of the family into its primary justification. Indeed, the pursuit of love through family life has become, for many, the very purpose of life itself.

Love, however, is defined in terms of this notion of shared growth. It is seen as a beautiful mesh of complementary needs, flowing into and out of one another, fulfilling the loved ones, and producing feelings of warmth, tenderness and devotion. Unhappy husbands often complain that they have "left their wives behind" in terms of social, educational or intellectual growth. Partners in successful marriages are said to "grow together."

This "parallel development" theory of love carries endorsement from marriage counsellors, psychologists and sociologists. Thus, says sociologist Nelson Foote, a specialist on the family, the quality of the relationship between husband and wife is dependent upon "the degree of matching in their phases of distinct but comparable development."

If love is a product of shared growth, however, and we are to measure success in marriage by the degree to which matched development actually occurs, it becomes possible to make a strong and ominous prediction about the future.

It is possible to demonstrate that, even in a relatively stagnant society, the mathematical odds are heavily stacked against any couple achieving this ideal of parallel growth. The odds for success positively plummet, however, when the rate of change in society accelerates, as it now is doing. In a fast-moving society, in which many things change, not once, but repeatedly, in which the husband moves up and down a variety of economic and social scales, in which the family is again and again torn loose from home and community, in which individuals move further from their parents, further from the religion of origin, and further from traditional values, it is almost miraculous if two people develop at anything like comparable rates.

If, at the same time, average life expectancy rises from, say, fifty to seventy years, thereby lengthening the term during which this acrobatic feat of matched development is supposed to be maintained, the odds against success become absolutely astronomical. Thus, Nelson Foote writes with wry understatement: "To expect a marriage to last indefinitely under modern conditions is to expect a lot." To ask love to last indefinitely is to expect even more. Transience and novelty are both in league against it.

TEMPORARY MARRIAGE

It is this change in the statistical odds against love that accounts for the high divorce and separation rates in most of the techno-societies. The faster the rate of change and the longer the life span, the worse these odds grow. Something has to crack.

In point of fact, of course, something has already cracked—and it is the old insistence on permanence. Millions of men and women now adopt what appears to them to be a sensible and conservative strategy. Rather than opting for some offbeat variety of the family, they marry conventionally, they attempt to make it "work," and then, when the paths of the partners diverge beyond an acceptable point, they divorce or depart. Most of them go on to search for a new partner whose developmental stage, at that moment, matches their own.

As human relationships grow more transient and modular, the pursuit of love becomes, if anything, more frenzied. But the temporal expectations change. As conventional marriage proves itself less and less capable of delivering on its promise of lifelong love, therefore, we can anticipate open public acceptance of temporary marriages. Instead of wedding "until death us do part," couples will enter into matrimony knowing from the first that the relationship is likely to be short-lived.

They will know, too, that when the paths of husband and wife diverge, when there is too great a discrepancy in developmental stages, they may call it quits—without shock or embarrassment, perhaps even without some of the pain that goes with divorce today. And when the opportunity presents itself, they will marry again . . . and again . . . and again.

Serial marriage—a pattern of successive temporary marriages—is cut to order for the Age of Transience in which all man's relationships, all his ties with the environment, shrink in duration. It is the natural, the inevitable outgrowth of a social order in which automobiles are rented, dolls traded in, and dresses discarded after one-time use. It is the mainstream marriage pattern of tomorrow.

In one sense, serial marriage is already the best kept family secret of the techno-societies. According to Professor Jessie Bernard, a world-prominent family sociologist, "Plural marriage is more extensive in our society today than it is in societies that permit polygamy—the chief difference being that we have institutionalized plural marriage serially or sequentially rather than contemporaneously." Remarriage is already so prevalent a practice that nearly one out of every four bridegrooms in America has been to the altar before. It is so prevalent that one IBM personnel man reports a poignant incident involving a divorced woman, who, in filling out a job application, paused when she came to the question of marital status. She put her pencil in her mouth, pondered for a moment, then wrote: "Unremarried."

Transience necessarily affects the durational expectancies with which persons approach new situations. While they may yearn for a permanent relationship, something inside whispers to them that it is an increasingly improbable luxury.

Even young people who most passionately seek commitment, profound involvement with people and causes, recognize the power of the thrust toward transience. Listen, for example, to a young black American, a civil-rights worker, as she describes her attitude toward time and marriage:

"In the white world, marriage is always billed as 'the end'—like in a Hollywood movie. I don't go for that. I can't imagine myself promising my whole lifetime away. I might want to get married now, but how about next year? That's not disrespect for the institution [of marriage], but the deepest respect. In The [civil rights] Movement, you need to have a feeling for the temporary—of making something as good as you can, while it lasts. In conventional relationships, time is a prison."

Such attitudes will not be confined to the young, the few, or the politically active. They will whip across nations as novelty floods into the society and catch fire as the level of transience rises still higher. And along with them will come a sharp increase in the number of temporary—then serial—marriages.

The idea is summed up vividly by a Swedish magazine, *Svensk Damtidning*, which interviewed a number of leading Swedish sociologists, legal experts, and others about the future of man-woman relationships. It presented its findings in five photographs. They showed the same beautiful bride being carried across the threshold five times—by five different bridegrooms.

MARRIAGE TRAJECTORIES

As serial marriages become more common, we shall begin to characterize people not in terms of their present marital status, but in terms of their marriage career or "trajectory." This trajectory will be formed by the decisions they make at certain vital turning points in their lives.

For most people, the first such juncture will arrive in youth, when they enter into "trial marriage." Even now the young people of the United States and Europe are engaged in a mass experiment with probationary marriage, with or without benefit of ceremony. The staidest of United States universities are beginning to wink at the practice of co-ed housekeeping among their students. Acceptance of trial marriage is even growing among certain religious philosophers. Thus we hear the German theologian Siegfried Keil of Marburg University urge what he terms "recognized premarriage." In Canada, Father Jacques Lazure has publicly proposed "probationary marriages" of three to eighteen months.

In the past, social pressures and lack of money restricted experimentation with trial marriage to a relative handful. In the future, both these limiting forces will evaporate. Trial marriage will be the first step in the serial marriage "careers" that millions will pursue.

A second critical life juncture for the people of the future will occur when the trial marriage ends. At this point, couples may choose to formalize their relationship and stay together into the next stage. Or they may terminate it and seek out new partners. In either case, they will then face several options. They may prefer to go childless. They may choose to have, adopt or "buy" one or more children. They may decide to raise these children themselves or to farm them out to professional parents. Such decisions will be made, by and large, in the early twenties —by which time many young adults will already be well into their second marriages.

A third significant turning point in the marital career will come, as it does today, when the children finally leave home. The end of parenthood proves excruciating for many, particularly women who, once the children are gone, find themselves without a *raison d'être*. Even today divorces result from the failure of the couple to adapt to this traumatic break in continuity.

Among the more conventional couples of tomorrow who choose to raise their own children in the time-honored fashion, this will continue to be a particularly painful time. It will, however, strike earlier. Young people today already leave home sooner than their counterparts a generation ago. They will probably depart even earlier tomorrow. Masses of youngsters will move off, whether into trial marriage or not, in their mid-teens. Thus we may anticipate that the middle and late thirties will be another important breakpoint in the marital careers of millions. Many at that juncture will enter into their third marriage.

This third marriage will bring together two people for what could well turn out to be the longest uninterrupted stretch of matrimony in their lives—from, say, the late thirties until one of the partners dies. This may, in fact, turn out to be the only "real" marriage, the basis of the only truly durable marital relationship. During this time two mature people, presumably with well-matched interests and complementary psychological needs, and with a sense of being at comparable stages of personality development, will be able to look forward to a relationship with a decent statistical probability of enduring.

Not all these marriages will survive until death, however, for the family will still face a fourth crisis point. This will come, as it does now for so many, when one or both of the partners retires from work. The abrupt change in daily routine brought about by this development places great strain on the couple. Some couples will go the path of the post-retirement family, choosing this moment to begin the task of raising children. This may overcome for them the vacuum that so many couples now face after reaching the end of their occupational lives. (Today many women go to work when they finish raising children; tomorrow many will reverse that pattern, working first and childrearing next.) Other couples will overcome the crisis of retirement in other ways, fashioning both

together a new set of habits, interests and activities. Still others will find the transition too difficult, and will simply sever their ties and enter the pool of "in-betweens"—the floating reserve of temporarily unmarried persons.

Of course, there will be some who, through luck, interpersonal skill and high intelligence, will find it possible to make long-lasting monogamous marriages work. Some will succeed, as they do today, in marrying for life and finding durable love and affection. But others will fail to make even sequential marriages endure for long. Thus some will try two or even three partners within, say, the final stage of marriage. Across the board, the average number of marriages per capita will rise—slowly but relentlessly.

Most people will probably move forward along this progression, engaging in one "conventional" temporary marriage after another. But with widespread familial experimentation in the society, the more daring or desperate will make side forays into less conventional arrangements as well, perhaps experimenting with communal life at some point, or going it alone with a child. The net result will be a rich variation in the types of marital trajectories that people will trace, a wider choice of life-patterns, an endless opportunity for novelty of experience. Certain patterns will be more common than others. But temporary marriage will be a standard feature, perhaps the dominant feature, of family life in the future.

THE DEMANDS OF FREEDOM

A world in which marriage is temporary rather than permanent, in which family arrangements are diverse and colorful, in which homosexuals may be acceptable parents and retirees start raising children—such a world is vastly different from our own. Today all boys and girls are expected to find life-long partners. In tomorrow's world, being single will be no crime. Nor will couples be forced to remain imprisoned, as so many still are today, in marriages that have turned rancid. Divorce will be easy to arrange, so long as responsible provision is made for children. In fact, the very introduction of professional parenthood could touch off a great liberating wave of divorces by making it easier for adults to discharge their parental responsibilities without necessarily remaining in the cage of a hateful marriage. With this powerful external pressure removed, those who stay together would be those who wish to stay together, those for whom marriage is actively fulfilling—those, in short, who are in love.

We are also likely to see, under this looser, more variegated family system, many more marriages involving partners of unequal age. Increasingly, older men will marry young girls or vice versa. What will count will not be chronological age, but complementary values and interests and, above all, the level of personal development. To put it another way, partners will be interested not in age, but in stage.

Children in this super-industrial society will grow up with an ever-enlarging circle of what might be called "semi-siblings"—a whole clan of boys and girls brought into the world by their successive sets of parents. What becomes of such "aggregate" families will be fascinating to observe. Semi-sibs may turn out to be like cousins, today. They may help one another professionally or in time of need. But they will also present the society with novel problems. Should semi-sibs marry, for example?

Surely, the whole relationship of the child to the family will be dramatically altered. Except perhaps in communal groupings, the family will lose what little remains of its power to transmit values to the younger generation. This will further accelerate the pace of change and intensify the problems that go with it.

Looming over all such changes, however, and even dwarfing them in significance is something far more subtle. Seldom discussed, there is a hidden rhythm in human affairs that until now has served as one of the key stabilizing forces in society: the family cycle.

We begin as children; we mature; we leave the parental nest; we give birth to children who, in turn, grow up, leave and begin the process all over again. This cycle has been operating so long, so automatically, and with such implacable

regularity, that men have taken it for granted. It is part of the human landscape. Long before they reach puberty, children learn the part they are expected to play in keeping this great cycle turning. This predictable succession of family events has provided all men, of whatever tribe or society, with a sense of continuity, a place in the temporal scheme of things. The family cycle has been one of the sanity-preserving constants in human existence.

Today this cycle is accelerating. We grow up sooner, leave home sooner, marry sooner, have children sooner. We space them more closely together and complete the period of parenthood more quickly. In the words of Dr. Bernice Neugarten, a University of Chicago specialist on family development, "The trend is toward a more rapid rhythm of events through most of the family cycle."

But if industrialism, with its faster pace of life, has accelerated the family cycle, super-industrialism now threatens to smash it altogether. With the fantasies that the birth scientists are hammering into reality, with the colorful familial experimentation that innovative minorities will perform, with the likely development of such institutions as professional parenthood, with the increasing movement toward temporary and serial marriage, we shall not merely run the cycle more rapidly; we shall introduce irregularity, suspense, unpredictability —in a word, novelty—into what was once as regular and certain as the seasons.

When a "mother" can compress the process of birth into a brief visit to an embryo emporium, when by transferring embryos from womb to womb we can destroy even the ancient certainty that childbearing took nine months, children will grow up into a world in which the family-cycle, once so smooth and sure, will be jerkily arhythmic. Another crucial stabilizer will have been removed from the wreckage of the old order, another pillar of sanity broken.

There is, of course, nothing inevitable about the developments traced in the preceding pages. We have it in our power to shape change. We may choose one future over another. We cannot, however, maintain the past. In our family forms, as in our economics, science, technology and social relationships, we shall be forced to deal with the new.

The Super-industrial Revolution will liberate men from any of the barbarisms that grew out of the restrictive, relatively choiceless family patterns of the past and present. It will offer to each a degree of freedom hitherto unknown. But it will exact a steep price for that freedom.

As we hurtle into tomorrow, millions of ordinary men and women will face emotion-packed options so unfamiliar, so untested, that past experience will offer little clue to wisdom. In their family ties, as in all other aspects of their lives, they will be compelled to cope not merely with transience, but with the added problem of novelty as well.

Thus, in matters both large and small, in the most public of conflicts and the most private of conditions, the balance between routine and non-routine, predictable and non-predictable, the known and the unknown, will be altered. The novelty ratio will rise.

In such an environment, fast-changing and unfamiliar, we shall be forced, as we wend our way through life, to make our personal choices from a diverse array of options. And it is to the third central characteristic of tomorrow, *diversity*, that we must now turn. For it is the final convergence of these three factors—transience, novelty and diversity—that sets the stage for the historic crisis of adaptation that is the subject of this book: future shock.

The Battle Between the Sexes

Rudolf Dreikurs

From *Social Equality: The Challenge of Today*, by Rudolf Dreikurs, M.D., 127–150. Copyright © 1971 by Henry Regnery Company. Reprinted by permission of the publisher.

Emeritus Professor of Psychiatry at the Chicago Medical School, Dr. Dreikurs has taught at the Universities of Rio de Janeiro, Northwestern, Vermont, and Oregon. Chief among his studies are The Challenge of Marriage *(1946),* Fundamentals of Adlerian Psychology *(1950), and* Social Equality: The Challenge of Today *(1971).*

Perhaps in no other area of social living is the rapid progress toward equality as obvious as in the relationship between the sexes. The difficulties we encounter are not the consequence of the *inequality* women labor under but of the *equality* that women have achieved. It is true that equal rights do not yet exist and will have

to be established. But women do not realize that the rights of women have been recognized much earlier and more fully than the rights of Negroes and of children. (As far as children are concerned, their "needs" have been recognized but never before their claim for treatment as equals.)

During most of our civilization's history society has been patriarchal. According to ancient Jewish law, for example, a husband can divorce his wife for adultery, but infidelity on his part gave his wife no right to divorce him. In many feudal societies the wife could be divorced if she bore no son. But the male has not always been dominant. There is historical evidence that, in the early phases of our civilization, certain matriarchal cultures in Greece, Crete, and Egypt awarded women many privileges denied to men. Even some primitive societies, which cannot be easily compared with civilized cultures, gave—and give—women dominant rights.

The dominance may have changed from one sex to the other, but at no time—except for a few instances of limited scope—has there been equality between the sexes approximating that which exists today, particularly on the American scene. The present degree of equality between the sexes corresponds to the growing tendency toward equality in all other areas of personal and group relationships. And as in the other areas, the process is still going on, and the ensuing friction is the source of many of our most urgent domestic problems.

THE FOUR RIGHTS
OF THE DOMINANT SEX

Four rights have been the exclusive privilege of one sex, whenever its dominance was firmly entrenched: political, economic, social, and sexual. Until recently, only men enjoyed these rights and privileges. They alone had political power, with the few exceptions of feminine rulers in otherwise male-dominated governments. Men alone could possess, will, or inherit property. The social position of woman depended entirely on that of the man on whom she depended—father, husband, or brother. Woman had no sexual "rights"; man all. Rigid religious and secular laws *demanded* purity and monogamy; yet the restrictions were *applied* only to women. Social conventions permitted men pre- and extramarital relationships. If a woman lost her "virtue," she lost everything—respect, social status, even her place in family and society. For men, it was almost obligatory to have sexual "experience" before entering marriage.

Now let us examine our present situation. *Political* equality of suffrage has been achieved, and women can be elected to office, though few of us can imagine a Congress consisting of a majority of women and most of us accept the present masculine majority without much objection. Only in the last few years has there been serious discussion of the possibility of a woman becoming president of the United States. Political equality between the sexes is growing, but it has not yet been fully achieved.

Regarding *economic* equality between the sexes, much has been made of the fact that most of the wealth in the United States is owned by women. Women may now inherit property and will it. The husband no longer owns whatever his wife earns or receives. But women do not yet have *complete* economic equality. Most of the wealth possessed by women is managed by men. High economic positions are almost exclusively held by men. Despite exceptions, the wages for women are still generally lower than those for men in the same positions. In a time of unemployment, it is still the woman who is expected to give up her job, under such rationalizations as are always found to support social conventions in favor of the dominant group.

It is perhaps more difficult to recognize that women have *not* yet gained the same *social* rights as men. True, their social position no longer depends on that of their husband, father, or brother. They can climb or descend the social ladder on their own merit. A woman who marries a man below her in status does not necessarily sink to his social level; she may elevate him to her position. Women do, however, assume the husband's name, a traditional sign of patriarchal structure socially, and divorce affects a woman more adversely than a man, though in this area, too, conditions are rapidly changing.

Discussion of *sexual* rights is a precarious undertaking. Established sexual morals are regarded by many as so fundamental that any deviation, as a result of social change or whatever, is considered amoral and offensive. Moral concepts, however, do reflect social conventions and change with each culture. Legal and moral conventions are not imposed upon man by any authority outside himself; they are man-made. Nevertheless, the contemporary social changes toward democracy are inevitably producing new moral standards, and no authority can stay this process.

The growing equality between the sexes is responsible for the gradual breakdown of the double standard for sex activities, heretofore largely accepted by men and women alike. On the one hand, the demand that men now be as chaste as women, attributed to Puritan influence, is an expression of growing equality between the sexes. Stricter observance of monogamy is one way of depriving man of his one-sided privilege. On the other hand, as restrictions are imposed on men, bringing them to the level of chastity previously demanded from women, so the democratic evolution has led to new freedoms for women. Participating in increasing numbers in industry and commerce and—for the first time in history—serving in the armed forces with equal rank to men, women have taken upon themselves the right to be sexually as free as men. Society is changing its conventions and beginning to accept women in a new role. As a sign of this change, the stigma attached to an unwed mother is fast diminishing, so that a woman who decides to bring up a child who has no legal father no longer loses her self-respect or her social status.

The sexual code for women varies greatly with each community and is influenced by racial and national compositions, economic and educational levels, and prevalent religious orientations. These factors largely determine the rights of women, and wherever woman is accepted as an equal, she acts with greater sexual latitude. This freedom implies not merely greater laxity but also greater aggressiveness. Under patriarchal conditions women were supposed to be passive, to wait, to be chosen, although they learned to direct men's decisions in many subtle but effective ways. Today, however, many men are worried that women may become the dominant sex as they gain independence and privileges. Indeed, women have already become, in many regards, the dominant sex, at least in the family.

The change in the status of women has actually affected their approach to marriage. As long as women could find their place only through marriage, they tried their best to get married. Today, women hesitate before marriage as often as, and as much as, men—and sometimes more.

In the choice of a mate they are more confused than their sisters of yesterday. Then the choice was simple, especially since it often was out of the girl's hands altogether. Her parents acted on her behalf; any male who could support a wife and did not show any glaring faults and defects was considered a good prospect. Today the girl herself chooses; the standards are more complex. Two factors confuse modern girls: one often a conscious consideration—so-called romantic love—the other an inner conflict of which most are not aware—male-female competition.

ROMANTIC LOVE

Confusing and yet characteristic of the growing equality of women is the importance attached to romantic love. Sociologists and psychiatrists have long recognized that love alone is not an adequate basis for the choice of a mate. When there were fewer opportunities for the girl and she had virtually no choice, other qualifications of pairing were considered more important. Falling in love, often merely an expression of physical attraction, was not then —nor is it now—enough to assure fulfillment in marriage. When the first intoxication is over and husband and wife find themselves confronted with each other as persons and not as enthusiastic lovers, they often find that they have little in common. The ensuing disappointment frequently hampers their willingness to adjust to each other. Mutual interests, common backgrounds, corresponding personality traits, on the other hand, may eventually evoke a deep and lasting love, based on a strong feeling of belonging and of wanting each other. Ironically, when women marry only the men with whom they have "fallen in love," they imitate the masculine manner of choosing a partner: in a patriarchal setting physical attractiveness is the main asset of a woman. Under such conditions no man has to worry about his bride's personality traits; he has every reason to expect her to do as he wants anyhow. And since the bride is supposed to be innocent and inexperienced, it is up to him to shape her personality to his own liking.

The search for romantic love expresses modern woman's quest for sexual and sensuous gratification. We have evidence that frigidity is relatively common when sex gratification is considered a "natural" prerogative of men, and women merely a means to provide it. To a degree in various cultures it was considered improper for women to become sexually aroused—even by their husbands. "Good wives" were without any sexual desires or demands, and the sex hunger of modern women, freeing themselves of the traditional shackles of past centuries, presents our generation with new problems, both before marriage and after. And while oversexed men could always find willing submissive subjects, the demands of women on masculine performance may create more serious problems.

COMPETITION BETWEEN THE SEXES

The second factor affecting and confusing the minds of many modern girls when they think of marriage is even more destructive. To make it worse, they often are not even aware of the problem and are therefore perplexed by their subsequent marital tribulations.

Modern woman faces a peculiar predicament. On one hand, she is the product of thousands of years of feminine submission. Consequently, she still looks for the superior man on whom she can lean, who is strong, reliable, and capable of protecting her. In her growing years she may have experienced such a man in the person of her father, the last remnant of masculine superiority. And she may seek such a superior male as a mate. But he is hard to find. It is difficult for any man to be superior to a girl who has had the same education, worldly experience, and training as he, and who, in many instances, may have been more successful than her male peers. On the other hand, modern woman is also the product of the twentieth century, a human being who does not want to be inferior and submissive to anyone.

The consequences of the predicament often are disastrous. She may avoid any strong male who threatens to dominate her and marry someone who succumbs to her superiority, then com-

plain bitterly that her husband is not a "real" man whom she can respect. Or she may yield to one who seems to be strong and superior, then endeavor in her marriage to prove to herself and to him that his "superiority" is a sham. In the ensuing disillusionment he appears to be a weakling, or, if he successfully resists her efforts to "cut him down to size," a bully. In any case, the struggle for superiority and domination replaces cooperation and mutual respect, often with fatal consequences for the marriage.

Whether or not both partners appreciate the extent of their mutual efforts to gain superiority, marriage today is often the battleground on which husband and wife, each dubious about his own place, fight for dominance. All predicaments and hardships serve as tests. Yet, financial difficulties, in-laws, sexual problems, infidelity, incompatibility—whatever may be considered as the cause for marital trouble—is not in fact the *cause* of trouble but the *occasion* at which each feels defeated. As long as the relationship between husband and wife is friendly, as long as they are not in competition and do not resent each other, difficulties and predicaments bring them closer together and stimulate their common effort to deal with the dilemma. But in an atmosphere of rivalry and competition, each blames the other for their common plight; each feels neglected, humiliated, or abused, and consequently each makes the partner feel unfairly criticized and rejected.

In the past it was the men who frequently sought separation and divorce; in recent years it is more often the women. This fact, of course, reflects woman's greater independence, her realization that even without a man she can now maintain her place in society, but there is a more serious implication. The increase in the divorce rate attributable to women's dissatisfaction is evidence of the fact that men often fail to come up to the standards women are now setting. There was a time when women wanted to be as good as any man; today they want to be better. Women are becoming so "good" that their husbands and children have great difficulty in amounting to something, at least within the family.

MAN'S RESPONSE

It is difficult for a man to extricate himself from the traditional assumption that he is superior to woman *by nature.* Is he not taller, physically stronger, endowed with a deeper voice and a larger brain? Although women's athletic records may soar above those previously established by men, the top achievement in sports in most fields is still held by men. Therefore, are not men entitled to a superior social role and to a "natural" position of dominance in the relationship between the sexes?

The assumption of a "natural" masculine superiority has always been a threat to women *and* to men. Adler coined the term "masculine protest" to indicate how women rebel against an assumed masculine superiority, and men feel frustrated by their assumed superiority, uncertain of their own masculine prowess and unable really to feel like the strong men they were supposed to be. Actually, man's superior physical strength and height may be merely the result of traditional patterns of mating. It may well be that women felt embarrassed at being coupled with shorter men and that men chose smaller spouses. In the process of "natural selection" tall women had difficulty in finding mates. Whatever the reason, since the trend toward equality permits women to marry shorter men, and men have begun to choose older and even bigger partners, the sex determination of height and strength may well slowly disappear.

The change in masculine and feminine patterns causes considerable confusion, both to boys and to girls. A new concept of feminine superiority, based on intellectual and moral qualities, is emerging, and it leads to a new "feminine protest." Concurrently, however, women increasingly feel that they cannot live up to *the* feminine ideal, often presented to them by their mothers, and men resent the newly emerging superiority of women.

Actually, by renouncing the obligation to play a superior role, men free themselves from an almost intolerable burden, if only they knew it. As long as man clings to the myth of masculine superiority, he can never live in peace with women who constantly, and with increasing success, challenge every vestige of that "superiority."

MUTUAL SUSPICION

In the circumstances, it is difficult for the sexes to recognize their essential equality. Men often cannot believe that they themselves are esteemed and appreciated; women are prone to assume that they themselves are dominated and subdued. Every disagreement in the social and sexual function, every argument, from highly intellectual contentions to trivial daily occurrences, offers ample opportunity to inject the question of who is the boss. As long as a man or a woman is not sure of his own value and equal status, each assumes defeat by a partner who feels equally defeated. It is hard for each to believe that the other shares the same sense of failure. Each is afraid of the other and cannot see why the other should have any reason to be afraid of him. And the eternal struggle between the sexes is injected into every predicament, controversy, and difference of opinion; it not only precludes the possibility of a solution but engenders hostility and distrust between two groups that cannot live without each other and have not learned to live peacefully with each other.

An incident may demonstrate this intrinsic tendency to inject the "battle between the sexes" into every form of interaction. Many years ago in Vienna I had lectured to a women's group about equality and the rights of women. The chairman of the meeting expressed her delight in having found a man who did not assume masculine superiority. According to her, very few men respected women. I disputed this claim and assured her that I knew many men who shared my opinion. Maybe it was she who looked for humiliation—and perhaps provoked it—I suggested.

There was no opportunity at the time to pursue this discussion. But she was an educator, and we were both interested in the same problems, so she invited me to tea to exchange our experiences. As we discussed various aspects of child guidance and personality development, it became obvious that we operated on different and contradictory scientific premises. She was a Freudian; I an Adlerian. The discussion became hotter. Each defended his own position and challenged that of the other. Suddenly, my hostess interrupted the discussion to voice her disappointment in me. She had thought that I—in contrast to other men—had respect for a woman and her opinion, but now she could see that I, like the rest, was only interested in establishing my own masculine superiority over her.

Yet all we had done was to discuss conflicting psychological theories in the same way that two men would have done.

INCOMPATIBILITY

Whether incompatibility in interests or incompatibility in sex is blamed for marital failure, the frequency of such complaints clearly demonstrates the effects of equality in modern family life.

Differences of interests do not necessarily disturb a relationship. A young girl in love is more than willing to follow her young man's interests, even if they are foreign to her. She accompanies hm to ball games without any previous knowledge of the sport, and before long she may enjoy it as much as he. Her ability to participate in his interests depends on their relationship. Indeed, both partners in a marriage can stimulate new interests in each other. But once they reach a stage in which both feel neglected, their different inclinations and tastes are used by one to feel rejected and by the other to feel imposed upon.

Thus the frequent discrepancy in interests between men and women is often the result of their competition. Men still attempt to reserve certain activities, such as politics, business, and sports, to themselves. For here they feel safe in a "man's world." Likewise, women, more than men, are interested in fine arts, theater, literature, psychology, and education. Such interests are possibly the result of women having a greater amount of leisure time than men, but, in any case, the interests do provide women with a sense of superiority.

Differences of interests *can* enrich a marriage, when the vision of each partner broadens the vision of the other, but a division of interests that serves as a competitive weapon is highly destructive. The wife may "try" to induce her husband to participate in intellectual, cultural, and social activities but may unwittingly use her background and training as a subtle assertion of her superiority. Instead of encouraging her husband, she may make it almost impossible for him to follow her lead. Impressed with his inability to keep up with her and concerned with the preservation of his masculine superiority, he may avoid situations where he can only play second fiddle. Thus many successful businessmen and executives shy away from social activities because they can function only when they are on "top," and they have not developed the skill to shine at parties or social gatherings.

Literature and art offer many opportunities for mutual enjoyment. But the wife's perfectionism, her impatient and eager criticism, may prevent her husband's enjoying them. Similarly, many men deplore their wives' lack of business sense, yet become resentful when their wives have and use it. In a competitive relationship each partner finds it difficult to acknowledge the other's ability.

SEXUAL DISSATISFACTION

It seems that full sexual gratification is found less frequently in than outside marriage. But here again, dissatisfaction is less the cause of marital discord than the result of it. It does not necessarily reflect a clash of personalities, temperaments, and inclinations; for the same two people can have highly satisfying sexual experiences at the beginning of their marriage and later become unable to satisfy each other—all without any real change in their personalities.

The term "incompatibility" assumes that there are basic discrepancies, but such discrepancies often do not exist at all. Naturally, sexual temperament and training vary in any two adults. Two people who meet in marriage cannot possibly have the same past experiences and attitudes. But these differences can be utilized to the advantage of both, each supplementing and enriching the other. As long as both partners want to please each other, each can adjust to the other's desires, training, and needs. In this mutual adaptation both partners change and find a common ground for enjoyment. Consequently, it is no accident that many sexual difficulties arise later in marriage, when antagonisms and frictions have piled up; for then the most intimate union that requires full cooperation has ceased.

The newly acquired equality of women also is a disquieting factor. In the past, sexual frustrations were probably less frequent. Men had no difficulties in finding gratification, and they cared little for what women desired. Sex was their right by social consent, and women were merely useful. Women recognized and accepted their obligation to serve men as sexual objects. It was their "duty" to submit, regardless of how they felt. Today, having gained the status of full-fledged members of society, women demand the same right of gratification.

It is impossible for two people to always want the same thing at the same time and to the same extent. As long as the relationship is good and harmonious, differing demands pose no problem. But in the strife for mutual equality differences are the occasion for contest. Marriage is considered a "50-50" proposition, and this assumption is at the root of most marital problems. Each partner is constantly watching to ensure that he gets his 50 percent and is afraid of getting only 49—or less. Yet a harmonious marriage is possible only if each mate is willing to give 100 percent—all he has. Only then is he able to look at any contingency as a challenge he can meet.

The limited commitment to marriage has a direct bearing on the sexual function. As soon as one partner wants more than the other, both feel abused. One feels rejected and the other imposed upon, and once this stage is reached, a vicious circle starts. To prove his rights and point to the other's lack of cooperation, one partner increases his demands, and the other, in resentment, becomes more reluctant to give in.

Concern with "success" and "failure" disturbs the sexual function even further. It is impossible to function fully in a sexual relationship if one partner is preoccupied with extraneous problems, and concern with one's "adequacy" necessarily inhibits one's sexual performance. Thus the fact that in times of increased women's equality men become impotent or seek escape into homosexuality is not mere coincidence. Homosexuality is a cultural phenomenon, as was the case in classical Greece when the democratic process affected woman's status.

Obviously concern over success leads to the desire for perfection. Whatever we do has to be "just right"; otherwise, we are failures. This attitude, too, injects a disturbing note into marital sex activities. Each act should be "perfect." Deviation from that standard becomes distressing, particularly to women. Even if they do something wrong, it has to be done "in the right way." In this area of intimate interaction, all the flaws in interpersonal relations become accentuated. At work and in social contacts it is possible to get by with limited cooperation; there is no need to *give* oneself. Marriage does not permit such distance; it requires that we give ourselves completely, an impossibility if we are tense, fearful, and apprehensive. Sex fulfillment presupposes the ability to relax and to enjoy.

INFIDELITY

The disturbed sexual relationship in marriage and the desire for escapades and sexual "victories" make infidelity more common. In modern marriage, as contrasted with those in the past, infidelity poses an increasingly serious problem. In the past, masculine promiscuity received tacit social sanction. Today, women are no longer willing to accept "infidelity" as a man's privilege. They feel personally humiliated and either retaliate or consider an act of unfaithfulness as tantamount to putting an end to a marriage that otherwise may be healthy.

The terms "infidelity" and "cheating" need

to be reevaluated in our present democratic setting. The philandering husband of yore did not consider himself to be "unfaithful" to his wife. He treated her respectfully, as the mistress of his household, as the mother of his children, as a social companion. His sexual escapades were considered to be a necessary outlet for his masculine needs. Women were supposed to have different needs; therefore, their sexual transgressions were not justifiable. Women, as the mothers, had to be chaste—so the dominant male society decreed. Women had to remain "faithful" and "clean"—otherwise, they had no right to any consideration and respect.

It is obvious that the requirement of faithfulness among women reflected male possessiveness. The husband "possessed" his wife, as one can own property and jewelry. But only as part of possessiveness has the term "infidelity" or "unfaithfulness" any significance. The wife of the past never "possessed" a husband. He owned her; therefore, his extramarital relations constituted neither unfaithfulness nor infidelity. Yet what constituted transgression or infidelity on her part depended on the state of subjugation in which she was held. Muslim women were unfaithful if they showed their faces to another man. In other countries, women were not permitted to go out in the street without a companion; a married woman was unfaithful if she as much as looked at a stranger. With the increase in their independence and freedom, women increasingly ventured out into the world by themselves as free agents. But still, the question remained unanswered as to what extent a married woman could go without becoming unfaithful.

Is it an act of unfaithfulness and infidelity if we go with a person of the opposite sex to lunch or dinner or to a movie? Or does it depend entirely on our feelings about that person? Then, is it no infidelity if we think romantically or sexually of another person or dream of him or are aroused by him? Is it infidelity to give a kiss or to hug, or is this state of unfaithfulness limited to physical contact beginning with holding hands? Is such contact only permissible at parties and not in private? Or does infidelity only

involve sexual intercourse? To be sure, almost everybody has a definite idea about these questions, but his ideas may differ greatly with those of his neighbor.

A NEW SEXUAL CODE

It is obvious that our sexual code is no longer what it was, and many complain about immorality simply because few adhere to the code of the past.

The newly established equality between men and women confronts us with the task of determining a new sexual code, since the old pattern of double standards is no longer acceptable.

With the disintegration of traditional moral concepts, confusion sets in. Since the rigid sexual code of the past is rejected by many, and a new one not yet firmly established, everyone is not only free but also almost obliged to reach his own conclusions, to develop his own attitudes toward sex and about proper sexual conduct. Group identifications play an important part, but by no means diminish the confusion, since various cultural, racial, national, religious, and economic groups establish different patterns for themselves.

At any time we can distinguish three levels of sexual norms. There is first the *openly declared code*. Usually, this code conforms more or less to accepted religious and secular prescriptions. Monogamy is accepted, as a rule, and women are still considered in the same way as they have been throughout the ages; they are still expected to be chaste and faithful, and, for some people, virginity is still sacred. Even men who have doubts about these rigid demands usually do not fail to impose them on their own women: wives and daughters. A son is usually "excused" for what a daughter would never be permitted to do.

However, what people say about sex and propriety is not necessarily what they really consider to be right and wrong. The *private code* in which each one really believes is on the second level. And there is still a third level sexual code, namely, *actual practice*. Many do what they themselves consider to be wrong. Their actions are not in line with their value systems.

Kinsey did a disservice to the contemporary concept of sex. He mainly recorded what people actually did, giving the impression that, by their actions, they expressed their value systems. This is not correct. For instance, a girl may believe in "free love" but not practice it. Conversely, a boy who masturbates may not consider masturbation a "proper" thing to do. In other words, it is the *belief* that expresses moral codes, not the actions. Belief and conviction alone can form the basis of value judgment. Unfortunately, few realize what their own moral beliefs are and know even less about that of others. It is almost impossible at the present time to recognize any definite code of sexual behavior that would be acceptable to most people and represent contemporary conventions.

The absence of a well-defined set of sexual mores is particularly felt by the younger generation; few young people still accept unequivocably adult standards, particularly since they are fully cognizant of the many contradictions and uncertainties in the attitudes of adults toward sex. Young people want answers, but who is to give them answers?

One cannot predict the sexual code that eventually will emerge and be generally accepted. However, it is certain that women and children will play an important role in determining new sexual standards.

THE FUTURE OF MARRIAGE

Many people have questioned whether marriage as an institution will survive. Certainly marriage today no longer fulfills the three functions that it fulfilled throughout the ages. First, marriage was the basis for economic survival. Without a provider, the family could not exist. Today, many women are quite able to support a family without a husband. Second, only in marriage was sexual gratification permitted, at least for women, and a certain moral code did not permit extramarital relationships for men, either, unless they were "discreet." Today, sex-

ual activity outside marriage is common. As far as the third marital function, that of raising children, is concerned, we find not only that many parents are presently ill-equipped to raise their children properly, but that many women raise their children without fathers.

A distressing fact that may contribute greatly to the growing doubt of the need for marriage is the increased availability of sexual gratification outside marriage. Many reasons are given for this development, the chief of which probably is that extramarital relationships allow unattended "time outs" away from the other partner and cut down on the pressures a couple face. But there are also the lure of the forbidden and the constant search for the new conquests.

Despite such developments, there can be little doubt that a marital union to which both partners give themselves totally, spiritually as well as physically, is still one of man's highest aspirations. Unfortunately, our inability to function as equals in close relationships impairs such a union. This is why sex continues to be a disturbing factor in marriage. However, we may assume that man, once he has learned to live as an equal among equals, will find monogamy the ideal institution because it will not be imposed upon him by pressure of society and maintained by law. Monogamy will be chosen because it satisfies deeper needs. It means partnership and sharing what may come for better or worse. Only then will sex lose its faculty of arousing anxiety, fear, and guilt feelings.

If fears—of failure, humiliation, censure, economic hardship, detrimental impact on the children—are absent, the sexual function will appear altogether in a different light. Impotence, frigidity, and homosexuality are consequences of such fears, materialized by anticipation. Possessiveness and jealousy, with their inevitable consequences—resentment and retribution—may become obsolete. Each one will be free to do what he decides since he respects the same rights of his spouse. The attraction that a spouse may feel for another person may be tolerated without resentment and fear. Sex will stop being sin, and the desire of the partners to belong to each other will preclude restrictions to each one's full freedom of movement. The real uniting force will be the decision to be and live with each other, regarding the other as part of one's life, independent of unavoidable emotional fluctuations. Marital partners do not have to regard each other as threats; both can contribute to the richness of their union.

THE ROLE OF THE PARENT

How does equality affect the father's function within the family? Obviously the effect is great because the strong father figure is mostly gone for good—and where it still exists, it exerts a dubious influence. The most capable and virile men often affect their children quite adversely. Their sons despair of their ability ever to be as strong and capable as their fathers; therefore they doubt their ability to be "real men." Daughters of strong men receive the picture of a superior man that few contemporary males can ever match. Neither realizes that the father is the last remnant of a vanishing masculine superior power.

Any assumption that a certain type of mother or father is necessary for the proper upbringing of children is fallacious. A parent who knows what to do with his children and how to influence them can be highly successful, regardless of his personality. A father who is interested in influencing his children can learn how to do that as well as can their mother. But one thing can never be done in a democracy: the father cannot tell the mother what to do, nor can she tell him. Neither has the power or authority to tell others what to do, but each has a full opportunity to exert his or her own beneficial influence.

The changing status of woman also involves a change in her role and function as a mother. The father, no longer universally recognized as the head of the family, is often replaced as such by the mother. As a consequence, he either withdraws from the task of raising children or opposes his wife in her methods. In any case, we can no longer say, "Father knows best,"—in most cases, Mother does!

The competitive atmosphere in the family affects the relationship between parents and children and between the children themselves. In a feudal family the firstborn son was supreme; no other child could challenge his superior status. Today each child fights for his own position against the rest, often siding with one parent against the other. We no longer find definite masculine and feminine patterns in the family. No longer is the masculine pattern of a family followed exclusively by boys. Girls may follow the traits of the father and boys those of the mother, resulting in mixtures and confusing patterns seldom found in a static social order where masculine superiority is well defined.

Mothers pay a high price for the position they have obtained within the family. Their prestige becomes gravely involved when the children do not accept their authority and the rules they establish. Consequently, there is a growing sense of inadequacy among mothers. They take every act of misbehavior and every misdemeanor of their children as a sign of personal failure. The high moral and intellectual standards that many women have chosen as part of their striving for equality do not necessarily stimulate the children to emulation; rather, they inhibit them. Many ambitious and perfectionistic mothers discourage their husbands and children, who simply cannot live up to the expectations of their wives or mothers. Then the women are surprised and shocked by inadequacies and failures, which they themselves have induced. An "efficient" mother is often the greatest obstacle to a child's development.

The greatest price is paid by such mothers when the children grow up. Then they lose their queenly status. When the children grow up, get married, and settle down, there is nothing left for the mother to do. The children remove themselves from her supervision and leave an emptiness in her life. The husband is often little involved with the children and when they leave, the mother no longer has any function in the family.

Herein lies the reason for many of the nervous breakdowns experienced by efficient mothers around the period of their climacterics. The "change of life" is less a change within the glandular system than a change in the social function of a woman. Any modern woman who devotes herself entirely to her family and to rearing children exposes herself to such a crisis.

Thus as women gain equality, they can no longer confine their functions to the family circle. Indeed, women who had been accustomed to studying and holding a job and who are suddenly thrust by marriage into the traditional roles of housewives find themselves at a loss when their function as mother has ended. They have either lost their occupational skills or failed to develop them sufficiently; therefore, they cannot find jobs that will give them status and responsibility equal to what they had enjoyed within their families. They have become mature and efficient, and they cannot start from scratch vocationally without losing prestige and significance.

MOTHERHOOD OR CAREER?

An important challenge for a modern woman, therefore, is to find a new equilibrium for herself between a career and motherhood. It is no longer possible to choose one course at the expense of the other. Many who have realized the full impact of our cultural development believe that a woman can—and even must—choose between career and family. But consider how silly it would be to tell a man that he would have to choose between a job and having a family.

Naturally, the responsibilities of a woman as a mother entail greater obligations in time and effort than are required from a father. But the discharge of her obligation as wife and mother does not require as much time as many women —or men—are inclined to believe.

Technical progress has made housekeeping less time-consuming than ever before, and a woman's domestic work load will decrease even further as housework is recognized by husband and wife to be a common task—an inevitable result of progressive equality between the sexes. And as housework ceases to be an inferior task assigned to the "inferior" sex, domestic help may once again be available in the form of professional workers instead of the servants traditionally held in low esteem.

In any case, the *length* of time a mother spends with her children is not important. What is important is *how* she spends it. It has been declared that the child needs the physical proximity of the mother to develop emotionally and socially. If great emphasis is placed on feeding, weaning, toilet training, and the gratification of instinctual needs, the time the mother spends with the baby naturally becomes all-important. But if, on the other hand, the importance of social relationships is recognized, a different picture evolves. Then it is no longer the *time* that counts in the relationship between mother and child but the *kind of relationship* she establishes. Moreover there is some evidence that women are better mothers if they also have outside activities and interests. When they devote all their time and energies to the child, they run the danger of being wholly dependent on the child for their value and significance, thus smothering the child with their expectations.

Dealing with the Aged: A New Style of Aging

Margaret Mead

Reprinted from the November 15, 1971 issue of *Christianity and Crisis*, copyright © 1971 by Christianity and Crisis, Inc.

One of the world's distinguished anthropologists, Dr. Mead has contributed hundreds of articles and books since her Coming of Age in Samoa *(1928). When not on expedition to New Guinea or Bali, she has taught at the University of Cincinnatti and Columbia University. She is emeritus curator of the American Museum of Natural History. One of her many honors was President of the American Anthropological Association.*

A NEW STYLE OF AGING

It is useful in discussing aging to talk about different cultural styles, to look at what is happening in other societies, in older societies. I would like particularly to talk about the need to develop a new style of aging in our own society, and to suggest that we could do more for the older American than we are doing at present. Everyone who is aging has a chance to develop this new style. Everyone who is working with old people can contribute to this new style.

Young people in this country have been accused of not caring for their parents the way they would have in the old country, in Puerto Rico, in the Old South or in Italy. This is true, but it is also true that old people in this country have been influenced by an American ideal of independence and autonomy. The most important thing in the world is to be independent. So old people live alone, perhaps on the verge of starvation, in time without friends—but we are independent. This standard American style has been forced on every ethnic group in the country, although there are many groups for whom the ideal is not practical. It is a poor ideal and pursuing it does a great deal of harm.

This ideal of independence also contains a tremendous amount of unselfishness. In talking to today's young mothers, I have asked them what kind of grandmothers they are going to be. I have heard devoted, loving mothers say that when they are through raising their children, they have no intention of becoming grandmothers. They are astonished to hear that in most of the world, throughout most of its history, families have three- or four-generation families, living under the same roof. We have overemphasized the small family unit—father, mother, small children. We think it is wonderful if Grandma and Grandpa, if he's still alive, can live alone.

We have reached the point where we think the only thing we can do for our children is to stay out of their hair, and the only thing we can do for our daughters-in-law is to see as little of them as possible. Old people's homes, even the best, are filled with older people who believe the only thing they can do for their children is to look cheerful when they come to visit. So in the end older people have to devote their energies to "not being a burden."

We are beginning to see what a tremendous price we've paid for our emphasis on independence and autonomy. We have isolated old people and we've cut off the children and the young people from their grandparents.

One of the reasons we have as bad a generation gap today as we do is because grandparents have copped out. Young people are being deprived of the thing they need most—perspective, to know why their parents behave so peculiarly and why their grandparents say the things they do.

In peasant communities where things didn't

change and where people died in the beds they were born in, grandparents taught the young what the end of life was going to be. So you looked at your mother, if you were a girl, and you learned what it was like to be a bride, a young mother. Then you looked at your grandmother and knew what it was like to be old. Children learned what it was to age and die while they were very small. They were prepared for the end of life at the beginning.

It is interesting to realize that early in human society we developed a method of keeping old women alive. Human beings are the only primates that have a menopause. So women do stop having babies, and if they haven't died by the time they stop, women can become quite strong and can live quite a long time. For countless centuries old women have been around who knew things that no one else knew—that 10, 20, 30 years ago there was a hurricane or a famine and people survived. The old women remembered what people did in the past. Today, however, such memories are no longer useful. We can be dead certain that when our grandchildren reach our age, they will not be living as we live today.

Today grandparents and old people in general have something quite different to contribute. Their generation has seen the most change in the world, and the young today need to learn what this change has been. They need to know about their past before they can understand the present and plot the future.

Young people also need reassurance that change does not mean an end to the world, but merely an end to the world as they first saw it. Older people remember that we have had periods of disorder in this country before. Some of them can remember the Time of Troubles in Ireland. Some of them remember the riots after World War I and those during World War II, and they remember that we lived through them. Because the ties between generations have been broken, young people have lost their perspective.

Normally we talk about the heartless young people who don't have room for their parents in their lives, much less in their apartments. But old people today have tremendous advantages, and these advantages make them much less dependent.

We all look so young to each other. Sometimes we kid ourselves that we look young to the young, which is nonsense. But we have our hair cut and styled in the most modern fashion, dye it in the most modern colors. It is wonderful how young your old friends look. Old people have never been cheered up in this way before.

My grandmother may have been treated with a certain respect, but she was formally dressed in a way that her grandmother had been, in a way that made her feel old. Today we dress old people in a way that makes them feel young.

On the subways I've been riding for fifty years, two things have happened: people have stopped giving up their seats to the old, and old people have stopped accepting seats when they are offered. "I'll stand, thank you."

WHAT OLDSTERS CAN DO

What we need to do is to find a style of aging that will keep and foster this independence, but will encourage old people to think in terms of what they can do for someone else. If we are going to change the style, the relationship between young and old, older people will have to take the lead by finding ways to relate either to their own grandchildren or to someone else's.

As long as we say that youth has no need for age, that young people in this country aren't interested in old people, in seeing them or listening to them, there will be an enormous number of things in our society that are not being done, but which could be done, by old people. It is true that it is very hard to get employment if you look the least bit old. But there are many things to be done in society that don't have to be done under the auspices of employment agencies.

What we need in this society more than anything else is warm bodies who can sit by a door, answer a telephone, stay around until the plumber comes. There are masses of people sitting around being independent and keeping healthy who could be sitting in somebody's house freeing that person to get out and go to work.

We are beginning to think about day care centers and we ought to bring older people in. PTA's should encourage older people to participate, not throw out the mothers the minute their children leave the school.

The Soviet Union now has "block grandmothers." People who have been social workers or teachers and have had experience caring for people are paid a regular salary in a housing project to be a "grandmother." When there's an accident in the playground, the mother can hand her the baby. When a mother doesn't know what to do, she can ask the advice of the "grandmother." The grandmother function has been institutionalized.

The country is filled with widows who sit around in eight-room houses polishing furniture instead of being of any use to the world. They'll tell you that nobody wants them, that nobody listens to old people anymore, but it isn't true. Or it's only as true as they make it true.

There isn't any reason society shouldn't be reorganized along new lines by finding places where old people are really useful. Old people themselves have to begin asking the question, "Where and how can I continue to make a contribution?"

What we want is for people when they are about 50—when they begin to think about aging —to consider also the end of their lives. People need to know that you can make living wills. You can decide to let your eyes be used by somebody else or your heart or your kidneys. If you start very early thinking that you can make a contribution when you die, you will develop a different attitude toward death.

You can also stipulate that you do not want to be kept artificially alive, by blood transfusions or in other ways. You can feel that you have some control over the end of your life, making sure that your relatives don't beggar themselves for the funeral or exhaust the family's financial resources prolonging life in a hopeless illness.

There are a thousand ways old people can contribute if we only set up the housing, the neighborhoods, the living arrangements that make it feasible for them to do so.

18 AUTOMATION— LABOR'S LOVE LOST?

The Job Blahs: Who Wants to Work?

Newsweek Magazine

From *Newsweek* (March 26, 1973), 79—82, 84, 89. Copyright Newsweek, Inc. 1973, reprinted by permission.

The sullen refrain, it sometimes seems nowadays, is heard everywhere—at a Kaiser Steel Corp. plant in Fontana, Calif., at a blue-collar saloon in Houston, Texas, at a production workers' conference called in Atlanta by the United Auto Workers union. "The one thing I have is security," says Fidencio C. Moreno, a $5.60-an-hour Kaiser steelworker. "But it's a boring, repetitious job—nasty, hot and dirty work. I go there 'cause I have to." "It's getting to be a bore to me," grumbles J. E. (Andy) Anderson, a $15,000-a-year machine-shop manager in Houston, who seeks companionship over a couple of lunch-hour beers in Jimmie's Bar. "Every day, for eight hours, we fight that black devil-chain [the assembly line]," said R.J. Soptic, a Kansas City, Mo., autoworker at the recent UAW conference in Atlanta. And even James M. Roche, the retired $790,000-a-year board chairman of General Motors, wisecracked recently: "What is more boring than lugging home a big briefcase of papers to be read before going to bed every night?"

Roche, presumably, was just being sardonic. But the other complaints reflect the discontent of an angry new breed that some say is growing faster than the labor force itself. These men and women are the new problem children of the American economy: the "alienated" workers, afflicted with the blue-collar blues, the white-collar woes and the just plain on-the-job blahs. They are bored, rebellious, frustrated; sometimes they're drunk on the job or spaced out on drugs. And though they are the newest darlings of the sociologists and industrial psychologists, they're still largely a mystery to many of the people who should understand them best: their bosses and their union leaders.

Today some 83 million Americans are holding full-time or part-time jobs. Of the total—62 percent of them men—about 19 million are engaged in manufacturing and 1 million of these are tied to the dull, routine tedium of an assembly line like that satirized four decades ago by Charlie Chaplin in "Modern Times." But there are actually more white-collar workers (49 percent of the total) than blue (35 percent)—the rest are service workers and farm workers. There are more women at work in the nation today than ever before, and more young people.

The mood of this vast work force is obviously of tremendous importance to the country as a whole as well as to the individuals themselves. Worker attitudes affect productivity—how competitive the nation is versus nations such as Japan (box, page 248) and how high America's

240

standard of living can go. On a more philosophic but no less significant level, a nation's attitude toward work is a reflection of its sense of itself. The work ethic President Nixon is so fond of celebrating involves not only a job but a way of life.

THE 'ENRICHMENT' BOOM

While people have been complaining about work since it was invented, there is a widespread feeling that there is something different about today's discontent. As a result, the managers of American business and industry are now coming up with plan after plan—some pure public relations, some quite innovative, but all designed to pacify unhappy workers. From giant General Motors Corp. to a tiny, 50-worker unit of Monsanto Chemical's textile division in Pensacola, Fla., literally hundreds of companies have instituted "enrichment" programs to give workers a sense of satisfaction on the job and send them home with a feeling of accomplishment.

And the movement is growing rapidly. Lyman Ketchum, a manager of organizational development for General Foods and the father of a pioneer enrichment program at GF's Topeka, Kans., Gaines Pet Food plant, has been practically forced to get an unlisted telephone number. "I was getting ten to twelve calls a week from corporation executives who wanted to talk to me about it," Ketchum reports. "I have just had to say no. I have too much of my own work to do."

In the automobile industry, where about 25 percent of the work force assembles cars with robot-like monotony, General Motors is experimenting with a "team" approach to the assembly of its new $13,000 motor home. Rather than having the chassis roll down an assembly line, with each worker performing only one or two functions, teams ranging in size from three to six workers are now building selected coaches from hubcap to horn. Ford is trying a team assembly program at its Saline, Mich., parts plant while Chrysler has given some Detroit-area plants virtual carte blanche to try any experiment they choose. So far, these have ranged

from employees operating without a foreman to assigning assembly-line workers the relatively pleasant chore of test-driving the new cars they have just built.

While experiments by the auto industry's Big Three are still inconclusive, others are not. Indiana Bell Telephone, for example, used to assemble its telephone books in 21 steps, each performed by a different clerk. It now gives each clerk individual responsibility for assembling an entire book. One result: employee turnover in recent years has been cut by as much as 50 percent.

At Kaiser Steel in Fontana, Calif., a group of 150 workers literally kept the continuous-weld pipe mill from closing—at least temporarily—when they were given full responsibility for making it competitive with Japanese pipe producers. Recalls Timon Covert, a grievance committeeman for the United Steelworkers union and a leader of the worker group: "I told management, 'Look, we don't believe anybody in the damned world can outproduce us.' I hear all this bunk about how good they do it in Japan and Germany and we told management to let us try some things." The workers overhauled some tools, rearranged the production flow to make it more efficient and worked out changes in the production schedule. The result: production jumped 32.1 percent during the final three months of 1972, while the spoilage rate dropped from 29 percent to 9.

THE SEARCH FOR SOLUTIONS

As another example, the 50 workers at the Monsanto plant in Pensacola set up task forces to restructure certain jobs through automation, and managed to eliminate certain "dirty" chores that nobody wanted or did well. The workers also became their own managers. In the first year of the new deal, waste loss dropped to zero and productivity improved by 50 percent.

With such programs proliferating, the search for the roots of the problem and for possible solutions goes on apace. In New York next week, a group of major firms and labor unions will gather to discuss "The Changing Work Ethic." In Washington, the Nixon Administration, for all its reluctance to accept job dissatisfaction as a matter of serious concern, is at least reported willing to spend $2 million this year to study it. In the Senate, Sen. Edward Kennedy has introduced a bill calling for a $20 million investigation to determine just how serious the problem is and what efforts might be taken by the U.S. to solve it.

But even as businessmen and government officials search for new solutions to worker alienation, a lively debate goes on in business, labor and academic circles over the basic question of whether the whole thing hasn't been blown out of all proportion to begin with.

On one side are such social scientists as Harold L. Sheppard and Neil Q. Herrick, whose book *Where Have All the Robots Gone* is considered by some to be a definitive work on the subject. After an in-depth study of 400 male union workers, Sheppard and Herrick concluded that one-third of them—particularly the young ones—were alienated from their jobs and could not be assuaged with the typical rewards of more money, shorter hours or longer vacations. Sheppard and Herrick went on to assert: "Worker dissatisfaction metamorphosed from a hobby horse of the 'tender minded' to a fire-breathing dragon because workers began to translate their feelings of dissatisfaction into alienated behavior. Turnover rates are climbing. Absenteeism has increased as much as 100 percent in the past ten years in the automobile industry. Workers talk back to their bosses. They no longer accept the authoritarian way of doing things."

'DULL, REPETITIVE, MEANINGLESS'

In large measure, Sheppard and Herrick are supported by a controversial Health, Education and Welfare Department report issued last December. While short on specific evidence, the HEW report indicated that nearly half of American workers are dissatisfied with their jobs and suggested that something had better be done to make work more attractive, interesting and meaningful. According to the 200-page HEW study, the work force in America is changing and more and more workers are growing restless because of "dull, repetitive, seemingly meaningless tasks, offering little challenge or autonomy."

These are foreboding words indeed, but they don't pass unchallenged—and the challenge often comes from the very workers who are supposed to be unhappy. "I like it all right," says 30-year-old Rico Veneas of his job as a paint sprayer for a lighting-fixture firm in Inglewood, Calif. "I mean, I know how to do it so it doesn't tire me out." This may seem like an unscientific sample of one when arrayed against the Sheppard-Herrick and HEW studies. But in actual fact, the thesis that most Americans are indeed contented with their jobs finds powerful support among public-opinion specialists and some thinkers.

For example, a Gallup poll reports that, contrary to what HEW and the others say, eight out of ten Americans are satisfied with the work they do. And the situation is getting better, not worse, says Gallup. Back in 1949, "Three out of ten whites and nearly half the blacks said they were dissatisfied or had qualifications about the work they were doing," vs. the two out of ten for today, according to Gallup.

More than that, the Sheppard-Herrick and HEW studies start out with preconceived notions and then find statistics and other evidence to "prove" their point, charges Irving Kristol, professor of urban values at New York University. George B. Morris Jr., General Motors' vice president in charge of industrial relations, compares the current debate with the furor over automation a decade or so ago. "The academics started talking about it and pretty soon they were quoting each other. They said people were on their way out, which simply wasn't true," he says. "Well, today the same thing is happening; there is a lot of writing being done on this subject of 'alienation' by people who don't know what they are talking about."

For their part, most union leaders seem to be gingerly skirting the subject, waiting for someone to offer some definitive answers. UAW president Leonard Woodcock concluded a meeting of his union's production workers not too long ago with a blast at "academics" whom he accused of writing "elitist nonsense" that degraded factory workers. "Sure," Woodcock said, "work is dull and monotonous. But if it's useful, the people who do it are entitled to be honored and not degraded, which is what's going on in this day and time." But a few weeks later, UAW vice president Irving Bluestone said that the blue-collar blues were indeed a problem and called for an intensive search for answers. As one UAW source summed up: "I guess you could conclude everybody's confused about things."

Indeed, perhaps the best sense on the subject these days is being made by observers far removed from the industrial-relations firing line. One is Fred Foulkes, an assistant professor at the Harvard Graduate School of Business and author of the book *Creating More Meaningful Work*. As Foulkes sees it: "Jobs haven't changed. People's expectations have, and this has been expressed in high absenteeism, low morale, high turnover, etc." Greater educational achievement has helped raise expectations. The average worker in 1940 had an eighth-grade education, he notes, but now about 80 percent of the work force has gone beyond high school. Changing life-styles outside the job affect attitudes at work. Says Foulkes: "[Workers] want some sort of participation. There's more freedom around. So why should employees want regimented, autocratic jobs?"

So far, the White House hasn't taken a public position on the alienated-worker issue. But according to insiders, President Nixon has privately expressed displeasure with the HEW report, claiming that it is the work of soft-headed sociologists who don't know much about work and worker motivation. This may be so. The amount of actual discontent and alienation may be limited in scope. But where it exists, it is important, and increasing numbers of companies are trying to do something about it. Among the best-known and most successful are ongoing programs in Topeka, Hartford, Fort Lauderdale and Medford, Mass.

"I used to work as a construction laborer and every morning I hated to get up," 21-year-old Andy Dodge recalled as he relaxed in the comfortably furnished employee lounge at the Topeka Gaines Pet Food plant. "Now, it's different. I'm still just a laborer, but I have something to say about my job. If I get sore about something, I bring it up at the team meeting in the morning. If I want to go to the bathroom or make a phone call, I do it. I just ask someone else on the team to cover. I really feel more like a human being than a worker. After this, there is no way you could get me to go back to regular employment."

Andy Dodge is one of the lucky 72 production workers at the revolutionary, five-story Gaines plant, a brainchild of General Foods' Lyman Ketchum. Until two years ago, pet-food production was limited to the company's plant in Kankakee, Ill., run along conventional lines and plagued by conventional factory problems: a lackadaisical work force, a 5 percent absentee rate and occasional acts of sabotage. (Someone once dumped a batch of green dye into a hopper and spoiled an entire day's production of dog food.) Thus, when the demand for pet food outstripped Kankakee's capacity, Ketchum persuaded his superiors to try something new: a plant designed around people, not jobs. The result is the Topeka facility.

While it is highly automated, the plant is still burdened with a number of menial jobs with a sizable potential for boredom. So, to insure that both the rewarding and unrewarding jobs are shared equally, Ketchum devised a model workers' democracy. The employees are split into semiautonomous teams, ranging in size from six to seventeen, depending on the operation. Each team selects its own foreman and, at the start of each shift, determines how to meet production quotas, divides up job assignments and airs grievances. Moreover, each worker is trained to do practically any job in the plant, from filling bags on an assembly line to monitoring the complicated controls of machines that cook and mix the pet food.

Even more unusual, the team leaders interview and hire replacements, and the teams discipline malingerers. "If someone is goofing off," says William Haug, 38, "the team members get on him. If this doesn't work, we have a team meeting. If there is a personal or family problem, team members often help. Sometimes it is just a matter of time off to straighten out problems, but we don't have many of them."

To further expand the individual worker's feeling of involvement and responsibility, Ketchum erased most of the lines dividing the white- and blue-collar workers at the Topeka plant. There are no time clocks, no special parking privileges for executives and everybody eats in the same cafeteria. At lunchtime, it is not unusual to see plant manager Ed Dulworth, a 38-year-old graduate of General Motors Technical Institute, playing Ping Pong with a production worker.

Predictably enough, the result is an exceptionally high level of worker contentment. "Everything is left up to the individual to expand himself," sums up 26-year-old Joe Ybarra. "We are responsible for the product we turn out. A guy can come to work here without a feeling that management is on his neck." As one result, the absenteeism rate at Topeka is less than 1 percent, vs. 5 percent at Kankakee.

Even more important to the executives back at General Foods' headquarters in White Plains, N.Y., the Topeka plant is a glowing financial success. "Even after [allowing for the new] technology, we get a productivity rate here that is 20 to 30 percent higher than at Kankakee," says Dulworth. "We need only about two-thirds of the Kankakee work force to get the same production."

Could the Topeka plant work in a larger, more complicated setting? To a degree, says Ed Dulworth. "I think it is transferable in terms of the basics, and the basics are that work can be organized for both business needs and people needs and it pays off both ways," he told *Newsweek*'s Tom Joyce. "The problem with this is that managers are looking for models. They want a package you can put in place and have it pay off. Well, the nature of job design is com-

plex and each program must be developed to fit specific situations."

DIVERSITY BOOSTS MORALE

At the huge, 21,000-employee Travelers Insurance Co. headquarters in Hartford, Conn., the raw material is punch cards rather than dog food, but the problem was the same: high absenteeism and low morale and productivity. So three years ago, Travelers hired Roy W. Walters and Associates, a New Jersey management consultant firm, to undertake a job-enrichment program.

As a pilot project, the Travelers selected a key-punch operation involving 100 operators and ten supervisors. "What we attempted to do here is create a structural change for employees and supervisors which forces a behavior change and eventually an attitude change," said Jewell Westerman, second vice president in charge of management services.

Basically, the project involved transferring some supervisory functions to the operators and broadening their jobs so that instead of dealing day after day with only one phase of an operation they carried it through from start to finish. Ordinarily, a worker would handle receipts or collections or any of the separate punch-card functions. But work was rearranged so that one employee is now responsible for the entire punch-card operation for a particular corporate or individual customer and establishes a firm operator-customer relationship. "Typically, work is assigned on the basis of who has the least to do," explains Norm Edmonds, Travelers' director of management services. "So the operator has no commitment to the job. That's been reversed, and people are aligned with their own group of clients."

The first-year results of the pilot project were dramatic: a 26 percent increase in productivity and a 24 percent decline in absenteeism. The enrichment program has since been expanded to cover some 2,000 employees in four departments at Travelers' headquarters and eight branch offices. As Dale Menard, a 27-year-old supervisor in the premium-collection department, sums up his "new" job: "I'm much more involved in decision-making than my peers at other insurance firms. Before, we went down the syndrome of 'the more you specialize the more efficiency you have.' It got to the point where tasks were divided into smaller and smaller bits and pieces. Now, with combining certain jobs, the problem takes care of itself."

STUDIES IN BOREDOM

At the Corning Glass plant in Medford, Mass., the attitude is so gung-ho that work teams give themselves such nicknames as "The Dirty Half Dozen" and stick around after the 4:30 afternoon whistle to discuss the best way to meet their production schedule. At the Motorola Corp. plant in Fort Lauderdale, Fla., the work teams compete in production races and the winning team is treated to a dinner each month by the company.

The Medford plant turns out such products as hot plates, while the Fort Lauderdale facility produces a pocket-size electronic signaling device called the Pageboy, both of them prime candidates for the impersonal attention of an assembly line. However, in each plant, the hot plates and the Pageboys are assembled in their entirety by a member—usually a woman—of work teams that set their own production goals and, in the case of Corning, even decide when they will take some of their holidays.

The results have been highly encouraging. Last year, the Medford plant increased its hot-plate production by 20 percent and it is expecting an even larger increase this year. And while the plant increased its work force by 50 percent last year, efficiency improved by 100 percent. Even though the pay is relatively low ($2.95 an hour), the plant has many more job applicants that it can satisfy. Margie Bell, a 54-year-old mother of three, sums up: "I love this place. It's not like at Raytheon where I used to work. Here

you start with nothing and you make something yourself."

At Fort Lauderdale, Motorola officials say that productivity is about 5 percent lower than it would be on a normal assembly line, but that the quality is better and the morale of employees vastly improved. "It's technology having advanced to a state that permits this kind of operation," one official notes. "We're now back to something simple enough for one girl to make a total contribution, and that is very significant, I think."

Admittedly, the experiments at Gaines, the Travelers, Corning and Motorola would be impossible to impose on many operations; it would be ridiculous, for example, to split the 30,000 employees of Ford Motor's River Rouge plant into work teams and allow them to decide production schedules and assembly-line speeds. However, there is no question but that job enrichment will continue to grow as a subject for both management soul-searching and collective bargaining between companies and their unions. The Ford Foundation has found the subject worthy of further study and plans to spend nearly $500,000 evaluating experiments industry has undertaken to stimulate worker satisfaction. And the conference on "The Changing Work Ethic" in New York next week will enjoy the full-scale participation of labor for the first time; autoworkers, steelworkers and machinists will all be represented.

But all of the conferences, all of the studies, all of the books may be too late to help some workers, such as steelworker Fidencio Moreno. "I should have quit long ago," he said sadly last week. "Now my dad, he ran a bar. When he'd come home, us kids would run up to him and say, 'How'd it go?' My dad always had pride in his work. He'd talk about all the things the customers would say and do. Me, I go home, they don't understand a damn thing. All I do is dump a little coal into an oven. Why would my wife or my kids be interested in that?"

Modern Times: Workers Speak

Grousing about work is as American as, well, cherry pie. Whatever their complaints, millions of Americans are essentially satisfied with their jobs. Still, the thread of discontent runs deep and eloquent in the work force. A sampling of the gratified and the disenchanted:

* * *

One by one, the cases of swimming pool cleaning acid move relentlessly down the conveyor belt and into the shipping department of the Purex Corp.'s Los Angeles plant. If the machinery is working properly—and it often is not—as many as 800 cases come down each hour. And for the past four of his 26 years, Cal Shaw has been earning his living by pulling the heavy cases off the belt and shoving them toward the loading docks. "You're on a half hour and you're off a half hour," Shaw says. "That's four hours of real physical labor. The other time you're looking for leakers."

Shaw and the other men sometimes get violent headaches from the fumes let off by the chlorine and muriatic acid. But the worst part of the job is its tedium. Echoing many workers, Shaw says: "The job is *very* monotonous." During the summer, production spurts and there is plenty of overtime, but he sometimes refuses it. "The taxes just eat me up," says Shaw, who is married but has no children.

Shaw has the typical small-cog-in-the-wheel feeling. "Being a peon, I don't have any say in the company," he complains. "The waste bothers me, but I'm not in the situation where I can say anything." He doesn't plan to make a career of his job—and like many others, he lives from day to day with only vague goals. "Maybe I'll work here ten years," he says, "but what I want to do is have my own antiques store." Still, he confides: "I don't project years ahead."

* * *

After she graduated from college, Deanne Rogers thought she would join the Peace Corps, study in Europe and return home to an exciting job. Today, at 25, the tall and pretty executive secretary for an Atlanta firm can't figure out just what went wrong. "Where did the get-up-and-go get knocked out?" she wonders. "It seems that after I went to work, nothing I had planned to do became worth the trouble anymore."

Like many other people, Miss Rogers basically likes her job but complains that she has never really been challenged. "After six months, you've got the system down," she says. "You spend the next six months finding upward mobility and the following six months looking for a new job." More responsibility would make her happier—again, a reaction typical of many workers. "Executive secretaries, and especially those that end up making a lot of decisions for the boss without his realizing it, should have the chance to be in on policymaking decisions," she says.

Her job takes so much of her time and energy that, she says, there's nothing left to do after work but go home to her apartment, "wash my hair, watch a little television and fall into bed." The result, predictably enough, is frequent depression. "I actually go on crying jags," she admits. "I begin to analyze my job too much, question whether I'm really making any impact." But her $10,000 annual salary makes it difficult for her to leave. "I can't get another job in what I'm doing because I'm overpriced," she says. "The company makes you put up with all the crap by paying you well."

* * *

George Fradenburg is a lucky man. The Hewlett-Packard factory in Palo Alto, Calif., where he works is clean, pleasant and quiet enough to permit Fradenburg to talk with the other workers. Fradenburg, whose job is to assemble Hewlett-Packard's complicated electrical-signal analyzers, takes a craftsman's pride in his work. "It's a cute little outfit," he says of the device. He has even come up with a couple of tools to make the assembling go faster. "They like you to come up with new ideas," he says of his employer. "When they have this policy, you think more."

Fradenburg is pleased with other Hewlett-Packard personnel policies, such as a profit-sharing plan. The 46-year-old worker, who earns $4.80 an hour, owns 360 shares of the company's stock. "You feel you're more a part of the company," he says. Last month, the factory initiated a flexible schedule that allows Fradenburg to come to work anytime between 6:30 and 8:30 a.m. and leave between 3:15 and 5:15. Fradenburg is usually at his workbench by 6:30. "These hours give you so much freedom in the afternoon," he points out. When he goes home, Fradenburg does chores around the apartment building that his wife manages. "One of the problems today is that people have too much idle time," he says. "I just can't sit around."

* * *

All too often, the career ambitions of a young man or woman are blocked by the reality of the labor market—and economic necessity forces a compromise choice. Sandy Cook is a case in point. Back home in Clinton, Iowa, the pixyish 23-year-old envisioned a career as a glamorous airline stewardess. Dreams of jet travel and "crowds of interesting people" evaporated when her application was rejected. Now, as a secretary to two lawyers in one of Chicago's largest firms, Miss Cook finds that she is "dead tired, exhausted" at day's end, that her monthly salary of $650 is too low and that, some days, she "just feels like a machine."

Some 50 secretaries work on her floor and each morning, Miss Cook says, "we come in like a thundering herd." At work, Miss Cook and the other secretaries are constantly supervised by old "field marshals," who have been with the firm "since Blackstone was written"—and she reacts with the impatience and distaste younger workers often show toward established patterns. As she tells it, the supervisors distribute debits or credits for tardiness or overtime, look over Miss Cook's shoulder as she types and warn her not to have a drink at lunch because it makes her sleepy. The system, she says, "just grinds you down."

Miss Cook's father, an accountant, is a driving, ambitious man. "He always told me that when you're work-ing and making money, you're happy," she says. "But it's not as simple as that. To be happy, you have to feel that you're making some sort of contribution. And that's difficult when you have a supervisor staring at you every minute like you're going to do something wrong." Another thing that rankles is not being told why she has to do certain things. Still, Miss Cook plans to stay with her job for a while. "After all," she says, "it is a job."

* * *

Many of the men who toil on Detroit's assembly lines call their work "dehumanizing," but to John Johnson, a job at Chrysler Corp.'s Lynch Road factory was "the only break I got in three years." Johnson (not his real name) is grateful for a special reason: the job allowed him to support—then kick—the costly heroin habit he acquired as a soldier in Vietnam. When he was interviewed at Chrysler, Johnson recalls, "I had needle marks and everything. But they'll give anybody a place on the line, even a dope fiend." Still, it was hard work. "This job was my first auto plant," Johnson says. "The first day was a really long one. I wanted to get out, find something easier. But, you know, I didn't have no choice. I had to do it—either do that or go back on the streets."

Johnson had plenty of company. According to an official of the union local's methadone program, at least 500 of the factory's 4,000 workers are heroin addicts. By Johnson's account, life for a junkie in an auto plant is simple enough—if he can score. "If you're hurting, man, that's all you can think about," he says. "Production, whatever, nothing matters. If you're high, you can get by. Mostly everybody is too occupied to be worrying about who's a dope fiend. They just try to leave you alone."

Since Johnson kicked his habit, he has been working as a counselor to the methadone program. A black high-school dropout, Johnson says that he'll go back to the line but that he won't like it. "The jobs that you do degrade you," he says. "You don't feel like a man."

The Japanese Yen for Work

The well-known Japanese willingness to work is the envy of many a Western entrepreneur. What makes them labor so hard? *Newsweek*'s veteran Tokyo bureau chief, Bernard Krisher, offers this analysis of the Japanese yen for work:

Japanese workers aren't motivated primarily by money or the prospect of climbing to the top. Basically, they work for the team. Their attitude is a throwback to feudal days when *daimyo* (feudal lords) protected and provided for their followers and demanded loyalty and obedience in return. Today, the daimyo are gone, replaced by corporations—but the tradition of obedience remains. Company presidents often take a paternalistic interest in their employees. For example, Takeshi Hirano, president of one of Japan's leading fishing and canning firms, attends ten or more employee weddings a month, and members of his board go to "many, many more."

As a result, the Japanese worker usually feels a deep loyalty to his firm, which almost always employs him until he retires or dies. Working for the advancement of the company is elevated into a life goal for the worker. Japanese society encourages this by identifying a man not by his profession, but by the company he works for. "If you ask a man what he does," says one Japanese businessman, "he will say he is with Mitsubishi regardless of whether he is a driver or vice president." Often a Japanese employee's life revolves more around his company than his family. A 1971 government poll revealed that almost one-third of Japanese employees felt that work was the most meaningful part of their lives.

Company officials work hard at maintaining a team spirit among employees. In many firms, the work day starts with group exercise, the chanting of a company song or a slogan-packed speech by the president. Sometimes whole plants are shut so that workers and employers can go off together for company-paid overnight trips. Along with teamwork comes harmony. Most firms have management-labor councils that hold year round discussions with employees—not just on wages and vacation issues, but also on production rates, new machinery and how to improve working conditions. As a result of this team effort, strikes are infrequent, and when they occur, they are usually symbolic and end after a day; workers just care too much that other companies will get ahead of their own. Niroshi Naruse, a 29-year-old checker in Kinokuniya, a Tokyo supermarket, puts it this way: "We all have pride working here, knowing it is the most reputable supermarket in Japan."

There is also a philosophic basis for the Japanese work ethic of which Westerners are often not aware. It is based on Confucianism, which promulgates the doctrine that work is a virtue.

And, of course, there are practical reasons Japanese work so hard. One is to save for retirement. While U.S. social-security payments now average $270 a month for a retired couple, Japanese at present receive only $75—hardly enough even in a country with a lower standard of living. Many company-financed pension programs in the U.S. are six times bigger than those in Japan, and the Japanese employee must work hard when younger to provide for his retirement, which starts at the age of 55. In recent years, young Japanese workers have been muttering about this and about other aspects of their work life. A few even reject the traditional hard-work ethic that created the Japanese economic boom. But Japan still has a long way to go before it has to worry about a slackening of the national passion to work.

The Real Cause of Workers' Discontent

Emanuel Weintraub

From *The New York Times* (January 21, 1973), 21. Copyright © 1973 by The New York Times Company. Reprinted by permission.

Mr. Weintraub is a management consultant and the President of Emanuel Weintraub Associates, Inc.

Job enrichment and job redesign are becoming fashionable new phrases when discussing the seemingly growing discontent of workers in this country today. Interestingly, however, we have found that what is an "enriched" job to one worker may not be all that attractive to another.

In the recently issued study by the Department of Health, Education and Welfare, "Work in America," a major point raised was that the key step in the road to universal worker harmony and increased productivity was the redesign and enrichment of jobs, including a greater voice for workers.

Job enrichment is both a subjective and an ambiguous term to anyone who has grappled with the knotty issue of attitudes and productivity of our work force. There has certainly been considerable controversy over what elements make for job satisfaction and whether enrichment is the dominant force in that equation.

The H.E.W. report takes a point of view that discards the concepts of Frederick W. Taylor and his principles of scientific management that form the basis of most production systems in today's industrialized society. In support of the enrichment theory, H.E.W. describes job redesign as the "keystone" of its recommendations and contends that tightly structured, repetitive jobs are the least interesting; therefore, this is where most dissatisfaction could be found.

Discontent in the work force is hardly a new subject. It has been bedeviling management and labor, not to mention unions and management consultants, for generations. It was the underlying reason for an extensive study that was designed and initiated by our concern in the middle of 1971.

The focus of our study, concluded last summer, was to determine whether female blue-collar workers in very tightly structured jobs found their work unsatisfying and to investigate the elements of work dissatisfaction.

We used a test method that isolated attitudes of people willing to quit (highly dissatisfied) and those not likely to quit (less dissatisfied) and then compared these attitudes by computer analysis.

The study covered 17 factories from New England to the Southwest United States and encompassed 2,535 sewing-machine operators whose pay was based on an hourly guarantee plus a direct productivity incentive. The product lines involved men's wear, women's wear and home furnishings. Seventy percent of the total work force of about 5,000 belonged to unions.

How these people answered some of the questions raises many questions about what really constitutes job enrichment.

For example, only about 1 of 10 did not like their kind of work, while approximately 2 of 10 couldn't say their jobs were interesting. Replies of this magnitude would fly in the face of a great deal of what has been said and written recently about job enrichment.

The nagging question is how can workers in very tightly structured jobs overwhelmingly like their work and only a lesser number find it interesting? Apparently "interest" and "like" don't go together in equal proportions.

The highly engineered nature of the surveyed plants was such that the respondents' work, which must be performed while seated, was clearly fractionalized and repetitive with little opportunity for variations.

Definite areas of dissatisfaction were uncovered and they were rooted strongly in economic reasons. Of the total work force, only 43 percent felt they made enough to make ends meet. Also, less than half (48 percent) of the women considered their pay comparable to that of nearby factories.

It was clear that both the highly dissatisfied and less dissatisfied workers are not particularly enamored with pay. It's just a matter of intensity. Among those likely to quit, 66 percent thought they would earn more elsewhere, while only 33 percent of the less dissatisfied thought that way.

An interesting pattern showed up to the question of workers having a voice in how the actual work is done. Sixty percent of the total force felt they didn't have a voice.

Here again, a matter of intensity surfaced. Almost 8 of 10 workers ready to quit felt they lacked a voice in the decision-making process. Among the less dissatisfied, about 16 percent felt the same way, but neither group considered "a voice" as one of the four important elements they would look for in another job.

The responses from both groups about a voice in work procedures seemed significant since 70 percent of the plants were unionized. This certainly points out that, in the eyes of the workers, management of both unionized and nonunionized plants is not doing a good job in creating and maintaining two-way communications.

To test the validity of the true-false section of the study, a multiple-choice segment was included. It revolved around the question: "If I ever left this job it would be most of all for the following things. Check off the four that would be most important to you."

Given 13 choices, including economics, job enrichment, leisure time, physical working conditions and a voice in work procedures, they were asked to select the four most important to them. The results were: (1) more job security; (2) pay equal to other plants; (3) more or different fringe benefits, and (4) a four-day, 40-hour week.

The conclusion that seems clear from these responses is that people would leave their jobs for a "package" of substance, including more security, more pay, better fringe benefits and an opportunity for more time away from work to pursue their personal needs.

The call of leisure-time activities, which is being aggressively promoted from all quarters—the vacation home, the camping trip, the pursuit of hobbies and interests—are compelling factors, obviously.

The wish for a voice in their workplace, a real need, is nevertheless subordinated by greater, though less dramatic-sounding desires by working people. This was obvious when workers ranked in eighth place "weekly or monthly meetings with supervisors to talk about how work is done and how it can be done differently."

Even lower on the scales of desires (11th of 13) was the wish to switch to a plant producing a totally different product.

It appears that there is obviously a different blueprint of satisfaction for different individuals. It is not necessarily nonfinancial improvement alone, nor solely financial betterment.

Where the danger lies is in convenient presumptions that vast flaws exist in the work ethic; that structured jobs are universally unsatisfying, and that the needs of people in such jobs can be easily defined beneath the umbrella of a single generalization.

We are decidedly at a time when our work force is more knowledgeable. As a group, it is better educated and, through mass communications, exposed to more information than ever before.

With much more research, I believe we will find that a pluralism of needs will be the response from our working population; that there are those who are most content in tightly structured work, providing that the structure is encompassed in a framework appropriate for these times.

If we contrast the attitudes of people in very

structured work with those in presumably unstructured jobs, might we be in a position to identify an interesting job?

Consider, for a moment, the status of civil servants, transportation workers, education employes, people performing services that are not regarded an extension of the machine. We find almost constant strife among these employes even though their work is not considered tightly structured in the traditional sense.

Or is it? Are the needs of the factory worker the same as the school teacher? These are questions that cry out for increasing analysis.

From our studies of manufacturing employes, we do know that our study group has no serious complaint about the very character of the rigidly structured job.

Since their pay is based on a guarantee plus direct productivity incentives, these manufacturing workers volunteered the strong opinion that they objected to any change in job or assignment that might reduce their productivity and therefore interfere with their earnings opportunities. All through our study the economic package came through as a strong element.

In any work-oriented situation, the more productive person invariably will demand additional compensation for the productivity, including, perhaps, more time to enjoy leisure.

Even though payment by productivity is being down-graded in our society, most of us are really paid, one way or the other, on productivity and performance.

The question then is: Is it possible that an intelligent reinstitution of payment by productivity systems—which would offer money and fringe benefits and would respond to the increased demand for leisure time that working people have—may enable us more totally to meet the needs that we all have as human beings and to begin to create a work force more in harmony with itself?

What Workers Want Most			
The Weintraub survey of 2,535 sewing-machine operators showed the following order of preference in what the operators wanted in connection with their jobs:			
	Combined Total	Highly Dissatisfied Workers	Less Dissatisfied Workers
More job security	1	2	1
Pay equal to other plants	2	1	1
More or different fringe benefits	3	3	3
4-day, 40-hour week or other shift changes	4	4	4
Supervisors who are nice to people as well as knowing their job	5	6	5
A rest from working at all	6	8	6
Work in a company where people get along better	7	5	7
Meetings to talk about how the work is done and how it could be done differently	8	9	8
Renovated plants, including cleaning, painting, new washrooms, better cafeteria	9	7	9
Supervisors who pay more attention to my work and equipment	10	10	10
Work in a company that manufactures a different product	11	12	11
Supervisors who can make more decisions	12	11	12
Day care center for my kids	13	13	13

19 THE ESTABLISHMENT— AT THE CROSSROADS?

The Military Establishment: Its Impacts on American Society

Adam Yarmolinsky

From *The Military Establishment: Its Impacts on American Society*, 395, 404–408, 411–412, 413, 414–417, and 418. Copyright © 1971 by Twentieth Century Fund. Reprinted by permission of Harper & Row, Publishers, Inc.

Adam Yarmolinsky is Professor of Law at Harvard University. In addition to journal articles and his study on the military establishment, he has written Recognition of Excellence *(1960) and has an extensive public service career.*

THE MILITARY ESTABLISHMENT AND SOCIAL VALUES

The impact of the military establishment—as of any other institution—on the nation's value system is not easily measured. Easy stereotypes of authoritarianism, conformity, aggression, and brutality are common. The evidence to support or refute them is less readily come by. What is clear is that the effort to sort out reality from myth is a crucial one. It is useful to survey so far as possible the character and range of military influence, tangible and intangible, on the quality of American life.

The history of the United States can be measured as it can for most nations from war to war, as many textbooks and children's book series bluntly indicate. It took one war to create the Union and another to preserve it. For most Americans, the military continues to be the most obvious manifestation of the federal presence, apart from the Post Office. Its influence extends nationwide more than almost any other institution. Soldiers are trained and serve far from home with comrades from every class, race, and region. Only at the executive level of large corporations—and perhaps not even there —does the pattern of movement begin to match the mobility of the military. During the lifetime of those now in their seventies the nation has engaged in five wars in which the United States was a major participant; those now over thirty have lived through three wars that have covered more than a third of their lives.

Until the time comes, if it ever does, when regional differences within the United States are significantly reduced by national television and the spread of other communications, broadly based educational influences and the architectural uniformity of shopping centers, housing developments, and office buildings—and until wars diminish or cease—the separate influence of the military will continue to serve as a unique and potent common national experience. . . .

The coincidence between the cycle of military popularity and the cycle of military expansion is not peculiarly American. Other nations have experienced the same phenomenon. When the military has been strong it has, by and large, been popular and accepted as necessary to national defense. Yet, for the first time in American history, a phase of increased popularity and expansion occurred in a time when there was no declared war. Then, at the end of the sixties and the beginning of the seventies, when the United States military establishment was at the height of its strength and power, after an era of unprecedented popularity, in the eyes of a significant element of opinion leadership in the United States (as well as abroad) and particularly in the expressed views of some of the nation's most articulate young people, the American military became an object of fear and hate.

The war in Vietnam is not the single nor even the dominant issue that divides our society today. The issue of race is clearly primary; it has imposed strains on the structure of the country greater than those of all the other issues put together. But the military establishment is a major divisive issue as well. Several thousand young Americans have chosen to put their citizenship at risk by fleeing the country rather than accept service in the armed forces. Tens of thousands of others, young and old, have joined in demonstrations designed to obstruct recruiting and the movement of troops within the United States.

Violent protest against the military establishment seems to be confined to issues directly related to the Vietnam war—and, at least at this writing, to a small segment of the population. But the violence of this protest tends to exacerbate the violence of protests on other issues, and it has been accompanied by the general alienation of a much larger minority from the military establishment. During the march on the Pentagon in the summer of 1967 large-scale violence was avoided only by the deep concern and extraordinary ingenuity of the federal officials directly responsible for handling the demonstrations. The leaders of the November 1969 peace demonstrations in Washington made heroic—and generally successful—efforts to prevent those who sought to provoke violence with violence from involving the mass of the demonstrators. At the same time, administration spokesmen retreated, under popular pressure, from potentially self-fulfilling prophecies about the likelihood of serious violence attending the demonstrations.

The severe alienation of many youths from the military or other governmental service is relatively new. In the early 1960s, the Alianza para el Progreso and the Peace Corps—and, originally, the Green Berets—were expressions of a concern for social justice that transcended national interests and captured the attention of youth. The increasing disaffection of young people from government in the late 1960s has focused particularly on the uses of violence, which took some of the most promising young leaders of the country by assassination, and involved many thousands of others in urban riots or foreign combat. The military establishment and the police, as symbols of officially condoned force, became primary objects of this alienation. The confidence of youth in their country had been eroded by the growing awareness of the problems of race and poverty, and of the poisoning of the environment, by the growing recognition of the deterioration in the general quality of life, and by the resentment of the personal sacrifice which is demanded from them for service in a war many think immoral in ends as well as means. They believe—and their elders find it hard to deny—that the massive misuse of military power in Southeast Asia threatens the careers and the lives of succeeding generations, and siphons off resources desperately needed to resolve domestic problems. In the face of such profound antipathy, the traditional function of the military is grudgingly accepted at best or at worst rejected outright by those few, but articulate, young people—among them many potential leaders—who feel that a society so defective is not worth protecting. Many have opted out, as a consequence, through drugs or other escapist devices.

The prototype of the young political activist,

as a result, is no longer the whiz kid or the political candidate challenging the bureaucracy from within the system in order to make it more effective, but the lawyer or the community organizer confronting the system in order to change its fundamental goals and purposes. And the prototype of the young radical is no longer a disciplined, institutionally oriented cell member, but an anti-institutional individual capable, at one extreme, of naïve and childlike concern for simplicity and purity and, at the other, of random amoral violence.

The military is not only the nation's largest bureaucracy, but it is probably the most entrenched, and the least amenable to confrontation or to change. All established American institutions have felt the shock of alienation of the young, but none more than the military.[1] Perhaps even more seriously, there seems to be growing cynicism among the more moderate youth about the validity of American institutions and their capacity for constructive change. If the military establishment is not to be a continuing source of bitterness and divisiveness within the country, and if it is to be effective even in limited ways, it must assume a lower and more flexible posture, not only in the demands it makes on national resources, but in the justification that it offers for those demands.

The symptoms of student alienation—ostracizing or banishment of college ROTC units and violence directed against ROTC buildings, opposition to defense-supported research, and, for a small but articulate and committed minority, the choice of prison or exile rather than military service—are growing in number and in scope. Even apart from the destructive consequences for individuals, alienation between the

military establishment and the minority endangers the political cohesion of the country. Whether the primary target is the war in Vietnam, in which they may be called to serve, the size of the military budget, or the pervasiveness of military influence in American life, the disaffection of young people tends to overflow the limits of the military establishment and to poison the attitudes of these youths toward American government in general and American society at large. The military is regarded not as a passive beneficiary of a skewed system of national priorities but as a wicked, greedy aggressor conspiring with other vested interests to subvert the American dream.

Alienation, in a way, begets alienation, for polarization in the nation increases as vehement minority reaction evokes a response from the "silent majority," young and old, which takes criticism of the military and demands for institutional change as an affront and a danger.

A disturbing related question goes to the core of contemporary American values. Many middle Americans have tended to embrace the concepts of authority and conformity that are associated with military life, and have increasingly opposed traditional American liberties. How far this civilian rigidity is a reaction to the disconcerting styles of radical youth, how far a response to the unrest in society generally, and how far an effect of the extensive influence of the military itself is unclear. The evidence suggests that all are relevant. Moreover, the most articulate antimilitary spokesmen are under thirty, and the most articulate defenders are over forty, which only accentuates the gap and hardens the polarization. And since so many of the alienated minority are among the brightest of the young, their disaffection makes more difficult the development of a rational philosophy of public policy, including a rational strategy for the uses of military power at home and overseas.

As citizens of the only nation to employ nuclear weapons to attack human targets, many in the United States have suffered a recurrent sense of guilt, a guilt that may have been prolonged and accentuated by the Dulles doctrine of massive nuclear retaliation.

---

[1] The resistance to conformity has touched the military elite as well. At one of the service academies the students could be divided, according to an informed observer, into three categories: "engineers," who accept the system as necessary, "Eagle Scouts," who accept the system enthusiastically, and "mods" and rebels. See *Administration of the Service Academies, Report and Hearings of the Special Subcommittee on Service Academies of the House Armed Services Committee*, 90th Congress, 1st and 2nd Sessions. 1967–1968, pp. 10912–10913.

Many American scientists, particularly, have been greatly troubled at the uses to which their knowledge has been put in the service of war. As recently as February 1970, Dr. Charles Schwartz of the University of California at Berkeley circulated a pledge of conscience among his colleagues of the American Physical Society. It carried a drawing of a mushroom cloud and read: "I pledge that I will not participate in war research or weapons production; I further pledge to counsel my students and urge my colleagues to do the same."[2]

But this burden of conscience probably has escaped the majority of the American people. For those who had guilt feelings, the Kennedy administration's substitution of the doctrine of flexible response, designed to deploy military force at the low end of the spectrum, was a matter of considerable moral relief. The sense of reprieve was soon broken by American action at the Bay of Pigs, and later intervention in the Dominican Republic, producing a moral as well as a political division on the propriety of offensive military action. With the extension of the war in Vietnam, and the gradual revelation of the despoliation of land and villages and the extent of civilian casualties, the moral liability for the use of United States military power impacted on the consciousness of American society with splintering force.

An articulate minority, made up primarily of young students and old liberals, reacted with shock and horror to the delayed revelations of My Lai and other military atrocities. Others either refused to believe the stories, or chose to regard the alleged atrocities as justified by the exigencies of war. The division on the moral issue heightened the political tension between hawks and doves, and polarized the civilian society even further. When a fund-raising campaign to pay for civilian counsel was launched on behalf of one of the military defendants, many responded in defense of the conduct itself, although others perhaps did so in protest against what they regarded as unfair exploitation of a scapegoat for the military establishment as a

[2] *New York Times*, February 1, 1970.

whole. West Point cadets cheered their commandant, Major General Samuel Koster, when he announced his resignation from the academy, citing the charges against him as the commander of the division involved at My Lai. Many doubtless cheered in affirmation of their loyalty to the Point, at a time when it seemed under attack, but those who read or heard of the event could legitimately raise serious questions about the moral discrimination of young men chosen for military leadership, and the choice they might later make as officers, if called upon to do so, between their loyalty to the military institution and their obligation to hold the institution accountable to the country.

The popular reactions to My Lai stimulated grave reflections about national dedication to fundamental principles of human conduct. One began to hear troubled references to possible parallels, in kind, although certainly not in degree, to the national guilt and the moral indifference of "the good Germans." The apparent cover up of earlier investigations of My Lai at all levels of military command has implicated the system as a whole in the minds of many. Only when a former soldier brought the events to the public, did the military respond and consider indictments. But there was no overwhelming public outcry. Whether the acceptance by a sizable portion of the population of conduct previously considered contrary to the laws of war is a consequence, in part, of the growing public reliance on the military, or a contributing cause, it may well produce a brutalizing effect on the moral sensibilities of the country, extending beyond the immediate precipitating events. Insensitivity to unwarranted police violence and insensitivity to brutality in military actions—abroad and at home—may be unrelated phenomena, but they cannot escape mutual reinforcement.

HOW MUCH IS ENOUGH?

The United States military establishment is the largest institutional complex within the United States government. It is so much larger than all the other institutions of government that its operations, and its impacts—on the economy, on class and racial minorities, on science and research, on higher education, on the legal system of justice, on the national scheme of values—are literally of another order of magnitude. Not only is it larger but it is more pervasive than any other governmental institution except the Post Office and the Internal Revenue Service, extending its impacts into almost every community in the United States.

The military establishment is not growing. In fact, it is shrinking, both as a percentage of our rapidly increasing gross national product, and in absolute terms, measured in constant—and even in inflating—dollars. But it is shrinking slowly. It remains the single most powerful and pervasive establishment in our society.

The magnitude of the impact of the military establishment derives from two primary factors: its absolute size, and extensive ramifications; and its size relative to other important public enterprises, international and domestic: health, education, foreign aid, family planning and community organization at home and abroad, environmental controls, and the war against poverty.

The absolute size of the establishment makes it uniquely difficult to control (although it is by no means monolithic) and encourages expansionary tendencies for which internal or even external checks and balances are, as we have seen, often inadequate. But it is difficult to imagine early changes in the international climate that would permit the reduction of the United States military budget by more than, say, 50 percent, and a military budget of $40 billion—or even of $20 billion—presents the same kind of problems of management and control as a budget of $80 billion, although such a reduction might well make a qualitative difference in the society.

The problem of relative size, which was implicit in the smaller military budgets of the mid-1950s, did not then become explicit because other critical national problems had not surfaced, and the costs of dealing with them had not been generally realized. It will continue to be a major issue even as the military budget continues to decline as a percentage of the gross national product and of the federal budget.

The size and impact of the military establishment is likely, therefore, to remain a special problem in America for the foreseeable future. Whether it becomes a manageable problem, or whether it turns out to be the rock on which the country is split depends first on general understanding of and control over the uses of military power in the nuclear age; and second on the achievement of a general agreement that no automatic priority attaches to the stated requirements of the military establishment as against the stated requirements of other contenders for a share of national resources.

Any general understanding of the uses of military power, however, is obscured by the traditional ambivalence in American attitudes toward the military establishment—an ambivalence that is exacerbated by the threat of thermonuclear destruction and by the continuing drain of the war in Southeast Asia on the nation's human, material, and moral resources. It is difficult to be rational about a military establishment consisting of a nuclear component that can destroy us all if it is ever unleashed, and a nonnuclear component of which a large part has been engaged for the last five years in a tragic demonstration of the ineffectiveness of military force in controlling violence in the Third World. But a rational perspective remains essential if the proper uses of a military establishment in the United States are to be settled, so that the elements not required for those uses can be eliminated without cutting out vital functions, and a foundation can be laid to answer the perplexing question, "How much is enough?"

The underlying rationale for the nuclear establishment is less difficult to state than for the nonnuclear forces, although still full of uncertainties. It begins with the prevailing situation of nuclear parity between the two nuclear superpowers, and recognizes that neither side can profit from disturbing the balance, because the other side can and must respond by restoring it at a higher level of expenditure—and possibly with new weapons that are themselves destabilizing (because, for example, they are, like MIRV, harder to count). Since there are so many uncertainties in the balance, neither side can afford to take a "worst case" approach. . . .

There can be and there are sharp differences of opinion on the necessary size and shape of the nuclear arsenal; the danger of a runaway nuclear arms race is always present; and the actual size and shape of the arsenal is probably still determined as much by political exploitation of irrational fears, and by pressures from within the military establishment, as it is by rational analysis. But at least there is a framework for discussion, more and more generally accepted, of the question, "How much nuclear armament is enough?"

On the nonnuclear side, the question is even more difficult to spell out, let alone to answer. It is obscured by the distortion of history and the perpetuation of cold war ideology that have issued from the official apologists for the Vietnam war. So long as this or similar processes of justification continue, it is difficult for Americans to recognize the limits of the national interest that would call for the use of nonnuclear military force, or the options for impact on other societies that do not include military force at all. The country tends to be polarized, one group regarding the United States as a global policeman, ready to intervene in internal revolutions or to counter blatant or insidious aggression, and the other group—growing in numbers —willing to withdraw into a fortress America or hoping to substitute policies embodying a narrow interpretation of national interest. . . .

The complex issue of nonnuclear force levels is even more difficult to resolve than issues of nuclear force levels. Nor can those nonnuclear issues be resolved by opting always for the higher force level or the more sophisticated weapons system, even if there were no budgetary constraints. Too many American troops in Europe might be as destabilizing as too few, and ultrasophisticated weapons are not as ready or as flexible as less sophisticated ones. These difficulties point up the impossibility of making any absolute determination of the amount of military spending necessary for national security. There are too many unknowns, too many vari-

ables, and too many elements of judgment, including nonmilitary judgment, and even if every doubtful issue were decided in favor of more spending, the net effect, both on the nuclear and on the nonnuclear side, conceivably might be to decrease our security. In any event there are the ubiquitous facts of diminishing returns and opportunity costs.

In the face of these uncertainties, the automatic priority for military spending that has prevailed over the last decade demands reconsideration. The argument that the military establishment should have first claim on the public purse finds support from a number of sources, as has been indicated above, but when the military claim is met first, other national needs, some of them vital needs, are neglected. So long as the civil-military budgetary relationship assumes the primacy of the military, even temporary subordination of military demands indicates to the public that the demands have been unreasonable, and to the military that not only their drafts on the public treasury but they themselves are being dishonored. Such a division can become a national political issue, and a dangerous one for the country. In other societies, and in other ages, it has been a fatal division.

If, however, the military is recognized as one of a number of valid claimants, the necessary periodic adjustment of priorities can be accomplished. Of course, the transition from primacy to competition among equals is never easy; it will be as difficult for this generation of the American military as for the first-born who has to learn that while his parents still care for him, he is not an only child any more. But the transition has to be made; one way—among others—to encourage it would be to make the opportunity to draw on a national service pool available to other priority claimants on public spending, or to make voluntary service with such other claimants grounds for exemption from military service.

No other institution, private or public, is now authorized to use compulsory processes to make up its manpower deficit—and even in periods of peace, or undeclared war. The United States has experienced and is experiencing critical shortages of health services personnel, teachers and teachers' aids, and police officers—to name only a few areas of scarcity. But the nation has never assumed a responsibility for ensuring that these shortages are met. If, for example, the principle of mandatory service were not only accepted but also applied beyond the military to other forms of national service, equally urgent and important for the country, the military would have the benefits of a public policy declaration in favor of a priority allocation of manpower as befits a critical public function, but it would not be identified as the sole repository of the responsibility for safeguarding the nation's security and its most sacred values. Other activities— the education of disadvantaged children, the delivery of health services to groups whose health needs are badly neglected, the organization of communities to achieve genuine participation in American society, the preservation of domestic public order with justice—all these and more could then be recognized, as they are not now, as essential in the same sense that the military function is regarded as essential.

How a national service pool should be organized raises a host of questions as to scale, timing, coverage, supervision, the selection of functions to be performed, and institutions to be included. The fundamental issue is the extent (if any) to which compulsion can or should be substituted for incentives and voluntary action. These are all issues to be debated before decisions can be made. Initially, the selective service principle might be employed for essential civilian as well as military service (i.e., by requiring service of a limited portion of the age group), perhaps with a more inclusive lottery. General acceptance of the national service principle, on the other hand, might permit abandonment of compulsory military service, without giving way to a wholly professional military, made up of career volunteers. It is doubtful, too, whether a program of this kind could be begun during wartime. As a first step, however, a major national program of voluntary service, administered by state and local government and private organizations with federal financial help, could be launched immediately.

A program of national service would serve another broader purpose as well, softening the impact of other establishments in addition to the military establishment on the society. American society is increasingly professionalized, and at the same time, the dominant role of the professional is increasingly challenged from outside the organizations that he dominates. In schools, in hospitals and clinics, in social service agencies, professional qualifications are multiplied, and extended into lower ranks, while consumers of services become increasingly restive. The injection of young nonprofessional, noncareer people into increasingly professional organizations, even at the bottom of the organizational pyramid, tends to restore useful communication between the institution and its clientele, and to remind the career bureaucrats of the needs and demands of the world beyond organizational horizons. It may also reduce the impact of professionals on nonprofessionals, by putting some of the nonprofessionals on the professional side of the encounter.

The issue will be resolved only when the partisans of a better quality of life can persuade the American public to invest national resources in implementing their goals on an equal—or superior—basis to the investment of natural resources in the goals of the military establishment.

An enormous organization, growing less recognizable as distinctively military with the convergence of military and civilian styles, more bureaucratized, and more and more expensive, and without effective countervailing power to balance its own power, cannot be permitted to regulate itself without comprehensive and workable external controls. The internal controls within the military establishment, both on the governmental and on the industrial side, must also be further refined and developed. On the government side, the primary need is to reduce some of the expansionary forces generated within the organization by loosening up the bureaucratic structure. More nonbureaucratic influence must be brought to bear, particularly on issues of strategy and force structure. A larger role for short-term or non-career people not only loosens up the system, but makes it more responsive to enlightened public opinion. Persons who come into the Department of Defense from outside the military establishment, and who expect to return to careers outside the establishment, are better able to see the claims of the establishment in perspective, against other high-priority claims on the increasingly beleaguered resources of the United States; and they are better able to communicate this perspective to the general public, always provided the civilian impact on the military is at least as great as the impact of the military on the civilian. . . .

The key instrument of presidential authority in control of the military is the budgetary instrument. The President controls the over-all size and shape of the military budget as it is transmitted to the Congress, and unlike, for example, the rivers and harbors appropriation, it is unusual for the Congress to make major additions to (or subtractions from) the budget as the President submits it. One can argue that the military budget is essentially the product of pressures exerted by generals, defense contractors, labor leaders, and their allies and supporters; but in fact the President has a good deal more freedom of choice than he ordinarily uses in controlling the military expenditures. . . . As Commander-in-Chief, the President is the ultimate authority over all military actions and responsible, therefore, for all excesses, however difficult they are in practice to control.

The Congress, for its part, needs to apply more effective countervailing power to the military establishment and its industrial and scientific components than it has done to date. It must overcome self-interest in major contracts for districts, states, and regions; and in wasteful development and procurement procedures. It must break through unnecessary secrecy, which impedes full public debate and constituent response, and ensures self-perpetuation and expansion of the establishment without public decision. It must avoid timidity in the face of technical expertise, complex data, and projected images of alarm and danger based on the "worst" view of potential enemies. It must overcome a sense of ambivalence, one part awe and one part hostility, toward military power, which

reflects the public's own ambivalence and inhibits rational decision-making on military methods and goals. With the Executive, it must assume the responsibility necessary for a civilian-controlled society in critical review of the military-industrial establishment, in setting the goals which the military is required to carry out, and in evaluating how consistently the military holds to these goals. The goals must not be set, by default or momentum, by the military itself. Indeed, there are signs that this role, to a considerable extent abdicated since World War II, is now being reassumed by the legislative branch. . . .

In the last analysis, the key to defense policy in a democratic society is still the attitude of the general public. As de Tocqueville observed: "The remedy for the vices of the Army is not to be found in the Army itself, but in the country."[3] By and large, the American people get the kind of military establishment they deserve.

Public attitudes depend on public information, and the military establishment is a powerful and effective advocate on its own behalf. Critical comment and evaluations of the establishment must be made publicly available for genuine debate. At present much is kept back from the American public that is readily available to espionage agents of our allies and of our actual and potential enemies.

The public, through its representatives in government and through strengthened countervailing institutions, must keep a wary eye on where the military is heading and why and at how much cost. The demands of the military, moreover, must be compared to the demands and the cost of competing national needs.

The public must watch and check the reach of the military as it appears to threaten the effectiveness of countervailing groups—whether through overclassification of research data, through surveillance of civilian dissent, by encouraging industrial monopolies dependent on its support, or by reinforcing general decision-

[3] Alexis de Tocqueville, *Democracy in America* (New York: New American Library, Mentor Edition), Book III, Chapter 49, p. 279.

making in terms of rational quantifiable options without testing the primary assumptions or the qualitative nature of consequences. It must refrain from undermining civilian control of domestic order by calling on the military to intervene increasingly—and preventively—to put down civic unrest; it must go beyond containment of violence to get at the root causes of violence. If the United States is to avoid becoming a militarized society, the public and its civilian representatives must retain the ultimate right of decision on such central political issues as counterrevolution and insurgency, war and peace.

20 PRIORITIES—AND NEXT?

Priorities for the Seventies

Robert L. Heilbroner

Robert Louis Heilbroner is Professor of Economics at the New School for Social Research. His list of contributions include The Worldly Philosophers *(1953),* The Future as History *(1959),* The Great Ascent *(1963),* The Limitations of American Capitalism *(1966), and* The Economic Problem *(1968).*

To talk about national priorities is to talk about precedence, the order in which things are ranked. It is not difficult to establish what that order is in America today. Military needs rank above civilian needs. Private interests rank above public interests. The claims of the affluent take precedence over those of the poor. This is all so familiar that it no longer even has the power to rouse us to indignation. There is no shock value left in saying that we are a militaristic nation, or a people uninterested in the elimination of poverty, or a citizenry whose only response to the decay of the cities is a decision to move to the suburbs. To get a rise out of people, these days, one has to say something really outrageous, such as that the main cultural effect of advertising on television is to teach our children that grown-ups tell lies for money.

But I do not want to expatiate on the present order of things. For I presume that to talk of priorities is to determine what they *should* be. What should come first? What ought to be on top of the agenda?

To ask such questions is to invite pious answers. I shall try to avoid the pieties by grouping my priorities into three categories. The first has to do with our immediate survival—not as a nation-state, but as a *decent* nation-state. The second has to do with our ultimate salvation. The third with our moving from survival to salvation.

The initial set of priorities is simple to specify. It consists of three courses of action necessary to restore American society to life. The first of these is the demilitarization of the national budget. That budget now calls for the expenditure of $80-billion a year for military purposes. Its rationale is that it will permit us to fight simultaneously two "major" (though, of course, non-nuclear) wars and one "minor" or "brushfire" war. This requires the maintenance of eighteen army divisions, as against eleven in 1961; of 11,000 deliverable nuclear warheads, compared with 1,100 in 1961; of a navy far larger than that of any other nation. . . .

Politically, economically—even militarily—this budget is a disaster for America. It has sucked into the service of fear and death the energies and resources desperately needed for hope and life. Until and unless that budget is significantly cut, there will be little chance of restoring vitality to American society.

By how much can it be cut? The Nixon administration proposed to reduce it by $4- to $6-billion by June 1971, and by an equivalent amount each year for another four years. *Fortune* magazine claimed it could be cut faster— $17.6-billion less by June 1972. Seymour Melman, professor of industrial engineering at Columbia University, has stated that it could be slashed by over $50-billion—and his reduced budget would still leave 2,300,000 men under arms, an obliterative power aimed at 156 Soviet cities, and an air and naval armada of staggering dimensions.

This conflicting testimony suggests that the question of how much the budget can be cut depends not on expertise alone, but on outlook —on how much one wants to reassign into other channels the resources absorbed by the military. Here let us make a first approximation as to how much the military budget can be cut by determining how large are the life-giving aims to which we must now give priority. I see two of these as being essential for the attainment of decency in American society. One is the long overdue relief of poverty. In 1967, 10 percent of all white families, 35 percent of all black families, and 58 percent of all black families over age sixty-five, lived in poverty—a condition that we define by the expenditure for food of $4.90 per person per week. *Per week.* To raise these families to levels of minimum adequacy will require annual transfer payments of approximately $10- to $15-billion. This is half the annual cost of the Vietnam war. I would make this conversion of death into life a first guide to the demilitarization of the budget.

A second guide is provided by the remaining essential priority for American decency. This is the need to rebuild the cities before they collapse on us. This means not only replacing the hideous tenements and junkyards and prison-like schools of the slums, but providing the services needed to make urban living tolerable—regular garbage collection, dependable police protection, and adequate recreational facilities.

It has been estimated that New York City alone would need $4.3-billion per year for ten years to replace its slums. To provide proper levels of health and educational services would add another billion. And then there are Chicago and Newark and Washington and Los Angeles. It would take at least $20- to $25-billion a year for at least a decade to begin to make the American city viable.

These objectives are minimal requirements for America. Fortunately, they are easy to accomplish—at least in a technical sense. There will be no problem in cutting the military budget by the necessary $30- to $40-billion once that task is entrusted to men who are not prisoners of the military-industrial superiority complex. There are no great problems in the alleviation of poverty that the direct disbursement of money to the poor will not tolerably remedy. And whereas I do not doubt that it will be hard to build new cities handsomely and well, I do not think it will be difficult to tear down the rotten hulks that now constitute the slums, and to replace them with something that is unmistakably better.

Thus the essential priorities have the virtue of being as simple as they are compelling. This does not mean, however, that we will therefore attend to them. On the contrary, the chances are good that we will not do what must be done, or at best will act halfheartedly, in token fashion. The power of the vested interests of business and politics and labor in the preservation of military spending is enormous. The unwillingness of the American upper and middle classes to assist the less fortunate is a clear matter of record. The resistance to the repair of the cities is too well documented to require exposition here. Hence, we may never rise to the simple challenge of making America viable. In that case it is easy to make a prognosis for this country. It will be even more than it is today a dangerous, dirty, and depressing place in which to live. There will be an America, but it will not be a civilized America.

There is, however, at least a fighting chance

that we *will* cut the military budget, that we *will* declare poverty to be an anachronistic social disease, that we *will* begin to halt the process of urban deterioration. Let me therefore speak of another set of priorities—one that many people would place even higher on the list than my initial three. They are, first, the elimination of racism in the United States, and second, the enlistment of the enthusiasm—or at least the tolerance—of the younger generation.

I have said that these priorities have to do with our salvation rather than with our survival. This is because their achievement would lift the spirit of America as if a great shadow had been removed from its soul. But like all salvations, this one is not near at hand. For unlike the first set of priorities, which is well within our power to accomplish, this second set lies beyond our present capabilities. Even if we manage to cut the military budget, to end poverty, to rebuild the cities, the bitter fact remains that we do not know how to change the deep conviction within the hearts of millions of Americans that blackness spells inferiority. Neither do we know how to win the enthusiasm of young people—and I mean the best and soberest of them, not the drop-outs and the do-nothings—for a society that is technocratic, bureaucratic, and depersonalized.

Thus the second set of priorities is considerably different from the first. It constitutes a distant goal, not an immediate target. Any projection of what America should try to become that does not include the goals of racial equality and youthful enlistment is seriously deficient, but any projection that does not expect that we will be a racist and alienated society for a long while is simply unrealistic.

What then are we to do in the meantime? How are we to set for ourselves a course that is within the bounds of realism and that will yet move us toward the long-term goals we seek? This brings me to my third set of priorities—a set of tasks neither so simple as the first, nor so difficult as the second. I shall offer four such tasks—not in any particular order of urgency—as exemplifying the *kinds* of priorities we need in

order to move from mere survival toward ultimate salvation.

I begin with a proposal that will seem small by comparison with the large-scale goals discussed so far. Yet, it is important for a society that seeks to lessen racial tensions and to win the approbation of the young. It consists of a full-scale effort to improve the treatment of criminality in the United States.

No one knows exactly how large is the criminal population of the United States, but certainly it is very large. Two million persons a year pass through the major prisons and "reformatories," some 300,000 residing in them at any given time. Another 800,000 are on probation or parole; a still larger number lurk on the fringes of serious misbehavior, but have so far escaped the law. Our response to this core of seriously disturbed and dangerous persons is to send a certain number, who are unfortunate enough to get caught, to prison. These prisons include among them the foulest places in America—charnel houses comparable to Nazi concentration camps. At Tucker State Farm in Arkansas, inmates have been reported to be forty to sixty pounds underweight, and have been subjected to acts of unspeakable cruelty, and even to murder. The sadistic practices in military stockades have become notorious. But even the more humane institutions largely fail in their purposes. In New York State the rate of recidivism for crimes of comparable importance is 50 percent. A recent FBI study of 18,000 federal offenders released in 1963 showed that 63 percent had been arrested again five years later.

Indeed, as every criminologist will testify, prisons mainly serve not to deter, but to confirm and train the inmate for a career in criminality. These institutions exist not for the humanization but for the brutalization of their charges.

What is to be done? One inkling of the course to be followed is provided by reflecting on the statistics of prison care. In federal adult institutions we average one custodial person per seven inmates; one educational person per 121 inmates; one treatment person per 179 inmates. In local institutions and jails the ratio of educational or treatment personnel to inmates broadens to one to 550. In some state correctional institutions the ratio is as high as one to 2,400.

Another clue is suggested by the fact that work-release camps, widely used abroad to bridge the gap between prison and normal life, are available here in only four states. Still another is the clear need for the early detection of asocial behavior among school children, and for the application of therapy before, not after, criminality has become a way of life.

It must be obvious that an all-out effort to lessen criminality is not nearly so simple to achieve as slicing the military budget or tearing down the slums. But neither is it so difficult to achieve as racial tolerance. I suggest it is an objective well worth being placed high on the list of those "middle" priorities for which we are now seeking examples.

Recently, the Administration has declared the reform of prisons to be a major objective. Let us now see if this rhetoric will be translated into action.

My second suggestion is not unrelated to the first. Only it concerns not criminals, but those who represent the other end of the spectrum—the symbols of law and order, the police forces of America. I propose that an important item on the agenda must be an effort to contain and control a police arm that is already a principal reason for black anger and youthful disgust.

First, a few words to spell out the problem. In New York City, the Patrolmen's Benevolent Association, itself a potent force for reaction (as witness its key role in the defeat of the Civilian Review Board), is now outflanked on the right by "law enforcement" groups of super-patriot vigilantes who on several occasions have taken the law into their own hands. . . . In Detroit the United Press reports "open hostility" between the city's mainly white police force and the city's 40 percent black population. At Berkeley, Harvard, and Columbia we have witnessed the dreadful spectacle of policemen smashing indiscriminately at students and using tear gas and Mace.

There is no simple cure for this ugly situation. Police forces are recruited largely from the lower middle class; they bring with them deeply ingrained attitudes of racial contempt and envious hostility to privileged youth. But there are at least a few measures that can be taken to prevent what is already a dangerous rift from widening further. To begin with, one way to minimize police abuse of Negroes is to minimize occasions for contact with them. The obvious conclusion is that black ghettos must be given the funds and the authorization to form their own police forces. Another necessary step is to lessen the contact of police forces with college youth; the legalization of marijuana would help in this regard. So would the training of special, highly paid, *unarmed*, elite police forces who would be used to direct all police actions having to do with civil demonstrations.

I do not doubt that there are many other ways to attack the problem. What is essential is to take measures now that will prevent the police from driving a permanent wedge between white and black, between student and government. Mace, tear gas, and billy clubs are weapons of repression, not of order. Few steps would contribute more to the return of American self-respect than those that would assist the growth of law and order among the forces of law and order.

Here, too, the report of the Eisenhower Commission signals an overdue awakening of public consciousness. But here again we shall have to see whether this awareness will be translated into action.

My third suggestion seemingly departs markedly from the first two. It concerns a wider problem than criminality or police misbehavior, but not a less pressing problem. It is how to rescue the environment from the devastating impact of an unregulated technology.

I need mention only a few well-known results of this ferocious process of destruction. . . . The air in New York is dangerous to breathe. We are drowning in a sea of swill; in a normal year the United States "produces" 142 million tons of smoke and fumes, seven million junked cars, twenty million tons of waste paper, forty-eight billion used cans, and fifty trillion gallons of industrial sewage. And presiding over this rampant process of environmental overloading is the most fearsome reality of all—a population that is still increasing like an uncomfortable cancer on the surface of the globe. I know of no more sobering statistic in this regard than that between now and 1980 the number of women in the most fertile age brackets, eighteen to thirty-two, will double.

Aghast at this terrific imbalance between the power of technology and the capacity of society to control and order the effects of technology, some people are calling for a moratorium on technology, for a kind of national breathing space while we decide how to deal with such problems as the sonic boom and the new super-tankers. But this approach ignores the fact that it is not new technology alone that breeds trouble, but the cumulative effect of our existing technology; perhaps no single cause is more responsible for air pollution than the familiar combustion engine.

Hence, I call for a different priority in dealing with this crucial question—not for less technology, but for more technology of *a different kind.* For clearly what we need are technological answers to technological problems. We need a reliable method of birth control suitable for application among illiterate and superstitious peoples. We need an exhaustless automobile, a noiseless and versatile airplane. We need new methods of reducing and coping with wastes—radioactive, sewage, gaseous, and liquid. We need new modes of transporting goods and people, within cities and between them.

The priority then is technological research—research aimed at devising the techniques needed to live in a place that we have just begun to recognize as (in Kenneth Boulding's phrase) our Spaceship Earth. There is a further consideration here, as well. Many people wonder where we can direct the energies of the engineers, draftsmen, scientists, and skilled workmen who are now employed in building weapons systems, once we cut our military budget. I suggest that the design of a technology for our planetary spaceship will provide challenge enough to occupy their attention for a long time. We have not hesitated to support private enterprise for years while it

devoted its organizational talents to producing instruments of war. We must now begin to apply equally lavish support while private enterprise perfects the instruments of peace.

There would be an important side effect to such a civilian-industrial complex. It is that young people who are bored or repelled by the prospect of joining an industrial establishment, one of whose most spectacular accomplishments has been the rape of the environment, will, I believe, feel differently if they are offered an opportunity to work in research and development that has as its aim the renewal and reconstitution of this planet as a human habitat.

The items I have suggested as middle priorities could be extended into a long list. But what I am suggesting after all, are only the *kinds* of tasks that cry out for attention, not each and every one of them.

But to speak of priorities without mentioning education seems wrong, especially for someone in education. The question is, what is there to say? What is there left to declare about the process of schooling that has not been said again and again? Perhaps I can suggest just one thing, aimed specifically at the upper echelons of the educational apparatus. It is a proposal that the universities add a new orientation to their traditional goals and programs. I urge that they deliberately set out to become the laboratories of applied research into the future. I urge that they direct a major portion of their efforts toward research into, training for, and advocacy of programs for social change.

It may be said that there is no precedent for such an orientation of education toward action, and that the pursuit of such a course will endanger the traditional purity and aloofness of the academic community. The reply would be more convincing did not the precedent already exist and were not the purity already sullied. Scientists of all kinds, in the social as well as in the physical disciplines, have not hesitated to work on programs for social change—financed by the Department of Defense, the Office of Naval Research, NASA, etc.—programs designed to alter the world by high explosives in some cases, by cooptation or skillful propaganda in others.

Some members of the academic community, aware of the destruction they have helped to commit, have now begun to withdraw from contact with the war machine. That is to their credit. But what is needed now is for them to redirect their energies to the peace machine. We live in a time during which social experimentation—in the factory, in the office, in the city, in economic policy, in political institutions, in lifestyles—is essential if a technologically dominated future is not simply to mold us willy-nilly to its requirements. The forces of change in our time render obsolete many of the institutions of man-agerial capitalism and centrally planned socialism alike; new institutions, new modes of social control and social cohesion now have to be invented and tried.

In part the university must continue its traditional role, studying this period of historic transformation with all the detachment and objectivity it can muster. But that is not enough. As Marx wrote: "The philosophers have only *interpreted* the world; the thing, however, is to change it." As the last item on my agenda, I would like to make the university the locus of action for the initiation of such change.